THE NEW FOX TERRIERS

Silent Sorrow (circa 1910) by Maud Earl depicts "Caesar," King Edward VII's favorite terrier, as he mourns the death of his royal master. This eloquent testimonial to a Fox Terrier's fidelity is part of the art collection of the American Kennel Club and is reproduced here with permission.

THE NEW
FOX TERRIERS

by HAROLD NEDELL

**A Colorful Odyssey Into the Respective Origins of
Both SMOOTH and WIRE Fox Terriers Together
With an In-Depth Presentation of the Breeds
as They Exist Today.**

First Edition

HOWELL
BOOK HOUSE
New York

Howell Book House
Macmillan Publishing Company
866 Third Avenue, New York, NY 10022
Collier Macmillan Canada, Inc.

Library of Congress Cataloging-in-Publication Data

Nedell, Harold.
    The new fox terriers.

    1. Fox terriers. I. Title.
SF429.F5N43   1987   636.7′55   87-22649
ISBN 0-87605-122-0

Macmillan books are available at special discounts for bulk purchases
for sales promotions, premiums, fund-raising, or educational use.
For details, contact:

          Special Sales Director
          Macmillan Publishing Company
          866 Third Avenue
          New York, NY 10022

10 9 8 7 6 5 4 3

Printed in the United States of America

Contents

Foreword   7

Introduction   9

1. Historic Overview   11

2. Fox Terriers in the Twentieth Century   38

3. British Impact   148

4. A Dog for All Reasons   176

5. Preparing for a Dog Show   223

6. Judging—Light a Candle, Don't Curse the Darkness   254

7. How to Become a Breeder   270

8. The Fox Terrier and Obedience   294

9. The Fox Terrier Legends   311

10. Back Through Time: Pedigrees   325

English, Irish and American Ch. Galsul Excellence, owned by William MacKay and Ruth Cooper, is one of the foremost show dogs of the 1980s. The top show dog of the year for 1986, "Paddy" has prevailed under all-breed and all-terrier authorities as well as under Fox Terrier experts. Bred in Ireland by John Galvin, he is presented in the ring by Peter Green.

Foreword

THE FOX TERRIER has captured the hearts and the imagination of dog lovers for over a century, offering as they do, two varieties to satisfy the widest possible range of interest. The smooth-coated type, requiring a minimum of maintenance, would seem to suggest broader acceptance, but not so, as there are four times as many wire-coated Fox Terriers produced currently.

These statistics would not have been available in 1984, since both varieties throughout their long history were regarded as one breed. Not until June 1985 were they separated, with the American Kennel Club providing individual registration and the resulting statistics.

Although few breeds have enjoyed the broad historical recognition and documentation given to the Fox Terrier, there has always been a "cloud of mystery" covering its early history. Harold Nedell is the first historian to consider this "cloud," and has done so with remarkable insight.

I was first introduced to Mr. Nedell in September 1980, after having selected his Smooth bitch, Quissex Upsadaisy, as Best in Sweepstakes at the Lone Star Fox Terrier Club Specialty. Although his involvement in pure-bred dogs covered several previous decades, he had only recently embarked on a new breeding program involving both varieties. "Daisy" would serve as his foundation in Smooths, and what an extraordinary matron she proved to be, producing multiple first-class champions in each and every litter. Just 10 months old at the time of our meeting, this was all to follow, and our discussion of her future prospects convinced me that Harold had a clear and thoughtful plan.

When he embarked on this writing project, he also had a clear and thoughtful plan, and the results are of even greater consequence. *The New Fox Terrier* is a most welcome addition to any terrier fancier's library. It is comprehensive, covering all aspects of the two breeds, and is researched with unprecedented care and accuracy. It is the first definitive work on Fox Terriers, and well deserving of the title "New."

DAN KIEDROWSKI

Ch. Brookewire Brandy of Layven achieved a permanent place in Wire Fox Terrier history when she was named "Supreme Champion" at the 1975 edition of the world-renowned Crufts show. A daughter of Ch. Sunnybrook Spot On, she was owned by G. Benelli and P. Dondina of Florence, Italy and handled by Alfred Langley.

Introduction

WHILE MY NAME APPEARS on the cover of this book as the author, it really should read: written by lovers of Fox Terriers from around the world. I received help from Allan Bailey in Australia; Mary Blake, Elizabeth Winstanley, Vera Goold, Elsie Williams, George Hocking and two unnamed clerks at the Kennel Club in England; Emilie Farrell, Winnie Stout, Roberta Vesley, Lisa Sachs, Eva Sasovetz, Janie Bousek, Ric Chashoudian, William Brainard, Tom and Kay Gately, John Medeiros, Virginia Ashlock, Arden Ross, Laura Forkel, Shirley Koehler, Eve Ballich, Howard Nygood, John Marvin, Dan Kiedrowski and all the members of The American Fox Terrier Club who responded to my pleas for help with speed and encouragement. These were the real authors. Special recognition should go to the following: Dan Kiedrowski for coming to my aid with research and photographs; Lisa Sachs and Eva Sasovetz for the chapter on obedience and the photos of their Fox Terrier TV stars; Arden Ross for her artistic contributions and the section on Grooming the Broken Coated Terrier; Arden Ross and Laura Forkel also made a major contribution to the Wire Standard amplification; Janie Bousek for preparing most of the Standard vizualizations; Winnie Stout who got me back into Smooths and then guided my efforts as I worked my way through this project; Winnie also prepared the amplification on the Smooth Standard; Roberta Vesley, The American Kennel Club librarian for helping me over some very rough spots; the Gatelys and Ric Chashoudian for their firsthand observations.

The authors who so carefully preserved the information that appears in these pages: Rawdon Lee, Theo Marples, Hugh Dalziel, Irving Ackerman, E. Lindley Wood, Macdonald Daly, J. H. Pardoe, Evelyn Silvernail, George Skelly, Elsie Williams just to name a few. In England, the Wire Fox Terrier Club for publishing their annuals and, of course, the American Fox Terrier Club for its effort every ten years.

To all of those mentioned and to many more who just kept the breeds alive during troubled times, I offer my heartfelt admiration and gratitude.

Finally, I could not have completed this effort if not for the loving, cooperative atmosphere provided by Ruthie, my devoted mate for 34 years.

To all those mentioned herein, I dedicate this book.

1

Historic Overview

$\mathbf{I}$N 1983 AND 1984, a committee appointed by the American Kennel Club voted to restrict Group representation for those breeds that had varieties to one Best of Breed Group contestant. At that time I was Secretary of the American Fox Terrier Club and the membership wanted to maintain our two-variety Group opportunity. It was decided that the only ways to assure the future of Group competition for Wires and Smooths was to obtain an exemption from the AKC or to divide the varieties into two separate and distinct breeds. Until then, I gave little thought to the question. The two Fox Terriers had co-existed for nearly 100 years in the United States and a bit longer in Britain. And while I recalled someone, sometime, telling me that there was a brief period when only one Fox Terrier competed in the Group, I attached little significance to the past. It was obvious that our club consisted of Smooth breeders or Wire breeders. Few members bred both. What's more, there was no intra-breeding of any consequence. The Club officers decided upon a two-stage effort to maintain the integrity of the Smooth and the Wire.

First, we would make our case to the AKC regarding the unique historical status of the Fox Terriers and, if unsuccessful, we would apply for separate breed status for each variety. As Secretary, I was to prepare the presentation for AKC. But once the presentation was prepared, I could not stop. I was like a snowball rolling down a mountain. As my research traversed back through the decades, the route became less reliable. Two conclusions make good sense. Reasonably reliable Smooth records begin around 1870 with a dog called Belgrave Joe and the comparable Wire dog was Meersbrook Bristles, born June 3, 1892. To state that the records preceding those two dogs have credibility is to believe in Jack Frost and the Tooth Fairy!

Another opportunity presented itself as my work progressed. Why not try to make this book a tool for judges as well? With the help and encouragement of the most knowledgeable fanciers, I have made that attempt.

Looking Back Briefly

There are thousands of pages written attempting to illuminate the dim past history of Fox Terriers. Early 18th century paintings seem to indicate the existence of Smooth and Wire Fox Terriers or at least individual dogs that resemble modern Fox Terriers.

Perceptions and conceptions people possess are frequently locked in a present time-warp. Through the eyes of a film director, the interpretation of the actor and the memory of the camera, movies and television have moved us back in time to man's obscure beginnings. And as we pass through history, just as certainly we ultimately return to reality. We cannot live in those historic times. We can only bend our minds, our imaginations, our attention for the length of the show.

So lend me your imagination, your minds and, most importantly, your imagination for a return to late Victorian England. The empire was at the height of its power, glory and majesty. There existed an unusual paradox whereby nouveau wealth from the industrial revolution and England's worldwide commercial interests were beginning to gain recognition and acceptance by the landed class that for generations looked upon commerce as a sordid enterprise.

Why this preoccupation with historic perceptions, conceptions, conditions and life style? Because I believe that it is the "X" factor missing from previous presentations of the history of Smooths and Wires. The certainty of today's pedigrees causes a myopic distortion of the period from 1800 to 1900. Nearly every litter of Smooths or Wires of the period had a bitch called Vic or, later on, Old Vic named for Queen Victoria, who reigned for over 63 years. In that time span, think of how many Vics and Old Vics were whelped. Not only were names duplicated but as late as the 1920s, owners were changing the registered name of newly-acquired stock. One of the most famous Smooths, Little Aristocrat, was first registered as Kidder Kompact. Suppose I bred my dog to your bitch in 1885 and, subsequently, we had a falling out. It would not be uncommon for you to alter the name of the sire of the litter to another stud owned by a person more to your liking. Other records read, "11/5/86—bred Old Tip to tan and white rough coated bitch." This is not an actual entry but is typical of records of the period. So, it is quite apparent, the early history of Smooths and Wires is unreliable.

Thornton's Pitch

An early Wire Fox or rough-coated terrier.

These exhibits clearly show the eighteenth-century characteristics of the two breeds. Note that the Smooth, Thornton's Pitch, is, at that early date, predominantly white.

13

Furthermore, the evidence that does exist points to the possibility that many of the existing conclusions on the origins of the breeds are in error. The net result is that our present understanding of Fox Terrier roots is made fact by repetition, not by evidence. Let us then examine some of this evidence together to see what conclusions we can draw.

There seems to be general agreement that the first modern Smooth was a dog called Old Jock who was from an early kennel called the Grove. He was born in 1859 and exhibited for the next ten years. Old Jock, more than any other early Smooth, established the modern "type." Beginning around 1800, throughout Britain, packs of hounds were kept. The Foxhound was the dog of the hour. Meticulous records were kept and anyone researching Foxhound history would have little difficulty tracing pedigrees to the late 18th century. Each pack had its terriers. Without a terrier the fox could go to ground ending the hunt prematurely, causing the Master of the Hounds no end of embarrassment. For all their importance to the hunt, few packs kept accurate records of their terriers' antecedents. antecedents. The exceptions were the Grove, the Oakley, the Quorn and the Belvoir. These four packs provide the ancestry of the present-day Smooth Fox Terrier. Anyone interested in Smooth roots can begin with the dog "Old Jock" and the bitch "Grove Nettle" from the Grove pack; "Old Trap" from the Oakley; while the Quorn produced "Psyche"; the period 1855 to 1865. From "Old Jock," "Old Trap," and "Grove Nettle" through "Belvoir Joe" and "Old Foiler" the Smooth's future was launched. For it fell to Belvoir Joe to produce "Belgrave Joe" born July 1, 1868. His breeder?

Well, the Fox Terrier Stud Book gives Mr. Luke Turner of Liecester the credit for bringing Belgrave Joe into the world but, in their "Monograph on the Fox Terrier," Marples and Castle made the following observation: "I believe this is not correct. (Belgrave) Joe was bred by John Branson on July 31, 1868 and he was well known in Liecester for many years and it was not until he was well on in years that Mr. Turner bought him for £.20."

Old Jock has a similar skeleton in his dog house. Rawdon Lee described "Old Jock's" breeding as follows: "Jock was to be bred by Jack Morgan, who when the dog was pupped sometime during 1859, was huntsman with the Grove. I have also heard it stated that Jock was born at the Quorn Kennels. The Kennel Club Stud Book gives the breeder as either Captain Percy Williams, who was then Master of the Grove, or Jack Morgan; but the uncertainty of the month in which the terrier was born, and "Old Foiler" the Smooth's future was launched. It fell to Belvoir Joe to produce "Belgrave Joe" born July 1, 1868. His breeder? terriers." If this account about Old Jock is accurate, then the ancestry of one of the first important Wires, Meersbrook Bristles, is just as confused.

Irving Ackerman was the first American to tackle the history of the Fox Terrier. In 1928 Ackerman's *The Wire-Haired Fox Terrier* was published. It was updated ten years later to include Smooths. In Ackerman's chapter SAM HILL AND THE MEERSBROOKS, he writes of Meersbrook Bristles and his impact as the double grandsire of Barkby Ben, the sire of Cackler of Notts. Cackler is credited by authors Williams, Silvernail, Skelly, Skinner, et al. as the "Patriarch of the Modern Wire." Ackerman details Bristles' beginnings, "Hill's Smooth Meersbrook Crissy with no trace of Wire in her pedigree had a litter to a mongrel. The whelps were drowned; and Hill, who subscribed to the discredited theory of telegony, thought that Crissy was forever ruined as a producer of purebred stock. He nonetheless mated the bitch again, this time to Albert Clear's Knavesmire Jest, by Young Jester, who was by Old Jester out of his own daughter. The puppies were two dogs and a bitch, one of them Meersbrook Bristles." Or was it? The AKC has Bristles' breeding as Meersbrook Nailer ex Rough on some of its records.

One small observation that most breeders will appreciate: In the following paragraph Ackerman describes how Hill's kennel manager re-acquired Bristles after selling the two dogs and the bitch. Bristles' brother was killed by a coach. Ackerman concludes with the paragraph, "The other puppy which was killed by the coach was said to have been a much better specimen than Bristles himself." All breeders believe that the puppy that is killed or doesn't make it to maturity is almost always *better*. Just like the fish that got away. The puppy that never grew up will haunt us for years to come and so it was with our earlier breeders and Sam Hill was no exception. He believed that the puppy killed by the coach was a better specimen than Meersbrook Bristles. However, if progeny is an indication of a dog's value, the right dog survived.

I have basic problems with Ackerman's account of Bristles' ancestry. The first is with the dam Meersbrook Crissy. The second is supported by Rawdon Lee's account of "Old Jock's breeding," indicating that pedigrees of the time were unreliable. If, in fact, Crissy was indeed Bristles' dam, there is no evidence regarding her ancestry to support the references to her as a "pure Smooth." I wonder if she was the dam because Ackerman's explanation raises the question of why Hill bred a "contaminated" bitch again and why develop an interest in re-acquiring a dog puppy of questionable value and purity regardless of his conformation? One answer is that those early breeders placed little consequence upon the accuracy of the names of the sires and dams. Names were changed. Dogs and bitches were entered under different names on occasion. Another answer is that Jest and Crissy were not the parents. Another book on the Fox Terrier was was authored by Evelyn Silvernail. In it she states, "An interesting fact about Bristles, who was whelped in 1892, was that his sire was a Wire dog, Knavesmire, who was nine times inbred to 'Old Tip,' and his dam was a Smooth bitch, Meersbrook Cristy, who was nine times inbred to Belgrave Joe." The sire of Bristles, from some accounts, was a dog called

Knavesmire Jest, not just Knavesmire (or Meersbrook Nailer). The dam, according to some, was Meersbrook Crissy, a Smooth bitch. According to others, Bristles' dam could have been any of Sam Hill's bitches including previously mentioned "Rough," certainly not a Smooth.

There can be little doubt that the great hunts of southern England in the mid-19th century developed the prototype for today's Smooth Fox Terrier leading to *Belvoir Joe (by Trimmer) to Belgrave Joe.* There exists an ancient and glorious history that dates back to the first printed work in the English language on "Field Sport" which appeared early in the 15th century but, then there were no stud books, no hard evidence as to the breeding records of the distant past. Was there a Beagle cross in the late 18th century or early 19th century as put forth by the "Duchess of New Castle"? Or was there a possible Bull Terrier or Whippet cross as reported without conviction by Mr. Rawdon Lee? Without conclusive evidence confirming one or the other theory, I will read them all with interest but believe none.

The unanswered question is: If, in fact, the eye, ear and skull faults that occur in our breeds today are as a result of Greyhound/Whippet crosses; and if, in fact, the head, muzzle, mouth, shoulder and general cloddiness faults are the result of Bulldog blood; and if, in fact, the ear and color difficulties are the manifestation of the Beagle influence, then why do we see these faults not in their entirety but in lesser degrees? Do we really have a "hound ear" or an ear that is larger, heavier and set lower on the skull? Are the heavy markings and the hound coloration the result of the Beagle cross or the natural development of coloring indigenous to canines in general? The lesson of genetics is that a large ear bred to a small ear provides a large ear/small ear result, not a medium ear.

The Fox Terrier elegance did not come from crossing a coursing hound with a terrier, at least not after 1800. Any examination of the paintings depicting terriers, rough or smooth, reveals a streamlined hunter that had the strength to do his job. And since all breeds develop an occasional undershot specimen and since we observe how strongly Bulldog influences regenerate themselves in the various terriers who were crossed with the Bulldog for fighting and baiting purposes and since our terriers have had the courage to hunt and go to ground since at least 1500, the report of the Bulldog cross has no basis in fact or characteristic.

The Fox Terrier enjoyed so much popularity so quickly at a time when genetic science was so young that the only explanation diligent breeders could resort to for the negative results of their carefully-planned efforts was the earlier infusion of strange blood rearing its ugly head or ear or eye or color. In the alternative, Whippets have wrong ears, Bulldogs have too prominent muzzles and last but not least was the fear some years ago of many Beagle breeders that the Beagle was becoming "terrier-ized" in ear and in action. In reality our dogs' faults are their own and they come by them honestly, simply because they are inherent in dogs.

16

After more research and additional soul searching I have come to a definite conclusion about the early history of the modern Wire Fox Terrier. The Wire and the Smooth developed from different stock. They were physically different. The Wire or Rough-coated Terrier was both larger and smaller but stockier, more suited to the rough terrain of Durham and Devonshire. Unlike the Smooth, I could find no early records of Wire breeding efforts. The premier Wire breeder was the Rev. Jack Russell of Barnstable, Devonshire. His story begins in 1813 with the purchase of a "Wire bitch, Trump" from a milkman. But the "Sporting Parson" cared little for appearances and pedigrees. He bred his Wires based solely on their hunting ability. Size, length, weight, appearance, style and symmetry all gave way to courage and working talent. Some of our present breeders would no doubt claim that our two standards were designed to produce the perfect worker. The parson would most certainly refute those purists.

We must leap from 1813 to the 1880's before coming upon a Wire breeder of any consequence, William Carrick, Jr. His Carlisle Wires were the Wildoaks and Evewires of his time. From 1880 through the mid-1890's, Carlisle Wires dominated the show ring. But with the exception of Rev. Russell, the indications are that Sidney Castle, in his *A Monograph on the Fox-Terrier*, presented an accurate summation of early Wire stock . . . "The origin of the wire-haired variety is unfortunately not so decided. That there were Wire-Haired Fox-Terriers centuries ago is proved by Dame Juliana Berners' (circa 15th century) treatise of 'teroures' both rough and smooth; also they appear in many old-time pictures and prints. They were mostly heavily marked with black-and-tan or blue grizzle-and-tan, and no doubt they have had their admirers in times that are gone, just the same as they have now. But even if they had the same care bestowed upon their breeding as their Smooth cousins, which I very much doubt, their record is lost, and it is impossible to trace their history in the same manner that we are able to do in the Smooth-Haired variety."

While his next paragraph adds little to clear up the obscurity of early Wire development, it is, nonetheless, worth reporting, for I hear the same comments today from some Wire handlers and breeders . . .

This, to my mind, is the reason why it is harder to breed Wire-Haired Fox-Terriers true to type, and is the cause of so much disappointment to the thoughtful breeder. Those who have tried and are still trying to breed high-class Wire-Hairs will understand what I mean. One may think one is breeding from ideal specimens, and we all use one's brains and infinite care in so doing, with the result in nine cases out of ten—disappointment.

There are far more bad terriers in the Wire-Haired variety than in the Smooths. In the latter it is not easy to obtain the very high standard that is necessary in these days of universal excellence, a terrier that can win in the best company, but it is easy to breed an average good one, good enough for the V.H.C. at any show, but in Wire-hairs a preponderance of animals not worth a card is the rule, not the exception.

This to my mind is because the breed in the past was not kept pure, was not cultivated and cared for in the same manner as the Smooths. There are no "Old Jocks," "Traps," "Foilers," "Grove Nettles," or "Belvoir Joes," as ancestors in the Wire-haired variety. No doubt the best Smooth dogs in the various hunt kennels were used to some black-and-tan or grizzle-and-tan nondescript, rough, earth stopper's terrier, and the best of the progeny bred from again, and so on, with the result that for years breeders were breeding in the dark.

It is fair to state that Smooth Fox Terriers in 1875 were a more consistent breed. The fancy was developing a standard. There were decent entries at the shows and accurate records were being maintained. While some confusion still existed, for the most part the breed was on its way and those historians who trace the history of the Smooth have sketchy but unchallenged data to draw upon.

Wires, on the other hand, presented a somewhat different picture. While there may be a direct line from Kendall's Old Tip to Meersbrook Bristles, reports exist that question the dam of Bristles; a challenge arose as to the relationship of Bristles to Meersbrook Ben; that would obfuscate the pedigree of Barkby Ben and through him, the foundation dog, Cackler of Notts. It is safe to infer that early wire breeders were a competitive, win-at-any-cost lot. In some ways it is merciful to students of Wire development that the great show dog of the turn of the century, Go Bang, had little impact as a producer because his ancestry was highly questionable.

Therefore, to state, with certainty, that "Bristles" came from a Smooth bitch is to totally ignore the conditions of the times. So, as is evident, were the records of the times, even those of the kennel terriers of the hunts, at best sketchy and at worst pure fiction. To make matters worse for Wire historians, most writers of the late 19th century were Smooth fanciers who seemed to take some personal glee in attributing Wire progress to this or that Smooth antecedent. Suffice to note that Meersbrook Bristles came upon the scene and the Wire as a show dog was on his way. Most plausible to me is that the modern Smooth started with "Belgrave Joe" and the modern Wire with "Meersbrook Bristles."

Now that I have cleared the air by clouding the past once again, there remains the mystery of the origin of our two wonderful breeds. The simplest and most obvious explanation is that there were always two different earth dogs, *terroures*, or terriers, one rough coated and the other smooth, in Europe and the United Kingdom. The climate of the British Isles and the sporting nature of its people provided the perfect environment for terrier development. They were rough coated or smooth, short legged or high stationed, drop eared or prick eared, but all were terrier. Sometime,

Meerbrook Bristles

Meersbrook Ben

Barkby Ben

Modern Wire Fox Terrier roots rest in the offspring of these three dogs.

probably around the middle of the 18th century, someone, someplace in Britain, developed an affinity for the predominately white color and began to breed the whitest to the whitest. It took place earlier in the smooths than in the roughs since Kendall's Old Tip is universally acknowledged to be the first mostly white Wire. By about 1850 the smooth-coated Terriers of the great hunts were the prototype for our modern Smooth Fox Terrier. In the colder northern country, sportsmen like the Rev. Russell were hunting the high stationed rough-coated terrier with little regard to color or type. However, other interested parties like Harding Cox and William Carrick, Jr. recognized the possibilities of the rough-coated terrier that had tasks identical to his smooth cousin to the south and began to breed them selectively. Then in 1876 a group of enthusiasts of both coats met to organize the Fox Terrier Club and the two distinct breeds became two varieties of the same breed.

One ray of light into the murky past of the Fox Terrier is the Castle-Marples description of the formation of the Fox Terrier Club.

CHAPTER II, THE FOX-TERRIER CLUB

The advent of dog shows, and increasing popularity throughout the country, induced many people to take up dog breeding as a hobby; and in selecting a breed the Fox-terrier soon became the most favoured one.

The keen, alert, game character of the Fox-terrier, his size, intelligence and sporting instincts soon obtained the preponderance of admirers over any other variety of dog.

Many men started breeding, some on an extensive scale, hundreds on a less ambitious basis, but all with the same object in view—viz., to try and breed something a bit better than anyone else.

The Fox-terrier Club was started in 1875, and as my old friend, Mr. Harding Cox, was largely instrumental in its formation, I cannot do better than quote his own words on the subject.

"It was about the year 1875," says Mr. Cox, "that I, having been to some extent instrumental in founding the original Bulldog Club (now incorporated), turned my attention to the inauguration of a similar society whose objects it should be to foster and further the interests of the Fox-terrier. In pursuit of this idea I summoned the clans to meet in convivial conclave and discuss the project.

"From north, south, east and west, they came—a party of earnest enthusiasts, amongst whom are names indelibly associated with success in the Fox-terrier world as judges, breeders, and exhibitors. Some of these have, alas! passed away, but many remain with whom the memory of this auspicious occasion will ever be cherished.

"Amongst those who gathered at the board—if recollection serves me truly—were the late Mr. Fred Burbidge, Mr. Gison, Mr. W. Allison, Mr. Abbot, Mr. Francis Redmond, the late Mr. Theodore Bassett, Mr. Sydenham Dixon, the late Mr. J. A. Doyle, Mr. Russell Earp, Mr. G. M. Southwell, Mr. Drake, and Mr. W. W. Jaquet.

"The Club, in its successful endeavors to encourage the breeding of high-class Fox-terriers, offers numerous specials at the leading shows throughout the country. It holds one *Club* show annually although previously there were two annual exhibitions, the venue being a changing one so as to suit the convenience of those in various parts of the country. At these shows the prize money is offered on a most liberal scale; Ten pounds is annually given for the best young Smooth dog, for the best Smooth bitch, for the best Wire-haired dog, and for the best Wire-haired bitch bred by a member of the Club.

"Various interesting stakes such as the Produce Stakes, the Birthday Stakes, the Derby, and the Oaks are competed for, and to give an idea of the money that is offered for competition I may mention that one member alone has been credited with as much as £.300 in cash by the success of his ambition.

"The Club possesses two fifty guineas Challenge Cups, given for the best terrier of each variety. These are perpetual cups now, but originally, when the older cup of the two, viz., that for Smooths was competed for, anyone winning it five times gained absolute possession of the trophy. Mr. Burbidge won it five times in the first three years that it was competed for, but with that generosity that always was so apparent in all that he did, he gave it back to the Club on the condition that it should be perpetual. The sister cup for Wire-hairs was subscribed for some years later."

What is significant to my premise of separate development is the last line . . . "The sister cup for Wire-hairs was subscribed for some years later." While in itself the statement is inconclusive it would seem to indicate that, at that early date, Wires were traveling their own path and were not necessarily developed from Smooth stock. Why then one breed with two varieties rather than two separate breeds? Once again, we must create in our own minds a time when there was no television, no mass transit. A time when "gentlemen of means" engaged in sport as a way of life. It was perfectly natural for gentlemen who had a deep interest in their dogs to come together to enjoy one another's company. Since Smooths and Wires were bred for the same purposes, the sporting men were naturally drawn together. The resulting club for Fox-terriers included the two. These were working terriers first, hardy companions second, and show dogs last. So whether the coat be rough or smooth was of little consequence in 1875 except to the individuals who supported one coat or the other within the club. Since their purposes were similar, the standards that developed were also similar. And while two standards are still in use in England, the founders of the American Fox Terrier Club, until recently, adopted the standard for the Smooth since the club's founders were predominately Smooth breeders and they added the coat variation for Wires. The dominance of Smooth breeders rapidly diminished as the new century approached and today the two breeds under the Fox Terrier banner are both enjoying exciting entries and good popular acceptance. Unlike other varieties that interbreed and share common antecedents, the two Fox Terriers share little or no common ancestry but do have a common trade.

And since the standard of any breed should reflect the image of the perfect specimen's ideal structural conformation to accomplish its assigned task or tasks, it is not surprising that Wires and Smooths shared the same standard until June 1, 1985.

In her book *The Fox Terrier Wire and Smooth*, Elsie Williams wisely avoids any early references to Wire and Smooth ancestry. Instead, she relies upon post 20th century information which is more accurate and reliable.

Mr. George Skelly, in Chapter 12 of his book *All About Fox Terriers* provides a list of "top sires" of Wires from 1892-1942. These were dogs who had a significant impact in Wires. If Meersbrook Bristles' ancestry remains a mystery, as it should, there is not a single stud dog in the list that was the direct result of a Smooth cross. As for the standard, no standard is so specific that it confines breeders to a narrow objective whereby interpretation is virtually eliminated. There must be room in any standard for the self-expression of the breeder. However, the Wire standard of June 1, 1985 provides far greater specificity than the older Smooth standard.

One approach to the flexibility of the standard is in the area of size and weight. The Smooth standard states "weight is not a certain criteria of a Terrier's fitness for his work." The present AKC standard goes on to say "General shape, size, and contour are the main points: and if a dog can gallop and stay, and follow his fox up a drain, it matters little what his weight is to a pound or so." As to symmetry, size and character, the standard uses words like "should," not "must." So the one standard applied equally to both breeds. Today the Smooths are on the whole a bit smaller than the Wires (although they are gaining on them, unfortunately). Smooth heads are a bit larger, and fuller in the skull as well. The Smooth also tends to be a bit longer and less angulated in the rear. The Wire has a shorter back, and while somewhat larger in appearance will probably weigh less due to lighter bone which usually indicates a weaker pastern, poorer feet. I believe the entire rear assembly of the top Wires differs from that of top Smooths. There may also be a noticeable difference in ear carriage. This may be due more to the narrower Wire skull than to the placement of the ear. There is a more basic difference between Wires and Smooths than the standards allow. I have never seen a tan-headed Smooth with black body markings.

The first record of a dog show in the United States or the United Kingdom took place in 1859 at Newcastle-on-Tyne. Fox Terriers competed in a *Variety Class*, a category that compares to our Miscellaneous Class today. The first show at which Fox Terriers competed with their own breed was in June 1862 at the North of England Second Exhibition of Sporting and Other Dogs, held in Islington Agricultural Hall. "Trimmer" topped an entry of 20 Fox Terriers—an extremely large entry for a new variety and the largest at the show. But it was at the National Exhibition in

Birmingham in 1862 that the Fox Terrier began to earn the popularity that was to dominate the sport for more than 50 years on two continents. The new variety was exhibited in a class for "White and Other Smooth-Haired English Terrier, Except Black and Tan." Fox Terriers placed one, two, three in dogs and first and second in bitches. This achievement by a new variety created quite a good deal of excitement and interest. Those of us who have witnessed the emergence of new breeds at today's shows realize that nothing succeeds like success. Everyone wants a winner and the fancy in 1862 was no different. By 1863 at London in March and in May, as well in Birmingham, the scene of their year earlier triumph, two classes for "just Fox Terriers" were provided.

Once again, we see that timing is critical to the success of our breeds. In *A History and Description, With Reminiscences of the Fox Terrier,* Rawdon Lee describes the existing canine world in 1862.

At that time there was an opening for a popular dog, the swell of the period was becoming a little less effeminate than he had been, and was tired of lolloping my lady's Toy Spaniel on his knees. He had tasted and enjoyed the Tom and Jerry days in the rat pit, at the public-housedog show, and in the occasional baiting of a semi-domesticated badger. Many of the ladies themselves had grown discontented with the continued snortings of their over-fed pets, and the unodoriferous smells which sprung from obese King Charles and Blenheim Spaniels. The Yorkshire Terrier was fairly well known in parts of the north of England and elsewhere, but his coat was troublesome, and the Italian Greyhound was far too delicate and fragile a creature for ordinary "comforting" purposes. The lovely Maltese, with his coat in texture and appearance like spun glass, was scarce and an uncertain mother with her puppies, whilst the appearance of the often goggle-eyed "apple-headed" black and tan Toy Terrier was not sufficiently aristocratic to tempt the connoisseur in such livestock. Besides, these black and tans were bred and reared in the east end of London, the back streets of Birmingham and of other large towns, so they were too plebian by half. Then the Dandie Dinmont and Hard-Haired Scotch Terriers were scarcely known out of the land on the other side of the border, and the Skye Terrier with his long jacket carried too much dirt into the house. The white English Terrier might have become popular had he not been so subject to chronic deafness, and no doubt the Bull Terrier and the Black and Tan Terrier lost their chance of becoming idols by reason that a barbarous custom had decided that their ears had to be in part amputated. This could only be done at considerable trouble and expense, and with inordinate suffering to the poor creatures themselves. So here was the chance for the Fox Terrier; he availed himself of the opportunity, and the public gladly accepted his enterprise.

Rawdon Lee wrote this in 1888. The analysis he provides, while written with the benefit of hindsight and a certain amount of Fox Terrier chauvinism, reveals an interesting insight into Victorian society. The Fox Terriers discussed thus far are all Smooths. It was in 1869 at Darlington,

England that classes for "Rough-Haired Terriers" were held. Ten years later the Birmingham catalogue listed classes for "Wire-Haired Terriers." Finally, in 1882 the English Kennel Club stud book changed the classification to "Wire-Haired Fox Terriers."

In a few short years Fox Terriers moved from obscurity to prominence. In 1859 Fox Terriers were exhibited as "Other Varieties" and somewhat of a novelty. At Nottingham in 1872, 276 Fox Terriers were entered. I have searched the records of our American shows and cannot find an entry to equal Nottingham in 1872. Later I discuss the question of size and it is interesting to report that from 1876 to 1886 classes were provided for dogs over and under 18 pounds and bitches over and under 16 pounds. Fortunately, good sense prevailed. By 1886 hardly a judge could be found that would put up a dog over 17 pounds and the classes for the larger dogs and bitches were eliminated.

Pedigrees and bloodlines were still a bit uncertain when in 1868 Belgrave Joe strolled upon the stage of Fox Terrier history. His accomplishments as a stud dog were so prodigious that when he died nearly twenty years later his skeleton was mounted and exhibited at the English Kennel Club. It is reported that Luke Turner purchased Belgrave Joe in 1878 for £.20 because he was still throwing remarkable puppies. While Belgrave Joe's virility and longevity guaranteed his unique status as "Father of the Breed" he was not without company. Luke Turner bred Fox Terriers that were always at or near the top in any competition in his day. So it was that young Francis Redmond sought him out when he was looking for a Fox Terrier. Not only was Belgrave Joe a part of Turner's kennel but another Smooth foundation dog, "Old Foiler," was Turner's as well. But while Belgrave Joe was undoubtedly the dominant sire of his time and was largely responsible for producing the type so sought after at the time, he, like Moses, was destined never to cross the river to the promised land. Few, if any of his male line descendants survive today. The distinction belongs to Old Foiler, born in 1871. Foiler had just two great-grandparents, Grove Tartar and Grove Nettle. Foiler's great-great-grandson, Champion Splinter, born in 1883, through his descendent, Champion Oxonian, had had more of an impact on modern Smooths. Splinter's sire, "Dickon," was purchased by Redmond for a few shillings from Turner and Totteridge Kennels was born.

One fact is obvious in the history of the Smooth Fox Terrier thus far. There are no other breed crosses. While some of the dogs exhibited between 1862 and 1890 may have had some wire or black and tan blood, none were Bulldog, Beagle, or Greyhound crosses. The Duchess of Newcastle subscribed to the Beagle theory. Others believed in a Greyhound cross and still others in the Bulldog thesis. I do not doubt for a moment that such experimentation took place. The question to be answered is, "Did crossing have any significant impact on the development of the modern Fox

Terrier?" There is universal acceptance of Belgrave Joe as the Father of the Smooth Fox Terrier. We can account for the purity of his sire, Belgrave Joe, with some credibility. Hugh Dalziel was an early reporter of the breed. In 1889 he wrote of W. Cooper, "A late huntsman to the Belvoir, Cooper took great pains in keeping the breed pure during his time at Belvoir and got several of the old black and tan sort, mentioned before from Mr. William Singleton of Caythorpe, near Grantham, a noted breeder of them, and he kept them free from Bull for over 40 years. I cannot trace the present breed of Belvoir Terriers further back than Tom Goosey's day, over 40 years ago."

The black and tan terrier referred to by Dalziel was not the Manchester Terrier but a smooth coated English Terrier who had many of the same characteristics as the Smooth. I believe the hound coloration resulted from the English Terrier rather than from any Beagle blood.

Francis Redmond, after acquiring Dickon, had no equal in Smooth Fox Terrier history. For more than 50 years he showed the way. In the history of the Smooth Fox Terrier Francis Redmond stands alone. His interest began in 1869 and from 1872 to 1880 he purchased several bitches in addition to the dog, Dickon, mentioned earlier. Dickon became his first champion as well as a fine stud dog. Dickon's son Splinter is one of the three dogs whose names appear in nearly all modern Smooth pedigrees. The 1926 Jubilee Year Book of The Fox Terrier Club contained the following accounting of redmond's legacy . . .

> Among the past winners in the Totteridge Kennel, and by Totteridge sires, may be noted—Champion Diamond Dust born in 1880, always revered by her owner as being the first champion. He bred Her Daughter, Ch. Diadem, Ch. Darkie, Ch. Dusky Trap, Ch. Dominie, Ch. D'Orsay, Ch. Despoiler, Ch. Devereaus, Ch. Donna Dominie, Ch. Dona, Ch. Donigton, Ch. Dame Fortune, Ch. Don Caesario, Ch. Duchess of Durham, Ch. Dukedom, Ch. Haydon Dark Ruby, Ch. Dunleath, Ch. Doralice, Ch. Dangler, Ch. D'Orsay's Model, Ch. D'Orsay's Donna, Ch. D'Orsay's Damsel, Ch. Darrell, Ch. Myrtus, Ch. Dusky Dinah, Ch. Dusky Doris, Champions from 1881 to 1922, etc. and in Wirehairs The Dusky Cackler, Ch. Dusky Cracker, Ch. Dusky Twitcher, Ch. Dusky Admiral, Ch. Dusky Siren, Ch. Dusky Gleaner, Ch. Dusky Courtly, Ch. Dusky Tweze, Ch. Dusky Tweak, Dusky Nipper, Dusky Collar, etc. By the aid of the above string of champions the Totteridge Kennel was successful in winning the special silver cup presented by "Our Dogs" for the greatest number of champions of any breed or various breeds bred by one owner.

Redmond's dogs all had names beginning with "D." His chief rival throughout the late 19th and early 20th centuries was Robert Vicary whose terriers had names starting with the letter "V." And so at each show through the years Venio, Vesuvian, Vesuvienne, Vice Regal, Valuator, Visto, Norfolk Veracity, and Veracious competed with Dickon, Diamond

Francis Redmond's Smooths captured by Arthur Wardle's 1897 painting "The Totteridge Eleven." On the straw, left to right: Dryad, Daddy, Dame Dalby, Dalby and Divorcee. Standing, left to right: Dominie, Donna Fortuna, Dame Fortune, D'Orsay, Donington and Diamond Count.

An early photo of Her Grace, Kathleen, Duchess of Newcastle, with a young Wire.

The late Francis Redmond with Ch. Daddy.

Dust, Diadem, Darkie, etc. Reports of the period indicate that the rivalry was a heated one since Redmond and Vicary disagreed as to what constituted a good Fox Terrier. In today's frame of reference, Francis Redmond was a believer in soundness. His dogs had good legs and feet, good rear ends and fronts. Robert Vicary's dogs were very stylish with marvelous heads, ears and expression. The rivalry was so intense that neither bred to the other's dogs. There is a familiar ring to that bell. While Francis Redmond also bred Wires, his impact was less than in Smooths. He never quite warmed to the practice of trimming Wires. The purist, Redmond showed his first Wire in 1888 at the Barn Elm show. A controversy had built up through the years about trimming or not trimming Wire Fox Terriers. In 1888 the Kennel Club decided in favor of showing Wires in their natural state. Francis Redmond abhored fakery of any kind and his exhibit was called "The Untrimmed." In accordance with instructions from the Kennel Club, the judge, Sir Lindsey Hogg, awarded the Challenge Cup to "The Untrimmed." Those active in dog clubs are all too familiar with the effects of controversy, and the natural adherents were convinced that right was on their side. Of course the sculptors were just as certain of their position. Both sides were tearing their hair out over this issue. The debate almost destroyed the Fox Terrier Club. The matter was settled with a Kennel Club ruling which permitted the removal of hair with brush, comb, or fingers, but not by such tools as knife, scissors, or taper. We got fingers and took an arm. I wonder how many professional handlers are aware of how much they owe to that early decision of the Kennel Club.

The early history of Wires as show dogs begins later than that for Smooths. The Wire or Rough coated terrier did not receive its own classification until 1869, seven years after the Smooth. Another factor in the early Wire years was the almost total lack of future significance of the Rev. Jack Russell's activities. As mentioned earlier, his dogs were hunters first, last and always. "Who" produced "what" was not critical, nor was conformation of any consequence. He kept records of his activities for over 50 years, but hardly a dog alive today can claim any kin to the parson's progeny.

William Carrick, Jr. should have been the Francis Redmond or the Robert Vicary of Wires. Carrick purchased a dog called Venture. He was by the dog believed to be the first modern white Wire Fox Terrier, Kendall's Old Tip. Tip was whelped in 1866. It is probably true that Old Tip's blood courses through the veins of every present-day Wire. From about 1875 to 1889 Carlisle Wires led the rest. Carrick's Trick, Ch. Carlisle Tack and Ch. Carlisle Tyro were just a few of Carrick's winners. But fate intervened to end the Wire career of William Carrick. I will let *The Fox Terrier Chronicle,* July 1889, recount the events:

> The news of Carlisle Tyro's having been objected to by the judge and of his dis-qualification by the Kennel Club committee came like a thunder-clap

upon the fancy; and when his ears had undergone several examinations and were found to be "suspicious" consternation reigned supreme.

On the bench Tyro has a most peculiar ear carriage, his ears having the appearance of having been fastened down to his cheeks at the tips. In the ring he carries his aural appendages perfectly and without any careful feeling nothing wrong could be detected about them, but upon passing them between the thumb and forefinger the tell-tale cicatrix can easily be felt. Mr. Sewell's opinion having been obtained, and it being an adverse one, and in accordance with the views of many present, the Kennel Club committee disqualified the dog on the grounds that his ears had been tampered with.

Mr. Carrick's long standing as a fancier, his social and monetary position, all point to one conclusion that he at least knows nothing about the faking of the dog, which it seems has always been kept at Barrow-in-Furness. Several hearings took place which finally led to a full blown trial. What a scandal and the dog world was abuzz. The decision, "that Carlisle Tyro's ears have been improperly tampered with, but by whom and with whose knowledge and consent, there is no evidence."

William Carrick, Jr. cut all ties with the fancy following the trial and this marvelous breeder was lost to Wire development. Just one more note on the subject. Prize money at shows was considerable in those early days. People were working and supporting a family on less than two guineas per week and prizes in excess of 100 guineas were not uncommon. Thus it was left to several Wire fanciers to steward the breed into the 20th century. Major Harding Cox, the originator and charter member of the Fox Terrier Club, exhibited Wires under the "Broad" prefix, but if Wires had no *father* they certainly had a *mother* in the person of the Duchess of Newcastle, who in 1893 bred her first Wire, Lady Tipton of Notts.

The early history of the Wire may be summarized by beginning with Kendall's Old Tip who begot Pincher who begot Old Jester who begot Young Jester who begot Knavesmire Jest who begot Meersbrook Bristles. Bristles was the foundation dog for Wire development on both sides of the Atlantic. He came to America in 1899.

The first American Smooth Fox Terrier was a bitch called Tort. She arrived in Boston around 1879 in whelp to Luke Turner's Turner's Dick, a Belgrave Joe grandson. F. B. Fay was responsible for acquiring Tort. Other imports arrived in America during those early days from Robert Vicary. Francis Redmond also sent Splauger to Lewis and Winthrop Rutherfurd. Edward Kelly of New York imported two more of Luke Turner's about the same time. With all this activity, it was just a matter of time until The American Fox Terrier Club came into existence. The American Fox Terrier Club Year Book 1934 describes the "founding of the club" as follows: In 1885 . . . "several gentlemen interested in the improvement of Fox Terriers in the United States, met this evening by appointment in the Madison Square Garden to take steps for the formation of an American Fox Terrier Club. Mr. Edward Kelly was the promoter, and he presided.

Those present were Messrs. A. E. Godeffroy, L. Rutherfurd, J. E. I. Grainger, Frank Hitchock, Joseph Kelly." This is the first entry in the minutes of the meetings of the American Fox Terrier Club. The Club was duly organized during the week of the Westminster Kennel Club Show, held in 1885. Mr. Lewis M. Rutherfurd was elected president, Mr. John E. Thayer, vice-president, and Mr. Edward Kelly, secretary and treasurer. At a later meeting held at Delmonico's, the English Fox Terrier Club's standard of excellence and points of the fox terrier was adopted as a standard for the American Fox Terrier Club.

These founders were soon joined by two marvelous early breed supporters, August Belmont, for many years President of the Jockey Club, and James Mortimer, who was to become one of our great all-rounders and manager of the Westminster show for some 30 years. Our breeds attracted the best of America's dog world. August Belmont, in particular, imported the best that England had to offer. Ch. Lucifer by Ch. Splinter out of Ch. Kohinoor was the most important.

The first show of the AFTC was held in Newport, Rhode Island. There were 75 Smooth dogs and bitches and four Wires for Francis Redmond to pass on. Lewis and Winthrop Rutherfurd's Splauger was his choice. A second show was held a year later in Newport but no other shows were held until 1904, when a show was held in Atlantic City. Formal Specialty Shows were not regularly held until 1920 and they have continued to the present. This did not prevent the Club from offering The Grand Challenge Cup competition at designated all-breed events. From 1886 through 1905 the Grand Challenge competition took place 52 times. August Belmont won it 15 times, G. H. Gooderham had 10 wins, G. M. Carnochan had six and the brothers Rutherfurd had six. Mr. Carnochan's victories were the first for Wires.

About three years after the first Smooth arrived in America, John Grainger, previously mentioned as an AFTC founder, purchased Tyke from William Carrick, Jr. after the dog had done some winning in England. Tyke was shown in the Miscellaneous Class at Westminster in 1882. The first 10 years that Wires were shown in America, they were exhibited for the most part by just six men. In addition to Grainger and Carnochan, James Mortimer, J. Lee Tailer, T. S. Bellin and Reginald F. Mayhew worked diligently to promote Wires during the late 19th century in the United States. As 1900 approached, Major Carnochan was determined to become the dominant Wire exhibitor and he had the resources to do so. In 1898 the Major imported the great Go Bang, a Meersbrook Bristles son. His most serious competition came from the great Bristles himself, who was imported by Charles W. Keyes of Boston. In 1902 Carnochan solidified the American Wire gene pool by importing Barkby Ben, one of the all-time great producers.

Before moving into the 20th century two more subjects must be explored briefly. What were the real origins of these two marvelous breeds of dogs? Earlier, I asked the readers to transport themselves to 1875. This was to try to develop a perspective from the existing knowledge and lifestyle. A judicious and sincere breeder plans a litter of puppies, he studies the current top dogs and selects his stud with the utmost of care. The litter arrives and the offspring are a disappointment. Their eyes are too large and soft and their ears are too large and hang down. This could not be!! Those characteristics are not indigenous to Fox Terriers. Somewhere, back in the early days of the breed, there must have been a Beagle cross and it manifested itself in that carefully planned mating. Or the skull was too round; the stop too pronounced; the bone too light and the set-ons not quite where they should be. It cannot be the fault of the two parents. It must have been some Whippet cross 50 years ago. How else could these abberations be explained? How indeed? The explanation that appeals to me most describes domesticated dog as the sum of its parts. Those parts can be eyes of varying shape and size; ears of differing configuration; shape that runs the gamut from stocky and short legged to tall, lithesome and swift. Man, to his credit, noticed that certain characteristics lent themselves to particular tasks. The terriers of Dr. Caius or Dame Berners were a nondescript lot whose only commonality was their purpose and even that was mitigated by climate and terrain. Aesthetic qualities were of little consequence, if the vermin were destroyed or the fox bolted. Slowly, imperceptibly at first, man became more conscious of his surroundings. Dress became functional but attractive. Horses were bred for speed and beauty. Sitting a mount well was a high tribute to any rider. And the appearance of the hounds and the terriers were a sign of gentility. The good-looking, courageous, hard-working terrier was bred to a similar animal and over the years evolved the Wire and the Smooth of 1875. The breed discrepancies that we still see today, we come by honestly. Not too long ago a Beagle fancier I know was lamenting the *terrierization* of the Beagle. She was seeing Beagles with shorter ears and smaller eyes and funny "terrier" movements. Had this occurred 50 to 100 years ago, people would certainly credit the "faults" to some terrier cross years back. I believe that while someone, sometime, may have crossed a terrier with other breeds, such activity had no material impact on the two Fox Terriers. Of all our terrier breeds today, Fox Terriers are the purists of the group.

The second observation is the good fortune Fox Terriers enjoyed by virtue of the wealth and position of the early enthusiasts. Major Carnochan paid $5000 to bring Go Bang and Barkby Ben to America. This at a time when a week's work in a factory produced a pay envelope containing $8.00. Family breadwinners earning $1000 per year were considered "well to do." That combination of wealth and enthusiasm propelled both coats to a level of popularity unique in the dog community.

In the members' room of the Kennel Club in London is the skeleton of Belegrave Joe bearing the following inscription:

The celebrated Fox-terrier "Belegrave Joe" who died at the age of 19, on the 15th of January, 1888. One of the last and most valued representatives of the renowned "Belvoir" strain, from whom most of the best Fox-terriers are descended.

He is justly described as one of the strongest pillars of the Stud Book in connection with his breed.

Presented to the Kennel Club by the widow of his owner, the late Luke Turner, Esq., in compliance with her husband's wishes in the year 1899. Restored in the year 1903 by the following members of the Kennel club—S. Castle, A. H. Clarke, A. W. Emms, W. Glynn, W. S. Glenn, F. Redmond, and J. C. Tinne, out of respect to the memory of their great personal friend, Luke Turner.

The Smooth Fox Terrier moved into the 20th century in the capable hands of some of the most dedicated, knowledgeable sportsmen the dog fancy has ever known. And the results bear witness to their success. A look at the paintings of Arthur Wardle of the Smooths of the period would exhilarate any current breeder. Ch. Meersbrook Bristles, Ch. D'Orsay's Donna and Model, Ch. South Cave Leger, Ch. Sandown Violet, Ch. Cackler of Notts, Ch. Dame Fortune, and Ch. Captain Double just to name a few, are Wardle's subjects. Of course Bristles and Cackler were Wires.

While Francis Redmond bred Smooths and Wires continually until his death in 1927, he always believed that his finest hour was in July 1896 when Ch. Donna Fortuna first entered the Totteridge world. She was the best of a great group of Smooths competing as the new century arrived. Her show debut was at Crufts in February 1897 as a seven-months-old puppy. This was the era of tremendous, highly competitive entries. And Crufts enjoyed the same respect then as it does today. One of the Fox Terrier Club founders, Mr. J. A. Doyle, awarded Donna Fortuna the Challenge Certificate from the veterans class at the Fox Terrier Club show at Cheltenham. In five years of campaigning she was never defeated. Another Club founder, Mr. J. C. Tinne, paid her the following tribute in 1903 . . . "She goes down to posterity as absolutely the best fox terrier of all time." A top show bitch of 1900, upon retirement, she enjoyed a life far different from the retired champions of our time. Ch. Donna Fortuna was placed with a keeper who, after a very brief training program, had her broken for ferret, fox and badger. It is reported that she was a game and clever worker.

I have attempted to convey to the reader the quality of gentlemen that fostered the early development of the Smooth Fox Terrier. Sidney Castles, himself a fine Fox Terrier breeder and exhibitor, as well as an early reporter of Fox Terrier activity, wrote of Mr. Frederick Burbidge who exhibited under the "Hunton" banner until about 1900:

Ch. Donna Fortuna—said to be the greatest ever. Unbeaten in five years of top competition, she was whelped in July 1896.

Redmond's Ch. Wire Dusky Reine, whelped 1899.

Mr. Frederick Burbidge, one of the most charming men it has ever been the author's privilege to know, was a most successful breeder, and though, to the regret of everybody, he was not spared to breed the perfect terrier on which he had set his heart, yet he did enough to stamp the terrier of to-day as a workman, with substance, bone, legs and feet.

Mr. Burbidge was a very keen cricketer, captaining the Surrey County Eleven for many years, but after he retired the fortunes of Surrey cricket fell to a very low ebb; they seemed unable to get any new players of merit, and their old ones were past first-class cricket. But their old captain, Burbidge, set his heart on doing something to put cricket at the Oval on its legs again. He used to tell the writer that two of his ambitions in life were to make Surrey champion country and to breed the best Fox-terrier of all time. The former he was successful in doing, and I have not the slightest doubt that he would have succeeded in the latter if he had been spared a few more years for this world.

A keen follower and liberal supporter of the Old Berkely Foxhounds, a good shot, first-class fisherman, a fine billiard player—in fact there was little Fred Burbidge did not excel at, and many there were who, when he died, lost a kind friend. His charitable hand was always in his pocket.

Amongst the many good terriers owned by Mr. Burbidge were his "Nettle", referred to previously and always associated with his name; "Bloom" by "Buff", and "Dorcas", by "Old Foiler". This trio of bitches would be hard to beat today, and although we produce many more good ones than in their day yet I very much doubt if three bitches could be produced today that could beat Burbidges's "Nettle", "Bloom" and "Dorcas".

"Nimrod" and "Bitter" were two celebrated importations into his kennel, also "Royal", whose statue in silver adorns the lid of the Fox-terrier Club fifty-guinea "Smooth" challenge cup. "Hunton Prince", "Hunton Baron", "Hunton Scrimmage", "Hunton Tarter" (brother to "Despoiler"), "Hunton Brigand", "Hunton Bridegroom", "Hunton Honeymoon", "Hunton Queenie", and "Hunton Justice", are a few names which will always do credit to the celebrated Hunton Kennel.

All of the early supporters from Luke Turner to Robert Vicary and Francis Redmond were true sporting gentlemen.

Coming into the last half of the first decade Robert Vicary was building his international reputation on the productive quality of the bitch "Vesuvienne" and the dog "Venio." There is a report that an American millionaire offered 200 guineas for these two fine terriers but Mr. Vicary refused, advising the bidder that the dogs were not for sale. The American persisted, sending cable after cable. Finally, when the offer reached 1000 guineas, Mr. Vicary replied, "Still much obliged but you don't have enough money to buy them."

Before moving on to Wires at the turn of the century there remains two more great Smooths to recognize. Ch. Result, a Belgrave Joe descendant, was bred by the brothers A. H. and C. Clarke. Result won the Fox Terrier Club's Fifty Guinea Challenge Cup 12 times and produced a number of fine Fox Terriers including the great bitch Rachel. Ch. Oxonian was born in

1904 and became so successful as a sire that many modern Smooth champions are directly descended from him or his marvelous grandson, Ch. Cromwell Ochre's Legacy. Mr. Desmond O'Connel was Ch. Oxonian's breeder and this fact alone assured him a place in history. Oxonian was a great, great grandson of Ch. Splinter.

Prior to describing the triumphs and contributions of the Duchess of Newcastle, I want to use her to reinforce my early basic premise about the confusion surrounding the accuracy of the early pedigrees. The Duchess was the only important breeder of Wires to Smooths. I consider that in spite of all her efforts in crossbreeding, her rewards were slim. It is difficult to pinpoint with any certainty a single significant success as a result of inter-breeding the two breeds. The Duchess was a determined and gracious lady who wanted to believe that her cross-breeding efforts were not only successful but significant in the development of Wires and Smooths. There is general acceptance that the great Wire Ch. Barkby Ben was by Meersbrook Ben, a son of Meersbrook Bristles. There had been some minor challenge to Barkby Ben's ancestry but it was dismissed with little notice at the time. However, Her Grace still raised the issue of the possibility of Barkby Ben's Smooth ancestry in her article appearing in The Fox Terrier Club's Jubilee Year Book published in 1926, 20 years after the controversy.

> There has always been rather more than a doubt as to Ch. Barkby Ben's true parentage, in fact there was a *cause celebre* tried by the Kennel Club over it. If Barby Correspondent was his sire instead of (as given) Meersbrook Ben then he traces back to Belgrave Joe. I own that in make, shape and terrier character there was a lot that reminded me of Correspondent about Ben. However, leave it at that, but because of these doubts I have started a family tree from Ch. Barkby Ben. Certainly I owe all of my "Of Notts" strain entirely to inbreeding to him.

With that statement by the Duchess and the other comments by previous breed scholars, I rest my case on the origins of the two breeds. They have developed separately and from different roots and no Smooth-Wire cross made any meaningful difference. If, in fact, the Smooth aided the development of the Wire or vice versa, then there would have developed a need to periodically inject the blood of the cross to prevent regression. In the absence of definitive data to the contrary, I will accept the records of the past 70 years and the evidence of my eyes and state that the two breeds are separate and developed independently of one another.

The withdrawal of William Carrick, Jr. from dogs was a severe setback to Wire development in England. His dogs were approaching parity with and indeed surpassing the quality of the Smooth. Mr. Harding Cox, the Fox Terrier Club founder, and Mr. George Raper were other early Wire enthusiasts but it was Carrick's results in the ring that gave the Wire its initial leap forward on both sides of the ocean. Her Grace, the

Duchess of Newcastle, to her credit, refused to engage in the financial competition that was prevalent in the 1890s. American money and the interest of the English gentry kept prices in the comparative stratosphere. But Her Grace would have none of that. In 1893 she bred a Smooth bitch, Partner Prude, to the Wire dog Tipton Slasher. While there is no evidence to support the story, rumor has it that she paid about five pounds for both! The mating produced Lady Tipton of Notts. The Duchess was breeding Fox Terriers with only moderate success until 1898 when she bred Lady Tipton to Ch. Barkby Ben. The result was Ch. Cackler of Notts, one of the great Wire foundation dogs. Wire students all agree that Cackler appears in the extended pedigree of almost every modern Wire. Cackler completes the early connection to Kendall's Old Tip. The line continues from Tip to Pincher to Old Jester to Young Jester in 1884 to Knavesmire Jest in 1885 to Meersbrook Bristles in 1892 to Meersbrook Ben in 1894 to Barkby Ben in 1897 to Cackler in 1898. From 1900 to the outbreak of World War I in 1914, "Of Notts" Wires won the Fifty Guinea Challenge Cup five times, twice with Cackler, once with Collar, and Mr. A. E. G. Ways won it twice with Collarbone of Notts. The Duchess of Newcastle left Wires and went into Smooths with equal success. According to most Wire historians her greatest contribution was the development of Comedian on Notts. Such significant future Wires as Fountain Crusader, Barrington Bridegroom, Crackler Supreme, and Wireboy of Paignton were direct descendants of Comedian.

There can be no reasonable accounting of Wire history without reference to George Raper. He was a judge of world renown, a breeder of consumate skill, a salesman rivaling P. T. Barnum, the premier conditioner and handler of Wires of his day, and a speaker of marvelous wit and charm.

Ch. Go Bang was the top winner in England from 1896 through 1898; during that period he won the Fifty Guinea Challenge Cup eight times in nine attempts including seven consecutive awards. This remarkable achievement was never duplicated. The Cup was offered from 1881 to 1935 but during the early years only a handful of Wires competed. The early Wire owned by P. Haywood Fields and later sold to the Earl of Lonsdale, "Briggs," won it six consecutive times and nine in all, but the 15-year time period between the two dogs produced dramatic changes in the quality and numbers of the competition. Raper first saw Go Bang as a puppy in 1895 when he judged at the Durham show. He bought the dog from his breeder-owner, G. W. Norman, for £.200 and campaigned him vigorously from 1895 to 1898. Raper's talent as a handler and groomer brought out the best in Go Bang. In 1898 Raper sold Go Bang to Major Carnochan for £.500. Such was the fame of the dog and the significance of the sale and acquisition that Raper personally delivered the dog to Carnochan. Ackerman describes his arrival as follows: "Raper brought Go Bang and the Smooth champion Claude Duval to America along with some other

Comedian of Notts. It would be difficult to find a modern Wire that does not trace back to Comedian.

Ch. Oxonian, whelped in 1902.

Ch. Orkadian.

These two Smooth links join the modern Smooths to their roots.

terriers. A crowd of fanciers greeted Raper at the Hoboken dock and it was the consensus of those present at the impromptu dog show that Go Bang was the best ever seen up to that time on American soil." Unfortunately Go Bang never fulfilled his promise as a sire. Raper was also Carnochan's agent in his efforts to acquire Barkby Ben. The combination of Raper's sales ability and Carnochan's pocketbook finally convinced J. W. W. Swingler to part with Ben for the inconceivable sum of $2500. Raper died in 1924. In his lifetime he was instrumental in bringing more great English terriers to wealthy Americans than anyone else in his time.

Francis Redmond applied his skills to Wires as well as Smooths. In 1901 and again in 1902, Major Carnochan applied for permission to show his American Wires against the British Wires. Permission was granted and in 1901 the first match was held at the Quarantine Station in Mitchum, England. In 1901 Mr. Redmond's Dusky Cracker was judged the winner and Dusky Admiral, another Redmond homebred, won in 1902. From 1901 to 1916 the following Redmond-bred Wires won the Fifty Guinea Challenge Cup: 1901—Dusky Reine, 1902—Dusky Gleaner, 1904—Dusky Siren, 1905—Dusky Courtly, 1906—Dusky Admiral, 1908 and 1909—Dusky Dairymaid. There can be no question that Francis Redmond was the major Fox Terrier force in his time and for generations yet to come. We will not see his like again and it is to the eternal good fortune of the Fox Terriers that he chose our breeds to devote his life's efforts.

Before moving on to the clearer, more discernible and more meaningful dogs and people in relationship to today's Smooths and Wires, the reader may ask, "If, in fact, nearly all modern Smooth stud dogs can be traced back to Splinter and not Belgrave Joe, why does Joe earn the distinction as the father of the Smooth?" Joe pre-dated Splinter by 15 years. Naturally, Joe sired many champions before Splinter saw the light of day. The first Smooths in the United States were descendants of Joe. Tort, a bitch that came to America in 1879, was a granddaughter of Belgrave Joe. Ch. Levenside Luke, a later descendant of Belgrave Joe, went to Australia to start Smooths in that great hotbed of Fox Terrier activity, and many of today's Smooths can trace their ancestry back to a Belgrave Joe daughter. It is reasonable to conclude that Belgrave Joe laid the foundation for our great house of Smooth history and Splinter completed the structure. As this history progresses, keep in mind that Oxonian and Orkadian are direct descendants of Splinter.

2

Fox Terriers in the Twentieth Century

IT IS NOT THE DOGS in our past that are important but the past in our dogs. The great saloon comedian Joe E. Lewis used to say, "Beauty is only skin deep, but ugly goes right to the bone." In dogs, beauty is superficial, but faults go right to the genes. The previous chapter describes the acquisition by Major Carnochan of the great show dog, Ch. Go Bang. In 1987 dollars the Major paid about $50,000 for Go Bang and, while he piled up an impressive career as a showman, he was a dud as a producer, whereas Meersbrook Bristles and his grandson, Barkby Ben, were not only great competitors but great producers, with a legacy of productive offspring on both sides of the Atlantic. The history of the Smooth Fox Terrier in America, from the early years of the 20th century to the end of World War I, can be condensed into three great names. Rutherfurd, Farwell, and Gooderham virtually dominated the breed for nearly 25 years. G. H. Gooderham of Toronto was included with Farwell and Rutherfurd because of his early success with his great dog, Eng., Am. Ch. Norfolk Veracity. Here was an outstanding show dog and an outstanding producer. The June 1902 issue of *The Fox Terrier Chronicle* contained the following report on American Fox Terrier activity:

The Fox Terrier in The States

Fox Terriers are about holding their own; the leading kennel in Smooths—that is Norfolk—is as strong as ever it was, whilst in Wires the strongest kennel—Cairnsmuir—has not lost any ground, but is, if anything, a bit more formidable than ever. There may be Mr. Belmont to reckon with before long. He is not the sort to play second fiddle for any length of time, so that likely enough his kennel will soon be quite as prominent as those just mentioned. Mr. Belmont's recent import, Don Cesario, is an acknowledged good stud dog, whereas his Blemton Victor was a distinct failure in this capacity. The new dog should be a very useful addition to the fancy, and he may be heard from next spring, possibly sooner. Trianon Kennels usually managed to breed a fairly good one or two every year, and they were in evidence at Pittsburg as usual; but the best youngster of the circuit shows was seen in Norfolk True Blue, bred by the Norfolk Kennels. Two good Wire stud dogs in Matchmaker and Barkby Ben have been imported. The former, especially, being very successful, and these, with two new Smooths, Don Cesario and Terence, the latter owned by Cairnsmuir Kennels, should help raise the standard some during the next year or two, although neither of the Smooths may prove as successful as Veracity. This, however, remains to be seen—

Source: Man's Best Friend

In the February 10, 1906 issue of *The Rider and Driver Magazine* the following was reported:

No kennel in our recollection has sprung into prominence and with greater prospects of success than those of Mr. Jennings Scott McComb, of Dobbs Ferry, New York, whose prefix "Rowsley" is making such havoc in the prize lists of our leading shows. Although only making his debut at the New York show a year ago his list of wins is too extensive to give in detail.

The article goes on to explain the purchase of Irish, Airedale and "wire-haired Fox Terriers" by Mr. McComb and some of the achievements of those imports.

Turning from the Irish Terriers and in another kennel were the best and most level team of wire-haired Fox Terriers it was ever our lot to see in one ownership, and it would not be too much to say, even at one time. When we mention that three of the bitches were first, second and third at the recent Crystal Palace Show, London, enough has been said as to their quality and value when it is said that they represented the cream of the wire-haired terrier world of England.

Rowsley Syren, late Dusky Syren, has to her credit 22 championships and nine times that for Best in Show of all breeds. Rowsley Courtly, her half sister, is the winner of firsts at Birmingham, Manchester, Burton on Trent, etc., etc., etc., the last win being at the Cheltenham Show, where she won the Fox Terrier Club Fifty Guinea Challenge Cup. (author's note 1905 Cheltenham C.C. winner Dusky Courtly) Rowsley Hope, although only 18 months old, has 56 firsts to her credit, and has, as it were, been knocking at the championship door for some time and only Dusky Syren has held it against her. Here is a case of what one cannot do, the other can. Last but far from least is the all-white dog Rowsley Jester. When we say not least we mean it in point of merit. Although unshown, his superlative quality commands attention from everyone to whom a private view has been given. Suffice to say he will be exhibited at the Garden and our readers can there form their own ideas what a good terrier is like.

A Public Challenge has been made to show him against any breed of terrier for $500 aside.

Later on in that same Westminster issue, the magazine provided a preview of the Fox Terrier competition.

Smooth Fox Terriers have nothing of conspicious note recently imported. However, with the famous Sabine Kennels, Warren Kennels and other prominent exhibitors competing with many real good domestic-bred the old-timers will not be in good form. In the wire-haired variety, however, there is a different tale to tell. The recent importations of Mr. J. Scott McComb, of Rowsley fame, are bound to make their presence felt. We have no hesitation in saying that on no previous occasion has such an array of quality ever been imported that could compare with the trio which landed last week consigned to the handler, George Porter. Dusky Syren is one of the most noted bitches of this decade and has won no less than 22 championships in England, against the cream of the terrier world. Dusky Courtly is another topper that has a similar record. The tid-bit of the lot, however, in our opinion, is the unknown, Rowsley Joker, a young dog that for all 'round terrier character and quality, is certainly a wonder. One most pleasing feature about this trio is their beautiful size and general type; they are on the "huntsman" type, cobby, with rare legs and feet, long, clean heads, sound shoulders and hindquarters, and "natural" jackets. Against this team will compete the noted Wandee team from San Francisco, owned by that good fancier, Mr. C. K. Harley, who owned the famous Ch. Wandee Coastguard, Wandee-Mearas, Wandee Manila and the beautiful Lucretia, all of which are in grand fettle.

While these articles are interesting period pieces, providing a feel for the time, they also signal the start of a tidal wave of imports that would descend upon the Fox Terrier world in future years. Hardly had the ribbon been presented in England than the winners were on a boat to the Colonies, leaving behind for the most part richer Englishmen and *a great number of American imports.* In many instances, the people who paid huge sums, hoping to buy what they could not produce, were never heard from again. The "Famous" Rowsley Kennel so glowingly described in the two articles did gain American titles for Rowsley Jester, Stylish, Courtly, Hope, Remnant, and Syren ne Siren. The "Joker" in article two, I can only assume was Jester. All finished in 1903-04. These is no other record of Rowsley Wires gaining a title before or since. But the fat was in the fire. The English were getting fat and the Yanks were getting burned for the most part. The balance of this book will confine itself to those Fox Terriers who proved worthy of their keep by producing the ancestors of today's winners.

Sabine

The Sabine prefix of Frederick Henry Farwell was the prevailing force in Smooth Fox Terriers for the first 20 years of the new century. He bred black and white to black and white and, if the reports are true, culled the tan and whites and all the white puppies. According to William Kendrick, who knew Farwell intimately, the master of Sabine never wanted to "contaminate" his look with the "muddy tans." The American Fox Terrier Club Year Book of 1934 states:

> by fearless buying of the best in England and by methodical and intelligent mating evolved a strain of Smooth Fox Terriers which, with never a tan marked or all white among them, bred so true to type that the veriest novice could pick out at a glance a Smooth which bore the Sabine prefix.

In 1910 Sabine Smooths were exhibited at 17 shows and went BIS at 12. Some of Farwell's top winners were Ch. Sabine Rarebit, a five-time winner of the AFTC Grand Challenge Cup and Best in Show at Westminster in 1910; Ch. Sabine Forever completed her American title and then challenged the best that England had, and earned her English championship. This was a first for any breed and accomplished wonders for the prestige of our American program. Farwell spent willingly to get the Reuge; each gained their American title. Of course, every Smooth breeder signifiant performer was Ridgewood Result, better known in the United States as Ch. Sabine Result. The Sabine home in Orange, Texas was a showplace and Mr. Farwell was a gracious host to all visitors who arrived at his place on the banks of the Sabine River. Farwell was a fierce competitor and he culled agressively, but when he felt that he had achieved his goals, he cut back his efforts to make room for other, newer exhibitors. And it is quite possible that the Sabine success did inhibit some from exhibiting Smooth Fox Terriers but not Winthrop Rutherfurd. While Farwell was a breeder and exhibitor of significance, it was Rutherfurd who was a founder and President of the American Fox Terrier Club. Farwell lived in Texas, a 40-hour train ride to New York, the center of club activity. Farwell rarely made an appearance in the ring except when judging. Rutherfurd frequently exhibited his own dogs. It is quite possible that had Farwell lived closer, he might have been more active, but that was not the case. Winthrop Rutherfurd was President of the AFTC from 1896 to 1921, and, when his cherished club needed him again, he served as President from 1931 to 1944. The first of Rutherfurd's Warren champions were exhibited in 1892. As mentioned earlier, the acquisition of Splauger from England was a great start and proved to be a good foundation for future winners. But in 1892 Lewis and Winthrop imported Warren Safeguard by Venio ex Eggesford Saphire and the bitch, Warren Captious, by Charlton Verdict ex Reuge, each gained their American title. Of course, every Smooth breeder

Winthrop Rutherfurd, one of the earliest exhibitors of Smooths. A founder and past president of the American Fox Terrier Club, he was also a great breeder.

Ch. Warren Remedy, Best in Show at Westminster in 1907, 1908 and 1909.

Ch. Sabine Rarebit, Best in Show at Westminster in 1910, the last Smooth to attain that honor.

is aware of Ch. Warren Remedy, the fantastic bitch whose major achievement has yet to be duplicated, three consecutive Westminster Bests in Show—1907, 1908, and 1909. And as mentioned earlier Ch. Sabine Rarebit won in 1910. These achievements were the beginning of the decline for the Smooth and the start of the ascendancy of the Wire in America. Just before World War I, both Farwell and Rutherfurd sold off many of their dogs; Farwell gave up exhibiting. Rutherfurd competed periodically in the ensuing years but never with the frequency of the pre-WWI years. Some of the Sabines that were sold off continued to compete and win, but no breed in those days could afford the loss of so dominant an influence as Rutherfurd and Farwell and continue to prosper.

To give the reader some insight into the decline of the Smooth from World War I to the early 1930s, let's examine some revealing statistics. The AKC recorded a total of 353 Fox Terrier champions born from 1884 to 1924. Of these, 175 were Smooths and 188 were Wires. Of the champion Smooths, just 15 completed their titles in the post-war years; less than 10%. Wires, on the other hand, had 52 titles or nearly 28%. And to further emphasize the Smooth drought, two of the 15 who finished after World War I were Farwell-bred Sabines, although owned and exhibited by others.

One individual who stepped into the breach was E. H. Ingwersen of Chicago. Under the Niola prefix he continued to breed and exhibit through World War I and into the 1920s. Several of the Sabine Smooths provided Ingwersen with the foundation for his program. Ch. Sabine Referee, Ch. Sabine Reckoner, Sabine Reserve, Sabine Rollway, Ch. Sabine Resist, and Sabine Red Gem all sired Niola champions, so even with Farwell on the sidelines, his dogs were still carrying on. Before writing a finish to this period in Smooth history, there is an experience I had that, I believe, will be of interest to any Fox Terrier fan. The Quaker Oats Company hosts an annual dinner, the date of which coincides with the Westminster Show. The seven individual winners from each of the groups are selected by a point system based upon the number of dogs defeated by the winner in its respective group. The seven winners, therefore, include one representative from the Sporting, Hound, Working, Terrier, Toy, Non-sporting, and Herding Group. Since the banquet was tied to Westminster and since the emphasis was on top-winning dogs, the Quaker Oats Company commissioned one of the generation's most successful and knowledgeable dog men, Richard Chashoudian, to create a bronze statue of Ch. Warren Remedy to be awarded annually to each Quaker Oats Group victor. Ric accepted the commission with pride and set about the task of recreating Remedy in bronze. There was one problem. All the pictures of Ch. Warren Remedy were too small to really be much help to the artist. One afternoon my phone rang and I recognized the gravelly voice immediately. . . . "Harold, this is Ric. Do you have a large photo or painting of Warren Remedy?" I remembered a large photo or painting of Remedy on the cover of an old issue of *Fox Terrier Magazine,* a publication of the 1940s. It went out that day, express, to Baton Rouge, Ric's home. He promised to return the rather rare copy just as soon as he finished the sculpture. Several months later, I had occasion to call Ric on another matter and inquired about his progress. "Oh, I just sent it to the foundry in Canada yesterday. That picture was terrific. The only thing was in those days they didn't show the dog's plumbing. There was no plumbing on the dog. I had to put that on myself." When I told Ric that the *dog* was a *bitch,* he was mortified and in a panic. He had to get the statue back from Canada and perform the *sex change* before the actual casting. I promised Chashoudian that I would not tell a soul . . . and I haven't. The only reason I'm sharing this with you now is that Ric still has my magazine!

The Smooth of the early 1920s sputtered along with Ingwersen's Niola representatives and the occasional Rutherfurd entry under the Warren prefix. Several years ago I had the opportunity to talk with Winthrop Rutherfurd, Jr. about the activities of his "Fox Terrier famous" father. I was curious about the actions of Rutherfurd Senior. Why did he sell off most of his Smooths and seemingly retire from breeding and exhibiting? And, then why the return to the ring, although more modestly in the '20s? Mr. Rutherfurd advised me that, to the best of his knowledge, it was difficult to get competent help during the war, but his father was always involved with Fox Terriers until his demise in 1944. And the Warren prefix can be found among the winners at many shows in the '20s.

Another Farwell protegé, Thomas Rice Varick, exhibited with some success. In 1918 Varick won the AFTC Grand Challenge Cup with Ch. Sabine Fernlike. From 1920 to 1922 Fernlike won the Sabine Result Trophy six times. However, Mr. Varick did little noteworthy breeding but was always on the lookout for a "good one." In 1928 he had some success with Ch. Southboro Satrap and again in 1932 with Ch. Dunsrex.

As the decade passed the mid-point for the Smooth Fox Terrier, four new names began to appear: Dr. and Mrs. Homer Gage, Q. A. Shaw McKean, E. Coe Kerr, and Robert Sedgwick. Homer Gage, Jr. died in September 1925 at age 30. The AFTC records his passing as follows: "Gentleman, Sportsman, Lover of Dogs, but above all, a devoted son and faithful friend, who met death as each day he greeted life, with a smile." The Homer Gage, Jr. and Welwire Memorial Trophies are offered each year in his honor, funded by a trust established by Dr. and Mrs. Homer Gage. The Gages continued to exhibit an occasional Smooth, but they made their significant contribution in the other coat.

Enter stage right: Quincy A. Shaw McKean of Prides Crossing, Mass., a Wire breeder of some success, who decided to try his hand with Smooths. Ch. Lady Crossfield of Prides Hill won the Sabine Result Trophy 10 times from 1925 through 1928. E. Coe Kerr and Robert Sedgwick rounded out the decade by discovering the Watteau Kennel of Mr. Calvert Butler in

Carnforth, England. Is there anyone breeding Smooths today who has never heard of Watteau? The bitch imported by Kerr and Sedgwick was Ch. Watteau Donzella. An eyewitness described here as "a feminine bitch, full of refinement and quality, who perhaps not overly burdened with substance, beautifully chiseled head, sweet front and a gladsome shower, trying all the time." Donzella was a five-time winner of the Sabine Result Trophy, but, I believe, her greatest contribution was the part she played in alerting the Smooth breeders in the United States to the existence of Mr. Butler, his daughter, Mrs. Anthony Blake, and their Watteau Fox Terriers.

Dog breeding and exhibiting, like all other things in life, exist in relationship to the times. Thus from 1885 to 1914 there was considerable activity between the United States and Great Britain. In 1914 war broke out and American breeders were forced to develop their own "flyers." The "over the pond" activity resumed once again for both breeds in 1919 but was interrupted one more time by the events of 1919 and the subsequent economic upheaval. For example, of those Wires whelped in 1922 that eventually became champions, 15 were imported from England, six were American-bred and one was Canadian. That same ratio held true until 1929, when 17 Wires born that year eventually qualified for the title, but only six were English imports, and, by 1931, as the Depression deepened, all the Wires whelped in 1931 that went on to the title were American-bred. The majority of Smooth champions were developed by American Smooth champions of which just 37 were English. One-hundred of the 174 Wire champions were exported from Britain. Between World War I and 1919 more than 2/3's of all champion Wires were imported. So while Wires outnumbered Smooths by as much as 8 to 1 at many major shows, domestic breeding programs were proportionately less effective. The emphasis was on winning, and breeding, in some cases, suffered.

Wires in 1905 were in a state of transition. There was no Wire fancier the equivalent of Winthrop Rutherfurd or F. H. Farwell. It appears the early exhibitors bought dogs through George Raper or George Thomas. There was no lack of buyers, only a lack of perseverance and tenacity. In 1904 Charles K. Harley purchased six Wires from George Raper, including Raby Coastguard, Lucretia, and Manilla. By 1906 Harley was out of dogs. Major Carnochan also dropped out around the same time. Some enterprising dog person with a flair for research and nose for mystery might develop enough material for an entire book on "Whatever Happened to . . ." this or that Wire import of the first two decades of this century.

Mr. J. Scott McCoomb's dilettante activities were referred to earlier. In 1912 Wire fortunes took a brighter turn. The breed had improved dramatically over the past 10 years and was giving better than it was receiving from the previously dominating Smooth. The first serious American Wire Fox Terrier breeders emerged in the persons of Mrs. Roy Rainey and the partners Mrs. A. V. Crawford and Charles H. Perrin. The

Crawford-Perrin combination developed the Vickery strain and were located in Barrington, Illinois. Mrs. Rainey's efforts established the Conejo Wires as a reckoning force in the ring for the succeeding 15 years. Vickery Wire Result and Vickery Bubbling Water were just two of the Crawford-Perrin charges that George Thomas acquired for them.

Conejo Kennel (Mrs. Roy Rainey) would have earned its place in the Wire Hall of Fame with one acquisition, Ch. Conejo Wycollar Boy. He was purchased from his importer, Andrew Albright, for $3,000. I won't bore the reader with comparative analogies as to the relative value of $3,000 in 1917, but it was a remarkable sum. Ch. Conejo Wycollar Boy in 1917 won BIS at Westminster and again in 1920. The 1917 win came after Vickery Kennel's import, Matford Vic, won in 1915 and 1916, the first Wire to achieve that prestigious win.

Mr. Quincy A. Shaw McKean, mentioned earlier in the Smooth discourse, was one of the first to successfully breed Wires in America that could compete with the English. Ch. Prides Hill Tweak'em was one of the first American-bred dogs to make a mark in the tough competition that prevailed from 1916 to 1920. Mr. McKean and Mrs. Rainey continued to raise Fox Terriers for years to come and were very active in the activities of the AFTC.

The decade closed with bright hopes for the development of American-bred Wires and a rather unusual event or, more descriptive, "series of events" in Great Britain. The year was 1919. The Great War to end all wars was over. In three different parts of England three great Wires were whelped, dogs that were to affect the conformation and competitiveness of the breed to the present day. It would be the equal to the foaling of Bold Ruler, Native Dancer, and Secretariat in the same year. This trio not only propelled the modern Wire into the 20th century but they also provided the link to Comedian of Notts and Kendall's Old Tip. Earlier, the link from Comedian to Old Tip was established as well as possible considering the conditions of the times. Comedian of Notts sired a number of top Wires of the period including Olcliffe Captain and Collar of Notts. Tracing two lines from Collar of Notts to 1919, they were responsible for Barrington Bridegroom and Wycollar Trail. Olcliffe Captain sired Fountain Crusader. Those three marvelously prepotent sires are in the pedigree of nearly all Wires shown today.

Homer Gage, Jr. imported Barrington Bridegroom and affixed the Welwire prefix. George Skelly describes Bridegroom's impact on American Wires:

> The comparative influence of Welwire Barrington Bridegroom in the breeding of American champions, as measured by his siring record and his appearance in the second and third generations, rates him in the upper dozen of super-studs. While each of 12 other sires produced a greater number of American champion sons and daughters than did Bridegroom, it is worth noting that all

Frederick Farwell's champion import,   Sabine Result.

Ch. Wireboy of Paignton, sire of Conejo Wycollar Boy, twice
Westminster Best in Show.

47

Ch. Barrington Bridegroom, rated by George Skelly as being in "the upper dozen of super-studs." He was imported by Homer Gage, Jr.

Ch. Prides Hill Tweak'em, five times Best in Show, 1918.

Mrs. R. C. Bondy (right) and Phyllis Robson with champions Eden Aristocrat, Weltona Frizette and Crackley Supreme.

12 of them were his descendants with most of them actually line-bred from him. Therefore, with deserved credit to him for some part of their prepotency, the superlative Bridegroom easily ranks as one of the greatest Wire stud forces in the history of American Wire breeding. To call him a pillar of the breed would be an under statement.

Eng. Ch. Wycollar Trail was the maternal grandsire of five American champions, among them Gains Great Surprise, referred to by many Wire breeders as the most influential Wire matron of all times.

Eng. Ch. Fountain Crusader was an outstanding stud who sired six American champions but most people will always remember him as the sire of the Adam of modern Wire Fox Terriers, the unique Talavera Simon. Ackerman on Talavera Simon:

Meersbrook Bristles; Bristles' great-grandson, Cackler of Notts; Cackler's great-great-grandson, Comedian of Notts; and finally Comedian's great-grandson, Talavera Simon, are what may be termed power-houses along the river of Wire blood as it flows from Old Tip to the most recent champion recorded in the stud books either of America or of England. That one dog should dominate his species for generations, that a single individual should be able to improve a breed to the point of revolutionizing it and to the point of rendering old-fashioned all that has gone before him is one of the facts to which breeders can never become accustomed.

Yet every breed of domestic livestock has such a Charlemagne. What Hamiltonian* was to the standard-bred horse, what Lexington was to the thoroughbred, what Longfellow was to Berkshire swine, so is Simon to the Wire Fox Terrier.

Somewhat loosely and all too freely dogs are called "pillars of the stud book," but Simon is a veritable structural steel framework for the improved Fox Terrier of today.

*Author's note—I believe ackerman was referring to Hambletonian.

Ah, but in this digression about these great antecedents of the modern Wire, I've let the scent grow cold. We are coming into the 1920s with the Wire future in the capable and talented hands of Homer Gage, Jr. and his parents, Mrs. Roy Rainey and Mr. Quincy A. Shaw McKean. And in this decade we see the emergence of the combination that was to insure continued breed improvement, the professional handler/kennel manager. Leonard Brumby entered the employ of Maurice Newton and took on the colors of Chappaqua Kennels. Leonard Brumby's father, W. L. Brumby, was an earlier terrier breeder in Yorkshire under the Briar prefix. Stanley Halle, not to be left at the post, brought Percy Roberts to Halleston. But, by far, the most successful combination of gifted owner/talented kennel manager was that of Mr. and Mrs. Richard C. Bondy of Wildoaks, Golden Bridge, New York and their redoubtable Mac Silver. Other writers on the breeds refer to the period from 1920 to 1935 as the Golden Age of Wires; a more accurate application would be "The Age of Wire Enlightenment," because for the first time Wire exhibitors recognized that it "takes two to tango." A good stud dog does not alone a champion make. Alas, Horatio, you need a good producing bitch. In truth, a great producing bitch can add lots of lustre to a rather ordinary stud dog if he is well bred, but a great stud dog can only do so much if put to commonplace bitches. The combination of resources, dedication, talent of the owners and the knowledge of men like Brumby, Roberts, and Silver ushered in "The Golden Age of Wire Enlightenment." In 1925, Wildoaks imported Courtwood Charmer and Watteau Paladin, bred by the same Mr. Calvert Butler, who a few years later sent Ch. Watteau Donzella, the gorgeous Smooth bitch to Kerr-Sedgwick. All breeders, regardless of breed, can learn an object lesson from the remarkable standards of quality produced by certain breeders who, as they have for decades, continue to produce specimens approaching the ideal encompassed in the standard. Charmer produced the first Wildoaks homebred champions, Rajah and Reveller, from a breeding to Ch. Signal Warily of Wildoaks, an earlier import. The next three imports proved to be pivotal to the future of Wildoaks. Crackley Supreme and Eden Aristocrat would have satisfied the needs of most breeders, but the Wildoaks effort was climaxed with the purchase of the "mother" of the modern Wire, Ch. Gains Great Surprise of Wildoaks. This daughter of Talavera Simon out of a Wycollar Trail bitch was bred to Ch. Crackley Supreme of Wildoaks, a Barrington Bridegroom grandson, and the union produced what can only be described as a truly unique result. A writer runs out of superlatives in attempting to describe a litter that produced Gallant Fox of Wildoaks and Gallant Knight of Wildoaks. Together, this pair sired 30 American champions, and Gallant Fox, after acquiring his English title, retired to stud and produced 15 English champions. This record might have been even more impressive if not for the interruption of World War II. Gallant Knight was too big for the ring, but he became the foundation stud dog of the Hetherington Kennel of Mr. and Mrs. Thomas H. Carruthers III.

The following was said of Ch. Barrington Bridegroom in Ackerman's book:

> Barrington Bridegroom, said to have cost the late Homer Gage, Jr. $7,000, was a magnificently built stallion terrier on the big side. He met defeat many times in England where judges faulted him for size, but just as often did he attain supreme honors in his native land.

Bridegroom's English record was unimpressive when compared to his American wins.

As for Ch. Gains Great Surprise, she lived up to her name. When bred to the Crusader grandson, Ch. Signal Warily, she turned out Beau Brummel of Wildoaks, who went to England before completing his American title but still managed to impact the breed in England and on the Continent in a typical Wildoaks' fashion. Before closing this decade and the Wildoaks achievement, mention must be made of Ch. Weltona Frizette of Wildoaks. Frizette was another astute import of Mrs. Bondy, who continued the Wildoaks tradition after the death of Mr. Bondy in 1930. This extraordinary bitch established a BIS record that lasted for many years, and in her first litter she produced three champions. That's right—a top winning show bitch actually took time out in her career to have a litter of puppies. Mrs. Bondy was a breeder first and then an exhibitor.

The Depression deepens. One third of the nation is unemployed, the flood of terrier imports from England is reduced to a rivulet. However, what the '20s were to the growth and prosperity of the Wire, the '30s had a similar, albeit less dramatic, impact on the Smooth.

Smooths were beginning to come alive with E. Coe Kerr's Millhill Kennels, Mr. and Mrs. Scott's Brandon Fox Terriers leading the way. They were joined by three significant breeders who were to do for Smooths what the Gages and the Bondys did for Wires a decade earlier. "FFA" in Smooth Fox Terrier lore does not stand for Future Farmers of America, but for Farrell, Fallass, and Austin.

In the winter of 1934, Mr. and Mrs. James A. Farrell, Jr. returned from an extended European honeymoon with two Irish Smooth Fox Terriers, Molten Fancy Man and Molten Kamala, and Foxden Kennels was off and running. Several times during the succeeding 50-plus years that the Farrell name was associated with Smooths, they would single-handedly keep the breed and the club from atrophy and despair. One slight correction to Ackermans work: he reports a dog called Gallant Fox as being their first Smooth. Gallant Fox was a Smooth and he did belong to a Farrell, but it was a brother of Jim Farrell; the same is true of Ch. Fox Finder.

Mr. and Mrs. James A. Farrell, Jr. began Foxden with Fancy and Kamala, and about a year later they turned once again to Mrs. W. L. G. Dean of Molten and acquired another bitch, Ch. Molten Zola. Percy Roberts then sold Ch. Flornell Springbok to the Farrells, and Zola, Kamala and Springbok formed the nucleus of the Foxden brood bitches with Fancy Man the first stud dog. If this section on the '30s appears a bit sketchy when compared to the other periods, blame it on the Depression. There were several Specialties held in the early '30s that had little or no Smooth entries. If Jere R. Collins, Charles Scott, the Gages, or Kerr-Sedgwick did not have a litter, or did not exhibit the latest import, there was no entry. The addition of serious breeders like the Farrells, therefore, was all the more significant. The support of the smaller breeders was simply dried up by the economic conditions. It took money to raise and exhibit dogs, and there was precious little of it around.

The mid-'30s saw most Smooth competition dwindle to just three or four prominent breeders. The Scott's Bandon Kennels, Kerr's Millhill prefix, Winthrop Rutherfurd's Warren Smooths still made an occasional

Ch. Gains Great Surprise of Wildoaks as a youngster. Photo supplied by Mr. Calvert Butler's daughter, Mrs. Mary Blake. Taken after the bitch was purchased by Calvert Butler for £1,000.

Ch. Gallant Fox of Wildoaks.

Prides Hill Tacks, a 1919 Best in Show winner for the Prides Hill Kennels of Quincy A. Shaw McKean.

Best in Show at Westminster in 1930, 1931, Ch. Pendley Calling of Blarney.

Ch. Molten Fancy Man and Molten Kamala were the nucleus of Foxden Smooths. Fancy Man was the first dog of any breed to earn its title under the Foxden banner. Circa 1934.

An important producer and outstanding bitch in the ring for Robert Sedgwick, Ch. Heathside Houri. She was a granddaughter of Kidder Karzan, whelped August 14, 1935.

appearance, and, of course, Foxden. In 1933, however, there was a bumper crop of new members to the AFTC, and among them was the squire of Wissaboo Kennels, James M. Austin of Old Westbury, N.Y.

On October 3rd, 1936, in Worksop, England, Mrs. M. V. Hughes was judging a dog show. She was an all-breed judge with good terrier credentials. She picked a seven-month-old Smooth as Best Fox Terrier and Reserve BIS. In her critique published in the English magazine *Our Dogs,* Mrs. Hughes remarked: "Should all go well with this child, he will have a starry future." One week later this pup was exhibited at the Notts Fox Terrier Club Specialty under Judge J. B. Hudson, whose critique read, "... An amazingly good youngster, without any doubt one of the best of this or any era, this eight-months youngster should create a furor when making his debut in classic circles." *Our Dogs* in 1935 still had a good American readership, along with the popular English publication, *Dog World.* James Austin read the critiques describing this new star and wired his handler, Alf Butler, that he wanted to bring Nornay Saddler to America. The price of £.100 was agreed to, and on the 20th of January, 1937, Saddler arrived on the Berengaria. For those readers unfamiliar with Ch. Nornay Saddler, he single-handedly gave the Smooth Fox Terrier a transfusion of enthusiasm and interest when the breed most needed it. And for those of my fellow exhibitors who occasionally feel victimized by less than knowledgeable judges, take heart and persevere. Saddler was 4th in a class of four and 3rd in a class of three in his first two shows. Nobody remembers the judges, and rightfully so, but every Fox Terrier breeder knows of Ch. Nornay Saddler. In addition to 59 All-Breed BIS awards, Saddler won the AFTC Challenge Cup six times. His last three BIS came when he was seven years old. Mr. Austin also imported Eng. Ch. Travelling Fox and Eng. Ch. Avon Peddler, Saddler's sire and grandsire. For breeders who advocate line breeding, Saddler will be a disappointment. The Saddlers of this world are gifts bestowed upon a breed by forces beyond our ken and we should just appreciate them for all of their many contributions.

Saddler himself was the sire of 27 champions, while two of his sons, Ch. Lineman and Ch. Desert Deputy, were responsible for 12 and 10 American titlists respectively. Saddler's sire, Travelling Fox, sired six more American champions after arriving on our shores. Saddler and seven of his get were painted by Franklin B. Voss in oil and reproduced in a limited edition print called *The Saddler Seven.* The same was done for Saddler, himself. I believe the originals are the property of the American Kennel Club in New York. Collectors can still find a rare print if they are fortunate.

Saddler accomplished one more feat as a result of his dramatic success. For several years prior to Saddler, only one Fox Terrier made it into the Group, and it was always a Wire. Since Wire people dominated the breeds, Smooth breeders were resigned to the situation. However, Saddler's string of victories generated enough sentiment among Wire Fox

Ch. Nornay Saddler, the dominant show dog of his era. A fine producer and a wonderful friend. Whelped March 12, 1936.

Saddler's fine son, Ch. Desert Deputy, brought Saddler blood to the West Coast after a fine show career in the East, whelped January 8, 1939.

Terrier breeders to petition the American Kennel Club to once again have two Fox Terriers in the Group. So, in his way Saddler made it that much easier to separate the breeds in 1985, nearly 40 years after his death.

The second "F" of my FFA triumvirate was Barbara Lowe Fallass (Mrs. Charles H.) who returned to the United States after 20 years raising Fox Terriers in France. I left Mrs. Fallass for last because her activities as a breeder of Smooths surpassed any previous effort in the area of home-bred champions. Upon her return to America she imported two fine Smooths, Avon Bondette and Buckland. These were soon followed by Oneway Storm. Another side of Mrs. Fallass' character that endears her to the writer is demonstrated in the following account. Ch. Buckland of Andely was bred to Avon Bondette and produced Heir Apparent of Andely, a dog, and Andely Lovely Lady, a bitch. The dog was marvelous. I've spoken to many knowledgeable Fox Terrier people who saw the dog, and they report that there was little to fault him on. Heir Apparent was over standard and Mrs. Fallass refused to exhibit him. Through 1964 Andely produced more than 40 home-bred champions, including Ch. Cream of Andely, who went to England and earned her title there as well, the first Smooth bitch to accomplish that honor. One final note about the two great pillars of modern Smooths, Saddler and Buckland. They both go back to Oxonian through Orkadian. Orkadian sired Cromwell Ochre and Southboro Sandman; Saddler goes back to Ochre and Buckland to Sandman.

As this account moves into more recent times, it will be seen that Heir Apparent had a very important influence on the progress at Foxden and at another significant kennel in Smooth archives. The Downsbragh Kennels of Mr. and Mrs. William W. Brainard, Jr. relied heavily on Andely blood in their program. While the Smooths were a poor second in the early '30s, Wires were blooming. Great Wire kennels were being established all across the country. In Texas, an Airedale breeder decided that wires were worthy of his attention, and he acquired another of the grandchildren of Talavera Simon, Westbourne Teetotaler. Forest Hall of Dallas had some success before Teetotaler with Ch. Hallwyre Heartburn, but it was the prepotency of the Simon grandson that made Hallwyre one of the top Wire kennels for decades to come.

No history of Wires in the '30s can exclude William Luther Lewis and his Glynhir string: eight home-bred champions from 1934 to 1942, winning in the stiffest competition in the history of the breed. Lewis judiciously combined Gallant Fox with Simon to produce his distinctive strain. Mrs. Bondy sold Gallant Knight, the larger brother of Gallant Fox, to Mr. and Mrs. Thomas H. Carruthers III of Cincinnati, Ohio. Their Hetherington Kennels, under the guidance of Jake Terhune, blossomed into the fourth member of the great wire quartet of the '30s and '40s: Wildoaks, Hallwyre, Glynhir, and Hetherington. All the marvelous efforts of these talented and dedicated people, however, produced only one competitor worthy of the

Barbara Lowe Fallass with an early Andely bitch, Blackedge Gentle Lady.

Ch. Buckland of Andely, the most important single Smooth import of the decade and perhaps the generation. His offspring and his descendents are still winning on both sides of the ocean, whelped September 14, 1935.

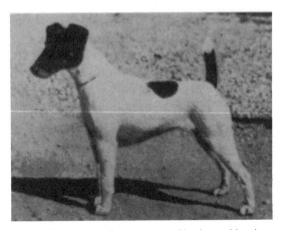

Ch. The Marchioness of Andely, a Buckland granddaughter, whelped August 28, 1942.

Westminster 1941, Best of Variety (Smooth), Percy Roberts and Len Brumby in the ring wth Ch. Flornell Checkmate and Ch. Desert Deputy. The third dog in the ring is Ch. Predictor of Etona. Predictor and Deputy were Saddler sons. The judge was C. P. Scott.

American and English Ch. Cream of Andely. She gained her U.S. title first and then crossed the pond to gain her English title. Whelped July 5, 1944, her sire was a Buckland son and her dam a Buckland daughter.

Andely Lovely Lady, litter sister to Heir Apparent of Andely.

grand award at Westminster. It was fitting that the winner was a bitch, because Tom Carruthers always had a top bitch on the campaign trail, but none better than Ch. Hetherington Model Rhythm, Westminster BIS 1946. She was the first American-bred Fox Terrier to gain that honor since Sabine Rarebit in 1910.

In the December 1943 issue of *The Fox Terrier,* S. M. Griffith, Jr. summarized Wire and Smooth activity on the West Coast. Mr. and Mrs. William B. Reis had been exhibiting since 1928 and in 1943 were campaigning Ch. Battlehill Bernadette to 16 Wire variety wins and ". . . several Bests in Show."

> Mr. and Mrs. Frank Bilger, Jr.'s Reglib Kennels are established at Lafayette, California, and this establishment has set many a record on the Coast with their great wires. In 1935 they acquired Ch. True Charm of Wildoaks and this grand bitch proved to be their goldmine. By breeding True Charm to Humberstone Surething they secured two lovely dogs—Ch. Triwyre Resemblance, a great stud dog, just took Best in Show at the Sacramento Show.

Other Wire activists on the West Coast in the early '40s include Mr. and Mrs. Roy Jones and Mr. and Mrs. David Gardner. The article then reports on Smooth activity on the West Coast and starts with a name many readers will recognize.

> Derek Glenon Rayne, formely of Carmel and now living in Monterey, adheres to the Smooth coat. He finished Ch. Andely Personal Property which set quite a record out this way. Derek is now campaigning The Young Pretender of Andely, another nice one. As can be told from the prefix, both of these were acquired from Mrs. Barbara Lowe Fallass' Andely Kennels at Cross River, New York.

Later on, Mr. Griffith tells of

> Ray Parker, an all-breed handler (he handles the Reglib Wires) now has a Smooth in his kennels which I'd say is one of the greatest specimens of his coat to come out of California. His name is Desert Dynasty and he is sired by Ch. Nornay Saddler out of Dr. Cushman's great brood bitch, Ch. Braw Lass. Dynasty has not been shown to date but is certainly a real one.

Heir Apparent and Saddler made their way to the West along with Wildoaks Wires providing the breeders with the sound basis that was developed in the East.

We have completed 60 years of Fox Terrier chronicles and, aside from some early experimentation, there is no evidence of productive cross breeding. Another emerging factor is that without a specific Wire standard (the standard is the Smooth with a Wire coat) there emerges an inclination to "encourage oversize if the individual suits other aspects of the standard." Ackerman, Skelly, and Silvernail cite comments of Wire judges referring to

Ch. Westbourne Teetotaler

Ch. Flornell Spicy Piece of Halleston.

Ch. Glynhir Gobang II, one of the many fine Wires shown by
William Luther Lewis. Whelped March 4, 1940.

Ch. Hetherington Model Rhythm, the only American-bred Wire to go Best in Show at Westminster, 1946. Owned and bred by Mr. and Mrs. Thomas H. Carruthers, III. Handled by Jake Terhune.

Ch. Hetherington Model Rhythm and Ch. Hetherington Navy Nurse win Best Brace in Show, 1946 Westminster. Mr. T. H. Carruthers is showing Navy Nurse.

a "great stallion of a dog" as though such a description was a virtue. One further observation. Gallant Knight was oversize. Mrs. Bondy did not exhibit him and sold him to the Carruthers. Mrs. Fallass refused to show the oversized Heir Apparent but used him successfully, although judiciously, in her breeding program. This is not an editorial comment but a re-statement of facts; the reader can draw his or her own conclusion.

World War II cut off the English connection for six years but the American Fox Terrier clan had stocked up well in the years just before the outbreak of hostilities. The war also curtailed some exhibiting by limiting travel for non-essential reasons. But the war was not without its positive effects. Progress in air travel that might have taken 30 years was condensed into five, giving birth to a commercial aviation industry that brought coasts and continents closer than ever before. Another casualty of the war was the Depression. A strong, wealthy middle class emerged that was to significantly broaden the base of participating exhibitors, spawning kennel clubs and breed clubs all across the country in numbers heretofore unthinkable. With the strong base of well-to-do exhibitors leading the way, a whole army of newcomers began enlisting in the sport.

Spurred on by the fame and glory of Saddler, Smooths attracted newcomers in significant numbers. At a time when we conduct over 2000 all-breed dog shows a year and when fanciers promote their latest champion, it is all the more difficult to imagine the impact Saddler had on the dog community of less than 300 dog shows per year. James Austin was 25 years ahead of his time in his skill in promoting a champion. Saddler was everywhere, raising money for the war effort here, encouraging people to contribute to one or more British causes, and each appearance had some press coverage. Saddler died in 1948. Two years after Saddler's death, James M. Austin encouraged Don Reynolds to write a book about him, and in 1950 Random House published *Champion of Champions,* the story of Nornay Saddler. In the February 1944 issue of *Popular Dog,* the magazine conducted a poll of judges "licensed to pass upon all breeds and those approved for one or more groups." They were asked to . . .

> go back in your memory for five years. Line up the great show dogs of now and the time between, go over them carefully and pick the best. Put another entry up for second and a third dog behind the second. Then—and this is harder by far—think back ten years to 1933, when S. M. Stewart's Ch. Warland Protector of Shelterock ruled as the Garden King and John Bates' Wire, Eppingeville of Blarney was Madison's (author's note: Madison was Morris & Essex) winner. Set up all those older champions right beside your three five-year winners and again take your choice—one, two, three.
>
> Forty-three dogs were selected in the polling. The votes ranged from one point to a top-scoring of 121 points made by James M. Austin's Smooth Fox Terrier, Ch. Nornay Saddler. Saddler, with a razzle-dazzle show career behind him—it includes well over 50 finals, the last Morris & Essex among them,

Gone to Ground, a Saddler daughter and a foundation bitch for Mr. and Mrs. William Brainard, Jr.

Foxden Sundowner, sire of the first Downsbragh home-bred champion, Downsbragh Groundwork.

The Downsbragh Five: Top Sawyer, Red Vixen, Jumpin Powder, Diana's Dream, Two O'Clock Fox.

Ch. Canadian Ambassador, Best Smooth, American Fox Terrier Club Specialty, May 24, 1946.

Ch. Downsbragh Fuse, a foundation dog for many of today's Texas-bred Smooths, brought to Texas by the Arthur C. Gays of Gaycliffe Kennels.

Ch. Downsbragh Two O'Clock Fox, the only American-bred Smooth to ever win Best in Show at the Montgomery County all terrier event.

since his landing at Wissaboo from England in 1937—was well ahead of another much discussed dog, the black American Cocker, Ch. My Own Brucie, shown to win two Westminsters by his late owner, Herman E. Mellenthin. Although Brucie died last June at Dungarvan, he was remembered in the poll with 75 points.

As Smooths enter the mid-'40s, Saddler's influence is felt in his children and grandchildren. Mr. and Mrs. William Brainard, Jr. proved to be breeders of extraordinary competence, perhaps because they recognized the virtues of selecting the best of Wissaboo and combining it with the best of Andely. They started with a Smooth bitch called Paddy Be Gone of Drummond and bred her to Saddler. From that breeding they kept a bitch named Gone to Ground, a good name for a game terrier. The first Downsbragh home-bred champion that I could uncover was out of Gone to Ground by Foxden Sundowner. So early in the development of the Downsbragh Smooths the pattern emerged. A Saddler bitch bred to a son of Heir Apparent of Andely produced Ch. Downsbragh Groundwork, that first titlist. Gone to Ground was bred again to Saddler's most famous son, Ch. Desert Deputy, half-brother to half-sister, producing the bitch, Downsbragh Land Mine. Gone to Ground and Land Mine were the foundation bitches for the Brainards. The Gone to Ground/Sundowner match up also produced Downsbragh Mickey Finn, the sire of 22 champions. The Brainards, Mrs. Fallass, and the Farrells were patient breeders steeped in the tradition that a good horse takes several generations to produce. Three well-bred sires, who never had a successful show career, were, nevertheless, vital to the success of all three great kennels: starting with Buckland's son, Heir Apparent, the sire of five champions, on to Foxden Sundowner, the sire of six champions, and finally to Mickey Finn, the all-time top producer of his era after Saddler, with 22 champions. Altogether, from 1944 to 1946 Mr. and Mrs. Brainard bred and exhibited more than 23 Downsbragh champions. They affected the breeding programs of Foxden, Barberry, Stoney Meadows, Gaycliffe, Woodcliffe, and other less prolific fanciers. Perhaps the crowning achievement of Downsbragh was Ch. Downsbragh Two O'Clock Fox. He was an extension of the plan rigorously adhered to by the Brainards and discussed earlier. A study of his pedigree reveals that he was by Ch. Foxden Bracer, who was by Downsbragh Mickey Finn, who was by Foxden Sundowner, he by Heir Apparent. The distaff side of Two O'Clock Fox reveals the heavy Saddler influence. His dam was Downsbragh Land Mine, who was mentioned earlier as a double Saddler granddaughter. Ch. Downsbragh Two O'Clock Fox, as of October 1986, remains the only American-bred Smooth to win Best in Show at Montgomery County, an all-terrier annual event. That is one prize coveted by all terrier breeders and exhibitors.

The Brainards, Farrells, and Mrs. Fallass led the way as the war ended and life returned to normal. But for America and the dog community, life was never the same. Whereas, in years past, one or two large breeders would dominate the scene, a new synergism began to develop. Smaller breeders discovered that by working with one of the competent professional handlers offering their services, the competitive gap between themselves and the large breeders could be narrowed and, in some cases, eliminated altogether. This new alliance had the impact of broadening the base of the participating public in our sport, and, because of the care required to present a Wire properly, this breed was the primary beneficiary of the new synergism. The Smooths welcomed the Hon. James P. O'Connor and his Ronnoco Smooths handled by Tommy Gannon. His Honor followed the path of the other successful breeders by getting to Saddler through his son, Ch. Lineman, and to Heir Apparent of Andely through any one of several Wirehart bitches obtained from George Hartman of Lampeter, Pennsylvania. Judge O'Connor remained active until his death in 1955. Ch. Ronnoco Resolute and his brother, Ch. Ronnoco Rajah produced 18 champions with Resolute siring 12. Resolute was also Best of Variety at the February 1949 Specialty and Best of Opposite Sex at two later events.

Smooths began to work their way west; in Missouri the Welcome Kennels of Abigail Gross Jones had some success. She drew heavily on the Sabine bloodlines to get her start and was active for nearly 20 years; the Sandhill prefix of Charles Kurash brought Smooths to the Michigan area by starting with Brainard-bred stock; Arthur C. Gay had Smooths in the Dallas area and was one of the founders of the Lone Star Fox Terrier Club. The Gays also brought Downsbragh to Dallas. Ronnoco Resolute and Downsbragh Fuse were two important Gaycliffe antecedents. Some of the fanciers, whose account appears in this book, had some success and got out and all they left behind is a postscript in the record book. The Gays left a good deal more. They became a sphere of influence that rekindled Smooth Fox Terrier interest in the Southwest. Another Missouri breeder was Charles Wheeler, whose Pennridge Smooths were a strong factor in the Midwest as the post-war years progressed. Silver Ho Smooths of Thomas Lenfesty was one of the most productive kennels of the time from the standpoint of champions finished. Lenfesty was another protegé of the Brainards. No account of the post-war years would be complete without Robert Neff of Fenbor and Barberry's Frank Appleton. Both were active exhibitors and strong club supporters.

As the Korean War came to a close, another star was beginning to ascend to join Foxden, Andely and Downsbragh. Once again the positive impact of the three great forces is apparent in the founding of Stoney Meadows Smooths and development of Mr. and Mrs. Potter Wear. But before ringing down the curtain on "Give 'em hell Harry," and moving on to "Liking Ike," I must, for purely selfish reasons, comment upon Ch. Farnhan First Flight, the first BIS Smooth in my life. "General" was owned

Ch. Flornell Prestonian Jewel, imported for the Farrells by Percy Roberts.

Ch. Ronnoco Resolute, a BIS-wining Saddler son and the sire of 12 champions.

Ch. Saffron Hi-Hat of Gaycliffe (Ch. Asset of Andely ex Ch. Hi-Princess Joannie) at the Lone Star Fox Terrier Club Specialty, Dallas, Texas, November 16, 1958. The judge is John Kemps, owner-handler Arthur C. Gay.

67

by J. W. Block, who at one time ran over 40 Smooths with Len Brumby, Jr. My first lesson on the subject of the same dog looking completely different on different days was given to me by "General." When he was in the mood, he was lovely; when he wasn't, he could suck in his neck, drop his ears, pull his rear legs under him and gaze at the judge balefully. But he did do quite a lot of winning for Mr. Block, who left dogs as quickly as he arrived.

Imports played a smaller part during the late '40' and early '50s. One standout was Ch. Flornell Prestonian Jewel, imported by Percy Roberts for Mr. and Mrs. James A. Farrell, Jr. of Foxden. She was an outstanding show bitch and a marvelous producer.

Past breed observers tend to view the post-war years as the Dark Ages for the Wire Fox Terrier. After all, the breed won Westminster ten times from 1915 to 1940 and again in 1946, but from 1946 to 1986 only Ch. Zeloy Mooremaide's Magic turned the trick in 1966. If that is the criteria used to determine the health of a breed, then, of course, the assumption is correct. However, the breed has other, more vital requirements than Westminster wins. The Wire is a more demanding dog to exhibit, especially for a small breeder. Dog people like to follow the circuit and show dogs, but most Wires cannot be campaigned every week. Their coats need to be removed periodically. For the one-dog exhibitor, this means "nothing to show" at that time. And there are few owner-handlers who can compete on equal terms with the professionals in Wires. "Many's the heart that was broken after the ball," by a judge's decision that was swayed by presentation. But the Wire fate after World War II was affected by other forces that had little to do with coat or public acceptance. More than 10 million men took up arms in defense of their country from 1941 to 1945. They traveled more, saw more, were subjected to more new and strange sights than any previous generation. They returned with Boxers, Bouviers, Briards, and over the next four decades added 13 new AKC-recognized breeds. The parents of these men and women were, for the most part, depression deprived adults seeking new outlets, new sports, new entertainment, new ways to enjoy and display their newly acquired wealth. This new base of economic strength had none of the background early terrier exhibitors enjoyed. There was no affinity, no contact with Europe. As a matter of fact, Europe held only harsh memories for most of them, but their children, the lucky ones, were returning home bearing gifts in the form of strange-looking but interesting four-legged friends. And so other breeds gathered strength or gained renewed vigor.

It was these two factors, the rise of middle-class interest in the sport, which for the most part shunned the Wire challenge, and the growth of interest in other breeds that impacted Wires negatively. In point of fact, the number of Wire champions earning that title remained fairly constant during the post-war years; other breeds just grew right past them. By the year 1951, Wire champions totaled 42 as compared to 36 Smooths, whereas

Ch. Glynhir Gladly, owner-
handled by William Luther Lewis
to the top of the Terrier Group,
Westminster 1943.

Wynwyre's Pamela, owned by Mrs. Edmund A. Kraft, pictured winning Best in Show, Bryn Mawr
Kennel Club, June 15, 1946. Handler: George Ward. Judge: Mrs. Milton Erlanger.

in 1946 48 Wires earned titles as compared to 27 Smooths. In 1950 the terrier that won the most groups was a Smooth, Ch. Ronnoco Resolute; the second most successful Fox Terrier in terms of group success was Ch. Lucky Fella, another Smooth. In February 1950 Percy Roberts wrote in *Popular Dogs*:

> It was pleasing to note that Smooth Fox Terriers have more than held their place both in entries and quality.
>
> Wires have not made the headway in entries that Smooths have, although there are a number of very high class dogs and bitches ready to hold their own with any breed. This is another breed that is going very well on the West Coast, having some very interested fanciers and some very good dogs, with competition amazingly keen at the bigger shows.

For nearly six years Wire fanciers in America were cut off from their annual British transfusion, but once the war was over, British Wires once again found their way to America. From 1946 to 1956 the AFTC Grand Challenge Cup and Meersbrook Bristles Awards were in competition 34 times, twice it was void, and 14 times it was won by an import.

The combination of Wildoaks and Tom Keator's Derbyshire breeding gave birth to Wynwyre Wires bred and exhibited by Mrs. Edmund A. Kraft of Royal Oak, Michigan. George Ward was their handler, so we know they were well-advised. Two other names to join Glynhir, Hallwyre, Hetherington, and Wildoaks in the '40s and early '50s were Gayterry of Tom and Kay Gateley and Mr. and Mrs. Paul Silvernail, whose Crack-Dale Wires were very successful on the East Coast. Tom and Kay were all-breed professional handlers at the top of their profession, but they still raised a few outstanding Wires and also had some success with imports. Ch. Chief Barmaid was an outstanding example of the Gateley's acumen in bringing outstanding Wires from England. Another interesting Gateley product was Ch. Sirius of Gayterry, a home-bred who had a fine show career. The Gateley's could also recognize a bright star when they saw one in this country and in 1947 had exciting results with Ch. Boarzell The Brightest Star, bred by Joy Swann. Silvernails' Crack-Dale Wires were still in the East; while the kennel was not necessarily prolific, Crack-Dale kept a top Wire in contention for nearly 30 years, and, of course, Evelyn Silvernail was the last authority to write a book on the Fox Terrier. Another successful West Coast combination was Harry Sangster, handler for Mr. and Mrs. M. W. Rombaugh, who campaigned their dogs under the Ar-For banner. The Rombaughs got their start from the Hallwyre Kennels of Forest Hall. Mrs. Leonard Smit imported a pair of smashing Wires in 1952, Ch. Wyretex Wyns Traveler of Trucote and Wyretex Wyns Priceless, handled flawlessly by, to my mind, the best terrier man I ever knew, Phil Prentice. The Monstalla Kennels of Mrs. Munro Lanier drew upon some imports, e.g. Crackley Solution; some Bondy, e.g. Ch. Citation of Wildoaks; and some Lewis, e.g. Glynhir Great Guns, to compile a respectable record. She, like Harold Florsheim, was more an exhibitor than a breeder. The heartland was the home of Peg and Fred Bookstrom, who started in 1946 with a bitch called Striking Florate Foxfinder and by 1955 had bred five Bookwin champions. The Bookstroms were responsible for bringing Wire interest to the Nebraska area and the adjacent states. Their interest spanned more than 20 years. The period came to a close with another import, this one by Mr. and Mrs. Harold M. Florsheim, Ch. Travella Superman of Harham. He was handled by Tom Gateley to 26 Bests in Show and 54 Terrier Groups.

As for the "Big Four," they continued to provide the competition with a standard to shoot for that was not easy to attain. Another contribution of Lewis, Carruthers, and Bondy was the launching in 1944 of the Wire Fox Terrier Club of the Central States. During the post-war years Forest Hall bred nearly 50 additional champions, Carruthers nearly 30, and Bondy and Lewis, who, as the Eisenhower years progressed, were in the twilight of their activities, still managed well over a dozen homebred titlists and many, many Groups and all-breed Bests.

In the mid to late '50s some of the great East Coast terrier people began a migration west. "California, here I come," was the anthem of Jimmy Butler, Mrs. Leonard Smit, who became Mrs. Joseph Urmston, but kept the Trucote prefix, and several others. The membership of the American Fox Terrier Club in 1956 was composed of just three members from California. And while Ackerman, Bilger, and Rombaugh did their best, they were only as good as the dogs they had to work with. By 1966 the California membership in the AFTC swelled to 21. While the Smooth needed less care than the Wire, neither breed representative from the West Coast could compete on even terms with the East Coast entries. But with the migration to the West of Fox Terrier people in the East, soon West Coast entries were coming East and, as often as not, coming back to California with the ribbons. Richard Chashoudian, Jimmy Butler, and an English emigré named Harold Duffy provided the nucleus of professional skills required to properly present the Wire, and Mrs. Urmston, Mrs. Vassar, and Mr. William Meyers Jones provided the financial support and enthusiasm so essential for success to be achieved in our sport.

In preparation for this section on the growth of the Fox Terrier in California, I interviewed Ric Chashoudian. His career was directly tied to and impacted by the California migration. According to Chashoudian, the West was far behind the East in every respect in the '50s. Those few brave Californians who dared to venture to the Eastern shows returned home sadder but wiser for the experience. In the East, each coated terrier breed had one or two handlers who specialized in that single terrier breed. And it wasn't just the conditioning and the presentation. Those specialists knew their dogs, and if the people they showed for did not breed a good one, they had the resources and the English contacts to buy the best.

Ch. Radar of Wildoaks, BOV at the Wire Fox Terrier Club of Central States. The judge is George Hartman, the handler is Pete Snodgrass.

Ch. Fox Hunter of Wildoaks.

Tom Gately with Ch. Boarzell Brightest Star, Kay Gately with Ch. Sirrius of Gayterry and Frank Brumby with Brightest Star of Gayterry at the AFTC Specialty, May 23, 1947. Sirrius and Brightest Star were son and daughter to Ch. Boarzell Brightest Star.

Ch. Foxbank Entertainer of Harham, a standard bearer for Harold Florsheim.

Ch. Chief Barmaid, owned by Shirley Angus, Best in Show at the Harrisburg Kennel Club. The judge is George H. Hartman and handler is Tom Gately.

A Who's Who of Dogdom in 1946: The dog, Crackley Startrite of Wildoaks; the people, left to right: Sherman R. Hoyt, handler Robert Snodgrass, Judge Thomas M. Halpin, owner Mrs. R. C. Bondy and Mrs. Sherman R. Hoyt.

Judge Percy Roberts awards BOV at the Wire Fox Terrier Club of the Central States Specialty, June 10, 1950. George Ward on left is handling Ch. Penda Tropen Twinkle of Harham, owned by Harold Florsheim, and Robert Kendrick is shown with BOS winner, Tom Keator's Ch. Derbyshire Duelist.

The circumstances contributing to the inferior quality and competitiveness of West Coast Fox Terriers stemmed from those two significant conditions: lack of good dogs and the inexperience of the West Coast handler. All that began to change after World War II. According to Chashoudian, the first great terrier trimmer to arrive on the West Coast was Harold Duffy. He was not only a fine terrier man but a patient instructor, and Ric was his best pupil. As he was developing his skills in the early '50s, another top terrier trimmer and handler arrived on the scene in the person of Jimmy Butler. As the '50s drew to a close, Mrs. Joseph Urmston settled in California bringing with her the long record of success of the Trucote prefix. She teamed with Jimmy Butler and West Coast Wires gained respectability.

The real breakthrough occurred when Chashoudian came East with Ch. Miss Skylite, a bitch imported by Wyldwest Kennels of Charles and Nedra Vassar. Evelyn Silvernail reported on the 1961 and 1962 New York Specialties in the 1956-1966 American Fox Terrier Club Annual:

The late George Hartman judged our 1961 New York Specialty and as usual sorted through his entry of 42 with ease and precision. He found his Winners Dog in the Florsheim's Harham's Hard Sauce, his Winners Bitch in Seth Campbell's Denbeigh Denouement (a bitch with a very short show career) who he carried through to Best of Winners. His Specials class I found most interesting; it contained such dogs as Mrs. Urmston's Ch. Mitre Miss Adorable (a Caradochouse Spruce daughter). The Carruther's new import, Ch. Purbeck Pride of Helenstowe. The late Mrs. Saunders Meade's Ch. Weltona Dustynight's Warrior—who to my mind a great little dog, never shown enough to give him the chance he deserved, although he did acquire, I believe, three Bests-In-Show before Mrs. Meade's death, after which he was never shown; Barbara Worcester's Ch. Stoneygap Short Story; Mrs. Lanier's Ch. Mac's Revelation and the western winner owned by the Wyldwest Kennels—Ch. Miss Skylite—all had fine show records. Miss Skylite built up a fabulous show record for herself. This all white bitch was a very feminine show girl, lean head, arch of neck, short back, good mover. As usual, like all top winners she was rated high by those who admired her and dragged down by those who didn't. I found that she was the type animal that judges either liked immediately or couldn't see her at all. This was Mr. Hartman's Best of Variety; she also scored a repeat at the Garden the next day. His Best of Opposite Sex was my favorite, Ch. Weltona Dustynight's Warrior.

At our 1962 New York Specialty with Tom Carruthers judging we had a wonderful entry of 46 for him to pass on. Always a popular judge with amateurs, it is interesting to note the variety of breeders he drew from around the country. However, it was all imports that captured the top awards, and all owned by the same kennels and it was father and daughter, who were Winners Dog and Winners Bitch—Kirkmoor Coachman and Kirkmoor Cockleshell, then owned by the Wyldwest Kennels of California. His Best of Variety was also owned by the same kennels—Ch. Miss Skylite. Best of Opposite Sex went to Mrs. Lanier's Ch. Evewire Extra Edition.

George Steadman Thomas awarding Best in Show at the 1952 Morris and Essex event to Ch. Wyretex Wyns Traveller of Trucote. Mrs. M. Hartley Dodge, club president, and handler Seth Campbell are also pictured.

The 104th Specialty of the AFTC February 13, 1955. Shown are BOV Ch. Madam Moonraker, handler Phil Prentice and Judge Alva Rosenberg.

A sense of the attitude of the time may be revealed in the writings of Mrs. Silvernail. All other contestants were referred to by name except the California entry. The same was true in her account of the 1962 Specialty when Mrs. Vassar's entry handled by Chashoudian completely dominated the day. I cannot recall another instance where a reporter second-guessed the judge in print, as Mrs. Silvernail did in describing the '61 event. It was as if to say, "Who are these upstarts?"

And while Nedra Vassar faded as quickly as she burst upon the scene, the Wire picture on the West Coast made the transition from comic strip to Renoir almost overnight. The interest kindled by the spectacular, though brief, success of Wyldwest Wires attracted the kind of people and resources required to promote a breed.

Of course, there were a few entrenched stalwarts in the last '50s and early '60s in California and the rest of the West Coast. And there were some who brought their skills and knowledge with them from the East Coast. Among the former was William Meyers Jones, whose Heathcote prefix took on new luster when challenged by Mrs. Vassar. No true Sportsman likes to be beaten at his own game, and Mr. Jones was a sportsman in the finest tradition of the dog game. In 1961 he imported Ch. Falstaff Lady Fayre and, four years later, Ch. Gosmore Kirkmoor Storm.

William Meyers Jones and Mr. and Mrs. Raymond Splawn of Spokane, Washington provided the staying power necessary to nurture the West Coast Wire renaissance. The Splawn's Wyrequest prefix is prominent in many of today's fine Wire representatives from the West. In the late '60s Mrs. Joseph Urmston settled in California, where her Trucote Wires were presented and conditioned by the great Jimmy Butler. Other prominent Californians included Mr. and Mrs. Henry Sayres. Mrs. Sayres was the former Barbara Worcester. Both Barbara and Henry were born into dogs and added to the increasing Wire expertise on the West Coast.

The California drive for parity and recognition climaxed in February 1966, when the Westminster Kennel Club Best in Show was won by a California-owned import. English and American Ch. Zeloy Mooremaide's Magic with Jimmy Butler at her side brought glory and excitement to Mr. and Mrs. Walter Bunker of Los Angeles. Magic's Garden win did more than provide glory and excitement for Jimmy Butler and the Bunkers, she focused the attention of American Wire breeders on her sire, Eng. Ch. Zeloy Emperor, who proved to be as significant as any sire in Wire history. Most present Wires have at least one line going back to Emperor. Since Magic won the Garden, Emperor's champion offspring have numbered in the hundreds, worldwide. Eng. Ch. Zeloy Emperor stands alone as the most outstanding sire in Wire history.

The major contributor to the West Coast development, aside from the people mix, was air travel. As the '60s succeeded the '50s transcontinental flight was under 10 hours. In earlier decades, if a West Coast dog enthusiast wanted to go to England, it meant a train to New York or an extended voyage through the Panama Canal and then on to England. Even those more fortunate individuals had to think twice before taking two months off to look for dogs. West Coast handlers, even those few with contacts in England, rarely invested in so extensive and expensive a journey. It was the Eastern established breeders that had the edge in contacts and convenience relative to England's best.

It has been estimated that George Thomas, in his lifetime, sold over one million dollars worth of Fox Terriers to American exhibitors and breeders. He was responsible, as well, for bringing over or discovering great terrier handlers. These efforts were at the behest of the Fox Terrier folks east of the Mississippi.

As the airplane made the world smaller, the course of this chronicle must, of necessity, condense. The next 25 years which take us to the present will not be sectionalized. Air travel made it possible for people of moderate means, from anywhere in this country or the world, to visit Westminster or Crufts. And importing dogs, once the private preserve of the well-to-do, became a viable option for many serious breeders and exhibitors. The resulting years saw an influx of Emperor sons, grandsons, and double and triple great-grandsons, all made possible by air travel.

Post-war Smooth activity in the early '60s in California saw three important families emerge: Corinne and William Lyons, and Pat and Henry Speight of California, and Mr. and Mrs. Andrew McDowell of Ireland. The McDowells were well-known breeders whose Mullantean Fox Terriers had been exhibited for nearly half a century. Once again, I am indebted to Dan Kiedrowski for the following account:

> It was through the late Anton Rost that the first Mullantean Smooth was imported to California. Mullantean Miss Marian, a half-sister to Mullantean Miss Nora, came to the home of the late Corinne and William Lyon. Marian had both quality and personality and became an easy champion.

Further correspondence with the McDowells told of Nora's litter of two, by Eng. Ch. Watteau Snuff Box, whelped November 13, 1963, that would be for sale.

It was here that Mr. and Mrs. Henry Speight entered into the story, as the Lyons and Speights decided to go together and import the pair. The Lyons showed the dog, Ch. Mullantean Mr. Pickles, and the Speights the bitch, Ch. Mullantean Miss Lou Ann. Both were so well received by the fancy that Corinne decided to import Nora's next litter, sired by Maryholm Seahawk. This litter arrived just prior to Corinne's untimely death from cancer. Five days before Corinne died, Pat and Hank went to visit her, and she prevailed upon them to take one of the puppies as an assurance that her dream might continue—and well it did.

My first introduction to the Mullanteans was in June 1965, when six

Ch. Miss Skylight.

Ch. Derbyshire Dazzler,
one of Tom Keator's
many fine Wires.

Ch. Falstaff Lady Fayre created enthusiasm on the West
Coast by winning major Fox Terrier events in the east.

79

Ch. Zeloy Mooremaids Magic, owned by Marion Bunker, goes Best in Show at Westminster in 1966. Pictured are Judge James A. Farrell, Jr., Westminster President William A. Rockefeller, handler Jimmy Butler.

Evelyn Shafer

Ch. Sunshower Strike, owned by Barbara Keenan, one of the many Wires she has campaigned through the years.

Ch. Mullantean Miss Florence with Jimmy Butler.

Ch. Pathen's Some One Special with Henry Sayres.

Ch. Pathen's Sammy Sayres with owner-breeder-handler Henry Speight.

of the first seven to be imported, all future champions, were shown at the WFTBA Specialty in California. Mr. Pickles, already a champion, having finished a few months earlier as BW at the NCFTC Specialty, was handled to BOS by Ric Chashoudian. Miss Florence, in her debut, was handled by Jimmy Butler to WB and BW, with reserves going to Mr. Snowton and Miss Emily. Miss Florence was a standout even at this early age. She was sound and typey, with a showy personality and that elusive "touch of class."

The bitch responsible for all this success never saw America. She remained in Ireland. But her pedigree reveals some interesting combinations. Her sire was Brooklands Pippin, a dog solidly line bred to the great American sire, Downsbragh Mickey Finn, himself a Saddler-Heir Apparent product. The Mullanteans made West Coast bloodlines compatible to the East, in addition to enhancing breed quality in general.

The Speights and the Lyons were soon joined by other important West Coast breeders. Eleanor and Ivan Gilbert, Jane and Fred Kuska each began their activities in the mid-'60s. The Gilberts finished more than 13 champions carrying the Bronwyn name before cutting back in the '70s, while the Kuskas' Crag Crest Kennels are still active at this writing.

Before moving on the the late '60s and '70s as the two Fox Terriers move separately, but in tandem, through time, it is enlightening to stop and assess past events to determine what, if any, lessons can be learned. The oft-quoted coach of the Green Bay Packers, Vince Lombardi, said, "Winning isn't everything. It's the only thing."

Does that apply equally to breeding and exhibiting dogs? Draw your own conclusions from the following. Forest Hall, of the Hallwire Wires, was one of the most prolific breeders of this century, finishing 100 champions. Is there a winning dog today or a successful kennel with Hallwire at its roots? Forest is gone. He was well-liked and had many friends and acquaintances. He started handlers and judges alike. But what of his life's work in Wires? His dogs came from Westbourne Teetotaler, so we know he had a good start. But something happened along the way and he rarely had significant major wins and did not impact the Wire in any real sense. Where are the Hallwire descendants today? Somewhat less prolific were the Wyrequest Wires of the Splawns, and yet there is hardly a western pedigree of prominence that does not contain the Wyrequest strain whose roots are the Wyretex Wires of Mrs. Dorothy White. Mrs. White bred one of the first great producers of post-war England, Eng. Ch. Wyretex Wyns Tuscan.

I believe what we leave behind is far more rewarding than what we get while we are here. This is a purely personal and subjective observation. Luck, also, plays a seemingly unfair role in this scenario. So I will leave it with just this one example.

The early '60s, generally, were numerically lean years for the Smooth

Fox Terrier, but quality was maintained by active breeders all across the country. In addition to the Speights, the Lyons, the Kuskas and the Gilberts in the far West, the East and Midwest had its stalwarts. Continuing to improve her stock with help from the Brainards, Abigail Gross Jones' Welcome Smooths set the pace and standard for Midwestern breeders. Ch. Welcome Here and Now, finished in the late '50s, had a fine career with a number of Specialty Bests.

Stoney Meadows, the home of the Potter Wears, bred a real hummer in 1961, Ch. Stoney Meadows Buoy, who, at three years of age, made a clean sweep of the variety awards at all the AFTC Specialties. He was solidly rooted in the Downsbragh line so important to modern Smooths. From 1957 to 1966 the Wears bred eight champions and worked closely with Mrs. Wear's sister, Mrs. Steward Simmons, who exhibited under the Battle Cry banner. Mrs. Simmons began Battle Cry with a lovely import, Ch. Hampole Sincerity, bred by Miss Lindley Wood, by Eng. Ch. Hermon Parthing's Loyal Lad out of Eng. Ch. Hampole Housewife. "Lad" was a Lethal Weapon grandson, the bitch was from a line descended from Eng. Ch. Boreham Belsire. Mrs. Simmons continued to combine the finest American stock with judicious imports. Her most important import was another stylish bitch, Ch. Boreham Baranova. Baranova had six all-breed Bests, 16 Groups and seven Specialty Bests and was the dam of five champions, truly an all-around girl!

The Farrells, who had cut back for several years in the early '60s, revitalized their program with a real showstopper, when, in 1965 they imported a fine Snuff Box son, Eng., Am. Ch. Foremark Ebony Box of Foxden. Ebony Box not only had an outstanding show career, ably presented by Jane Forsythe, but he sired 26 champions and was used extensively by many active breeders of his time. While not quite achieving the results of the later Farrell import, Eng., Am. Ch. Karnilo Chieftan of Foxden, he was a dog of some stature. The most important Ebony Box legacy was represented by two bitches who were significant to the programs of Waybroke and Rebel Hills. Waybroke benefitted from the Ebony Box daughter, Ch. Foxden Titania, and Angeline Tillman's Rebel Hill Smooths enjoyed success with Ch. Rebel Hill's Midnight Serenade.

But he did bring new life and excitement, not only to Jim and Emilie Farrell, but, through his successes in the show ring, he reminded the fancy once again what a great show dog a Smooth is.

Mr. and Mrs. William Wimer of Pool Forge Farms, better known for their coated terriers, had some early '60s success with an imported Smooth bitch called Ch. Thermfare. She was a Chorister granddaughter, and when bred to Ch. Thurlsway Full Steam, a Chorister son, she produced the highly successful Ch. Pool Forge Gold Brick. He was BV at the New York Specialty in February, 1965, losing the breed award to Ch. Zeloy Mooremaide's Magic. He repeated that victory at the AFTC's floating

Ch. Wyretex Wyns Tuscan, one of the first significant post-World War II English stud dogs, bred and owned by Mrs. Dorothy White. The Wyretex strain played a prominent role in the activities of Virginia and Ray Splawn.

Ch. Stoney Meadows Buoy as a three year old. He won all the major specialties.

Ch. Hampole Sincerity, one of Mrs. Stewart Simmons' important imports.

Ch. Boreham Baranova, an all-around girl—top show bitch, top producer.

Ch. Stoney Meadows Comus, foundation sire for Dovenby Smooths of Jim Smith.

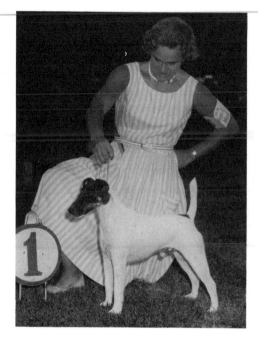

Eng. & Am. Ch. Foremark Ebony Box of Foxden began the rejuvenation of Foxden in 1965. Jane Forsyth compiled an impressive record with him which included BIS at Montgomery County 1966 under Percy Roberts.

Ch. Thermfare, imported by Pool Forge Kennels, shown BOV at the AFTC Specialty, February 1963. Handled by A. C. Ayers, the judge was Mrs. Paul M. Silvernail.

Specialty, held that year in Chicago over a disappointing entry of eight.

Watching today's Specialty entries of 50 to over 100 makes us realize the extent of our debt to those who carried the Smooth through the dark days of the late '50s and early '60s.

Another Jimmy Butler client who did yeoman service for the Smooth in those sparse times was the Kris-Vale Kennels of Mr. and Mrs. Theodore Veling, whose line stemmed from Andely. Mary Veling was a fine breeder and exhibitor who was taken away from us before her time.

I believe that the really great breeders are those who spawn interest in others and provide new people with quality dogs. Barbara Fallass was just such a person. Her Andely line started a number of outstanding kennels. One more was Twinbark of Mr. and Mrs. C. Huntley Christman. In their 15 year span they bred and finished over a dozen champions. Their most rewarding was Ch. Twinbark Tempest, who more than held his own, owner-handled, in tough Eastern competition.

This period, for Smooths, until the late '60s, was long on quality but short on exhibitors. It was as though the breed was somehow out of step with time. It began to lose some of its staunchest supporters; some by normal attrition that afflicts all sports, some by age, infirmity or death. And while the new crop of supporters was on the horizon, it was a particularly long winter night before sunrise.

The Wire, during the late '50s and '60s, fared much better. Mrs. Bondy died in 1966 at age 90, but the activity at Wildoaks was considerably curtailed before the end of the 1950s. When a breed renews itself with an Emperor and a Craftsman within the same decade, someone is doing something right. And when such a breed loses a Bondy and gains a Ballich and a Koehler, it is assured of a bright future.

With the passing of Mrs. Bondy, the Wire elder in point of service and success was Thomas Keator. Keator's Derbyshire Wires were always a force to reckon with. In the '50s and '60s, Bob Kendrick handled for Mr. Keator. His last champion was a home-bred dog, Derbyshire Dinner Jacket. His last bitch was Ch. Derbyshire Don't Tell—ninth generation with a bitch champion in each. Dinner Jacket was the last Wire Mr. Keator campaigned. He was a marvelous terrier man, a true sportsman and an active supporter of the Club. In 1968, the AFTC placed into competition the Thomas Keator Memorial Trophy. The legend describing the award reads as follows:

> Friends of the late Thomas Keator with the desire to perpetuate his memory, offer through the American Fox Terrier Club for competition at its separate Specialty Show only, a Sterling Silver trophy to be won outright each year by the Member's American-bred dog or bitch, Wire or Smooth, adjudged Best American-Bred Fox Terrier in Show; such judging to take place after the award for Best of Breed is made. The first member whose dog or dogs, as the case may be, win three such trophies will receive additionally a larger Sterling

Silver trophy in honor of such multiple wins which will be awarded outright to such member the same year that said third Annual award is recorded.

I knew Mr. Keator as a kind, considerate gentleman who was always on the lookout for newcomers to this beloved breed.

While on the subject of fine Wire folks, mention must be made of the Fred Dutchers, whose Copper Beech Kennels produced some fine competitors.

As the 1960s progressed, Wire action passed on to some newcomers. Do not misunderstand, Tom Carruthers was still King of the Hill, but the breed benefitted from an increasingly broader base of great competitors.

The 1960s were an important period for Wires. It is difficult to conceive that a similar period in the history of any other breed could have occurred. The decade's major event took place on March 10, 1960—the birth of Eng. Ch. Zeloy Emperor. This was most assuredly his decade. Examining pedigrees of the Wires of the '80s, a case could be made for March 10, 1960 as the most important date of the century for Wires. Emperor needs a book to himself!

Let's examine some of Emperor's American credits. He was the sire of Ch. Deko Dragoon, who produced 23 champions, and the great-grandsire of Ch. Brownstone's MacBroom. Then there is Ch. Meritor Bang On, who produced 12 champions and was one of the foundation dogs of Nancy Lee Wolf's Wyrelee Wires; Eng. Ch. Seedfield Meritor Super Flash, who, without setting foot on US soil, managed to sire 15 American champion descendants of Emperor, among them, Ch. Tava Bob, himself the sire of 15 champions. Super Flash also sired Eng. Ch. Harwire Hallmark, who, in turn, produced Eng., Am. Ch. Harwire Hetman of Whinlatter.

In all, 33 American champions were sired by Emperor, but that's not all. His blood flows through the veins of Bob Fine's Finewyre Kennels through Hetman; the late Jim Hook's Mountain Ayre Wires from Hetman through Eng., Am. Ch. Seawire Ellswyre Marksman to Eng., Am., Ch. Baglan Bertice. At the Libwyre Kennels of Ruth Libner, Emperor impacted through his son, Eng. Ch. Holmwire Tudor Renoun, the grandsire of Ch. Libwyre Legend. Emperor was the great-grandsire of Eng., Am. Ch. Sunnybrook Spot On, sire of 20 champions. Other outstanding American Wires that go to back to Emperor include Ch. Holmwire Tudor Reliant, Ch. Aryee Dominator, Ch. Bevwyre's Sovereign Escort, Ch. Terrikane's Tulliver, Ch. Yelsam Jumbo and many, many, more.

The sceptre of Emperor was awesome, his rule universal. He was the omnipotent potentate of the modern Wire. If your Wire has Townville behind it, chances are you will find Emperor. Eng., Am. Ch. Zeloy Mooremaides Magic, 1966 Westminster BIS, was an Emperor daughter.

Ch. Copper Beech Storm, owned by Mrs. Frederick H. Dutcher and handled by Jimmy Butler.

Ch. Derbyshire Don't Tell, campaigned by Mrs. Phillis Haage after Tom Keator's death.

Ch. Meritor Bang On, owned by William Meyer Jones, handled by Ric Chashoudian. Bang On was the sire of twelve champions.

Ch. Deko Druid, imported by Mr. and Mrs. Carruthers, had a strong influence upon Evewire and Glenarden Wires.

Ch. Seedfield Meritor Superflash sired fifteen American champions without leaving England.

Ch. Mutiny Mainstay of Glenarden, a homebred Best in Show winner, Arden Ross breeder-owner.

Many Blackdale Wires are four generations removed from Emperor. The Penda Wires of Elsie Williams had a heavy dose of Emperor. He would have had a far more imposing ring record if he could have kept his offspring away from the shows. When he did lose, it invariably was to one of his kids!

The great Welsh-bred import of Elizabeth and Tom Carruthers, Ch. Deko Druid, arrived in 1964. His offspring heavily influenced two marvelous Wire breeders and great friends 3,000 miles apart, as well as many Hetherington champions. Eve Ballich began in 1959 and a little later on the West Coast came the Glenarden Wires of Arden Ross. While Mrs. Ross was less prolific than many of her contemporaries, she brings a deep knowledge of the breed gained first from Jimmy Butler and then Ric Chashoudian.

Several newcomers have been guided by the experience and artist's eye of Denny Ross. Among her successes are Ch. Mutiny Mainstay of Glenarden, Ch. Glenarden Firedrake, Ch. Glenarden Fire and Ice, Ch. Glenarden Morry's Dance, and Ch. Glenarden Teapot. Most of Mrs. Ross' dogs and bitches trace their immediate roots to Druid.

Forest Hall was winding down his breeding activity to concentrate on judging. But Hetherington was bustling. The Carruthers were active as breeders and judges, and waiting in the bullpen to relieve Forest Hall was Eve Ballich.

Mrs. Eve Ballich purchased a pet from the Bondys, a son of Radar of Wildoaks. This narrative clearly shows the significance to breed development of people who not only breed and exhibit but affect the lives of others by encouraging them to become active breeders. Mrs. Bondy, even though it was "just a pet" sale, kept in touch with Mrs. Ballich. Eve Ballich, by her own admission, had no interest in Wire Fox Terrier activity. But Mrs. Bondy kept in touch. One day Eve Ballich received a phone call from a lady who had a Wire bitch, probably bred by Mrs. Lanier, called Eclat of Monestella. It seems that the owner of the bitch called Mrs. Bondy to inquire about a stud dog for Eclat. Today it would be an hour by plane, but in the mid-'50s dogs were shipped via Railway Express. Mrs. Bondy suggested that Eclat's owner contact Eve Ballich and breed to the Radar son. The result of that chance encounter was the beginning of Evewire Kennels. Mrs. Ballich took two bitches for the stud fee and kept them both "as pets," still with no knowledge or desire to exhibit. But she was beginning to look around and notice things. She named the two bitches Little Bit and Big Bit. In 1956 she bred Little Bit to Ch. Travella Superman, a Harold Florsheim import, handled by Tom Gately. Ch. Little Bit's Sassy Bit was one of the puppies from that litter and like many of her successors over the next thirty years was owner-handled to her title. A few years later she acquired a bitch from George Hartman, Smart Move of Wirehart, who, when bred to the great import Ch. Mac's Revelation produced Ch. Evewire

Extra Edition, the first champion with the Evewire prefix. Mrs. Ballich is the first to admit that Wire people at that time were encouraging, warm and ready to give advice when asked. The people to whom she went for advice were like a Wire *Who's Who*. To begin with, there was Mrs. Bondy, then Mrs. Munro Lanier, George Hartman, Tom Gately and Jimmy Butler. Eve Ballich was of that rare breed herself who, when given advice from experienced people, followed it. The dedication to the breed and the standard of consistent quality through the years, combined with the energy and intelligence Mrs. Ballich brought with her, indelibly place the seal of greatness on her work. One-hundred years from now, whenever Wire breeders gather, they will still discuss the contributions of Evewire.

Evewire averaged three home-bred champions per year for nearly 30 years finished in tough competition. Ch. Evewire Extra Ediition won the Homer Gage, Jr. Memorial Trophy in Wires from 1961 through 1966, Exemplar in 1968 and 1969, Escort in 1971, Page One in 1972. Ch. Evewire Stylish Design won the Welwire Kennel Memorial Trophy in 1963, 1968, 1974, and 1975. The Thomas Keator Memorial Trophy was won with different exhibits, all home-bred and frequently owner handled, in 1969, and again in 1975 as co-breeder; the Champion Meersbrook Bristles Challenge Cup in 1961, 1963, 1969, and again in 1975. From 1961 through 1975 in competition with Carruthers, Gately and other top Wire breeders at National Specialties, Evewire won Winners Dog five times, Winners Bitch three times, Best of Opposite Sex 13 times and Best of Variety six times. Mrs. Ballich started people in Wires from her home base in Stevenson, Maryland as far away as Honolulu. I selected the period from 1960 through 1975 because this was a great period for the Wire and because it was the time when the Specialties became truly national in representation. If Bobby Barlow was Mr. Wire Fox Terrier in the '20s and '30s, then Eve Ballich is now and forever will be Madam Wire Fox Terrier.

The Wire had other fine breeder-exhibitors during this period. The following histories appeared in the January 1983 *Terrier Type* published by Dan Kiedrowski.

> Ray and Virginia Splawn are well into their third decade, both as husband and wife, and as Fox Terrier breeders. It all started when Ray purchased a Wire Fox Terrier ("like Asta") from the Montgomery Ward catalog. He later bought a Wire from Virginia, and they, according to Ray, "got together and got their wires crossed."

Their original breeding stock from the late '50s was based on old established British lines and gave them their first few champions, including Ch. Wyrequest's Kimie Kim Kim Again, who has champion descendants to the present.

Two Nugrades from John Holmes' outstanding British kennels were to provide the real base for most of the 46 homebred champions from Wyrequest. The Splawns chose well this pair—Ch. Nugrade Regent (by Eng., Am. Ch. Bengal Ryburn Regent) and Ch. Nugrade Countess (by

Ch. Nugrade Countess, the fountainhead of Wyrequest.

Ch. Wyrequest's Pay Dirt, a homebred Best in Show winner.

Am. & Can. Ch. Tava Bob, an all-time producer, handled by Ray Splawn.

Ch. Evewire Exemplar, owned by Eve Ballich and Mrs. Munro Lanier, winning Best in Show at the Eastern Dog Club Show. The judge is E. Irving Eldridge, handler Sheena Garrett.

Ch. Baglan Bertice and Ric Chashoudian.

Ch. Country Squire of Crack-Dale, one of the many champions bred by Mr. and Mrs. Paul Silvernail, is shown going BOW at Montgomery County, October 1966. The judge is Stanley Halle.

Eng. Ch. Wintor Statesman), both out of the Emperor daughter Nugrade Bridget—and, as expected, their combination was a winning one. From this litter came two champions and two other champion producers, with Ch. Wyrequest's Pay Dirt (14 champions) the most important. A little later on, the Splawns brought over from Arthur Davison's Tava Kennels Ch. Tava Bob (15 champions), who was to give them their next generation of producing bitches, Ch. Wyrequest's Devil May Care (5 champions) and Wyrequest's Naughty But Nice (4 champions), the latter foundation for JoAnn Dutton's Rodans. Others have started with a Wyrequest bitch, as far away as Georgia, where Tom and Sue Yates have done well with Ch. Wyrequest's Wildfire.

Wyrequest has imported and bred from a host of Group and BIS dogs, but when asked about them, and particularly about Countess, Virginia wrote mostly about what really seems to matter.

> Tina (Countess) was a good mother, puppies and bed always in good order. She carefully reared her puppies—teaching them to play, to fight and to love. She put into her pups her greatest attribute—a sensible, gentle and kind nature—always pleasing—giving all she had to give.
>
> Living with Tina was pure pleasure. She came to us a nine-months pup and fit right into our home immediately, as well as our bed. In no time at all she ruled the house and kennel, and seemed to know it. Tina greeted everyone at the door, but defied them to sit in her favorite chair. If they did, she would stare at them until they occupied another. Any and all house guests shared the pleasure of her company, as she moved from bed to bed during the night to complete her welcome.

Ch. Nugrade Countess is the kind one thinks of when hearing the expression, "all it takes is one good bitch." Countess, with 10 champion children and over 40 more in succeeding generations, is truly "one of a kind."

When Darrell and Annette Jorgensen vacationed abroad in the fall of 1970, the purposes were twofold: a well-earned rest for both, and a good Wire bitch to take home with them. They spent four weeks in Scotland, Ireland and England, attending shows at Leicester and Birmingham. How fortunate for them to see two breed "greats" in competition—Ch. Seedfield Meritor Super Flash and record setting Ch. Gosmore Kirkmoor Craftsman. Darrell recalls that . . .

> Vincent Mitchell was showing Craftsman who was, in my opinion, the class of the entry and best put down of the lot, but failed to gain the ticket at either show.

Among the many breeders the Jorgensens wanted to visit was the Zeloy master, Ernest "Robby" Robinson. This was arranged and they were able to see the great Ch. Zeloy Emperor at 10 years of age and still in his prime.

He had him stripped out, so he was short of hair, but clearly well put together. He had a lovely head, good ear set, straight front and a short, level back. He held his head up on a loose lead and showed every minute. He moved out well and was good coming and going.

When Mr. Robinson took the lead off Billy, he followed him right along to the kennel, where he went around to each pen and visited with all the dogs. Billy went to the pen where Peggy (Holmwire Tudor Radiance) was tending her new litter. He sniffed them all, then sniffed Peggy. There was never any disturbance or barking while we were looking the dogs over. They were truly a sensible lot.

I finally asked him about buying Peggy. We agreed on a price and arranged that she stay at Zeloy for a repeat mating to Emperor. She was bred the 23rd of January 1971, but due to a mail strike, Mr. Robinson was unable to get an export pedigree until nearly a month later. When she arrived in Salt Lake City, Peggy was so heavy with pups her back was sagging. She looked all in.

On March 24th, she had seven puppies, six males and one female. It took her all night. We saved them all, and they turned out to be a fun litter right from the start.

That was to become a record-setting litter—six of seven finishing, but none before Peggy herself became a champion, less than seven months after whelping.

Ch. Holmwire Tudor Radiance produced three more litters at Ana-Dare, from which came five more champions, and in the decade that followed there would be 40 more champions in succeeding generations.

When Mr. Jorgensen developed heart problems in 1976, he arranged that Sam and Fredda Rothlein (Winsorhill) care for Peggy. She was the adored pet of the family until her death in 1979.

The family based on Ch. Holmsire Tudor Radiance, along with the line based on her brother, Ch. Holmwire Tudor Radiant, have been embraced by several breeders nationwide, and pedigrees carrying their names shall be evident for years to come.

Two other long-time Wire supporters, Gene S. Bigelow and M. J. "Jim" Hook, began their string with imported lines. Bigelow's Raylu strain started with a son of Ch. Crackley Supreme Again and Jim Hook with a sensational show and brood bitch, Ch. Baglan Bertice, line bred to Emperor.

Terrier Type had this to say about the Browns and Brownstone:

John and Ann Brown had enjoyed some success with Standard Schnauzers before "Penny" (Heathcote Enchantress) changed their ways. As Ann recalls it . . .

"We met Heathcote Enchantress after a canoeing trip in the mountains near Fort Collins, Colorado. Fred Hiigel had mentioned he had just purchased this good Wire bitch. When I saw her it was love at first sight. Penny went right to her championship, winning groups at a little over a year. We got to see her win now and again, a record that eventually earned her four

Bests in Show and 14 Group 1sts—a showing spitfire all the way.

"Once I had an opportunity to show a Wire in the Group, and had such a good time, that John and I decided to call Fred (who was retiring and going into judging) about leasing Penny. We ended up owning her—and her owning us—to this day. Penny is 16 years old now—and a dear friend who is our house dog. We're very proud of her and love her dearly."

The Browns hit the jackpot with their first breeding of Penny to the great Eng., Am. Ch. Gosmore Kirkmoor Craftsman, sharing honors with him at the 1973 Central States Specialty, where Mrs. Hartley gave Craftsman B, Brownstone's Hey Freddie BW and Brownstone's Breeze Away WB. "Breezie" was also Best in Sweepstakes under Pam Running (Runwyre). Penny was bred twice to Craftsman, twice to another top winning Britisher, Eng., Am. Ch. Axholme Jimmy Reppin, and for her last breeding, to her grandson Ch. Brownstone's Johnny One Spot (ex Hey Day). There were champions in every litter, and most were owner-conditioned and handled to their titles. In the decade since Penny produced her first champion, she has lived to see 10 children become champions, as well as 21 grandchildren, 17 great-grandchildren and 2 great-greats. She serves not only Brownstone, as her blood flows strongly in the East at Rhapsodale, in the South at Jadee, the Midwest at Blyre and in California at Criswood, Mowyre and Wyrelee.

As this is writen, two more Penny descendants can be added . . . an 11th champion for Broom and a third for Storm Warnng. And so the story goes . . .

This author would just add one comment to the Brownstone account. Ch. Heathcote Enchantress was bred by William Meyers Jones, another of those wonderful terrier people who is responsible for bringing others into the game by sharing their good dogs. So many breeders are afraid to part with good ones but I have found that nothing helps my program more than selling a good one for a fair price that someone else can win with and, therefore, whet their appetite for the sport. There is no greater contribution a breeder can make to the future than to engender excitement and enthusiasm in newcomers.

In 1956, Mrs. Franklin Koehler finished a bitch who became the foundation for Merrybrook Wires. Ch. Merrybrook's Fair Reward combined the bloodline of Lewis' Glynhir Kennels with the English Travella line. Ch. Merrybrook's Dancing Star and Ch. Merrybrook's Beautiful Belle were Fair Reward daughters. Mrs. Koehler devoted herself to her breed and her breed club with dedication and enthusiasm.

Before going on to the Smooths of the period and then to the current condition of the two breeds, homage must be paid to Elizabeth and Tom Carruthers and Evelyn and Paul Silvernail. Their activities spanned decades and transcend efforts to place them in one or two categories. The Silvernails began breeding Wires in 1928 and were active until the early '70s, when illness forced them to reduce activity and relocate to California. Evelyn wrote the most recent work on the Fox Terrier and had good success with her program through the years. The Rhapsodale Kennels of

Ch. Heathcote Enchantress launched John and Ann Brown into Wire Fox Terrier prominence. She is shown in a BIS win at Town & Country KC under Clara Alford, handler Dora Lee Wilson.

Ch. Brownstone's MacBroom, at eleven years of age, was BOS over the cream of Wire champions at the Greenwich KC show, June 1985. She is shown with owner Ann Brown handling.

A great bitch for Merrybrook Wires, Ch. Merrybrook Fair Reward was BOV and Best Fox Terrier at the AFTC Specialty, February 1959 under William Kendrick.

Jack Dewitt got its start from the Silvernails, and Evelyn was a dedicated hard working member of the AFTC.

Elizabeth and Tom Carruthers picked up where the Bondys left off and did it with skill and dedication, bringing to Wire breeders in the United States England's best. Their many fine imports include Ch. Deki Druid and Eng., Am. Ch. Gosmore Kirkmoor Craftsman. The Carruthers were deeply involved in the WFTC of the Central States and provided the delightful show site for their annual Specialty. There are many wonderful people who work hard for the breed and who are essential to a breed's success—but there are few giants. Elizabeth and Tom Carruthers were GIANTS. Hetherington is and will continue to be in back of many outstanding American Wires.

As the 1970s descended, Hetherington imported another great Wire sire. Once again I defer to Dan Kiedrowski, who wrote,

English and American Gosmore Kirkmoor Craftsman whelped October 23, 1967, was bred by the Kirkmoor masters, Mr. and Mrs. William "Billy" Mitchell, and was campaigned in England under Mrs. Audrey Dallison's Gosmore banner. This team of fanciers has incredible credentials. Billy Mitchell has been in dogs since early boyhood. As a youthful "pro" handler, his first Wire champion was Eng. Ch. Bluecollar Bramble and Billy had the honor of breeding and showing the breed's first post-war Wire champion, Kirkmoor Carefree. There were many great Wires which were to carry the famous Kirkmoor prefix, and many more were to become champions under his supervision, not the least of them being Eng. Ch. Madame Moonraker, winner of seven BIS before being exported to America to continue a spectacular career. Mrs. Dallison has probably owned more great terriers than anyone in the world. She has had champions in more than a dozen breeds, and must consider Craftsman and Eng. Ch. Kirkmoor Tessa among the best. Tessa won BIS at Manchester over some 6,000 dogs in her very first show—from the *Novice* class. She again won BB and Group in her second outing, at just 13 months of age, and finished at her third show. A Crufts Group winner, she went on to make more breed history having earned more CCs than any other Wire bitch. Craftsman was brought out for the first time at Birmingham at just two weeks past his first birthday and won the Reserve CC under W. M. Singleton. Two weeks later, at Richmond, Mary Blake of the famous Watteau Fox Terriers awarded him BB and gave him these glowing comments:

"I consider him the best Wire dog out for a very long time; beautiful long, lean head and real terrier expression, little beady eyes and well carried ears. Very well laid shoulders, short back, good spring of rib, well made hindquarters; moves with great drive and really covers the ground; good coat and a great showman who really looks the part. Given another few months to really mature and round off, I predict he will be another Best in Show winner for this famous kennel."

Craftsman went on to Reserve in the Group, and in 1969 ran up the finest record ever achieved by a Wire enroute to gaining the title *Dog of the Year,* as top among all breeds. Handled by the Mitchells' son, Vincent, Craftsman won 22 CCs out of the 29 shows giving Wire CCs in 1969. He was absent from only four of these shows, and his complete record that year was as follows: shown 25 times, he had 1 third place, in Open 24 firsts, 1 Reserve CC, 22 CCs, 20 Bests of Breed, 10 Terrier Groups, 3 Reserve Bests in Show and 3 Bests. In the next year he surpassed all breed records, earning a total of 35 CCs and 6 all-breed champion show Bests in Show.

Craftsman came to America in 1972, imported by Elizabeth Carruthers for her Hetherington Kennels in Glendale, Ohio. He was shown briefly that year, handled by long-time Hetherington kennel manager Frank Ortolani, gaining his title with 5 BVs, 4 Group 1sts and a BIS. His only appearance in 1973 was at the Central States Specialty, where he was Best in Show under Mrs. Heywood Hartley at 5½ years of age.

Among his credits as a sire can be found Ch. Bev-Wyre Conbrio Tim, Ch. Bev-Wyre Speedy Reminder (Sovereign Escort's dam), Ch. Brownstone's MacBroom, Ch. Rhapsodale Music Man, and Ch. Ana-Dare Admiral. All in all, a grand total of 30 American champions. But to his everlasting credit, he contributed to the development of many of the nation's breeders. That is the real bottom line.

Among the new breeders who joined Ballich, Koehler, Jorgensen and Brown were the Bouseks, Wayne and Joe, Rose and Linda and later on, in 1972, Wayne and Janie. Joe and Wayne finished their first Bowyre Wire in 1962, Ch. Bowyre's Cockney Girl. Rose Bousek, the family matriarch, encouraged her two sons by co-owning a couple of imports. Linda, Joe's wife, also bred a litter or two, but in the late '60s Joe's work limited his activities, and Wayne carried on until 1972, when he met and married Janie. Janie is a fine dog person in her own right, as well as an accomplished artist and craftswoman. Anyone fortunate enough to win one of her marvelous ceramic trophies will attest to her consummate skill. Since 1962, there have been more than two dozen Bowyre champions.

No Wire history of the '60s and '70s would be complete without Dr. John Masley (Yelsam), Harold Shook (Halsho), Mr. and Mrs. James H. Brown (Lynnwyre) and, finally, Dr. Charlotte Jones and Miss E. Stark (Koshare).

Hardly a year passes in the Wire ranks that does not have its crop of imports. Some years it is one or two, other years more. Some just gain their title, others win a few groups; still others, but far fewer, gain an all-breed Best or two. Most pass into breed oblivion. There is an occasional top performer such as the fine Dutch bitch of the early '80s, Ch. Dynamic Super Sensation. Even fewer win big and also impact the breed's future. I have attempted to present as many of the latter as is possible. The last dog to answer the description was Eng., Am. Ch. Sunnybrook Spot On. Once again, I believe the most accurate account of Spot On's achievements was chronicled by Dan Kiedrowski.

I first heard about Sunnybrook Spot On from Ric Chashoudian at Westminster in 1972. I had read his critique in the English dog papers—they were glowing. A decade later Ric had a lot more to go on when he wrote the following about "Duke" in the Souvenir Booklet published by the Western Fox Terrier Breeders Association to celebrate their 75th Diamond Jubilee Anniversary show, June 26, 1982 . . .

"I judged Spot On in England and gave him his second ticket. When I first laid eyes on this dog I told myself that this was a touch of class. He was a big one, a little too heavily marked, and had one ear slightly higher than the other. Peter Green had heard about the dog and called when I came home from judging at the Richmond show. He asked me about the dog, and I told him that if he had someone with enough money to buy him, to get him, and get him fast. I know that Peter never regretted it, and his final days were with Dan Kiedrowski of *Terrier Type* fame. Danny loved that dog until the day he died. I loved him, Peter loved him and so did a hell of a lot of other people."

My first real look at "Duke" was through the lens of my trusty old Nikon. It was at Great Western in '73. Early that Friday morning I just happened on a picture-taking session Pete had arranged with Joan Ludwig. Without really looking at him, I loaded my own camera, figuring I might as well work right along with Joan—which is what I did.

In minutes the session was over. Peter scooped him up, walked toward me with "Duke" in his arms and asked, "Well?" It was at that moment that I first really got to look at his expression. I don't remember replying—I was, to say the least, awestruck!

I didn't really get a proper look until a few hours later when "Duke" won the breed under the late, great Airedaler, Molly Harmsworth (Bengal). I got an even better look at him the next day in the Beverly Hills Group ring, where he covered ground as few Terriers can. He won that Group under Tom Kirk, and won 100 more in the years that followed, including Westminster in 1964 and again in '68 at 8½ years of age. (Author's note—it was 1974 and 1978.) He remained undefeated in a dozen Specialty attempts.

Ch. Sunnybrook Spot On was bred in England by Mr. E. Hardy (Sunnybrook). He was handled by Peter Green under the Springfield banner of Mrs. Robert V. Clark, Jr. throughout his career. "Duke" was a Quaker Oats Top Terrier winner and held briefly the record as the variety's all-time winner, a record strongly surpassed by his son, Ch. Aryee Dominator (75 BIS) and two grandsons (by Dominator), Ch. Terrikanes' Tulliver (45 BIS). They are called "Duke's Dynasty" now with over 200 Bests in Show between them.

I will remember "Duke" every day of my life—there is so much around to remind me. He is what a great dog is supposed to be—representing the breed well in the show ring, as a producer, in my community and wherever we went. I'll never forget the first time Peter came to visit us, about a year after "Duke" had settled in here. We were well into our walk through the woods and town before Peter could relax, as "Duke," without a lead, was more than he could handle. That night, with the Greens in the upstairs bedroom and me downstairs, produced quite a dilemma.

Smart dog, "Duke"—he spent half the night with them and half with me!

Ch. Sunnybrook Spot On, Terrier Group winner of the Ken-L-Ration Show Dog Award, 1974. He was owned by Mrs. Robert V. Clark, Jr., and campaigned by Peter Green.

Ch. Gosmore Kirkmoor Craftsman, a Wire immortal; imported by Mr. and Mrs. T. H. Carruthers, III.

As the Wire history works its inevitable way toward the present, tomorrow's past, there is still one more great stud dog to reckon with, and his roots are in the midlands of England. Among the fine Emperor sons standing tall is Ch. Seedfield Meritor Superflash, the sire of 15 American champions, most born in England and later exported to the United States. However, Superflash plays just a role in the drama surrounding this great dog. Eng. Ch. Hallwire Hallmark, a great bitch and winner of the 98th National Fox Terrier Show in 1975, was a Superflash daughter. In August of 1974 she was bred to the winner of the 99th National, Eng. Ch. Townville Tobias. It is the product of this union and the winner of the 100th National that this section is devoted to. As the producer of American champions, he has surpassed his famous ancestor, Emperor; gone beyond the fine record of the immortal Ch. Deko Druid; produced more champions than Craftsman or Dominator. Eng., Am. Ch. Harwire Hetman of Whinlatter was bred in England by Mrs. M. Harris, the owner of the Hallmark bitch. He was purchased by Mrs. Fisher May, the Whinlatter Lady, and handled to his English championship by the May brothers, Ray and Ernie.

Clifford Hallmark, one of our fine terrier handlers, acquired Hetman in 1976 for Mrs. Constance Jones of Sewickley, Pennsylvania. He made his American debut in September 1976 at Tuxedo, New York and went right from the classes to BIS. Hetman's next three outings netted his championship and another BIS. And in 1977 Hetman was Number One Dog All Breeds. When this was written, "Harry" was still alive and well going into his 12th year, still breeding a bitch or two but leaving the heavy work to his children and grandchildren. Some of the American breeders who made good use of Harry include Mountain Ayre, Finewyre, App's, Esquire, Wyrequest and Merrybrook.

One final comment about Harry—he was not a heavily-promoted dog. So for him to achieve so fine a record was a testimony to the greatness of the dog and the overall fairness of the game. He also proved that a great sire does not have to be a BIG ONE. Hetman was 15¾ inches but had ample bone and substance.

The Smooth of the '60s, as mentioned earlier, began a long climb back from the days of Saddler, Heir Apparent and Foxden Sundowner. Mrs. Farrell, writing for the Souvenir Booklet of the 75th Diamond Jubilee Anniversary Show of the Western Fox Terrier Breeders Association, June 26, 1982, observed,

Smooths suffered another sinking spell in the period from about 1955 to 1965. Entries at specialties were down in the twenties and worse. But most fortunately for the future of the breed, it was about this time that the Potter Wears (Stoney Meadows), Mrs. Stewart Simmons (Battle Cry), and Mrs.

Ch. Wintor Caracus Call Boy, Best in Show at the Virginia Kennel Club show, September 30, 1967. He was owned by Mr. J. Alford and handled by Tom Gately. Joseph C. Quirk was judge.

Ch. Harwire Hetman of Whinlatter with handler Clifford Hallmark winning Best in Show at the Troy Kennel Club show, October 22, 1978. The judge is William L. Kendrick.

Ch. Toofox Blazin' Saddler, bred by Betsy and Bill Dossett and owned by Kraehollow's Martha Riekenberg, cooling off from the hot Texas sun.

Ch. Kandihill's Digger O'Della, the Kraehollow foundation bitch.

Ch. Ellastone Vibart, imported by the Mar-Lor Kennels of Lorraine Creed.

Winifred Stout (Quissex) joined the cult on the East Coast. The Speights (Pathens), Kuskas (Crag Crest), and Lorraine Creed (Mar Lor) became active in California. The Arthur Gays kept things going in Texas and left a strong heritage to later breeders there. Newmaidley Lason (Author's note—I believe Lason is Jason) arrived in the Pacific Northwest and touched off the growth of an active and dedicated group of Smooth Fox Terrier breeders in that area.

Taking our cue from Mrs. Farrell, we pick up the Smooth development in the state of Washington. In 1964, Ms. Ann K. Broekins arrived from Holland where she had been breeding and exhibiting Smooths. She imported Dutch Ch. Newmaidley Jason from Mr. Gerhardt, who lost little time gaining his US title. Jason was by Brooklands Lucky Wishbone, a Midas grandson out of Newmaidley Destiny, another Chorister offspring.

Ms. Broekins, with Jason and a few Dutch champion bitches as her foundation, founded the Von Nassau prefix from which Mrs. Ray T. Robison and the Raybill's got their start. It is a strange coincidence that 25 years earlier a lady, this time returning home from Holland, had a profound impact on the Eastern Smooths that eventually led to the West Coast. Barbara Fallass returned from Holland and started Andely.

The Robisons acquired Ch. Von Nassau's Ter-A-Cycloon, a Jason son, from Ms. Broekins, and over the next several years, he sired a dozen Raybill champions.

Further south, in California, the Speights were building around Ch. Mullantean Miss Florence and her progeny and those of her half-sister, Ch. Mullantean Miss Lou Ann. Both of these great ladies were out of Miss Nora, described earlier. The Speights bred Miss Florence to an English import, Ch. Teesford Fanfare, resulting in one of the breed's great producing bitches, Ch. Pathens Some One Special. And in 1969, they bred Some One Special to another English import, Ch. Ellastone Vibart, to get Ch. Pathens Sammy Sayres. The Speights assume their importanc in the Western history of the Smooth, not so much for their success in the ring, which was considerable, but for their willingness to "share their fortunes with newcomers." Among the breeders whom the Speights helped are Dr. John Shelton and his Sheridan Smooths and Jane Swanson's fine Foxtrot effort. To give the reader so much perspective as to the depth of the Mullantean line in the West, the following kennels were impacted directly or indirectly by Miss Nora and her heirs—Raybill, Toofox, Kraehollow, Bellavance, Starkdom, Talisman, Royal Irish, Charbonne, The Priory and Lizebethan.

In Texas, Roy D. McGinnis started the Froy prefix, following some of the lines pioneered by the Gays. They exhibited throughout the early '70s, maintaining a presence and an interest until, in the mid-'70s, they were joined by Betsy and Bill Dossett (Toofox), Nancy Atwood (Blazin), Mr. and Mrs. R. L. Congdon (Foxfyne), James Grim (Guitpick), and Mr. and Mrs. M. J. Riekenberg (Kraehollow). It is difficult to play the "What If?"

game, but it is fairly certain that if it wasn't for the Gays and McGinnises, Texans would have had little real knowledge of Smooths.

Instead of a wasteland in Texas and the neighboring states, there exists a flourishing garden of quality combining the efforts of the Gaycliffe and Froy lines with the best of both coasts. I cannot leave the Texas area without referencing Mrs. R. L. Benedict of Ponca City, Oklahoma and her Kevrayno Smooths, most importantly, a home-bred dog, Ch. Kevrayno Sabre Jet, who took BV at the February New York Specialty in 1974 after going BOS in Atlanta Floating Specialty in 1973. At last count he had sired eight champions, and considering that his location limited his opportunities, that is quite a record. The mistress of Kevrayno, Ynona Benedict is quite a talented sculptress, providing an outstanding trophy for many years to the Sweepstakes winner at the Lone Star Fox Terrier Club Specialty.

To the south, the story was just the opposite. Mary Bowker of Bowmanor Kennels fought it out tooth and nail with Hubert Thomas and Madison Weeks and their Waybroke Fox Terriers. Starting with a royally-bred bitch, Bowmanor's Dolly of Beafox, who combined Andely and Downsbragh breeding, and making good use of an English import, Ch. Beechdene Replica, Mary Bowker bred close to 20 champions in the late '60s and early '70s.

Waybroke

Her efforts were surpassed in the South by only one kennel— Waybroke. Thomas and Weeks made good use of Stoney Meadows and Foxden strains. Their foundation bitch, Ch. Foxden Titania, proved to be that rare jewel that every successful program requires, a good producing bitch. Titania was by the Farrells' great import, Eng., Am. Ch. Foremark Ebony Box of Foxden out of a genetic powerhouse of a bitch, Irish, Am. Ch. Parkgrove Camphill Golden Fairy. The similarity in pedigree between Golden Fairy and Newmaidley Jason makes a strong statement. Jason was by Eng. Ch. Brooklands Lucky Wishbone, who also sired Watteau Chorister. His dam was a Chorister daughter, Newmaidley Destiny. Chorister, through Lucky Wishbone, goes back to Watteau Midas who, in turn, was a Laurel Wreath son. Wishbone was a Midas grandson. The resulting pedigree shows Jason solidly linebred back to Laurel Wreath on both sides of his pedigree. Golden Fairy was by Clondara Coach, a Chorister son, out of Camphill Bonny Girl, a Chorister granddaughter. So, at opposite ends of the country, two Smooths, one a dog, the other a bitch, with an almost identical gene pool, make a major contribution to the revitalization of the Smooth Fox Terrier after almost a decade of slumber. Dan Kiedrowski describes Golden Fairy as a bitch who had "the most profound influence, to date with nearly 200 American champion descendents through six generations." Following a careful plan, Madison Weeks and Hubert Thomas bred Ch. Waybroke Red Lobster, a Titania grandson,

Ch. Kevrayno Sabre Jet, a strong influence on Smooths in the Southwest, bred and owned by Ynona Benedict.

The important stud dog Ch. Waybroke Extra Smooth, owned and bred by Hubert Thomas and Madison Weeks.

Ch. Parkgrove Camphill Golden Fairy, a genetic powerhouse for Foxden and the breed.

to Ch. Waybroke Smooth as Silk, a Titania daughter. The result of that union was Ch. Waybroke Extra Smooth, the sire of over 30 champions as of this writing.

Another Southern kennel contributing to the Smooth resurrection of the '60s and '70s is the Rebel Hill prefix of Miss Angeline Tillman. Among the exciting experiences that emanated from writing this chronicle is the odd recurrence of certain dogs in the root pedigrees of breeders hundreds and even thousands of miles apart. The lesson learned is "Better not knock the other fellow's dogs; you may be attacking yourself." You recall the earlier account of the Texas activity of the Gays; well, Miss Tillman's original stock shared common, though not identical roots. Miss Tillman bred her first champion bitch to Ch. Lethal Weapon of Rocky Point. In addition to being a Laurel Wreath son, Lethal Weapon was a maternal grandson of Ch. Saffron Hi-Hat of Gaycliffe. Combining the Waybrokes, the Foxdens and a good deal of Quissex, Miss Tillman always has a good Rebel Hill string that provides keen, interesting competition.

One hundred years ago, many wonderful breeders and dogs ago this narrative began in the Northeast, and it is to that section that we turn our attention to now. And while the Farrells and Foxden have been the dominant stabilizing force in the ring, in terms of breed improvement and in support of American Fox Terrier Club, they were by no means alone.

Quissex

It is extremely difficult to write objectively about Mrs. Winifred Stout, whose Quissex products have assisted or started as many newcomers as anyone I know. How do you describe someone who unselfishly devotes her time, energy (which is considerable) and knowledge (which is prodigious) to the breed and to fellow breeders? If numbers impress you, since the mid-'60s there have been over 70 Quissex champions, including Ch. Quissex Deacon, one of the all-time top producing stud dogs. If you are impressed by knowledge, watch her on those occasions when she judges a sweepstakes, or, better still, ask her to discuss Smooth pedigrees, but be certain to allow enough time. If you are impressed by energy, she accomplished most of these achievements by studying all that has been written, pouring over English and American publications, working with various combinations of English and American strains, and handling most of her dogs herself.

Mrs. Stout, by her own admission, had more false starts than a nervous sprinter. Bloodhounds and Old English Sheepdogs were her early breeds, but she freely admits to a childhood admiration for the Smooth. As a child, horses were a part of her life. One of her favorite authors on equine subjects was Paul Brown, whose books contained illustrations of Smooths working with hounds and horses. She had a false start in the late '50s with a

Ch. Quissex Deacon, one of the great all-time Smooth producers, with owner-handler Winifred Stout and judge Elsie Simmons.

Ch. Foxden Fairy Godmother, winner of the Welwire Trophy for three consecutive years.

Ch. Quissex Upsadaisy, the Foxmoor genesis, won the puppy Sweepstakes at the 1980 Lone Star FTC Specialty under Dan Kiedrowski. The handler was Scott Sommer. The trophy was made by Ynona Benedict.

bitch bred to a Heathside dog. The Quissex story can be a model for any newcomer. After one or two other unsatisfactory acquisitions, Mrs. Stout began to read everything she could get her hands on about Smooth Fox Terriers, including the English publications. She became aware of the names Watteau, Hampole, Hewshott, Harkaway, Newmaidley, etc. After some correspondence with these breeders, Winnie Stout imported two bitches, sight unseen. They were Hewshott January and Newmaidley Dream. Dream was the sister of Newmaidley Destiny, mentioned so prominently earlier in this chapter. Dream gave Quissex its first home-bred champion, Quissex Pipe Dream. But there is a more interesting story about Newmaidley Dream that clearly presents the effect Winnie Stout has had on Smooths.

Winnie knew about Newmaidley Destiny and in corresponding with Linda Beak of Newmaidley she learned of the sister. To most people, acquiring Dream would have been goal enough, but not for the redoubtable Mrs. Stout. She had Dream bred in England to a newly finished but as yet unheralded young dog called Watteau Snuff Box. Dream arrived at Quissex in whelp to Snuff Box. There were four bitches and a dog in that litter. The dog was lost. One bitch went to the Potter Wears, another, Pipe Dream, went to Joe Bachmuth, the third stayed with Mrs. Stout, Quissex Tinder Box, and the fourth went to Mrs. Steward Simmons, Quissex Bandbox of Battle Cry, a major force in the Battle Cry success story.

This success after some failure only whetted her appetite and interest. There were more Smooth worlds to conquer. Again, she turned to England. Long an admirer of certain qualities of the Hampole line, as exemplified by Ch. Hampole Sincerity, imported by Mrs. Simmons, Mrs. Stout noticed that a gentleman by the name of Bevan Walker was doing some interesting crosses based upon that very strain. Mr. Walker's prefix was Viscum. Over the next several years she imported several Viscum products, among them Viscum Vellum, the dam of Ch. Quissex Tinsel and Ch. Quissex Stirrup Cup, and Viscum Veracity, the sire of Ch. Quissex Deacon. But once again, it was Mrs. Stout who found the Viscums, which were later utilized by several top breeders including the Kuskas of Crag Crest.

I began this review of Mrs. Winifred Stout by stating that it is difficult to remain objective when writing about this lady because she was responsible for my successful return to my first love, the Fox Terrier. She sold then four-months-old puppy, Daisy, now veteran Ch. Quissex Upsadaisy. Daisy is the dam of eight champions out of a total of 11 surviving. Three were never shown. Due to a need for life-saving surgery, she can have no more. But she is the grandmother of over 40 champions and has some strong Smooth offspring in England and France. Her son, Ch. Foxmoor Field Marshall earned the Challenge Certificate, Crufts 1986. Typical of Winnie, she was more delighted for me than I was for myself.

New York had its share of active successful breeders in the '70s. On Long Island, the Winsome Smooths of Sibyll Sommer did a fine job. Their foundation was mostly Watteau with an occasional infusion of Foxden or Battle Cry breeding. Further north from Long Island was Dovenby Kennels of Mr. and Mrs. J. W. Smith. Starting with Ch. Sprucehill Precious Jewel, a linebred Saddler bitch bred by Judith K. Wolff, Dovenby purchased Ch. Stoney Meadows Comus from the Potter Wears, Ch. Battle Cry on the Double, sired by a Quissex-bred Ch. Newmaidley Haig and Ch. Newmaidley Siffleur from Linda Beak, so if the pedigree of your Smooth contains the Dovenby prefix, chances are its roots are in one or more of the aforementioned Smooth Fox Terriers.

Pennsylvania was led, of course, by the mistress of Battle Cry, Mrs. Steward Simmons, who was capitalizing on the great imports, Ch. Hampole Sincerity and Ch. Boreham Baranova, whose records were presented earlier. One major reason for the consistent quality of Battle Cry offspring through the years can be found in the judicious blending of top available bloodlines. Mrs. Simmons, to her credit, knows a good one when she sees it. And she recognized the ability to produce quality in a dog no matter the owner. If she thought it was good, she bought it. If she couldn't buy it, she bred to it. If she couldn't breed to it, as in someone else's bitch, she bought a puppy from the bitch. For example, as mentioned earlier, she acquired the Snuff Box-Newmaidley Dream bitch, Quissex Bandbox, from Mrs. Stout. She then bred Bandbox to Ebony Box and kept a bitch who became Ch. Battle Cry Treasure Chest. Then, when Boreham Baranova arrived, her line was assured of continuing the high standard expected of Battle Cry Smooths.

In Maryland in the late '60s and '70s, Smooth activity was dominated by two kennels, one old and established, the other a relative newcomer to the Smooth but successful with Miniature Schnauzers. The former, Stoney Meadows and the Wears had a marvelous track record as breeders and exhibitors. By 1970, they had been at it for 20 years. By the late '70s, the Potter Wears were cutting back on their breeding program but not on their enthusiasm. They both continued to judge, and their services were much sought after.

Handful

The newcomer was Gene Simmonds; with the assistance of Susie and Bobbie Fisher, she really created quite a stir. Starting modestly with a bitch from Sibyll Sommer, Winsome Musical Bell, who was bred to Watteau Musical Box to get the first home-bred Smooth champion in 1972, Miss Simmonds pulled out all the stops in an effort to challenge the established leaders. From Frau Hetti Brinkman in Germany she acquired Ch. Dorle Von Silvertbach, Ch. Igor Von Silvertbach, and Ch. Domino Von

Eng. & Am. Ch. Karnilo Chieftan of Foxden, second on the list of all-time Smooth stud dogs.

Ch. Rusbridge Sallie's Secret, CG (Certificate of Gameness), bred and campaigned by Stanley March.

Ch. Royal Irish Reigning Baronet and Ch. Roughrider Cowboy in the ring at Devon, 1978. Both are Chieftan sons.

113

Silvertbach; from Linda Beak, Eng., Am. Ch. Newmaidley Jacko, a Whistling Jeremy son, and a Jeremy daughter, Newmaidley Flute. And while these efforts began to pay dividends, Miss Simmonds' health began to fail before she could really enjoy the fulfillment of her dream.

Another fine Maryland Smooth family is the Marches. Stanley March and his daughter, Judy Hazlet, are steady breeders on not so grand a scale as some of their contemporaries, but with certainly as much knowledge and dedication. Anywhere in the East that an important Fox Terrier event is taking place, chances are a Rusbridge Smooth will be there and be tough to beat.

No discussion of the Smooth in Maryland would be complete without Ida and Leon Seligman or, if you prefer, Dr. and Mrs. Leon Seligman. The Seligmans have been active supporters of the breed for half a century. Ida Seligman passed away in 1985, but Dr. Seligman continues as one of our good terrier judges.

In Connecticut, Foxden continued to turn out its annual roster of fine Smooth champions with the occasional infusion of new blood from Britain. With more than 80 champions to their name, in 1973 the Farrells once again turned to England and introduced to America yet another fine English breeder's product. Henry Holinrake of Karnilo Kennels bred his Snuff Box daughter, Karnilo Cavalena, to Eng. Ch. Laurel Drive, a Chorister grandson, and got for his efforts one of the truly great Smooths of the century. Henry Holinrake called his prodigy Karnilo Chieftan. After he gained his English title in 1972, the Farrells bought him and brought him to America. I saw Chieftan for the first time when he was ten years. At first glance, he was a decent Smooth, but when Archie Davis put a leash on him he turned into a very imposing dog. He had that unmistakable look of the "take charge" showman even at that advanced age. He made the most of every muscle. I've only seen that look a very few times in my nearly 40 years in dogs. But Chieftan was more than just another pretty face. His blood flows through the veins of most of the fine domestically bred Smooth Fox Terriers in the United States today. More than 40 American champions were produced by this great dog. His son, Ch. Foxden Warpaint, has more than two dozen. But it is from his bitches that he seems to carry through even more eloquently. Most of the leading kennels today have at least one linebred Chieftan bitch as a foundation producer. My own Ch. Quissex Upsadaisy is a linebred Chieftan bitch. Toofox, Foxboro, Quissex, Battle Cry, Royal Irish, Raybill, Rebel Hill and many more have Chieftan genes in their bloodstock. The Farrells have imported several fine dogs and bitches through the years, but none have done for the breed what Chieftan has done. Subsequent imports that have had fine ring careers and were successful at stud or in the whelping box include Eng. and Am. Chs. Higrola Horation of Britlea, Jonwyre's Galaxy and Jonwyre's Galore of Foxden.

Ch. Higrola Horatio of Britlea, owned by Foxden Kennels, winning the Terrier Group under Judge Dr. Leon Seligman with handler Jane Forsyth.

Ch. Foxden Warpaint has carried on as a fine stud dog in his sire's place. Paint is a Chieftan son.

115

Ch. Denidale Olga of Halsho, the foundation bitch for the Brookhaven Wires of Mari Morrisey, pictured at age six retiring the Challenge Trophy of the FTC of Northern California. Pictured are handler Wood Wornall and judge Annemarie Moore.

Ch. Dynamic Super Sensation, a Dutch import who established a great record in the show ring. Handled by Wood Wornall, she was imported for Barbara and Frank Swigart.

The Wire, in the '80s, is becoming, like the Smooth, a "cottage industry." Gone are the great Wire kennels, but, perhaps, what remains is healthier and better for the breed. The base of participants is far broader and the resulting competition is more multi-faceted. For example, California Wires in 1985 are better than ever in general quality. Instead of one or two leaders, there are several fine breeders who produce Wires of consistent quality.

In Southern California, Denny Ross may be less active, but she lends her knowledge and experience to Dorothea and Chuck Palmer, who have had some success with their Wyrdot Wires. With their foundation firmly rooted in Evewire and Glenarden, very few breeders can boast of a home-bred that can come East and win Winners Dog at Hatboro, Devon, and Montgomery County from the puppy class. Ch. Wyrdot Stop the Presses did just that.

Laura and Richard Forkel are really old newcomers or new old-comers. As of this writing, they have over 20 home-bred Wendywire champions. By intelligently blending their current stock with the best available new blood, the Forkels continue to turn out outstanding exhibits. A recent acquisition is Ch. Warwick Watchman, bred by Carol Hampton of Warwick Wires. He is by one of our most successful American-bred stud dogs, Ch. Brownstone's MacBroom.

The Brookhaven Wires of Mari Morrisey have given a good account of themselves in breed and specialty competition. Mari morrisey recently published a thank you to those who helped her off on the right foot.

> I would like to say a heartfelt thank you to so many who offered this novice help and encouragement. Most especially, I can never adequately acknowledge the patience, guidance, and care shown to me in those fledgling years by Arden Ross, the late Evelyn Silvernail and Harold Shook.

When a breeder shares success with those who encouraged and aided her through the breeder weaning years, that breeder enhances the reputation of all Fox Terrier enthusiasts. Mari Morrisey's success was due to the outstanding bitch, Ch. Denidale Olga of Halsho, who has seven champions for her efforts. As of this writing, there are nine more youngsters in different stages of development, so her final record could exceed 12 titlists. She was the top Wire in 1981, and five of her get were Specialty winners.

In the Bay area to the north, Wire activity is just as intense. The current "oldtimer" is an active schoolteacher, Nancy Lee Wolf. Her Wyrelees compete nationally and frequently walk off with the ribbons. As referred to earlier, the Halsho Kennels of Harold Shook was part of her beginning, but she blended the great dogs of the past—Craftsman, Spot On and William Meyers Jones' Heathcote—into her unique type of Wire. Ch. Wyrelee's Banned in Boston not only produced five champions but earned her obedience companion dog title as well. That is really what this is all about. The standard is a guide, and how each person interprets it is their creative expression. Wyrelee exemplifies that thought.

As for the Splawns, what can be added to so consummate a contribution to the breed? They provide a shining example for those who came after them, about 50 home-bred champions to date.

Newcomers to Wires in the early '80s in Colorado are Carole J. and Oscar Porter, who started beautifully with a William Johnson (Fairfield) bred bitch, who had several BIS, Ch. Redcap's Nell of Fairfield. Nell's sire, Ch. Terrikane's Tulliver, as of this writing, is the top-winning American-bred Wire of all time. He is by Ch. Aryee Dominator, the Spot On son.

Their Enchantress daughter, Brownstone's Hey Day, has seven champions to her credit, while her daughter, Ch. Brownstone Miss Kiss, has 10 offspring regal enough to claim their title.

Working our way east to Kansas, we have discussed the Browns of Shawnee, Kansas at length, but they have been an even greater factor in the '80s. Their home-bred Ch. Brownstone's MacBroom is proving to be one of the leading sires of the early part of the decade.

Wire Fox Terrier Club of the Central States Hall of Famer Bob Fine has curtailed his breeding activities at Finewyr in Louisiana in favor of a judge's career but not before encouraging Sherri and Dennis Terrill to establish Southwind Kennels in Kansas. The Terrills started with a wonderful young dog, Ch. Finewyr On the Spot. The Fines also shared the wealth with Paul Pruitt of Goldenwyr in North Carolina by parting with a lovely young bitch, Ch. Finewyr Carolina Debutante, and a dog, Ch. Finewyr's Mean Machine.

Eve Ballich spread her influence to Texas in the person of Marlene Middendorf of Corpus Christi. From a co-breeding of Ch. Evewire You Better Believe It to Ch. Evewire Limited Edition, Marlene reaped her first two champions, Memwyre's Tux 'N Tails and the bitch, Memwyre's Elegant Charm.

No study of Fox Terriers in Texas would be credible without the inclusion of Monsignor Joseph P. O'Sullivan. The challenge is to decide where he should be included. I do not believe anyone really knows how many champions "Father Joe" has seen through to their titles, both Wire and Smooth. His own prefix is Elton or Eltonwire, but since many of the dogs he has owned and titled were imports it is impossible to develop an accurate tally. One thing is certain—Joseph P. O'Sullivan, in more than 60 years, has done as much for Fox Terriers in Texas as anyone else. And since he prefers a good Wire to a good Smooth (but not by much), I've included him in the Wire section.

Before leaving the West, an account of Wire activity in Hawaii is in order. Mrs. Midori K. Fujii has exhibited and bred Wires for a number of years. Her Doriwyre exhibits have had a good deal of recognition on the mainland as well as the Islands. She has been a long-time supporter of purebred dog activities on the Islands.

We follow the Canadian border and travel east to the state of Michigan. Once again, a more experienced breeder willing to part with a good one seems to have been the catalyst for bringing the Libners to Wires. Ch. Libwyre's Prancing Fairy completed her title in 1974 and appears to be the first Libwyre titlist. She was bred by John and Jane Masley of Yelsam Wires. John has been active in Wire Fox Terrier activities for decades and is a WFTCCC Hall of Famer and a busy judge. Dr. and Mrs. John Masley from Charleston, Illinois have started a number of people into Wires, including the Libners. Libwyre Kennels is one of the Midwest's outstanding Wire breeders and exhibitors, headed by Eng., Am. Ch. Townville Tristanian, and beautifully supported by the marvelous homebreds Ch. Libwyre Legend (a top sire in his own right), Chs. Libwyre Crispy Katie, Advocate, Winter Storm, Landmark, Lady Guinevere and still others to come. Ruth Libner combines the best of the famous Townville Kennels of England with an occasional cross to the Harrowhill strain of Mrs. Howles. Mrs. Libner is a breeder who pleases herself first, and that is as it should be. Other Michigan breeders of note are the McIlwianes, whose Foxairn Wires are DOMINATED by Spot On. Finally, in Michigan, Mr. and Mrs. Harold Wainright have bred Smooths and Wires under the Halcar label, but I believe that they are better known for their Wires. A Carol Wainright-bred Halcar Wire earned its title more than 10 years ago, and they have competed consistently since then.

It seems so empty moving east through Ohio to Pennsylvania and not having a Hetherington success or two to report, but Mrs. Carruthers died recently. We never replace our great supporters, our great breeders, our breat exhibitors, nor our great judges, but we do carry on. Sometimes the contributions of a single exhibitor must now be matched by several, but if the breed is good and true, the people will be there.

Pennsylvania has a grand combination of old and new. The new in terms of Wire history is William Rawlings. He is an enthusiastic breeder and exhibitor who combines the blood of Townville and Emperor. His Ch. Warwood Townville Tarheel is a fine example of that breeding. The old consists of Wire greats like Irene Rhodes, who, I believe, is the only breeder currently active that started with a Forest Hall Wire. An early homebred champion was Foxglen Envoy's Tamora, bred in 1971. Her foundation bitch was the Whitham-bred Ch. Penda Townville Tanya, who gained her American title in 1971. Starting with a bitch bred from Tom Keator's last champion, Derbyshire Don't Tell, Mr. and Mrs. Joseph Haage have devoted the last 20 or more years to breeding fine Wire Fox Terriers. Mrs. Phyllis Haage is one of the few Wire breeders who have taken up the mantle of judge and has done the task honor. An example of the esteem her fellows have for her acumen was her assignment to judge Fox Terriers at the

Frances Thornton's Ch. Rom-Wyre's Tudor Bet.

Ch. Thornwyre's Heir Apparent. Frances Thornton of Converse, Texas, always has a top Wire and is a fine judge of terriers.

Ch. Townville Tristanian, an English, American and Canadian champion, owned by Ruth Libner.

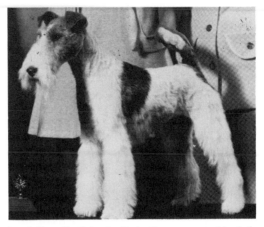

Am. & Can. Ch. Holmwire Vitoka Vanessa, owned by Ruth Libner.

Wayne Boucek with Ch. Cefnbryn Cookie, top Wire bitch 1981 and dam of Bowyre champions all sired by Ch. Bowyre Contender.

Ch. Evewire Druid Dynamic, a great early stud dog for Evewire Kennels.

121

American Kennel Club's 100th Anniversary show in 1984. Pennsylvania is also the home of Gayterry, Kay and Tom Gately's place. When they were professional handlers, they bred some wonderful Wires, including Chs. Sirius and Brightest Star of Gayterry. Three more great terrier Pennsylvanians are Mrs. William Wimer III and Mr. and Mrs. John Marvin. Bea Marvin has served as the American Fox Terrier Club's AKC Delegate for many years, and John has held almost every office in the parent club. Many of the photographs in this work were graciously supplied by Jack Marvin.

Along the Middle Atlantic and New England Coast the population is so dense that state or any geographic boundaries become blurred and unimportant. However, this density has not brought about a homogenization of bloodlines. For example, Mendham, New Jersey is the home of Mr. and Mrs. Clifford Hallmark. The Hallmarks were responsible for importing Eng., Am. Ch. Harwire Hetman of Whilatter, and "Harry" has resided with them all his life.

One New Yorker who deserves mention is Mrs. Murry Abrams. While Mrs. Abrams has competed less than some of the people mentioned in this work, she, nonetheless, has been a tireless worker and enthusiastic supporter of Wires for many years.

Connecticut is the home of Mr. and Mrs. Jack DeWitt. The DeWitts started with some of the Crack-Dale dogs that Mrs. Silvernail parted with before she left for California in the early '70s. Their Rhapsodale Wires are frequent and successful exhibits at most of today's Eastern shows. Jack DeWitt is much sought after as a judge for matches and sweepstakes, one indication of the esteem afforded him by his fellow breeders. Into the Crack-Dale line, the DeWitts have infused Ch. Axholme Jimmy Reppin, one of the fine imports of the '70s.

Newton Center, Massachusetts is the home of Norma Appleyard, who is carrying on the long and honorable program of the Appleyard family. Their prefix is simply App's. Starting with a bitch bred by the venerable Mac Silver (Wildoaks), the Appleyards bred to Ch. Evewire Exemplar to get their first homebred champion, App's Press Agent. Later they went out to a Townville linebred dog, Ch. Briartex Tavern, and that mating produced their most successful Wire to date, Ch. App's Prime Time. The Peter F. Daleys (Conwyre) are active in the 1980s. They obtained their start from Beatrice Turtle of Bakersfield, California. The Daleys of Massachusetts acquired a Bexleydale Wire from Miss Turtle, and Conwyre was off and running. Bruce Bentley (Bentleigh), Peter Green, and Penda's Elsie Williams combined to get Judith Anne Hunter started properly with Ch. Penda Painting. Hopefully, the future will be bright for this newcomer. Other Wire enthusiasts in Massachusetts are Bruce Bentley, mentioned earlier, and Grace Brewin, one of the busiest terrier judges around. Bentley has a great son of Eng. Ch. Townville Trail who has had considerable success at stud and in the ring, Eng., Am. Ch. Kilnhill Kinsman of Purston.

Connecticut is the home of a terrier legend. Barbara Keenan comes by her love of dogs from her mother and has had Wires since childhood. Wishing Well Wires were prominent in the '50s and '60s. Mrs. Keenan has also had great success in Westies and today is a leading judge. There is a third generation in competition in Barbara's daughter, Patty Ann, who has done well with Smooths.

I deliberately saved Col. and Mrs. Robert Bigelow and their Raylu Wires for this portion of Wire chronicles even though they have been successful since the early '50s. The Bigelows' early successes were in Hawaii, but they now reside in Virginia. Adhering to a wonderful program of linebreeding to the Wildoaks Wires, they have produced close to 30 champions. With the end of Hetherington, Raylu is one of the few remaining Wildoaks legacies. The Bigelows are WFTCCC Hall of Famers. Since they began in Hawaii and are still active in Virginia, it seemed best to include them in the last section of Wire history.

If Wire followers of the '80s were asked their favorite color, don't be surprised if the answer is brown. Mr. and Mrs. James H. Brown are WFTCCC Hall of Famers along with the Browns of Shawnee, Kansas. Marietta, Georgia is where the Brown's Lynnwyre Kennels is located with nearly 30 homebred champion notches on their totem pole. If you look back at their foundations and a little further, you would discover the influence of Raylu in the root structure of Lynnwyre, starting with a bitch called Berylean Spicy Rosemary (she had Raylu blood), who was bred to an English import, Ch. Exelwyre Elegance. The offspring was Lynnwyre's first taste of success, Ch. Lynnwyre Aristocrat, a dog. The year was 1966. Georgians Sue and Tommy Yates started Mystwyre with a Splawn-bred bitch, Ch. Wyrequest Wildfire, and later were influenced by the Lynnwyres. Is it any wonder that they have had so much success in a relatively short time?

Our final stop in this geographic chronicle of Wire activity is Florida. There are three breeders of significance in Florida starting in Miami with the breeders of Ch. Terrikane Tulliver, Mr. and Mrs. John Kane. However, the records indicate a working relationship between the Kanes and Alice Clay on the West Coast. The same can be said of the third Florida prefix, Carole and Bob Beattie's Sunsprite, although the latter appears to be more influenced by California foundation stock.

With the Florida summary, the Wire history is complete. The only question left to determine is when Wire breeders will rediscover the letter "i."

The year 1979 was momentous for the Smooth Fox Terriers. Some 40 years earlier, an eight-months-old puppy from overseas literally changed the course of Fox Terrier history in the United States. Nornay Saddler was so successful a show dog that the American Fox Terrier Club applied for and received permission from the American Kennel Club to once again

Ch. Littleway Haranwal Barrister, another successful Cliff Hallmark import, shown winning the Terrier Group at Westminster in 1973. The judge is John T. Marvin.

Ch. Terrikane Tulliver, shown winning Best in Show at the Paper Cities Kennel Club show, June 1980. He is handled by George Ward for breeder-owners Mr. and Mrs. John Kane.

have both Varieties represented in the group. In 1979, Ch. Ttarb the Brat arrived on our shores from overseas as a seven-months-old puppy, and once again Fox Terrier history was impacted. On June 1, 1985 the Wire Fox Terrier and the Smooth Fox Terrier became separate breeds. The reasons for the division are of little consequence to this work, but, in my judgment, without the Brat, the separation would have been more difficult to achieve. He brought the Smooth back to show ring prominence and parity. His offspring have continued to compete equally, not only with Wires, but with all Terriers. Imported to America from Australia by Ed Dalton of Oakland, California and discovered by then handler, now judge, Richard Chashoudian, the Brat was an instant sensation. I can only recall a couple of times when he lost in the Variety; his victories in the Variety numbered in the hundreds. It serves little purpose to compare Brat's show record with Saddler's. Comparisons of this kind are not comparisons, just cocktail party games. The Brat was a big dog and was not without his detractors. That is the price of greatness. Some people in this world prefer to talk about the glass chin of Joe Louis, the strike-outs of Mickey Mantle, Joe Namath's lack of mobility. Let them. As for me, I would not have wanted to be a heavyweight contender in 1937, or an American League pitcher facing Mantle, or a defensive back playing against Namath in his prime.

To compete in the Variety when Ch. Ttarb the Brat was in the ring was a very depressing experience. From the early days of my dog life, when Phil Prentice advised me to seek another career, I never set foot in the ring. Never, that is, until that summer day in 1983 when the Brat came out of retirement in search of his 60th all-breed BIS. Ch. Foxmoor One Tuff Cookie was in search of her title in California with Tony Giles. Unfortunately, instead of entering her in the American-bred class at Santa Barbara, she was in Bred-by-Exhibitor. So if Cookie was to be shown that day, it would have to be Ruth, my non-doggie but totally supportive spouse, or yours truly. The poor bitch was not a shower to begin with, but if this was a horse race, having me on the end of the leash would be equivalent to carrying top weight at the track. Fortunately, Phyllis Haage saw through the handicap of a handler who cannot handle and a show dog that hates dog shows and we were awarded Winners Bitch. A poll taken of handlers, spectators, exhibitors and the judge after the judging revealed almost unanimous support for Phil Prentice's original assessment; only my wife thought we both did "beautifully." But she also thinks I have a good voice. So, here I was in the Specials class with Cookie. I looked around at this marvelous class of nearly 30 champions, including about 10 or 11 all-breed BIS winners. They were all exciting to look at, and then my eye came to Peter Green and Ch. Ttarb the Brat, and, as far as I was concerned, the show was over.

The words to describe him are "impressive," "imposing," and "chal-

Ch. Ttarb the Brat—sixty all-breed Bests, nearly one hundred champion offspring—a Smooth immortal.

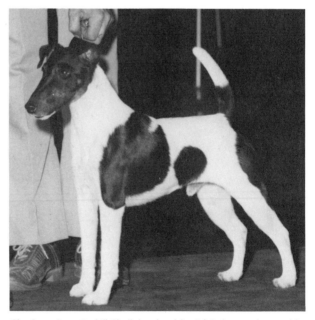

Ch. Crag Crest Foxhill Shallaha, bred by Ed Dalton and owned by Cragcrest Kennels—Jane Kuska.

lenging." He was like Sophia Loren in many ways. It you take her apart, her mouth is too large; her bust, over-generous; her hips too pronounced; but altogether, WHAT A WOMAN! Well, Brat, in his separate parts, can be faulted, but together, WHAT A DOG! Even amongst these entries that, on any given day, at any show, had the conformation and bearing to go all the way, he was a standout. As a Smooth Fox Terrier breeder, I have felt that Mrs. Farrell's Foxden Warspite, as a yearling, was a better dog, but he never intimidated me in the ring the way the Brat did that summer Sunday. He was truly awesome. For the record, he won the Variety, the Group and his 60th BIS and was permanently retired.

The pedigree of Ttarb the Brat is relatively unknown in the United States. His sire, Ch. Farleton Captain Sandy, is a son of Newmaidley Pennyworth, who goes back to Watteau Chorister on both sides of his pedigree. The balance of the Australian dogs, for the most part, go back to a dog called Eng. Ch. Brookland's Black Ace. He is by Eng. Ch. Brooklands Lucky Wishbone, which makes him a half-brother to Chorister. Black Ace was imported to Australia in the mid-'50s and was used extensively. Gothic Grand Gem, Redvan La Ronde Grenpark Amethyst all go back to Black Ace. Lucky Wishbone was a grandson of Watteau Midas, the Laurel Wreath son.

Another Brat ancestor was a dog named Lingfield Fame. He appears several times in the fifth and sixth generations. Lingfield Fame is a son of Eng. Ch. Brooklands Black Ace as well. However, Ch. Brooklands Sailor Lad, another multiple ancestor, is a Snuff Box Son. His remaining ancestry probably goes back to Levenside Luke, so that the Brat could be a direct male descendant of Belgrave Joe.

The Brat's offspring make up a recent Smooth Who's Who: Best-in-Show winners Chs. Bryan Wanda the Witch, Foxhill's Ttarb Baby, Crag Crest Shogun, Foxhill's Crag Crest Shillala, Foxmoor Macho Macho Man, etc. To date he has sired more than 100 champions.

One other interesting note about the Brat—he won Bests in Show with three different handlers. The dog could not be denied. Some of the active breeders he has impacted include Crag Crest, Laurelton, Quissex, Foxtrot, Foxmoor, Toofox, High Desert, Five Alarm, Foxfyne and, of course, Ed Dalton's Foxhill.

While it is still too early to assess the long range impact of Ch. Ttarb the Brat, the short term result has been a great renewal of attention to the Smooth and the feeling of parity so essential to the successful separation of the varieties into breeds.

Present-day Smooths are at the peak of quality. These fortunes change through the years, but as of 1986 the Smooth Fox Terrier in America is the class of the world. In my judgment, only the quarantine requirements and related expenses prevent the export to England and Australia of American Smooths. The hobby breeder is the impetus behind this rise in quality.

Following are some brief glimpses of a number of them in geographical sequence.

The Robisons and the Theels and Raybill are very active in the Pacific Northwest. The State of Washington is home for Foxhead Smooths of Ruth and Harold Turner. The Turners' beginnings are rooted in old, established lines. Watteau Chorister is behind an early import, Eng., Am. Ch. Watteau Sonnet; another foundation bitch, Ch. Foxhead Sylvia, is the product of the early Raybill-Von Nassau blood with the Mullanteans. Ten years later, the Turners are in the thick of the action. Two other Raybill protegés in Washington are Foxbow, owned by Susan Akin, and Sheez-beez, owned by Sheila Taylor Allen. The standard-bearer for Foxbow is Ch. Dragoon of Foxbow, linebred on Chieftan/Watteau. Sheez-beez is mostly Western in its roots, with a heavy dose of Raybill, but once again we find some Quissex breeding in the program.

California continues as a beehive of Smooth activity in the 1980s. Oakland is home to Aine and Ed Dalton and the Brat. The Kuskas are still active, while Lorraine Creed spends much of her time in the ring assessing the dogs of others; Ch. Ellastone Vibart produced 25 champions for her Mar-Lor Smooths and for those breeders who used him to their advantage. The Rev. Michael G. O'Sullivan maintains the Priory Kennels with the help of Barbara Cross. Lloyd G. Stark has produced some wonderful results combining the best of the East and West in his fine producing bitch, Ch. Starkdom's Blaze-N-Easy. He then sold her to Jerry Falkenstein who bred her to the Brat with really exciting results. The Falkensteins are not quite in California, but their High Desert Kennels is just over the border in Minden, Nevada. One other interesting bit of data concerns a dog called Newmaidley Pennywise, who was used by Jerry Falkenstein with his Starkdom bitch to produce a fine dog called Ch. High Desert Scout. The interesting item is that Pennywise is a litter brother to the grandsire of Brat, Newmaidley Pennyworth.

Starting with a champion bitch bred to Ch. Pathens Sammy Sayres, Mr. and Mrs. A. J. Baron launched one of the more successful California Kennels, Royal Irish. Their program combined the gene pool of Eng., Am. Ch. Karnilo Chieftan of Foxden and Ch. Pathens Sammy Sayres with such success that many of Chieftan's 40-plus champion offspring were from Royal Irish bitches. Royal Irish was another of those centers of influence so important to the future of the breed. The Lizabethan Kennels of Mary Lou Hammond had Royal Irish as startup blood, as did the Oakhill Smooths of Mrs. Jean Anton, but her foundation comes from the Toofox Kennels of the Dossetts in Texas.

The Dallas-Fort Worth metroplex is a hotbed of Smooth activity and the home of the Lone Star Fox Terrier Club. Without question, its most successful breeder and exhibitor is the Dossett family, Bill and Betsy. The Dossetts' Toofox Smooths are one of the surviving heirs of Ch. Nornay

Ch. Mullantean Arkle with owner Billie Lou Robison, Raybill Smooths.

Ch. Foxhead Sylvia (Ch. Halmor's Mullantean Mr. Carl ex Von Nassau Raybill Sequin), owned by Ruth and Harold Turner.

Ch. Foxhill Cash and Carry, another fine Brat son who challenged his dad in the ring on several occasions. The judge is Eve M. Ballich and the handler-breeder is Ed Dalton.

129

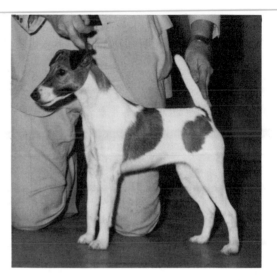

Ch. Starkdom Blaze-N'-Easy, foundation bitch for the High Desert Smooths of Jerry Falkenstein.

Ch. Foxboro Patent Pending.

Ch.Kraehollow Katy O'Della.

Two of Jane Swanson's Smooths
at Foxtrot.

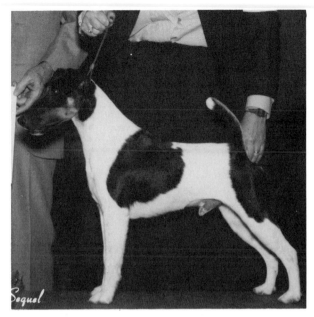

Ch. Toofox the Caribe Chief Spy, bred by the Dossetts and co-owned by Murrel and Joe Purkhiser.

Ch. Toofox the Colonel, multiple Specialty and BIS winner at Toofox.

Ch. Toofox Tribute to Gaycliffe, dam of Toofox the Colonel and a truly outstanding Smooth bitch.

Saddler. Their foundation bitch, Mini Echo, was bred to the Gay's Paragon of Gaycliffe. Paragon has at least three lines to Saddler, through Ch. Pericles. The Lenabergs were started by the Dossetts and are quite active along with Murrel and Joe Purkhiser. The Purkhisers have had a lot of fun with Ch. Toofox the Caribe Chief Spy, co-owned with the Dossetts. Toofox, however, really began to compete nationally after they went to the Brat with several bitches. One of their Brat daughters, Ch. Toofox Tribute to Gaycliffe, is as good a bitch as can be found anywhere. Ch. Toofox the Colonel was Montgomery County's variety winner in 1984 and the Caribe Chief Spy in 1985. Both dogs are heavily influenced by the Brat. Blazin Smooths of Nancy Atwood have done some winning, and the Kraehollow prefix of Mr. and Mrs. M. J. Riekenberg are surpassed only by the Dossetts in number of homebred champions. While their foundation stock is similar to Toofox, Martha Riekenberg went to the West Coast before the Brat arrived and infused the Pathens breeding into her stock. At the 1983 Westminster show, the Riekenbergs took the variety with a homebred bitch, Ch. Kraehollow Morning Mist. The author calls Houston his home, and a Houston suburb, Richmond, is the location of Foxmoor.

Colorado was home to one of the more prominent Smooth breeders of the past several decades. Patience Haller (Theiss) kept the Smooth flag flying with dignity and true sportsmanship during her lifetime.

William Potter II is active in the St. Louis area. Ch. Riever Angelica is a Potter Smooth who had great success in the ring.

Jane Swanson and her Fox Trot Smooths are difficult to characterize. Her efforts contain more variety of the leading kennels in America and England than any other. Examine the pedigrees of her Smooths; you will find Pathens, Kraehollow, Quissex, Foxden, Foxmoor and others, but Foxtrot began with Yvonne Burdick's Smoothglen breeding. Smoothglen used a Stanley March bred dog, Ch. Rusbridge Warlock, to good advantage. Warlock was by Ch. Foxden Riverboat Gambler ex Ch. Foxden Flammable.

Connecticut means Foxden and Mrs. James Farrell, Jr. is still producing great Smooths. Her most recent triumph has been Ch. Foxden Warspite. In the strongest terrier competition in the East in years, he compiled a record of Group and BIS wins that made him the most successful Foxden homebred ever. This is a truly great Fox Terrier.

Lisa Sachs is still an active breder and exhibitor, but her role in bringing Smooths to the attention of the public through television commercials and for obedience is significant. It is possible that one of Lisa's TV stars does more for Smooths in one year than was ever achieved by any breeder. Lisa Sachs is another Quissex associate. She collaborated with Eva Sasovetz on the obedience portion of this book. Mr. and Mrs. James Smith are still very active with their Dovenby Smooths, but Tom Partis (Karner) has opted for judging.

Ch. Foxmoor Macho Macho Man, sire of more than twenty champions through December 1985, owned by Ruth and Harold Nedell.

Eng. & Am. Ch. Maltman Country Life of Whinlatter.

133

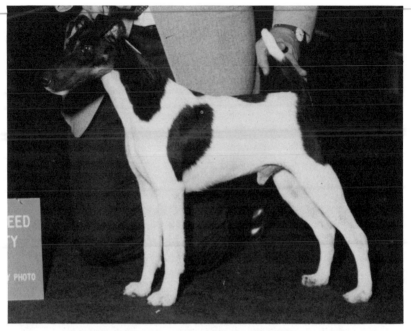

Ch. Charbonne Enfant Terrible, bred and owned by Ms. C. R. Le Vecque.

Ch. Talisman Second Coat of Paint, dam of eleven champions. Bred by Virginia Shames and owned by the Thorntons, Upcountry Reg.

Pennsylvania in the 1980s has its stalwarts in Mrs. Stewart Simmons (Battle Cry) and Judith Wolff (Sprucehill). Pennsylvania is the home of Newcomers A. G. Martin and P. T. Dwyer, who have started Five Alarm Kennels with a fine dog and victory at Montgomery County, Ch. Innana's Spurs and Saddles. The Greenvale Kennels of Sandra and Bayard Colfax have had a fine record in the 1980s. They are from Abington, Pennsylvania.

In Virginia, it is hard to write about anyone but the Brainards, but Virginia Shames has enjoyed real success in a comparatively short time. Talisman Kennels is rapidly becoming one of the more successful efforts.

South Carolina has several fine Smooth breeders. Taking a Virginia Shames-bred bitch, Ch. Talisman Second Coat of Paint, William and Mary Thornton went to Ch. Ttarb the Brat and came up with instant gratification. The litter produced Chs. Upcountry Jeremy and Jitterbug.

One of the oldest active prefixes, St. Asaphs Smooths makes its home with Burdette Bright in Kentucky, and one of the newest Smooth enthusiasts, Crovenay Kennels of Dr. Martin Marx, is in Kentucky as well.

While I have written much about Foxden, the late '70s and '80s cannot come to a close without pointing to the achievements of two of the Foxden imports, Eng., Am. Chs. Karnilo Chieftan of Foxden and Higrola Horatio of Britlea. Both of these fine producers have brought qualities sorely needed by breeders in America. Between them they are responsible for nearly 70 champions. Chieftan has provided more foundations than a commercial home builder. In the years ahead, whenever Smooth breeders get together, Foxden will always be in the conversation.

To make this section as helpful to breeders as possible, I have summarized the previous chapter for easy reference with a huge assist from Dan Kiedrowski. Who were the great dogs of the past? Who were the great breeders of the past? Those answers appear in the previous chapter. The following summary will, hopefully, supply a ready reference to what is detailed earlier.

Whom to list as the great Wire breeders in the United States is difficult if it requires ranking them. As a breeder, I know that opportunity, facilities, and resources play a significant role in this sport. The only fair listing is an alphabetical one. These, then, are the great Wire breeders:

Mrs. Eve Ballich . . . . Evewire
Col. and Mrs. R. C. Bondy . . . . Wildoaks
Mr. and Mrs. Wayne Bousek . . . . Bowyre
Mr. and Mrs. James H. Brown . . . . Lynnwyre
Mr. and Mrs. John M. Brown . . . . Brownstone
Mr. and Mrs. T. H. Carruthers III . . . . Hetherington
Mr. and Mrs. Robert Fine . . . . Finewyre
Mr. and Mrs. Richard J. Forkel . . . . Wendywyre
Mr. and Mrs. Tom Gately . . . . Gayterry
Mr. and Mrs. Forest Hall . . . . Hallwyre

Mr. George H. Hartman .... Wirehart
Mr. and Mrs. Myron Hook .... Mountain Ayre
Mr. and Mrs. D. E. Jorgensen .... Ana-Dare
Mr. and Mrs. Franklin Koehler .... Merrybrook
Dr. and Mrs. John Masley .... Yelsam
Mr. Harold Shook .... Halsho
Mr. and Mrs. Paul Silvernail .... Crackdale
Mr. and Mrs. Raymond M. Splawn .... Wyrequest
Dr. Charlotte Jones and Miss E. Stark .... Koshare
Nancy Lee Wolf .... Wyrelee

From 1900 to 1970, 25 dogs sired 10 or more champions. The leader, with 21 champions, was Ch. Fox Hunter of Wildoaks followed by Ch. Evewire Extra Edition. The production order is as follows:

21 - Foxhunter of Wildoaks
   by Gallant Fox of Wildoaks
   ex Ch. Crackley Sunray of Wildoaks

19 - Ch. Evewire Extra Edition
   by Ch. Mac's Revelation
   ex Smart Move of Wirehart

18 - Ch. Gallant Fox of Wildoaks
   by Ch. Crackley Supreme of Wildoaks
   ex Ch. Gains Great Surprise of Wildoaks

17 - Ch. Hallwyre Handy Jack
   by Ch. Hallwyre Huckster
   ex Ch. Hallwyre Hallie's Hildegarde

16 - Ch. Crackley Startler of Wildoaks
   by Eng. Ch. Beau Brummel of Wildoaks
   ex Pettigo Prudence

16 - Ch. Westbourne Teetotaler
   by Eng. Ch. Weltona Pebble
   ex Miss Marie

15 - Ch. Mac's Revelation
   by Eng. Ch. Weltone Exelwyre Dustynight
   ex Mac's Model Wire

14 - Ch. Striking Example of Wildoaks
   by Ch. Crackley Striking of Wildoaks
   ex Ch. Enchantress of Wildoaks

14 - Ch. Crackley Striking of Wildoaks
   by Eng. Ch. Crackley Supreme Again
   ex Eng. Ch. Crackley Social

Ch. Reiver Angelica, owned by William Potter, II.

Ch. Foxden Warspite, the top home-bred winner for Mrs. James A. Farrell, Jr. Sire of nearly twenty champions to date.

14 - Ch. Gallant Invader of Wildoaks
by Ch. Gallant Fox of Wildoaks
ex Ch. Weltona Frizzette of Wildoaks

14 - Eng. Ch. Talavera Simon
by Eng. Ch. Fountain Crusader
ex Kingsthorp Donah

13 - Ch. Florate Cwmbath Combine
by Emprise Double
ex Florate Festival

13 - Ch. Lone Eagle of Earlsmoor
by Eng. Ch. Talavera Simon
ex Firebrand Fairy

12 - Ch. Baros Marymount Ranger
by Eng. Ch. Lyngarth Scout
ex Baros Delight

12 - Gallant Knight of Wildoaks
by Ch. Crackley Supreme of Wildoaks
ex Ch. Gains Great Surprise of Wildoaks

12 - Eng. Ch. Lyngarth Scout
by Eng. Ch. Zeloy Crusader
ex Eng. Ch. Lyngarth Social Call

12 - Ch. Nemo's Magic of Lyvewyre
by Wyretx Wyns Copperstock
ex Mahonia of Freams

11 - Ch. Glynhir Great Guns
by Ch. Wyretex Wyns Jupiter of Glynhir
ex Glynhir Grenadine

11 - Ch. Miller Haven's Ike
by Ch. Whisk Broom of Waverly
ex Ch. Monona's Sunburst

10 - Ch. Evewire Little Man
by Ch. Baros Magic
ex Ch. Nugrade Nuflame

10 - Ch. Hetherington Parapilot
by Ch. Hetherington Co-Pilot
ex Quest's End Cinderella

10 - Ch. Hetherington Surprise Model
by Ch. Newbold Teetotaler
ex Ch. Hetherington Surprise

These wonderful studs established their place in the Wire cosmos. Their names will appear forever in the remote pedigrees of future generations but their gene pool is ever present. A study of a 10-generation pedigree will reveal a total of 2046 dogs and bitches. Nearly every great modern producer owes his or her "stamp" to the frequency of appearance in the pedigree of those producers identified in this chapter. The great contemporary Wire stud dogs begin with Eng., Am. Ch. Harwire Hetman of Whinlatter, who sired 52 American champions. He was by Eng., Am. Ch. Townville Tobias. I chose to cut off the list with those dogs who have sired 10 or more champions. Others who do not appear on the list are still active as of this writing so that their value is still being measured. Finally, serious breeders must keep in mind several important thoughts. No stud is perfect. Each brings certain negative baggage with his positive contributions. Secondly, promotion and exposure create breeding opportunities. It is possible that a stud with fewer opportunities may do more than a more famous one, and even the greatest stud cannot suit every bitch. Right behind "Hetman" are two more great imports followed by more great studs.

52 - Ch. Harwire Hetman of Whinlatter
by Eng., Am. Ch. Townville Tobias
ex Eng. Ch. Harwire Hallmark

32 - Ch. Deko Druid
by Vingo's Verve
ex Rumsam Duskie

31 - Eng. Ch. Zeloy Emperor
by Eng. Ch. Zeloy Endeavour
ex Zeloy Rhapsody

30 - Ch. Gosmore Kirkmoor Craftsman
by Ch. Kirkmoor Speculation
ex Kirkmoor Cygnet

27 - Ch. Aryee Dominator
by Eng., Am. Ch. Sunnybrook Spot On
ex Miss Vintage

27 - Ch. Sunnybrook Spot On
by Eng. Ch. Townville Tally 'O
ex Sunnybrook Gosmore Photogenic

23 - Ch. Deko Dragoon
by Eng. Ch. Zeloy Emperor
ex Deko Dieudonne

22 - Ch. Axholme Jimmy Reppin
by Worsbro Betoken Again
ex Axholme Zeloy Tanzy

22 - Ch. Evewire Druid Dynamic
   by Ch. Deko Druid
   ex Ch. Evewire Dyna-mite

22 - Ch. Wintor Caracus Call Boy
   by Eng. Ch. Zeloy Crusader
   ex Nugrade Nesta

20 - Ch. Trucote Admiral
   by Eng. Ch. Sandwyre Mr. Softy of Jokyl
   ex Eng. Ch. Helenstowe Pearly Queen of Jokyl

19 - Ch. Bowyre Contender
   by Eng., Am. Ch. Whitwyre Money
   ex Ch. Rancourt Platta Charmer

18 - Ch. Wyrequest's Pay Dirt
   by Ch. Nugrade Regent
   ex Ch. Nugrade Countess

16 - Ch. Evewire You Better Believe It
   by Ch. Evewire Evening Edition
   ex Evewire Vicky Jane

16 - Eng. Ch. Seedfield Meritor Superflash
   by Eng. Ch. Zeloy Emperor
   ex Maryholm Bitter Sweet

16 - Ch. Tava Bob
   by Eng. Ch. Seedfield Meritor Superflash
   ex Tava Claire

15 - Ch. Bev-Wyre's Conbrio Tim
   by Eng., Am. Ch. Gosmore Kirkmoor Craftsman
   ex Ch. Bev-Wyre's Can Anima

15 - Eng. Ch. Wintor Statesman
   by Wintor Townville Tuscan
   ex Wintor Twilight

14 - Ch. Meritor Bang On
   by Eng. Ch. Zeloy Emperor
   ex Meritor Springtime

14 - Ch. Seawire Ellswyre Marksman
   by Eng. Ch. Wintor Statesman
   ex Ellisa Luvseta Back Flash

14 - Ch. Terrikane's Tulliver
   by Ch. Aryee Dominator
   ex Ch. Terrikane's Tzarina

13 - Ch. Brownstone's MacBroom
   by Eng., Am. Ch. Gosmore Kirkmoor Craftsman
   ex Ch. Heathcote Enchantress

12 - Ch. Bev-Wyre's Sovereign Escort
   by Ch. Aryee Dominator
   ex Ch. Bev-Wyre's Speedy Reminder

11 - Ch. Caracus Cavalier
   by Eng. Ch. Wintor Statesman
   ex Caracus Crocus

11 - Ch. Holmwire Tudor Reliant
   by Holmwire Tudor Renown
   ex Seuchad Girl

11 - Ch. Whitwyre Money Market
   by Mitre Advocate
   ex Whitwyre Even Money

11 - Ch. Wyrecroft Penda Peerage
   by Eng. Ch. Penda Peerless
   ex Eng. Ch. Penda Purbeck Deborah

10 - Ch. Evewire Evening Edition
   by Ch. Evewire Evening Jacket
   ex Ch. Evewire Early Copy

10 - Ch. Evewire Exemplar
   by Ch. Evewire Druid Dynamic
   ex Ch. Evewire Even Start

10 - Ch. Mutiny Mainstay of Glenarden
   by Ch. Evewire Druid Dynamic
   ex Ch. Evewire Early Copy

10 - Ch. Rigador Right Again
   by Eng. Ch. Zeloy Endeavor
   ex Rathmore Pretty Pie

Smooth Fox Terriers have an equally outstanding array of past and present studs. Once again, the reader must look beyond the numerical records. Some studs have advantages and opportunities not available to others. Some studs that are among a string of dogs may suffer if their first few opportunities do not jell. The kennel owner will probably use the "more consistent proven producer" while delegating the newcomer to relative obscurity. It is wise when one is seeking a stud to not only examine the offspring, the record and the dog, but also the number of opportunities.

No Fox Terrier, Wire or Smooth, enjoyed more opportunities, more exposure, or captured the imagination of the public than did the great

"Champion of Champions," Nornay Saddler. In 1950 his owner for most of his life, James M. Austin, published a book titled *Champion of Champions*. Saddler was whelped in Worksop, England; his dam, owned by Mr. and Mrs. Frank Coward, was Wyrksop Surprise and in early January 1936 she was bred to Eng. Ch. Traveling Fox. On March 12, 1936, Wyrksop Surprise, call name Pat, had six puppies. Saddler was on his way. English judges prepare critiques after their assignments. At his first show on October 3, 1936, he was best Smooth Fox Terrier. Mrs. M. V. Hughes judged Saddler for the first time and wrote, "Nornay Saddler is a beautiful youngster; a great credit to his papa, Ch. Traveling Fox. Should all go well with this child, he will have a starry future." At his second show, the Notts Fox Terrier Show, he went BIS. Judge J. B. Heedson wrote of Saddler, "An amazingly good youngster, without any doubt one of the best of his age of any era, this eight-month-old youngster should create a furor when making his debut in classic circles." Saddler made his American debut in 1937. For those who want to compare records and show careers, in 1937 there were just 317 all-breed and Specialty shows, about 1/10th of the number held today.

Saddler retired after his 56th BIS, a wonderful win at the old Dodge estate in New Jersey, the Morris Essex extravaganza. That event attracted 3,480 dogs representing 91 breeds. He died on June 25, 1948, leaving a legacy of 27 champions to carry on. From 1900-1970, aside from Saddler, a dozen other dogs sired 10 or more champions. They are as follows:

22 - Downsbragh Mickey Finn
    by Foxden Sundowner
    ex Gone to Ground

15 - Ch. Danesgate Debtor
    by Chosen Collegian of Notts
    ex Danesgate Dot

15 - Ch. Heathside Headsup II
    by Ch. Mountmellick March Hare
    ex Ch. Heathside Hebe

14 - Ch. Upper Bay of Etona
    by Ch. Alwen Foxcatcher
    ex Star Emblem

14 - Ch. Vanguard of Andely
    by Ch. Avatar of Andely
    ex Ch. Ripe Plum of Andely

13 - Ch. Downsbragh Two O'Clock Fox
    by Ch. Foxden Bracer
    ex Downsbragh Land Mine

13 - Ch. Woodcliff Hiya Boy
by Downsbragh Mickey Finn
ex Ch. Silver Ho Sweet Talk

12 - Ch. Lineman
by Ch. Nornay Saddler
ex Ch. Braw Lass

12 - Ch. Ronnoco Resolute
by Ch. Lineman
ex Ch. Good Taste of Wirehart

11 - Ch. Sabine Rarity
by Ch. Predictor of Etona
ex Ch. So What of Milford Haven

10 - Ch. Buckland of Andely
by Eng. Ch. Corrector of Notts
ex Balgair

10 - Ch. Desert Deputy
by Ch. Nornay Saddler
ex Braw Lass

Fifteen Smooths since 1970 have produced 15 or more champions, but that statement fails to portray the remarkable impact of certain dogs on the list; for example, Eng. Ch. Watteau Snuff Box was the foundation stud for many top Smooth kennels. He produced 22 champions, among them Ch. Foremark Ebony Box of Foxden. Ebony Box was a top winner and himself produced 26 champions. Ch. Quissex Deacon is another top producer whose impact exceeds his 29 champions. Ch. Waybroke Extra Smooth labored 1,000 miles south of the center of any activity. That has changed now, but who knows what he would have achieved if he stood elsewhere. There is not enough space or sufficient adjectives to describe the contributions of the next two dogs, Ch. Karnilo Chieftan of Foxden and Ch. Ttarb the Brat. Chieftan at the end of 1985 had 47 champions, and Brat had over 80, but once again the numbers do not tell the whole tale. You could say that anyone who just looks at numbers is dealing with a "docked-tail." Chieftan equalled or surpassed Snuff Box as the foundation for great Smooth breeders, and Brat lifted the Smooth right out of the variety into a group to a BIS threat. Not since Saddler have Smooths enjoyed the respect that the Brat provided, and, again, good fortune decrees the Brat to be a terrific and prolific producer. The blending of linebred Chieftan-Deacon bitches to the Brat produced outstanding results in the immediate generation and for succeeding generations. The Brat also eclipsed Ch. Nornay Saddler's BIS record by gaining his 60th all-breed Best at Santa Barbara, California in July, 1983. The others in production order are:

80+ - Ch. Ttarb the Brat
by Aust. Ch. Farleton Captain Sandy
ex Ttarb Tuppence

48 - Ch. Karnilo Chieftain of Foxden
by Eng., Am. Ch. Laurel Drive
ex Karnilo Cavalena

41 - Ch. Waybroke Extra Smooth
by Ch. Waybroke Red Lobster
ex Ch. Waybroke Smooth as Silk

33 - Ch. Foxden Warpaint
by Ch. Karnilo Chieftan of Foxden
ex Ch. Foxden Dealers Choice

31 - Ch. Quissex Deacon
by Ch. Viscum Veracity
ex Quissex Nixie

29 - Ch. Higrola Horatio of Britlea
by Eng. Ch. Mosvalley Marksman
ex Teesford Teaser

27 - Ch. Ellastone Fireflash
by Ch. Ellastone Firecrest
ex Eatonwood Sufredon Treat

26 - Ch. Ellastone Vibart
by Wylhylda Black Magic
ex Wylhylda's Wiske

26 - Ch. Foremark Ebony Box of Foxden
by Eng. Ch. Watteau Snuff Box
ex Watteau Gaylord

22 - Ch. Foxmoor Macho Macho Man
by Ch. Ttarb the Brat
ex Quissex Upsadaisy

22 - Eng. Ch. Watteau Snuffbox
by Watteau Sculpture
ex Beechbank Olive

21 - Ch. Foxden Hercules
by Ch. Foxden Herbert
ex Ch. Watteau Pandora's Box of Foxden

20 - Ch. Foxden Warspite
by Ch. Foxden Warpaint
ex Ch. Foxden Gallivant

19 - Ch. Raybill's Breeze Away, CD, CG
   by Ch. Von Nassau's Ter-A-Cycloon
   ex Ch. Raybill's Windfall

18 - Ch. Teesford Fanfare
   by Ianneau Jeaves
   ex Teesford Dainty Girl

18 - Ch. Von Nassau's Ter-A-Cycloon
   by Ch. Newmaidley Jason
   ex Von Nassau's Ter-A-Countess

18 - Ch. Watteau Musical Box
   by Watteau Sculpture
   ex Beechbank Olive

17 - Ch. Boreham Bonanza
   by Eng. Ch. Newmaidley Whistling Jeremy
   ex Eng. Ch. Boreham Ballerina

16 - Eng. Ch. Newmaidley Whistling Jeremy
   by Eng. Ch. Newmaidley Vodka
   ex Newmaidley Dew

16 - Ch. Pathen's Sammy Sayres
   by Ch. Ellastone Vibart
   ex Ch. Pathen's Someone Special

14 - Ch. Bellechien New Addition
   by Eng. Ch. Solo Solus
   ex Bellechien Chorus Girl

14 - Ch. Watteau Snifter
   by Ch. Watteau Snuff Box
   ex Eng. Ch. Watteau Cantata

13 - Ch. Jonwyre's Galaxy of Foxden
   by Eng. Ch. Spaceman
   ex Jonwyre Spacegirl

13 - Ch. Lethal Weapon of Rocky Point
   by Scroggy Sandlebar
   ex Steward's Jumpin Ginger

13 - Ch. Mullantean Arkle
   by Maryholm Swingalong
   ex Mullantean Miss Nora

12 - Ch. Newmaidley Pennywise
   by Eng. Ch. Newmaidley Soapbox
   ex Newmaidley Soapbox

11 - Ch. Bachmuth's Cash Box
       by Ch. Foremark Ebony Box of Foxden
       ex Quissex Pipe Dream

11 - Ch. Newmaidley Jacko
       by Eng. Ch. Newmaidley Whistling Jeremy
       ex Newmaidley Orange Blossom

Before moving on to our Smooth Fox Terrier breeders' "Roll of Honor," just a word about Eng. Ch. Newmaidley Jeremy. I never had the good fortune to see Jeremy, but from those who have I hear he was a very pleasing dog. What I do know is that every time I see a Smooth that I really admire, Jeremy is back there two or three times.

Many breeders past and present contributed to the history and development of the Smooth Fox Terrier. Anyone who even showed a single Smooth or Wire made a contribution to the breeds. There are and were, however, a number of people who had the opportunity, resources and desire to work for the betterment of Smooths, without whom the breed's survival would have been in doubt. On October 6, 1964, at the Montgomery County Show, there were 28 Smooths and 65 Wires for Josephine Deubler to judge. The following February, Judge Thomas Keator had just 32 Smooths opposed to 59 Wires. The floating Specialty of the AFTC in Chicago in April, 1965 drew just eight for Jack Marvin's judging. Montgomery County in 1965 drew just 26 Smooths. Throughout the late 1950s and into the late 1960s, Smooths were in dire straights; with the exception of a few dedicated enthusiasts, there was little support. And so to these breeders who were active prior to 1960 and continued through the 1960s and saw the breed through to its present renaissance, we all owe a deep and significant debt. In the East, Mr. and Mrs. Potter Wear (Stoney Meadows), Mrs. Steward Simmons (Battle Cry), and the mainstays of the AFTC, who began in 1934 and never looked back, Mr. and Mrs. James A. Farrell, Jr. (Foxden). Out West, Mr. and Mrs. Fred Kuska (Crag Crest) kept the colors flying along with Maj. and Mrs. Robert Bigelow (Raylu). There were others whose activities made a major impact on Smooth Fox Terriers, and alphabetically they are:

Francis R. Appleton, Jr.	Barberry
James M. Austin	Wissaboo
Mr. and Mrs. William Brainard, Jr.	Downsbragh
Robert A. Brumby	Havahome
Leonard Brumby, Sr. and Jr.	Briar Kennels
F. H. Farwell	Sabine
Arthur C. and Marie Gay	Gaycliffe
E. H. Ingwersen	Niola
Thomas Keater	Derbyshire

146

E. Coe Kerr .... Millhill
Mr. and Mrs. Thomas Lenfesty .... Silver Ho
Robert Neff .... Fenbor
Judge James P. O'Connor .... Ronnoco
Winthrop and Lewis Rutherfurd .... Warren
Miss Gene Simmonds .... Handful
Mr. and Mrs. J. W. Smith .... Dovenby
Mrs. Winnie Stout .... Quissex
Mary Veling .... Kris-Vale
Mr. and Mrs. William W. Wimer III .... Pool Forge

3

British Impact

THE CREAM of British manhood was maimed or killed from 1914 to 1918. More than one man in three mobilized was never the same again. Who knows how many future Francis Redmonds never returned from France to make their mark in the development of our marvelous breeds?

Ch. Comedian of Notts, bred and owned by Her Grace, the Duchess of Newcastle, was another of those major dogs that periodically have an impact on the breed so that his time and the period beyond can be known as the Comedian Era. As the English Wire narrative unfolds it can almost be depicted as the Comedian Era, the Simon Era, the American Era, etc. For such was the impact of certain stud dogs that their effect significantly transcended their own lifespans. And while the English exported most of these great dogs, they usually managed to breed them several times first. Comedian sired three important Wire dogs, Collar of Notts, Chunky of Notts, and Olcliffe Captain. Chances are if you traced the pedigree of any present-day Wire, one or all of that trio would appear.

After years of almost singlehanded development of the Wire in England, Her Grace began to get some help. At first it was from small breeders who appeared at some local show where their entry was "discovered" and purchased by George Raper for his American clients. One of the earliest competitors of Notts Wires was the Paignton Wires of Miss M. E. Lewis. Miss Lewis in May of 1912 bred a bitch, Vanity of Paignton, to Chunky of Notts, a Comedian son. Ch. Wireboy of Paignton was the marvelous result: a super showman in England. Purchased by

Ch. Cackler of Notts, from an 1898 painting by Arthur Wardle.

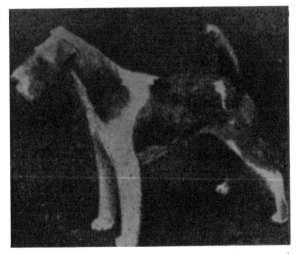

Olcliffe Captain, whelped 1912, was one of three significant sons of Ch. Comedian of Notts. He was sire of Ch. Fountain Crusader.

George Thomas for the reported sum of $4,500, he was sold to Mr. George W. Quintard of New York for the princely sum of $6,500, or so it was told. However, Wireboy did not leave England before being bred to a bitch called Queen Collar.

While all this was taking place, another unsung breeder had produced a bitch known as Matford Vic. His name for the record was Mr. Counter. I only report this bit of trivia because I feel that no one who breeds a Fox Terrier capable of two consecutive Westminster Bests should forever remain anonymous. Theo Marples describes the Matford Vic saga.

> Happily, things are better with the Wire-hairs, which in my humble opinion, were never so good as they are to-day as a whole, and which never contained such perfect individual specimens as for instance Mr. H. Trimble's bitch, Ch. Matford Vic, sold at the end of 1914 to the United States, and who won all before her at the New York Show in February 1915, including the challenge cup for best dog or bitch in the show, all breeds. She had, too, an unbeaten record in England. The price paid by Mr. Quintard for this estimable bitch was the record for a bitch of £.450. She was bought through my old friend, Mr. Geo. Raper, and "picked up" by astute Mr. Trimble for £.200. Miss Lewis obtained an even higher price for her great dog, Ch. Wireboy of Paignton, whom she bred, and who went to the same kennel as Ch. Matford Vic, and at the same New York show followed "Vic" home, by winning all his own heats and reserve for best dog or bitch in the show. In my opinion, Ch. Matford Vic is the acme of perfection in the breed, and the best Wire-hair dog or bitch that ever lived.

By 1915 a son by Ch. Wireboy of Paignton out of Queen Collar began to make his mark. Bred by J. W. Turner of Collar Kennels, Wycollar Boy was shown at the Wire Fox Terrier Association of England for the first time and from the puppy class he defeated England's best to earn BIS. Well, this feat could not go unnoticed and before you could say £.1500 he was on a boat to America, where he duplicated Vic's achievements of two Garden victories, although Wycollar Boy had to wait until 1920 for his second Westminster.

In 1919 the Comedian Era climaxed with the arrival of Barrington Bridegroom, Fountain Crusader, and Wycollar Trail. The first became Homer Gage, Jr.'s first major import. He was bred by Mr. F. Pearce and was whelped on May 10, 1919. Bridegroom was the maternal grandsire of Talavera Simon as well as the sire of eight American champions and a greater number of English champions, but the reader should bear in mind that his show career in the States was more successful than in England where his size presented a problem for many English judges. Their American counterparts were not quite so fussy and are not to this day.

The second of the triumvirate, Fountain Crusader, sired Simon. Skelly sums up the Crusader impact in a succinct paragraph.

Fountain Crusader the "wonder-coated dog" was well named, for he was a crusading fountain source of the better material then going into the makeup of the modern Wire. Keen breeders of the day early recognized his potential worth and sent their good bitches to his court with the result of four Crusader champions prior to Simon. The greatest of these was Ch. Signal Circuit of Halleston which sired Chs. Earlsmoor Choice (dam of Earlsmoor Snowflake) and Signal Warily. The last named in turn sired in one litter the two American Chs. Rajah and Reveller of Wildoaks.

Before leaving this remarkable dog to history, it is significant to recognize Crusader's major impact on the Wires in America today through his double grandson, Crackley Startler.

The third 1919 Wire prodigy, Wycollar Trail, may have been responsible in some small way for the "modernization" of today's Wire. He passed his elegance on to his granddaughter, Gains Great Surprise. The Comedian Era ended in 1924 with the birth of Talavera Simon. Ackerman describes the events that led up to Simon's acquisition by Capt. Phipps.

The Captain was riding in the spring of 1923 when he encountered a man exercising a very beautiful young Wire bitch which he tried unsuccessfully to buy. The man was A.J. Foster and the bitch was Kingsthorp Donah, which the following year was destined to be bred to Ch. Fountain Crusader and to produce Talavera Simon.

Captain Phipps saw the litter of five in the nest, but try as he would, was unable to induce Mr. Foster to part with any member of it; he again saw them at some five months of age when they had developed into incorrigible fighting little tigers. He still wanted one but still the owner would not sell. When they were about eight months, Mr. Foster approached the Captain with an offer to sell any one of the puppies, not because he was anxious to part with them but because they had developed into such demons that there was no doing anything with them and it seemed imminent that they would all die fighting. When Captain Phipps hastened over to choose his puppy he hit upon Simon, not as an outstanding specimen but as a rather likely youngster and one that both he and Mrs. Phipps considered as perhaps a shade the best of the lot. His eminence was not anticipated. He was even permitted to risk his life in the roads while exercising behind Captain Phipps' horses.

As the dog matured he was exhibited with but indifferent success. Not only was the dog not ready, but his demonic behavior spoiled whatever chances his good structure might have given him. His first championship show was Windsor in 1925 where he behaved so badly in the ring that he could not be fairly examined by the judge and was rightly defeated; and at that show Captain Phipps turned him over to "Bob" Barlow to try to turn a devil into a dog. By whatever legerdemain great handlers possess, Barlow in a few months turned Simon into not only a Fox Terrier but a gentlemen, after which he never looked back either in the show-ring or in stud.

This is as good a time as any to introduce Mr. George Raper's successor as the premier breeder, handler, talent scout and general all-

Ch. Fountain Crusader, whelped 1919, was sire of Ch. Talavera Simon.

Ch. Talavera Simon, whelped 1924, was said to be the most important Wire of the century.

Eng. Ch. Beau Brummel of Wildoaks and his kennelmate, Am. Ch. Gallant Fox of Wildoaks, dominated the British Wire scene until the outbreak of World War II.

round authority on the Wire, Mr. J. R. "Bob" Barlow of Coventry, England. He "discovered" and developed the considerable breed wealth of Talavera Simon; discovered and acquired Crackley Startler from his Welsh breeder, Mrs. M. Fogarty; had a hand in the Bondy's acquisition of Gains Great Surprise from J. C. Pickering and Weltona Frizette from Mr. Howarth. It is difficult to call to mind one single individual, before or since, whose activity so dominated his time. In addition to his efforts as a talent scout on behalf of the Bondy's, he brought those wonderful Wildoaks stud dogs to England. But Barlow's influence goes far beyond the 1920s and 1930s—he "redesigned" the Wire. By stripping a bit more here, less there, Bob Barlow established the pattern followed by all modern Wire handlers. His proteges include Mac Silver, who contributed so much to the Wildoaks Wires; George Bartley, a top English handler for many years; Joe Cartledge, who was active as a handler in England and the irrepressible Jackie Parker, who guided Glynhir for a time in the States. Barlow also influenced Jake Terhune, the Brumby brothers, Percy Roberts, Jimmy Butler, Seth Campbell, Tom Gately, Phil Prentice, and in fact any handler who ever put a finger or a knife to a Wire. In her book, Elsie Williams refers to J. R. Barlow as Mr. Fox Terrier. I can add no more to that. Barlow and his Wildoaks imports, Gallant Fox and Beau Brummel, dominated the English Wire scene until the outbreak of World War II in 1939.

Some other pre-war activists include the previously mentioned Capt. H. R. Phipps and his Talavera Wires; Florate Wires owned by J. Smith of York and linebred to Startler; Mrs. G. E. Pardoe's Cawthorne Kennels; and Alf Butler had the "of Marlowe" Wires of L. J. Heaton. However, all of these enthusiasts relied heavily upon the genes of Beau Brummel, Startler, and Gallant Fox. If you even slightly scratched the pedigree of an English champion or any English producing dog or bitch, a Barlow dog appeared.

The War took its toll of breeders. There were no dog shows and fanciers had to be content with "breeding for themselves." The War years tested the interest of each person associated with dogs. Items that, in peace time, were common and taken for granted became impossible to find. Things like dog food, cleaning solutions, soap, stripping knives, leashes, and tools of any kind were extremely scarce or non-existent. The War ended and the Wire team that took the field in post-war England was a bright one indeed. The captain was still Bobby Barlow and as shows commenced he finished Crackley Straightaway. Sir Charles Hancock's pre-war champion, Miltona Mahmoud, was still siring good ones. A Churchill and the Weltona Wires made it through, along with Elsie Williams and Capt. Phipps.

It is hard to assign a particular period or even periods to Miss Linda Beak and Calvert Butler. The November issue of *The Kennel Club Gazette* in the year 1933 noted Newmaidley Shock, a Wire dog, was bred to Newmaidley Susan, a Wire bitch, and produced Newmaidley Spark. In the mid-1980s Miss Beak is still successfully breeding Wires and Smooths. F. Calvert Butler was a very successful breeder of Wires in the early 1920s under the Watteau prefix. His daughter, Mrs. Mary Blake, and her daughter, Antonia, are at this writing still very active although mostly with Smooth Fox Terriers. More about these remarkable people later. The Newmaidley Wires were greatly enhanced by Barlow's Ch. Crackley Straightaway, who sired Newmaidley Ceasar. Ceasar sired the first Newmaidley Wire champions in 1946, subsequent Ch. Newmaidley Cleopatra, and in 1948 sired a 1951 titlist, Ch. Newmaidley Hob.

In 1949 Mr. J. W. Turner returned to breed his bitch, Wycollar Wondrous, to Barlow's Ch. Crackley Sailaway. The result was Turner's first post-war champion, Ch. Wycollar Duchess. The late '40s saw another newcomer, Mr. A. Clanachan, whose Maryholm Fox Terriers, both coats, competed successfully for the next 40 years. Ch. Waterton Maryholm Wendy became his first Wire champion in 1950. Another devotee, who enjoyed hard-earned success after struggling through "England's darkest hour," was Mrs. Dorothy White. From linebreeding to Simon and his heirs, her post-war effort was Ch. Wyretex Wyns Tuscan. Before leaving for America Tuscan produced Chs. Weltona What's This, Wyretex Wynns Wundar (exported to America), and Penda Callern Melody. Wundar in turn sired a number of English titlists but his most significant achievement was Ch. Zeloy Endeavour, the sire of what many believe to be the greatest sire of the postwar era, Ch. Zeloy Emperor. In addition to Tuscan and Wundar, Chs. Wyretex Wyns Priceless and Jupitor crossed the Atlantic; the former to Mrs. Leonard Smit, and the latter to Mr. Lewis' Glynhir Kennels.

The decade of the '50s closes with Ch. Penda Cawthorne Cobnut. He was bred by the J. H. Pardoes, whose Cawthorne Wires were prominent since the 1940s. Cobnut was purchased by Elsie Williams after she judged him at the Fox Terrier Club Show in 1958. "He did not win there, being placed second in his class, because he had not bodied up, but I liked his size, bone and shortness of back," explains Mrs. Williams. And she states further, "My prefix was added to that of Mr. Pardoe's and he became Ch. Penda Cawthorne Cobnut. Cobnut sired Ch. Baros Jewel, Irish Ch. Baros Cobbler, Ch. Wyrecroft War Bonus, and Ch. Penda Peerless. Ch. Penda Peerless proved himself to be an outstanding stud dog, having sired Ch. Penda Daleskirk Caress, winner of Supreme BIS at Bath and the Gold Cup at the Fox Terrier Club show, 1962, and the championship at Crufts, 1962 and 1963 shows. Also Ch. Penda Travatina, winner of the Gold Cup 1964."

The 1960s begin with two notable Wire dogs, Ch. Crackwyn Cockspur and Ch. Zeloy Emperor. Cockspur was bred by Mr. H. L. Gill and handled by Bobby Barlow to win 22 Challenge Certificates and a number of all-breed Bests. He then was sold to Belgium to M. Lejeune. He won BIS in Belgium, Holland, Italy, Germany, Luxembourg and Sweden. But while

Ch. Crackley Startler was a Barlow discovery whelped 1930.

Ch. Talavera Jupiter, whelped 1930. Captain Phipps would not sell him to America.

Ch. Castlecroft Contender, whelped 1935.

Ch. Miltona Mahmoud, whelped 1936, kept producing through World War II.

Ch. Crackley Supreme Again, whelped 1934, was more of the Barlow magic.

The first post-World War II English Wire champion was Barlow's Crackley Straightaway. He was also the grandsire of the first Newmaidley Wire champion.

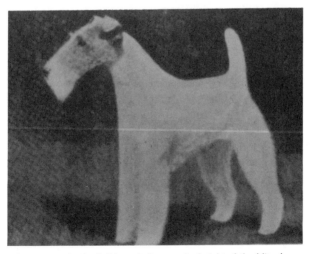

Ch. Wynstead What's Wanted. Born at the height of the blitz, he gained his title in 1948.

Cockspur was prancing through Europe, Ch. Zeloy Emperor was making his mark in the U.K. Emperor's place in Wire history is so profound that he warranted his own section in the January 1983 Special Fox Terrier Issue of *Terrier Type.* Dan Kiedrowski writes,

Not since the breed's heydays and the great American and English Ch. Gallant Fox of Wildoaks has there emerged so important a sire as English Ch. Zeloy Emperor. As the sire of 22 English champions, 31 American champions and numerous others throughout the continent, Japan, and Australia, he is by far the greatest producer of Wire Fox Terrier champions EVER.

Bred by Ernest "Robby" Robinson, Emperor represented the culmination of two decades of breeding—a zenith achieved with no small amount of skill, as the Zeloy dogs were for the most part owner conditioned and handled. Robby Robinson began exhibiting Wires in 1939. Although it took 20 years to produce his first CC winner in 1959, his successes thereafter are legion, and the "star" was clearly Emperor.

Whelped March 10, 1960, Emperor (call name Billy) was shown for the first time at Crufts, February 10, 1961; winning a puppy class of 14, as well as firsts in Undergraduate and Graduate, topping 7 and 8 entries respectively. The judge, John Hamilton of the Burntedge Wires, commented . . . "This puppy is most attractively hound-marked, short coupled, nice head, good reach of neck, uses his ears very well indeed, is possessed of good bone and feet; I thought that this could be my ultimate winner, but he has not yet the maturity to warrant this, but unless I am very much mistaken this is a rod in pickle."

"Billy" was beaten in the challenge by Ch. Penda Peerless and Ch. Crackwyn Cockspur—two top winners of that period. He was a class winner in his next three outings, and was Reserve at the Scottish and West of England Kennel Club shows in April, before winning his first CC and Best of Breed at Bath under the lady of Roundway, Josephine Creasy. Her critique was most interesting, and it is as follows. . . . "I have handled this dog twice before. I went over him as a puppy at Crufts, and could only see one possible *if.* I judged him last month, found his *if* had gone the right way, and he only needed to coat up to go places. A beautiful young dog, combining substance with great quality, and each time I have judged him he moved to my entire satisfaction. I stress this, as I had been told he had been put down for bad hind action, and so gave him very extended tests. He came through these at both shows under me, one indoors and on this wet, uneven grass, and later on the asphalt path, without any question."

In spite of these early successes and rather outstanding notices, he would go through seven more shows that year, frequently a class winner, but without that second CC. "Billy" was then transferred to the talented professional, Tommy Brampton, who finished him in the summer of 1962, quickly adding 4 more CCs with a total of 6 BBs. "Billy" was brought out once more in 1968, at the age of 8½ years, and was Best of Breed at the Scottish Kennel Club under USA judge Mrs. Augustus Riggs IV, handled by Robby.

By this time "Billy" was a sire of note, and even during his own title quest was frequently competing with his get, most notably his daughter, English and

Ch. Zeloy Emperor, the greatest of them all.

Emperor with his handler, Tommy Brampton, winning Best in Show at Cardiff.

159

American Ch. Zeloy Mooremaides Magic . . . Best in Show at Westminster 1966. It is said that Robby Robinson thrice refused sums of £.1,000 or more for Emperor, even in his later years, but could not be tempted to part with his favorite. As it was, with Robby's death in 1972, "Billy" did leave England, living out his remaining years in Holland as the housepet of the Van der Hoevens, long-time fanciers, whose Pickwick Kennels already housed Chs. Zeloy Select and Escort. In a tribute to Emperor the Van der Hoevens wrote . . . "Billy was a sensible dog; he was soon accustomed to his new life and nothing was more appreciated than a walk in the fields or a drive in the woods. He liked to accompany me when shopping; he was eager to examine everything and twice he saw his chance to snatch a bun or some sweets! Owing to his excellent disposition everybody was fond of him. In March 1973, a sudden stroke made an end to his happy life. A great sire had passed away and I am proud that I could give 'Billy' a comfortable and happy old age."

It has been less than two decades since the first champion from "the Emperor line" emerged. Since then more than 100 English champions trace to Emperor, and in America they number in the many hundreds. No dog has had a greater influence on the breed in modern times.

Some of his more important offspring include Eng., Am. Ch. Zeloy Mooremaides Magic, Ch. Zeloy Select, Ch. Zeloy Escort, Ch. Rancourt Kirkmoor Cowslip, Ch. Seedfield Meritor Super Flash, Ch. Holmwire Tudor Regent, Ch. Holmwire Tudor Renoun, Gosmore Kirkmoor Clinker, and on and on and on. His American champion offspring include Ch. Deko Dragon, Ch. Meritor Bang On, Ch. Seedfield Conqueror of Reglib, Ch. Gosmore Kirkmoor Storm, and many more. Emperor's grandchildren and great-grandchildren include Eng., Am. Ch. Harwire Hetman of Whinlatter, Ch. Brownstone MacBroom, Eng., Am. Ch. Sunnybrook Spot On and Ch. Tava Bob.

And so while English breeders are hard at work to produce the next "Super" dog, Emperor remains, to this day, the long shadow that is cast over today's Wire. Since the beginning of the 20th century, there have been five major eras in Wire chronicles. Five milestones; five individuals that have changed the direction of the Wire Fox Terrier for all time—Bristles, from unclear antecedents; Comedian, the first modern Wire; Simon, the glory dog; Gallant Fox, who returned Simon to England; Emperor, in the present era. Who will be the next super dog? Will he be an American-bred or, as in the past, an English Wire? What is really exciting about the future of the Wire is the present diversity of interest. England still has stalwarts. But now the Irish invade the English shows and often come away with the top awards. Harry O'Donoghue and his Blackdale Wires have competed successfully in recent years. In Germany, H. Schmiedner has produced a few top winners.

The period from 1907 to 1916 in England was a watershed for attracting new and important breeders and exhibitors to the Smooth cause. Redmond and Vicary were joined by F. Calvert Butler (Watteau), H.

Tudor Crosthwaite (Bowden), Sidney Castle, Mrs. T. Losco Bradley (Cromwell). This determined and dedicated group shepherded the Smooth fortunes through The Great War so that by the start of the 1920s, the Smooth Fox Terrier in England was in great shape. While the impact of super studs was more pronounced in Wires, Smooths, nonetheless, had their dominant dogs like Oxonian and Mrs. Losco Bradley's Ch. Cromwell Ochre.

Mrs. Bradley and Capt. Crosthwaite played significant roles in the future development of the Smooth in England and later in the United States. Mrs. Bradley, in 1917, bred Ch. Cromwell Ochre's Legacy. He was a son of Ch. Cromwell Ochre, who went back to Oxonian through Orkadian. Legacy sired nine champions, a record for his time; Myrtus, Blybro Top Note, Blybro Beggarman, and Wrose Indelible were the dogs; and the bitches were Cromwell Miss Legacy, Cromwell Dark Dorothy, Dunsting, Hermon Bequest, and Mint. He, also, was the sire of Cromwell Raw Umber, who in turn produced Kidder Karzan.

Kidder Fox Terriers were the property of Messrs. G. Grimley and S. R. Clay. Their unheralded stud dog, Kidder Karzan earned his place in history as the sire of Ch. Little Aristocrat and Watteau Battleshaft. Karzan was by Cromwell Raw Umber (Cromwell Ochre's Legacy ex Ch. Croswell Tangirl) ex Dunstable Princess (Cromwell Ochre's Legacy ex Lady Claudia). The dam of Dunstable Princess, Lady Claudia was linebred from Redmond's Dusky D'Orsay. Grimsley and Clay then bred Kidder Karzan to Kidder Kisabel, a granddaughter of Dusky D'Orsay and D'Orsay's Model and got Ch. Little Aristocrat. If the Smooth Fox Terrier roadmap needed a milestone, Ch. Little Aristocrat was just that. Born November 1, 1922 he was originally registered as Kidder Kompact (it was easy to change a name in 1922) by Grimley and Clay, his breeders. He was purchased as a puppy by Mr. A. E. Bishop of "Selecta" Kennels in Worcester, who changed his name to Little Aristocrat. Mr. Bishop advertised him as the "Bridegroom of Smooths." That says much about the relative strengths of the two breeds in 1925 when Aristocrat earned his title and was offered at stud. Bridegroom was never called the "Little Aristocrat" of Wires.

Let's leave Ch. Little Aristocrat for the moment and go to the Bowden Kennels of Capt. H. Tudor Crostwaite and another Cromwell Ochre son, a lovely dog called Dandifino. He was bred just after the War and he never earned his title. Arthur Wardle painted a beautiful portrait of Dandifino and his son, Bowden Hamish. Bear with me a bit longer for I believe that you will enjoy tracing the pedigree of your Smooth right back to Belgrave Joe or Splinter. Bowden Hamish sired Clanish of Notts, who in turn produced Ch. Corrector of Notts.

Now to pull it all together. In 1925 there was Ch. Little Aristocrat and in 1929, Ch. Corrector of Notts. Aristocrat produced at least five champions, among them Ch. Selecta Ideal. Ideal, in turn, produced

Watteau Surprise, Mr. Calvert Butler's first Smooth bitch.

Ch. Cromwell Ochre, whelped 1915, was a very important Smooth sire.

Kidder Karzan, the sire of both foundation dogs Ch. Little Aristocrat and Watteau Battleshaft.

Dandifino and Bowden Hamish, from an Arthur Wardle painting.

163

Homestead Little Man, who sired Homestead Dasher, who was the grandsire of the great Avon Peddler, Ch. Nornay Saddler's grandsire. What a marvelous mystery story could be developed from this history. I could start with Saddler and leave a few clues lying around. Then ask the reader to place Belgrave Joe or Splinter at the scene of the original crime.

Now, to return to Corrector of Notts. . . . He was the sire of Ch. Buckland, who was subsequently brought to the United States, where he sired Heir Apparent of Andely and Andely Lovely Lady. We've observed what wonders the crossing and recrossing of the descendants of Heir Apparent and Saddler have produced. But our old friend Kidder Karzan wasn't finished yet. He also sired Watteau Battleshaft, the foundation dog of much that was and still is Watteau.

As Britain entered the 1930s, new breeders joined the ranks. Their efforts strongly impacted today's Smooths in America and in England. To begin with there was the Molten Kennels of Mrs. W. L. G. Dean. In 1932 her standardbearers were Molten Cracksman, Molten Music Master, and a marvelous bitch called Molten Tan Maid. Mrs. Dean combined the Boreham strain of Dr. Miller with the Selecta line of Mr. Bishop, and a judicious dollop of the Duchess of Newcastle. Mrs. Dean remained active for the next 40 or so years. She provided the Farrells with the first Foxden Smooths, American Ch. Molten Fancy Man and the bitch, Molten Kamala. Mrs. Dean also did a lot to improve Smooths in Australia. During the mid-1920s she exported Molten Mikado, who gained his Australian title.

The late '20s and early '30s welcomed Dr. and Mrs. R. M. Miller, whose Boreham Kennels still produce competitive Smooths under the supervision of their daughter, Mrs. Winstanley. Their Ch. Boreham Baranova was a great bitch for Mrs. Stewart Simmons.

Earlier, this chapter mentioned Avon Peddler, as Saddler's grandsire. The Avon Kennels were the property of Mr. Frank Reeks. All of the people and dogs mentioned in this chapter had significant impact on the future of Fox Terriers. Their activities go far beyond the brief mention provided in this chapter. It seems a bit unfair to sum up the life's work of Frank Reeks with the development of Avon Peddler. After his demise his daughter carried on after World War II. But on the other hand, how many of us would be satisfied with breeding just one Peddler, or just one Ochre, or just one Karzan, or just one Saddler? Isn't that reward enough for one lifetime?

No history of Smooth progress in the 1930s can be complete without the following kennel prefixes: "of Notts," "Farleton," "Burmar," "Hewshott," "Solus," "Hermon," "Danesgate," and finally, a breeder that used his initials in naming all his charges, Mr. Lionel Wilson. His dogs' names consisted of two words—the first started with "L," the second with "W." With the exception of the Duchess of Newcastle, all of the aforementioned fanciers made their most significant contribution hus-

Ch. Corrector of Notts, whelped November 3, 1929, led the English Smooths into the next decade.

Watteau Battleshaft, the foundation of the modern Watteau Smooths.

Am. Ch. Molten Fancy Man.

Molten Kamala.

Mrs. W. L. G. Dean started Foxden with this pair.

Ch. Avon Peddler, Saddler's grandsire.

banding the Smooth through World War II and resuscitating the breed in the post-war years. But before moving on to that period there is one more product of the '30s that requires attention, Baron W. van der Hoop. While the Baron lived in Switzerland, his stock was all English and he competed actively in England and on the Continent under the "Flying" prefix. The Baron was much sought after as a judge as well.

World War II had the same impact on Smooths as on Wires. And the Smooth team reads like a *Who's Who* of outstanding breeders. The senior member of the team was Watteau. And although the founder, F. Calvert Butler, died in 1941, his daughter, Mrs. Anthony Blake, carried on the family tradition with a war baby called Watteau Golden Boy. The Duchess of Newcastle featured Correct Collar of Notts; the Solus Kennels of Mr. C. H. Bishop had Solus Congress and Solus Begorrah; the Padwicks had Danesgate Demijohn; Abberdale, owned by Mr. and Mrs. L. Ludford, carried on with Abberdale Flash and Abberdale Admiral; John Mitchell at Blyboro imported Irish Ch. Molten Moonlighter, a Danesgate Demijohn son (the Irish held championship shows during the War); in addition to sending Moonlighter to Blyboro, Mrs. Dean bred Molten Moonseed; Mrs. Forsyth Forrests had the nearly all-white Travelling Victory; Boreham Bedad was the Millers' mainstay; although not a war baby, Ch. Farleton Fusilier kept Mrs. Roy Richardson busy; and last but most importantly, was Leo C. Wilson, who bred Lethean Waters in 1941, and in 1943 acquired a Water's son, Lethal Weapon, who became Wilson's first post-war champion and the sire of the first post-war "era" quality dog, Ch. Laurel Wreath. From Dandifino, a World War I baby, to Ch. Corrector of Notts, to Danesgate Demijohn, to Laurel Wreath, a World War II baby, the line is straight and true.

Ch. Laurel Wreath was a major watershed Smooth of the post-war period. His get provided the rejuvenation of the Smooth in England. A lesser sire would have been satisfied with just one outstanding offspring. Wreath practically manufactured them. His first building block son was for Andres Clanachan's Maryholm Smooths, Ch. Maryholm Spun Gold. Next came his most important son, Ch. Watteau Midas. Midas lived only four years, but he made the most of it. In addition to the Maryholms and the Watteaus, the post-war Hermons, Harkaways, Borehams, and Brooklands all owe part of their success to Ch. Laurel Wreath. Dr. and Mrs. Miller of Boreham bred the first post-war champion. Ch. Boreham Belshire was by Boreham Bedad ex Boreham Belmalva. The Maharaja of Pithapuram bought him from the Millers and showed him to his championship.

Although Herbert Johnson worked as kennelman for the Blakes, he still had some outstanding Smooths of his own, who bore the Brooklands prefix. If the pedigrees of the Watteaus are studied, the mixing of Brookland with Watteau was a fairly common occurrence. While Mrs. Blake has expressed her admiration for Snuff Box as her finest creation,

Ch. Little Aristocrat, Ch. Selecta Ideal, Ch. Dunslaw and Ch. Dusky Knight.

Ch. Boreham Belsire. Almost every modern Smooth goes back to Laurel Wreath or Boreham Belsire.

Originally registered as Boreham Berene (shown as a five-month-old puppy), she was later renamed Call Up of Notts when acquired by the Duchess of Newcastle.

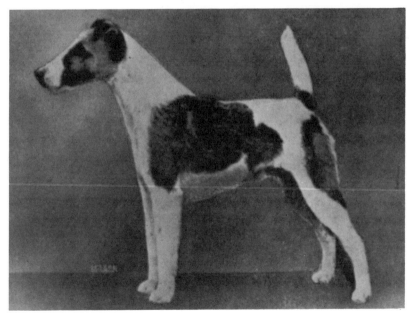

Ch. Laurel Wreath, one of two extremely important post-World War II Smooth sires.

Ch. Watteau Midas made the most of an all too brief career.

Ch. Watteau Chorister was the first of the great Watteaus to impact postwar America. He was the grandsire of Snuff Box.

many knowledgeable breeders, the writer included, think that that honor goes to Ch. Watteau Chorister, a son of Ch. Brooklands Lucky Wishbone.

Miss E. Lindley Wood started her Hampole Kennels in the late '40s. Ch. Hampole Tinkler, her foundation dog, was by Ch. Boreham Belsire. Miss Wood's Hampole Smooths are behind many of the early Quissex dogs.

Burmar is another prefix common in many American pedigrees. Mrs. E. Marshall and her daughter, Miss E. G. Burton, are the Burmar owners. The kennels were located on the grounds of The Manor House, Church Enstone, near Oxford, the Marshall family home since 1560. Their most famous products were Ch. Burmar Ted and Ch. Burmar Warrior; both form part of the base for Crag Crest Kennels. The Harkaway Kennels of Miss Barbara Stapley produced Ch. Harkaway Lancashire Lad, sire of Ch. Burmar Ted.

Hermon Kennels is another familiar prefix in many American Smooth pedigrees. Miss K. Emery produced her most significant Smooth in 1951, Ch. Hermon Parthings Loyal Lad. He was a combination of Leo Wilson's Ch. Lethal Weapon and the Belsire dog of Boreham fame. The Lanneaus were owned by John Lowe and Lanneau Jeaves was the grandsire of the bitch, Mini Echo, who provided Betsy and Bill Dossett with their foundation bitch and first success, Ch. Miss Me Too Spot.

What adjectives can possibly describe a family that has been dedicated to Fox Terriers for nearly 80 years? Dan Kiedrowski of *Terrier Type* says "incredible." Once again, that marvelous Fox Terrier issue of *Terrier Type* (Jan. 1983) provides a vivid analysis of the Watteau dominance in the Smooth representative.

Incredible as it may seem, the Watteau Kennels were founded more than three-quarters of a century ago in 1906 by Calvert Butler—not with a Smooth, but a Wire, Worsley Wrangler. Mr. Butler's first Smooth was Ch. Oxalis, by Ch. Oxonian and his first homebred champion, Miss Watteau. Since he had always admired the French artist of that name, he adopted Watteau as a prefix. A man of broad interests and skills, he made up dozens of Watteau champions in several breeds, including Airedales, Irish, Kerries, and Wires. Among the latter, he bred a dog called Watteau Warrior, the great, great, grandsire of Ch. Gallant Fox of Wildoaks, one of the most influential Wire sires of all time. In Smooths, Mr. Calvert bred 10 champions, but historically will be remembered for having bred Watteau Battleshaft, founder of the "B" line, which has champion descendents to this day.

World War II brought many a breeding program to an abrupt end, and with the death of Mr. Calvert in 1941, this might well have been so with Watteau, had not his daughter, Mrs. Blake, chosen to carry on. With the assistance of Herbert Johnson, who had successfully managed Watteau Kennels early on, and had the highly-regarded Brooklands, Mrs. Blake was to quickly reestablish Watteau's importance with her first homebred champion, Watteau Midas.

Ch. Watteau Snuff Box, perhaps the single most important sire worldwide from 1945 to 1970.

Ch. Newmaidley Whistling Jeremy, a Snuff Box grandson who appears in many pedigrees of top winning dogs.

Although Midas died at just four years old, he left an indelible mark as the sire of five champions from which have come, in succeeding generations, hundreds more. Virtually all the Brooklands and Watteaus of the post-war period carry at least one line to Midas, and almost all the top winners and producers of the last decade, worldwide, carry lines to Midas through his great-grandson, Ch. Watteau Chorister.

Chorister, whelped in 1954, was a great-grandson of Wreath on his sire's side, and a grandson of Warpaint through his dam, Ch. Watteau Songstress. He sired nine champions in England, five from matings to Watteau Marylyn. Yet another from this breeding, Watteau Cantor (2 CCs) has greatly influenced the breed in France.

Chorister offspring were to have a broad impact on the breed worldwide. His son, Watteau Concerto, was the founder of the famous von Silvertbach Kennels in Germany. Ch. Brooklands Present, from one of the Chorister-Marylyn breedings, along with Ch. Brooklands Black Ace, double bred to Midas, were exported to Australia by Mr. Johnson, where they have had a major impact on lines and families that have since found their way from "down under" to America.

Perhaps the single most important sire, worldwide, of the last quarter century is the Chorister grandson, Ch. Watteau Snuff Box. Sired by Watteau Sculpture, he is out of a Chorister daughter interestingly linebred to Ch. Lethal Weapon through both Ch. Laurel Wreath and Wreath's full brother, Parthings Laddie.

Whelped in 1962 Snuff Box was Watteau's biggest winner with 23 CCs under 23 different judges, beaten for Best of Variety only once, by previously mentioned Ch. Brooklands Present. As a sire, he is best known at home for his best-producing sons, Ch. Newmaidley Vodka and Ch. Harkaway Lancashire Lad, and in America for his sons, Eng., Am. Ch. Foremark Ebony Box of Foxden (26 Chs.) and the litter brothers, Ch. Watteau Snifter (14 Chs.) and Eng., Am. Ch. Watteau Snufsed of Crag Crest (8 Chs.). In America we also had Snuff Box's full brother, Ch. Watteau Musical Box (18 Chs.), who gave top producing bitches to Foxden, Quissex and Waybroke kennels.

An examination of the pedigrees of the top producing sires of the last decade shows a preponderance of Watteau, with virtually all carrying at least two lines to Midas and at least one to Chorister. So much is owed to Mr. Calvert, Mrs. Blake, and now her daughter, Mrs. Antonia Thornton, they were, are and will continue to be very special guardians of this very special breed.

Miss Linda Beak, who had labored so impressively in Wires for so many years, finished her first Smooth in 1963 and her second in 1964. Miss Beak, an outstanding breeder of livestock generally, recognized quality production when she saw it. Her first, Ch. Newmaidley Jehu, was by Ch. Brooklands Lucky Wishbone ex Newmaidley Destiny and her second, the outstanding Ch. Newmaidley Vodka, was by Ch. Watteau Snuff Box ex Newmaidley Destiny. Ch. Newmaidley Whistling Jeremy was sired by Vodka. It is curious how often this Snuff Box grandson appears in the pedigrees of some of our current winners and producers. While Miss Beak may disagree, I believe Jeremy to be her most important contribution to date.

Mrs. D. Roy Richardson campaigned her last Smooth in 1957, Ch. Farleton Salthome Saucy, but the breed cannot minimize her earlier contributions. Ch. Farleton Flavia, whelped in 1928, and his son, Ch. Farleton Fusilier, whelped in 1931, were an integral part of the Watteau story.

To Boreham, the breed owes a great debt. Dr. Miller's family continued active all through World War II and had the first Smooth post-war champion, Boreham Belsire. The Borehams maintained their line to Belsire and were among the very few lines that do not owe their type to Laurel Wreath and the early Watteaus. The Hampoles of Miss Wood, the Hewshotts of Mr. Glover, the Solus Smooths of Mr. Bishop and the Casterbridges of Mr. and Mrs. Rippingale all have roots in Boreham blood. An historical geneticist would find it difficult today to discover a Smooth whose ancestry avoids Lionel Wilson's Laurel Wreath or Mrs. Winstanley, nee Miller's Boreham Belsire and his sire Boreham Bedad.

The Boreham prefix still prospers under the guiding hand of Mrs. J. T. Winstanley, the former Miss Miller. Mr. C. H. Bishop, proprietor of the Solus kennels, went his own way picking and choosing judiciously of the best of Mrs. Forsythe-Forrest's Travelling blood, Mr. Clanachan's Maryholm representatives, the Hermon's and, of course, Midas. Solus has the distinction of spawning another successful English prefix, the Sidewaters, of Mrs. Vera Goold.

The book on English Smooths cannot be closed without recalling Henry Holinrake and his Karnilo Smooths. By shrewd use of Chorister and Snuff Box Mr. Holinrake has developed a Smooth Fox Terrier look that is his own. His great legacy is carried forward from the genes of Eng., Am. Ch. Karnilo Chieftain of Foxden. While Ebony Box preceded Chieftain to Foxden, it was Chieftain who produced the greatest impetus to the Foxden program. At last count he was responsible for 47 American champions. Only Ch. Ttarb the Brat has had a comparable impact in the last 40 years. I have a theory that the Brat owes much of his success as a stud dog to his "click" with linebred Chieftain bitches.

Smooths

109—Ch. Ttarb The Brat
 48—Ch. Karnilo Chieftain of Foxden
 46—Ch. Waybroke Extra Smooth
 37—Ch Foxden Warpaint
 33—Ch. Higrola Horatio of Britlea
 31—Ch. Quissex Deacon
 31—Ch. Foxmoor Macho Macho Man

27—Ch. Ellastone Fireflash
27—Ch. Nornay Saddler
26—Ch. Ellastone Vibart
26—Ch. Foremark Ebony Box of Foxden
22—Downsbragh Mickey Finn
22—Eng. Ch. Watteau Snuff Box
21—Ch. Foxden Hercules
21—Ch. Raybill's Breeze Away, CD
18—Ch. Foxden Warspite
18—Ch. Teesford Fanfare
18—Ch. Von Nassau's Ter-A-Cycloon
17—Ch. Boreham Bonanza
16—Eng. Ch. Newmaidley Whistling Jeremy
16—Ch. Pathen's Sammy Sayres
15—Ch. Danesgate Debtor
15—Ch. Heathside Heads Up II

Wires

56—Ch. Harwire Hetman of Whinlatter
32—Ch. Deko Druid
31—Eng. Ch. Zeloy Emperor
30—Ch. Gosmore Kirkmoor Craftsman
29—Ch. Trucote Admiral
27—Ch. Aryee Dominator
27—Ch. Sunnybrook Spot On
23—Ch. Deko Dragoon
22—Ch. Axholme Jimmy Reppin
22—Ch. Evewire Druid Dynamic
22—Ch. Evewire You Better Believe It
22—Ch. Terrikane's Tulliver
22—Ch. Wintor Caracus Call Boy
21—Ch. Fox Hunter of Wildoaks
19—Ch. Bowyre Contender
19—Ch. Evewire Extra Edition
18—Ch. Gallant Fox of Wildoaks
18—Ch. Wyrequest's Pay Dirt
17—Ch. Hallwyre Handy Jack
16—Ch. Crackley Startler of Wildoaks
16—Eng. Ch. Seedfield Meritor Superflash
16—Ch. Tava Bob
16—Ch. Westbourne Teetotaler
15—Ch. Bev-Wyre's Conbrio Tim
15—Ch. Bev-Wyre's Sovereign Escort
15—Ch. Mac's Revelation
15—Eng. Ch. Wintor Statesman

4

A Dog for All Reasons

$\mathbf{F}$ASHIONS COME, fashions go, but certain basic qualities make for a breed's continued success and acceptance. The Fox Terrier Club was started in 1885 and has flourished since that time with the same Standard until June 1, 1985. Many charming and endearing descriptions (other than the Standard) of the Fox Terrier have been offered by various owners since 1885. These excerpts were taken from the Anniversary Book of The American Fox Terrier Club to commemorate the 50th anniversary of the Club.

The Fox Terrier is a small black and white disturbance which afflicts and delights many family. The Fox Terrier has straight legs, an active, expressive face, a lean well-shaped head, talkative eyes, and a nose which leads him from one misdemeanor to another.

Originally he had a liberal tail, but it has been edited and revised by man. This was done because when a Fox Terrier's tail was as active as his head, it took two people to watch him.

The Reverend Rosslyn Bruce described the Fox Terrier as follows:

A Fox Terrier should be both active and strong with a brave, wise way with him to suit him either for the fields or the home. His head should be very long and lean, with much strength in front of his ears. His eyes should be small, and very dark and full of the pride of life. His ears should be small, and like a V set high on his head. His neck should be long and gently arched, tapering toward his shoulders, which should slope backwards and be long as well. His forelegs should be straight, round and thick; his hind legs strong but reachy, and his hocks should be near to the ground. His feet should be small and round, with thick pads. His body should have a deep but not broad chest with ribs making a round rather than a flat side; his back should be level, and his loins strong and firm. His tail should spring from the top rather than the back or the body; it must not be thin or curved but stout and straight, and carried uprightly, his coat should be smooth, straight, hard and dense. His color should be chiefly white; the marks which are black or tan or both (not red, blue, liver or brindle) may be of any shape, and carried anywhere; even-marks are of no show value. His weight should be from 16 to 18 pounds, more or less; bitches may be two pounds lighter. His character is very human; he is a faithful housedog, neither noisey or lazy; he is clever, clean, hardy, and very teachable; in town or country he needs little care, as he exercises himself anywhere. Bitches are very little more trouble than dogs, and both are obedient and full of good sense. His action is difficult to describe on paper; every novice should persuade an expert, preferably one familiar with horses and hounds, to show him the difference between good and bad action; briefly when a terrier approaches or leaves the onlooker, his legs should move straightly, and he should appear free, well-balanced, and sound, so as to waste no energy; he should move like Victorian poetry with Elizabethan grace!

How can anyone improve on that description written more than 60 years ago?

A Fox Terrier will out-rat a cat, out-guard a Doberman and out-play a two-year-old child. The Fox Terrier is economical. The breed is known for its longevity. It is not unusual for a well-cared-for Fox Terrier to live for 15 years or more. A good burglar alarm system would cost 10 times more and the system would probably be obsolete in five years. A furry Fox Terrier alarm will work even in a power failure. It is less expensive to feed a Fox Terrier than it is the larger breeds. While many of the larger breeds have great use and value commercially as police dogs and patrolling commercial establishments, the Fox Terrier is easily their equal in a home. Nothing escapes them, from a mouse to a moonbeam. So whether its job is to alert its master to the dangers of an intruder or to the existence of smoke in the home or just to notify everyone that something unusual is afoot, the Fox Terrier provides these services efficiently and economically.

The Fox Terrier is innovative and inventive. It spends most of its waking hours inventing ways to inveigle people into sharing its interests. With a mischievous eye and a head cocked to one side you can actually see the little wheels turning in its head. "Now let me see. I find this dead sock all in knots to be terribly interesting and attractive. How can I make it enticing to my idol so that he will see what I see? Perhaps if I march up and down in front of him with the sock in my mouth and shaking it rapidly from side to side, that is bound to work. Why are those two staring at each other and barking when I'm offering to share my dead sock with them? Some nerve!

Well, I'll just go over to one of them with the sock in my mouth and reach out with my paw to get their attention. They're still ignoring me and my dead sock. Impossible! I think I'll just drop my dead sock in someone's lap. They are bound to take notice of it and me. But maybe I won't get it back. Well, I'll just drop it but keep my nose up against it. When I'm sure they are interested I'll just snatch it away again. They actually ignored the sock. Incredible! I better get my chew bone and ball. Perhaps one of those possessions will interest those two." And so purposefully, but with high hopes and great expectations, the Fox Terrier proceeds to try to bring you into its world. At times, I find it is a much better place to be than where I am and I know you will, too!

The Fox Terrier is full of obvious compassion and understanding. You may use many adjectives to describe this marvelous breed—alert, merry, teachable, keen, intelligent, self-confident, sympathetic, intuitive, happy—but one word that does not fit is subtle. Obvious is the mark of the Fox Terrier.

No dog sighs or groans quite like a Fox Terrier. Remember that this is a workmanlike dog in a comparatively small, compact body. If you were blindfolded and placed in a room with a Fox Terrier and a Great Dane and if you could induce them to sigh, moan or groan on command and if your task would be to identify the breed by sigh, moan or groan decibel, I am reasonably certain that you would identify the Terrier's sounds as those of the larger dog. As dinner time approaches, your Fox Terrier might begin its campaign by staring at you and giving off a deep sigh. The result would do Sara Bernhardt credit in one of her more tortured performances. If that gambit fails, you may hear a moan equal to the best of a Hitchcock victim. There is a difference between a moan and a groan. A Fox Terrier's moan is a pleading moan. It retains some vestige of hope that you will stop whatever it is you are doing and fill its bowl with goodies. But the groan, no one can resist—the abject disappointment expressed by the low, guttural, totally despairing sound of the groan, lest you think your dog is dying, you had better stop what you are doing and fill that bowl if only to change the mood. As you can see, not one of these actions is subtle. No long suffering, pleading, tearful eye for this bloke. That's too risky. You might miss the meaning. As subtle as hitting a thumbtack with a sledgehammer. But the breed comes by these talents honestly. The English ladies and gentlemen who first bred these charmers wanted a dog fit for their company and lifestyle. The breed soon learned to take advantage of human nature. Just doing your job sometimes is not enough. There are times when a dog must draw attention to itself within the confines of the rules of polite society.

If you haven't already guessed, the Fox Terrier is intelligent, trustworthy, loyal, helpful, friendly, courteous, kind, obedient, cheerful, brave and clean. You might say the Fox Terrier is the Boy or Girl Scout of the canine world. They are always prepared. They are not thrifty. To be thrifty, you must plan ahead, think of your future. No such thoughts for a Fox Terrier. No other breed lives for the moment more than this marvelous breed. You, their master, are their future. They accept that fact totally. However, it is in the final virtue required of the Scout that the Fox Terrier turns its wagging tail and impish expression to. Reverent. The Fox Terrier is not reverent. It is an almost irreverent dog. All of its reverence and respect is heaped upon you, its master. It has none left for the rest of the world. A mouse, a cat, a cow, a lion, a bus are all treated with the same disrespect and irreverence. In strange situations, anxiety gives way to the spirit of adventure; the courage of a Fox Terrier overcomes prudence. They can be difficult, challenging, obstreperous, pesky, along with all their wonderful virtues, but they are never boring.

In December, 1984, the AKC recognized the Smooth Fox Terrier and the Wire Fox Terrier as separate breeds. The effective date was June 1, 1985. The establishment of a Standard for Wires necessitated minor changes in the Smooth Standard. All references to Wire coats and Varieties had to be expunged from the Smooth Standard. For American breeders, the Wire Standard was all new; however, the British have had a Standard for Wires since 1913. Virtually the same Standard the British utilize was adopted by the AFTC and the AKC.

Just printing both Standards would only provide students of the breeds with that which is easily available. On the following pages are the Standards for both breeds along with amplifications and visualizations. The goal is to provide a living Standard for the Wire and the Smooth so that judges and other students will have a point of reference, a starting place upon which to build their knowledge and understanding of the Fox Terriers. Language helps to unlock the door to knowledge. The sketch on page 177 provides a glossary of terms along with the applicable anatomy.

Standard interpretation is the prerogative of anyone associated with pure-bred dogs. Sometimes, when I listen to ringside comments, it is as if the individual making the comments has just invented the breed, or discovered new ground and that he or she was the first one to disagree with a judge's interpretation of the Standard. As secretary of the AFTC, when the varieties were divided into breeds and a new (albeit old) Wire Standard was adopted, I can tell you that there was considerable debate and discussion; more so on the Club's official amplification than on the Standard itself, because any amplification narrows the room for interpretation. Following is a quote by a famous breeder involved in Standard development.

A reference to the Fox Terrier Club's Standard has produced an avalanche of letters about it. A few asked where it can be had, and received the answer: from the secretary or from almost any Fox Terrier book; but the majority have it and know it, and write for light upon such phrases as "a pipe-stopper tail" etc., or for further enlightenment on some one or the other of the seven points:

(1) head and neck, (2) shoulders, (3) ribs, (4) quarters (5) legs and feet, (6) coat, and (7) action. The largest number ask for enrichment of the last—(7) action—including size, on which the inquiry originally arose, and symmetry.

These comments were made 60 years ago by Rev. Rosslyn Bruce but they could have been written today and will be just as topical tomorrow.

One hundred or more years ago Fox Terrier people were analyzing, discussing, debating, dissecting and, more importantly, using the Standard as the ultimate description by which to judge the results of their breeding efforts. One of the more interesting aspects of breeding and exhibiting any animal is the manner that different people view the Standard. Competent judges familiar with the Standard, or, as of June 1, 1985, the Standards, will vary in their mental image of a good Fox Terrier. Discussions arise as to correct bone. Is it the weight of the bone, its density and thickness or the shape of the bone that determines what is correct? Most knowledgeable people recognize a straight stifle, but how much angulation do the Standards mean by "well bent at the stifles"? Symmetry is another descriptive noun that encourages debate. And the discussion continues from generation to generation.

The Reverend Rosslyn Bruce was asked to describe "symmetry" in the early days of the 20th century. "Well, as to symmetry—which means, literally, measuring together—there is much that is common to all well-formed animals, such as shoulder well thrown back, which is as desirable in a biped as in a quadruped, as every mother and governess testifies when she scoldingly remarks, 'Gladys, you're stooping!' There is even more that is common to all four-footed animals, such as strong, muscular hindquarters; more still common to good, straight-legged Terriers, who are all built on the lines of a weight-carrying hunter; and this typical symmetry is found at its best and most obvious in a Smooth Fox Terrier, perhaps the most compact epitome of the qualities which constitute symmetry."

Symmetry can best be judged at a little distance. A general impression cannot be absorbed so well at close quarters. Symmetry can best be judged on level ground. A terrier standing uphill generally looks much bigger (but often considerably better) than he really is. Symmetry can best be judged broadside on, starting from the shoulder, as a sort of center of gravity, and looking both fore and aft. The shoulder should lie back in as sloping a position as possible; proficiency in judging this point—which does not permit of any very palpable divergence, and is indeed, often almost imperceptible to the untrained eye—arises only from constantly studying it in as many terriers as possible. The shoulder bone is obscured more or less by the muscles that cover it; but, even at the halt, an upright shoulder is a grievous eye-sore, and in walking it is a mighty handicap. Symmetry demands that a Terrier be long from chest to buttock—that is, covering plenty of ground space—but that his back or top line be very short, indicating strength. To achieve this combination the shoulder must slope, and also the thigh, viewed broadside on, must be almost as broad as possible.

Symmetry forbids that a terrier by "heavily topped"—the limbs, that is, appearing too slight for the body (like a beer barrel on four knitting needles). The forelimbs must not only be strong and round, like Norman pillars, but short and straight in all their lines, lest they show too high and too wide a display of daylight, and present that detestable "leggy" appearance which all terrier men hate.

Symmetry demands that a terrier be "well ribbed up," which indicates plenty of heart room and lungs and power to live. The hinder ribs must extend well back and be of good length. A Whippet is a delightful creature to look at, and so, too, is a thoroughbred horse; but we are dealing with terriers (who are to resemble hunters). An imaginary perpendicular line drawn in the middle of a terrier's back, half-way between withers and stern, from top to bottom, should be as long, or very nearly as long, as any similar line drawn nearer the withers. Then, if the under line continues without a kink up, the body has no "tucked-up" appearance and the whole is symmetrical.

Symmetry demands a "good set-on" at three points: (1) the joint of head and neck, (2) the adjustment of neck and shoulder, and (3) the position and direction of the terrier's flag. Each of these is often referred to as the "set-on," though recently I have noticed among terrier men that the third is generally intended. All are equally necessary to symmetry.

That heads should be long and lean and strong (Heavens! Who wants a weak head?); that necks should be long and slightly arched; that ears should be V-shaped and small; that eyes should be bright and dark and small; that mouths should be straight and underjaws strong; that coats should be hard and straight and smooth and abundant; that feet should be deep and small and circular—these are all points which bear upon the impression of symmetry which the broadside view presents. But a complete conception can only be formed of a terrier's symmetry when a glance both at his front, at rest and in action, and at his back view in the same two positions has assured us that he stands straight, and that he moves with rhythm; and when we have taken a last careful look down on to his back from behind, and observed the full spring of his ribs, with perhaps a reminiscent thought of the days when we thought saddles a stupid and unnecessary invention of parents and head-grooms, and loved rather to grip a living rib with a sympathetic knee, we may reasonably assume that we have found in that well-sprung rib the final necessary ingredient of true symmetry.

But some of you will say: "Padre, you old fraud, you have merely sketched all the points of a good terrier, and called the whole kerboodle 'symmetry.'" Kamerad, I own up, it is so; but the emphasis in your protest must be laid upon sketched. That delicate adjustment of the whole body, fitly joined together and compacted by that which every joint helps to supply, each part working effectually together with the whole—that is symmetry. And if you think this rather a wordy definition of something that you really understand better yourself, sit down quickly and write your description of it, that it may be recorded, if ever you come to die.

If Fox Terrier fanciers take pride in the constancy of the Standard, that pride is justified. The dog, either breed, is perfection itself. We know it. Its size and shape are perfect for any environment. Anyone who has attempted to keep a larger dog in an apartment or small rooming house must admit that larger dogs, under those conditions, require certain adjustments; not so with the companion of companions, the Fox Terrier.

Anyone who has tried a tramp through the woods with smaller breeds must be aware of the inherent hazards that activity places on a smaller breed. But, the "cleverly made hunter" meets each environment with aplomb and without the necessity for any major adjustment. The gentlemen who first fostered this fine breed in the late 19th century knew that they had encountered the "perfect dog."

Truly a sturdy, sensible dog with few health problems, it is pleasing and symmetrical to the eye and genetically sound. The Fox Terrier Standard should be cast in stone and then someone should remove all the hammers and the chisels from the fancy.

POINTS OF THE FOX-TERRIER CLUB ISSUED IN 1876

"SMOOTH"

1. Head—The skull should be flat and moderately narrow, and gradually decreasing in width to the eyes. Not much "stop" should be apparent, but there should be more dip in the profile between the forehead and top jaw than is seen in the case of the Greyhound. The cheeks must not be full. The ears should be V-shaped and small, of moderate thickness, and dropping forward close to the cheek, not hanging by the side of the head like a Foxhound's. The jaw, upper and under, should be strong and muscular, should be of fair punishing strength, but not so in any way to resemble the Greyhound or modern English Terrier. There should not be much falling away below the eyes. This part of the head should, however, be moderately chiseled out, so as not to go down in a straight line like a wedge. The nose, towards which the muzzle must gradually taper, should be black. The eyes should be dark in colour, small, and rather deep set, full of fire, life, and intelligence; as nearly as possible circular in shape. The teeth should be nearly as possible level—i.e., the upper teeth on the outside of the lower teeth.

2. Neck—Should be clean and muscular, without throatiness, of fair length, and gradually widening to the shoulders.

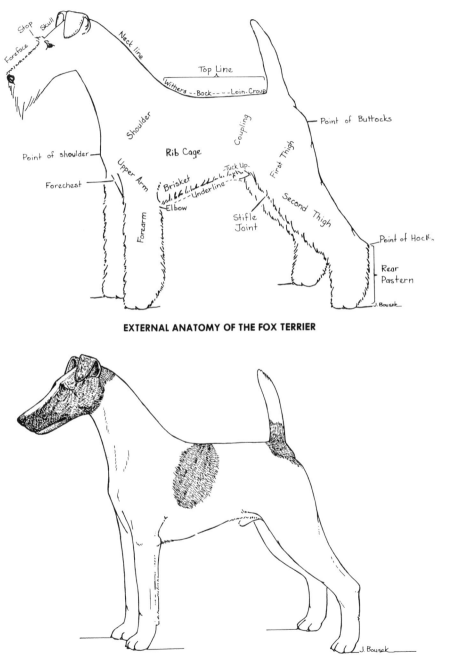

EXTERNAL ANATOMY OF THE FOX TERRIER

THE SMOOTH FOX TERRIER — GENERAL APPEARANCE

183

3. Shoulders—Should be long and sloping, well laid back, fine at the points, and clearly cut at the withers. Chest—Deep and not broad.

4. Back—Should be short, straight and strong, with no appearance of slackness. Loin—Should be powerful and very slightly arched. The fore ribs should be moderately arched, the back ribs deep, and the dog should be well ribbed up.

5. Hindquarters—Should be strong and muscular, quite free from droop or crouch; the thighs long and powerful; hocks near the ground, the dog standing well up on them like a Foxhound, and not straight in the stifle.

6. Stern—Should be set on rather high, and carried gaily, but not over the back or curled. It should be of good strength, anything approaching a "pipe-stopper" tail being exceptionally objectionable.

7. Legs—Viewed from any direction, must be straight, showing little or no appearance of an ankle in front. They should be strong in bone throughout, short and straight to pastern. Both fore and hind legs should be carried straight forward in traveling, the stifles not turned outward. The elbows should hang perpendicular to the body, working free of the side. *Feet*—Should be round, compact, and not large. The soles hard and tough. The toes moderately arched, and turned neither in nor out.

8. Coat—Should be straight, flat, smooth, hard, dense, and abundant. The belly and underside of the thighs should not be bare. Colour—White should predominate; brindle, red, or liver markings are objectionable. Otherwise this point is of little or no importance.

9. Symmetry, Size and Character—The dog must present a general gay, lively and active appearance; bone and strength in a small compass are essentials, but this must not be taken to mean that a Fox Terrier should be cloddy, or in any way coarse—speed and endurance must be looked to as well as power, and the symmetry of the Foxhound taken as a model. The terrier, like the hound, must on no account be leggy, nor must he be too short in the leg. He should stand like a cleverly-made hunter, covering a lot of ground, yet with a short back, as before stated. He will then attain the highest degree of propelling power, together with the greatest length of stride that is compatible with the length of his body. Weight is not a certain criterion of a terrier's fitness for his work—general shape, size, and contour are the main points—and if a dog can gallop and stay, and follow his fox up a drain, it matters little what his weight is to a pound or so, though, roughly speaking, it may be said he should not scale over 20 pounds in show condition.

The Scale of Values of Individual Points

1. Head and Ears 15
2. Neck 5
3. Shoulders and Chest 10
4. Back and Loin 10
5. Hindquarters 15
6. Stern 5
7. Legs and Feet 15
8. Coat 10
9. Symmetry, Size and Character 15

Disqualifying Points

Nose—White, cherry, or spotted to a considerable extent with either of these colours.

Ears—Prick, tulip or rose.

Mouth—Much undershot or much overshot.

Eyes "circular" not "round." Recently a very capable critic commented adversely on a bitch as being "a little round in eye," and he puzzled a student of the Standard, which urges that the eye should be "as nearly as possible circular in shape." The discrepancy arises from the use of the word "round," probably avoided on purpose by the all but inspired drafter of the Standard. In the dictionary round and circular would be almost identical, but in the technical language of the canine cult, "round" is used, and has for generations been used, to express a certain fullness which makes the eye appear to stand out with a bulgy effusiveness, which is just a shade pug-like, and not approved by sportsmen.

AMPLIFICATION OF THE SMOOTH FOX TERRIER STANDARD

A. Head

The *skull* should be flat and moderately narrow, gradually decreasing in width to the eyes. Not much "stop" should be apparent, but there should be more dip in the profile between the forehead and the top jaw than is seen in the case of a Greyhound. The *cheeks* must not be full. The *jaws*, upper and lower, should be strong and muscular and of fair punishing strength, but not so as in any way to resemble the Greyhound or modern English Terrier. There should not be much falling away below the eyes. This part of the head should, however, be moderately chiseled out, so as not to go down in a straight slope like a wedge. The *nose*, toward which the muzzle must gradually taper, should be black. It should be noticed that although the foreface should gradually taper from eye to muzzle, and should tip slightly at its junction with the forehead, it should not "dish" or fall away quickly below the eyes, where it should be full and well made up, but relieved from "wedginess" by a little delicate chiselling. The *ears* should be V-shaped and small, of moderate thickness, and drooping forward close to the cheek, not hanging by the side of the head like a Foxhound. The top line of the folded ear should be well above the line of the skull. The *eyes* and the *rims* should be dark in color, moderately small and rather deep set, full of fire, life and intelligence, and as nearly as possible circular in shape.

Anything approaching a yellow eye is most objectionable. The teeth should be as nearly as possible together, i.e., the points of the upper incisors on the outside of or slightly overlapping the lower teeth. There should be little apparent difference in length between the skull and foreface of a well-balanced head.

Discussion

The head should be flat and clean in all its planes. There should be no discernible rounding of the topskull from any angle, nor should there be bony protuberances over the eye ("alligator bumps"). The cheeks must be flat, with no bulging of bone or muscle. Backskull and foreface should be approximately equal in length. Viewed from the side, topskull and foreface should be in parallel planes. The muzzle should be slightly chiseled away from the topskull under the eyes. There should not be a prominent stop, which creates a dish-faced appearance. Neither should the area between the eyes be filled in, as in a Collie, Borzoi or—worst of all—a Bull Terrier! There should be a continuous but slight taper from backskull to tip of muzzle. An overfine muzzle will be snipy, while a too-heavy muzzle in proportion to backskull will make the head appear brick-shaped and lacking in refinement. The lower jaw should be well developed and in profile there should be a distinct "chin" rather than a jawline which recedes at a sharp angle from the lower front incisors. The lips should be clean and tight and there should be no loose skin under the throat.

Shape and placement of the eye, together with color, are very important in creating the correct expression. The eye should be *circular* in shape. An almond eye, or any deviation from the round orbit, is a fault. The eye must not be full. An eye may be small, dark, and round, but if it protrudes or is "poppy," the expression is mouselike rather than fiery. Light eyes create an undesirable soft expression. Eyes that are not circular in shape may appear to be set on a slant, creating an unpleasant fault in expression. An overlong foreface creates the undesirable "foreign" expression in which the eyes are no longer located at their appropriate position, the midpoint of the head.

Ears should be carried so that they break approximately at the midpoint of the leather. They should face forward, breaking in a clean fold so that the tip touches the skull.

The inside of the ear should never be visible when ear carriage is correct. Ears which are prick (erect), tulip (breaking much above the midpoint of the leather) or rosed (carried out to the side and breaking back against the side of

186

The Head in Profile

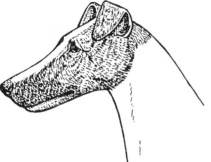

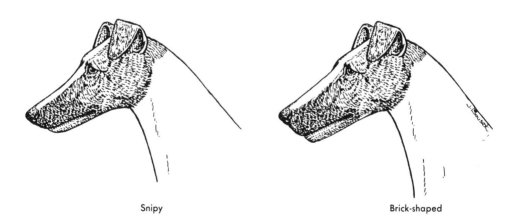

Head profile — Correct type

Well-balanced head. Skull and foreface (A and B) should appear equal in length. Top-skull and foreface (C and D) are in parallel planes.

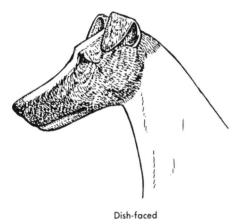

Dish-faced

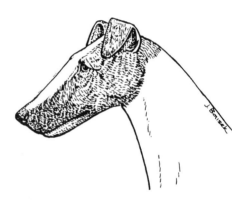

"Bull Terrier" look

Snipy

Brick-shaped

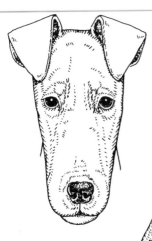

Correct head, ear and
eye type

Foreign expression,
tulip ear, almond eye

Cheeky, rounding top-
skull, rose ear, light
eye

Snipy foreface, prick
ears, large eyes

Houndy ears, mouse-
like eye

Bites (both Smooths and Wires)

Frontal view

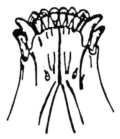

Inferior (bottom) view in normal occlusion (scissors bite).

Fig. 1

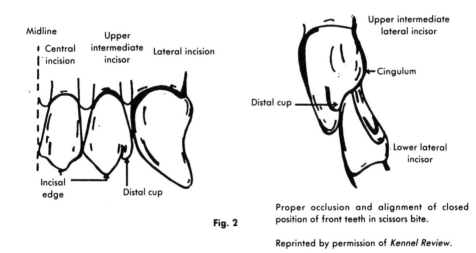

Fig. 2

Proper occlusion and alignment of closed position of front teeth in scissors bite.

Reprinted by permission of *Kennel Review.*

In the *scissor bite,* the upper central incisors (the two middle teeth) overlap the facial (outside) surfaces of the two lower central incisors and a small portion of the mesial (inside) surfaces of the intermediate lateral incisors (Fig. 1). The incisal (biting) edges of the lower central incisors contact the cingulum of the upper central incisors (Fig. 2). The lower lateral incisor rests on the small distal (outside) cusp (Fig. 2) of the upper intermediate lateral incisor, and on the mesial (inside) cusp of the upper lateral incisor.

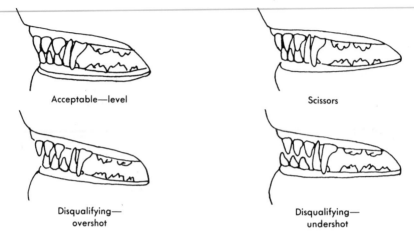

Acceptable—level

Scissors

Disqualifying—
overshot

Disqualifying—
undershot

the head like a Whippet) are cause for *disqualification.* Likewise, a nose must be solid black; any pink or white spotting of the nose leather is a disqualification. Furthermore, a scissors bite is called for with the points of the upper incisors on the outside of or slightly overlapping the lowers, and "much" undershot or overshot is a disqualification. What constitutes *much* is obviously a subjective judgement, but such deviations from the ideal as missing teeth and faulty alignment, although not mentioned in the Standard, are surely maladaptive and should be frowned upon by breeders and judges.

The term "level bite" used in the Standard describes the smooth joining of the incisors. A finger passing across the line where the upper and lower incisors meet should not feel a protrusion of the upper or lower teeth but, on the contrary, a level or smooth occlusion and alignment in a closed position.

B. Neck

Should be clean and muscular, without throatiness, of fair length, and gradually widening to the shoulders.

C. Shoulders

Should be long and sloping, well laid back, fine at the points, and clean cut at the withers. **Chest** should be deep and not broad. **Back** should be short and straight (i.e., level) and strong, with no appearance of slackness. **Brisket** should be deep, but not exaggerated. Loin should be very powerful, muscular and very slightly arched. The fore ribs should be moderately arched, the back ribs deep and well sprung, and the dog should be well ribbed up.

D. Hindquarters

Should be strong and muscular, quite free from droop or crouch; the

Structure: Forequarters and Hindquarters

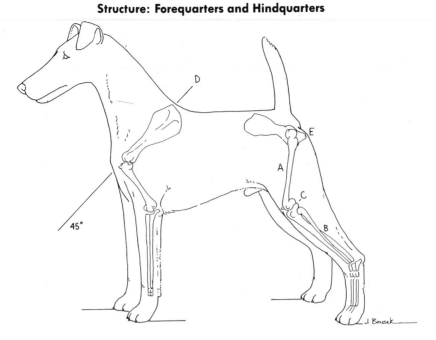

Thighs (A and B) are long and well-curved at stifle (C). Angle of shoulder layback (D) should be as nearly as possible 45×. The tail should be as forward of the rear projection of the pelvic bones (E) as possible.

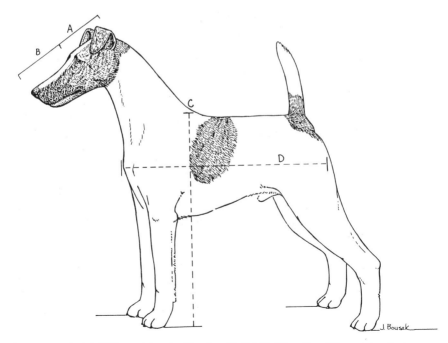

Balance—Length of skull (A) equals length of foreface (B). Height at the withers (C) equals length of body (D) from point of shoulder to point of buttocks.

thighs long and powerful, stifles well curved and turning neither in nor out; hocks well bent and near the ground and parallel with each other when viewed from behind, the dog standing well up on them like a Foxhound, and not straight to the stifle. The worst possible form of hindquarters consists of a short second thigh and a straight stifle.

E. Stern

Should be set on rather high, and carried gaily, but not over the back or curled. It should be of good strength, anything approaching a "pipestopper" tail being especially objectionable.

F. Legs

The forelegs viewed from any direction must be straight with bone strong right down to the feet, showing little or no appearance of ankle in front, and being short and straight in pastern. Both fore and hind legs should be carried straight forward in traveling, the stifles not turning outward. The elbows should hang perpendicularly to the body, working free of the sides.

G. Feet

Should be round, compact and not large; the soles hard and tough; the toes moderately arched and turned neither in nor out.

The neck should be well arched, especially in dogs. The angle of layback of shoulder should be as nearly as possible 45°. The withers should appear narrow when viewed from above, and the neck should fit smoothly into the shoulders with no bulge of bone or muscle. Length of neck will, with correct shoulder placement, be of graceful, but not excessive length, and the back will, as desired, appear short. The brisket should be at least deep enough to reach the elbow, giving the pleasing contrast in profile between chest and tuck-up called a "good turn of body." Viewed from the front, the chest should be somewhat narrow rather than broad and muscular like that of a Bull Terrier, but the front legs should not "come out of the same hole." The ribs should be well sprung, but the dog should not be barrel-chested. There should be no dip behind the withers. The topline should appear level, the arch in the loin felt rather than readily seen. The tail should be set as high (forward of the rear projection of the pelvic bones) as possible, and be carried either directly upright or slightly forward of the perpendicular. A gay or squirrel tail is a bad fault, and a "2 o'clock tail" spoils the dog's outline. Furthermore, no Fox Terrier of correct temperament should drop its tail in the ring; this denotes timidity. The rear legs should be well bent at the stifle, with hocks low to the ground, but angulation should not be excessive. Overbent stifles are weak in actual propulsive power. The forelegs must be neither "down in pastern" nor "knuckled over" forward at the pastern joint.

Action

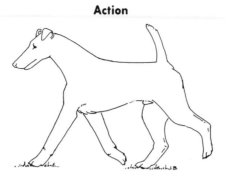

Correct Action

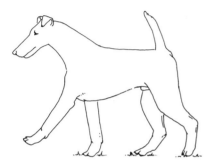

Goosestep action—incorrect

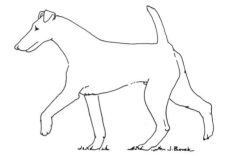

Hackney action—incorrect

Forequarters

Correct

Too Wide

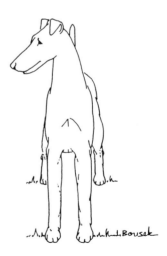

Too Narrow

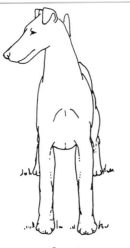

Correct

Out at Elbow, Toeing in

Tied at Elbow, Toeing out

. . . and Moving

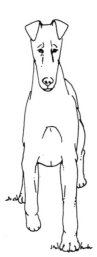

Tracking True

Weave and Dish Action

Paddling Action

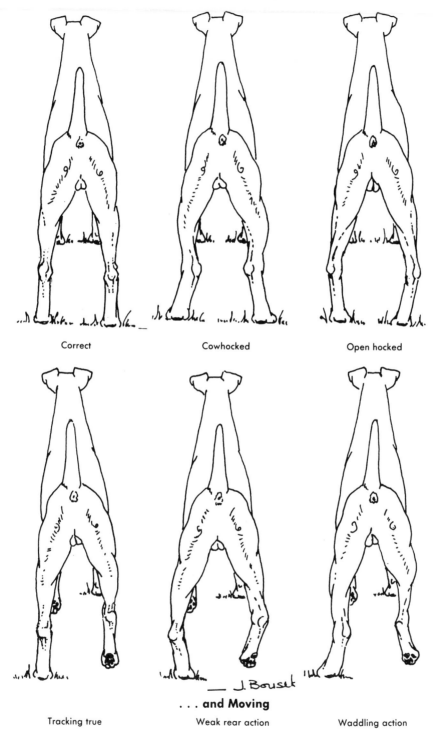

Correct Cowhocked Open hocked

_ J. Bousek

. . . and Moving

Tracking true Weak rear action Waddling action

H. Coat

For Smooth Fox Terriers, the coat should be smooth, hard, flat, dense and abundant. The belly and underside of the thighs should not be bare.

I. Color

White should predominate; brindle, red or liver markings are objectionable. Otherwise this point is of little or no importance.

> The coat of the Smooth Fox Terrier may vary in length and density according to breeding, grooming and climate, but should always be flat, with a hard topcoat. The hair under the tuck-up and inside the thighs is usually trimmed short, but the dogs should not be bald in this area, as in some single-coated breeds. The colors seen today in Smooth Fox Terriers may be solid white (eyerims must have dark pigment), white and tan, or black, white and tan—all "black and white" Smooth Fox Terriers are actually tri-colors, although the amount of tan that appears over the eyes, on the cheeks, at the vent, *etc.* varies considerably among individual expressions. These tan markings in the black are traditional and genetic and should never be colored out when grooming. "Tan" may be taken to mean any reasonably solid shade of reddish tan, with or without black points or shading. Many dogs are sable marked. Brindling (distinct stripes, as in a Boxer or Great Dane), if seen, should be penalized, but must not be confused with the sable shading that is so commonly seen. Although white should predominate, no preference of any kind should be given to placement of markings. The type, structure and character of the dog is paramount and the attractiveness or lack of it conferred by markings is extraneous to the intent of the standard. Ticking on legs and body is very characteristic of many strains and should on no account be penalized. Judges should bear in mind that in the scale of points makes no allocation for color and markings.

J. Symmetry, Size and Character

The dog must present a generally gay, lively and active appearance; bone and strength in a small compass are essentials; but this must not be taken to mean that a Fox Terrier should be cloddy, or in any way coarse— speed and endurance must be looked to as well as power, and the symmetry of the Foxhound taken as a model. The terrier, like the hound, must on no account be leggy, nor must he be too short in the leg. He should stand like a cleverly-made hunter, covering a lot of ground, yet with a short back, as before stated. He will then attain the highest degree of propelling power, together with the greatest length of stride that is compatible with the length of his body. Weight is not a certain criterion of a terrier's fitness for his work—general shape, size and contour are the main points; and if a dog can gallop and stay, and follow his fox up a drain, it matters little what his weight is to a pound or so. According to present-day requirements, a full-sized, well-balanced dog should not exceed 15½ inches at the withers—the bitch being proportionately lower—nor should the length of back from withers to root of tail exceed 12 inches, while, to maintain the relative proportions, the head should not exceed 7¼ inches or be less than 7 inches. A dog with these measurements should scale 18 pounds in show condition—a bitch weighing some 2 pounds less—with a margin of 1 pound either way.

K. Balance

This may be defined as the correct proportions of a certain point, or points, when considered in relation to a certain other point or points. It is the keystone of the terrier's anatomy. The chief points for consideration are the relative proportions of skull and foreface; head and back; height at withers and length of body from shoulder-point to buttock—the ideal of proportion being reached when the last two measurements are the same. It should be added that, although the head measurements can be taken with absolute accuracy, the height at withers and length of back and coat are approximate, and are inserted for the information of breeders and exhibitors rather than as a hard and fast rule.

It is as true today as it was in 1876, when this standard was first adopted in England, that a dog of correct size will seldom exceed 7¼″ in head length. At a recent match of the Smooth Fox Terrier Breeders Association, there was a class for the "best head." All contestants, including some notable winners, were measured. Irrespective of the size of the dog, none measured more than 7¾″. Terriers that are much oversize lack breed character and extremes are to be avoided. One should note the frequent use of the word "moderate" in the Standard. A current vogue for extreme length of head does little to promote the preservation of breed type. A balanced, active dog that can go to ground will not be of excessive size. Judges, breeders and exhibitors should make every effort to prefer the Fox Terrier of moderate size, spirited but tractable character, of substance combined with elegance and refinement.

L. Movement

Movement, or action, is the crucial test of conformation. The terrier's legs should be carried straight forward while traveling, the forelegs hanging perpendicular and swinging parallel with the sides, like the pendulum of a clock. The principal propulsive power is furnished by the hind legs, perfection of action being found in the terrier possessing long thighs and muscular second-thighs well bent at the stifles, which admit of a strong forward thrust or "snatch" of the hocks. When approaching, the forelegs should form a continuation of the straight line of the front, the feet being the same distance apart as the elbows. When stationary it is often difficult to determine whether a dog is slightly out at shoulder, but, directly he moves, the defect—if it exists—becomes more apparent, the forefeet

Composites of faults

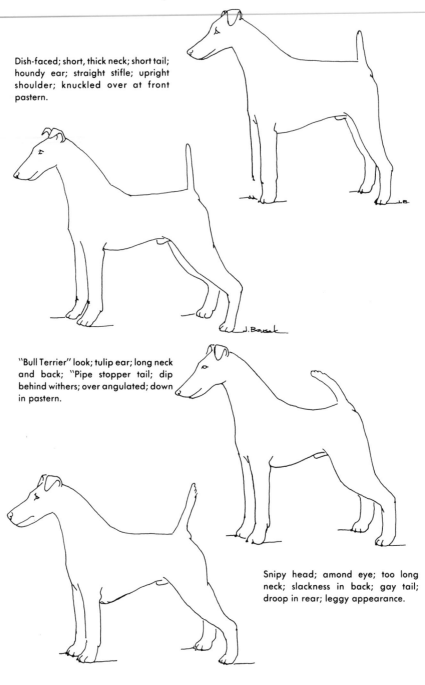

Dish-faced; short, thick neck; short tail; houndy ear; straight stifle; upright shoulder; knuckled over at front pastern.

"Bull Terrier" look; tulip ear; long neck and back; "Pipe stopper tail; dip behind withers; over angulated; down in pastern.

Snipy head; amond eye; too long neck; slackness in back; gay tail; droop in rear; leggy appearance.

Brick-shaped head, two o'clock tail; short-legged appearance.

having a tendency to cross, "weave," or "dish." When, on the contrary, the dog is tied at the shoulder, the tendency of the feet is to move wider apart, with a sort of paddling action. When the hocks are turned in—cowhock— the stifles and feet are turned outwards, resulting in a serious loss of propulsive power. When the hocks are turned outwards the tendency of the hind feet is to cross, resulting in an ungainly waddle.

M. N.B.

Old scars or injuries, the result of work or accident, should not be allowed to prejudice a terrier's chance in the show ring, unless they interfere with its movement or with its utility for work or stud.

WIRE-HAIRED FOX TERRIER

This variety of the breed should resemble the Smooth sort in every respect except the coat, which should be broken. The harder and more wiry the texture of the coat is, the better. On no account should the dog look or feel wooly; and there should be no silky hair about the poll or elsewhere. The coat should not be too long, so as to give the dog a shaggy appearance, but, at the same time, it should show a marked and distinct difference all over from the Smooth species.

The Scale of Values of Individual Points

1. Head and Ears 15
2. Neck 5
3. Shoulders and Chest 10
4. Back and Loin 10
5. Hind Quarters 15
6. Stern 5
7. Legs and Feet 15
8. Coat 15
9. Symmetry, Size and Character 10

Disqualifying Points

Nose—White, cherry, or spotted to a considerable extent with either of these colors.

Ears—Prick, tulip or rose.

Mouth—Much undershot or much overshot.

Movement: The Standard's description of desired movement is clear as it applies to "coming and going." The forelegs and hindlegs should swing perpendicular to the ground. If a dog is moved at a moderate speed, rather than so fast that he is forced toward singletracking, and is correctly constructed and trained—so that he is not pulling on the lead or being "strung up"—this movement is a realistic possibility and a standard from which we must not deviate. In profile, the terrier should move with the greatest possible length and freedom of stride, the legs swinging freely through a long arc. In front, there must be no hackney action (high, mincing steps) or "goose-stepping"—exaggerated extension of the foreleg with stiff, unflexed pastern. Judges should encourage exhibitors to move dogs on a loose lead. A tight lead can both cause and disguise faulty movement.

Endnote: The author has made every attempt to amplify those parts of the Standard which seem to need further description or clarification. Where the Standard makes a clear and full statement on its own, no amplification has been made.

AMPLIFICATION OF THE WIRE FOX TERRIER STANDARD

Characteristics

The terrier should be alert, quick of movement, keen of expression, on the tip-toe of expectation at the slightest provocation. Character is imparted by the expression of the eyes and by the carriage of ears and tail.

Amplification

Elegance combined with a lively sense of humor characterizes the Wire Fox Terrier; indeed so lively is he, that at times he seems likely to explode from sheer high spirits. He frequently stands "on the TIP-TOE of expectation" to the extent that he appears to have no feet at all. Some dogs will actually curl their front toes under, giving a "club-footed" appearance. This, though unsightly, should not be penalized as it is indicative of extreme animation, and animation is a key-note of the Wire Fox Terrier!

The ears and tail are its barometer, the tail straight up or slightly pulled over the back, and many times, quivering with repressed excitement.

The expression of the eyes, merrily mischievous, can change at a moment's notice to the hauteur of unamused royalty, while a cold, piercing stare, worthy of an avenging angel, gives ample warning of wrathful intentions. The Wire is one of the few dogs who will outstare a human.

NOTE: In the ring, the too exuberant Wire, lunging and leaping about, cannot be properly evaluated and therefore cannot be given top awards.

An intrinsic characteristic, not specifically mentioned in the Standard, is temperament. Intensely inquisitive, supremely happy, or aggressively combatant—all are attributes of correct Wire disposition. The Wire should not be shy; neither should he be foolhardy. Exploration or a few encouraging words should speedily return the dog to normal exuberance, an experienced adult recovering quicker than the unworldly youngster. In the ring, a Wire totally undone by an experience should not be given top awards.

This creates a ring-full of competitors, each wishing to impose leadership over the other. To prevent overt hostility, a judge should instruct his exhibitors to maintain one full dog-length between their charges, exhibitors making every effort to maintain this length. Should open hostility occur, the judge should quickly separate the warriors, sometimes placing one at the head, the other at the end of the lineup. This unfavorable attention is eliminated when EXHIBITORS RESTRAIN THEIR DOGS.

A Wire growls in play as well as anger; but, since the human ear cannot detect the subtle nuance between the playful growl and the "stay away from me" warning, the Wire should be discouraged from growling at humans while in the ring. Any dog displaying unwarranted aggression towards humans should neither be bred from, nor shown.

General Appearance

The dog should be balanced and this may be defined as the correct proportions of a certain point or points, when considered in relation to a certain other point or points. It is the key-stone of the terrier's anatomy. The chief points for consideration are the relative proportions of skull and foreface; head and back; height at withers; and length of body from shoulder-point to buttock—the ideal of proportion being reached when the last two measurements are the same. It should be added that, although the head measurement can be taken with absolute accuracy, the height at withers and length of back are approximate, and are inserted for the information of breeders and exhibitors rather than as a hard-and-fast rule. The movement or action is the crucial test of conformation. The terrier's legs should be carried straight forward while traveling, the forelegs hanging perpendicular and swinging parallel to the sides, like the pendulum of a clock. The principal propulsive power is furnished by the hind legs, perfection of action being found in the terrier possessing long thighs and muscular second-thighs well bent at the stifles, which admit of a strong forward thrust or "snatch" of the hocks. When approaching, the forelegs should form a continuation of the straight of the front, the feet being the same distance apart as the elbows. When stationary it is often difficult to determine whether a dog is slightly out at shoulder but, directly he moves, the defect—if it exists—becomes more apparent, the fore-feet having a tendency to cross, "weave" or "dish." When, on the contrary, the dog is tied at the shoulder, the tendency of the feet is to move wider apart, with a sort of padding action. When the hocks are turned in—cow hocks—the stifles and feet are turned outwards, resulting in a serious loss of propulsive power. When the hocks are turned outwards the tendency of the hind feet is to cross, resulting in an ungainly waddle.

Amplification

"All things in moderation" is the key-note of Wire Fox Terrier anatomy. At first sight, the correct "Wire" forms such an aesthetically pleasing whole, that NO ONE PART OR PORTION of him calls attention to itself. This is called Balance!

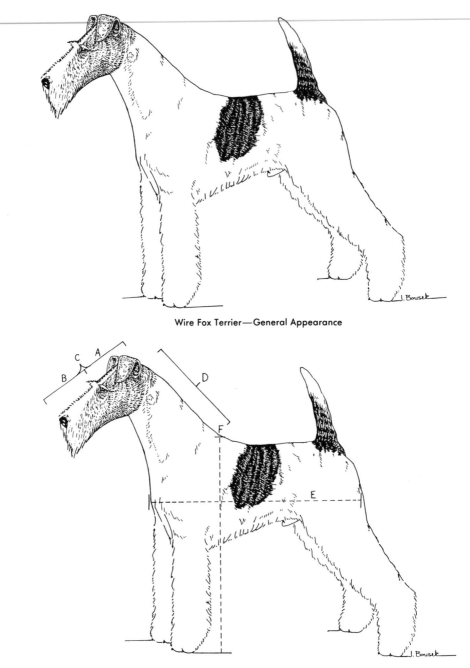

Wire Fox Terrier—General Appearance

Balance—Length of skull (A) equals length of foreface (B). Length of head (C) equals length of neck (D) from base of skull to withers. Length of body (E) from point of shoulder to point of buttocks equals height at withers (F).

The Structure of the Front and Rear

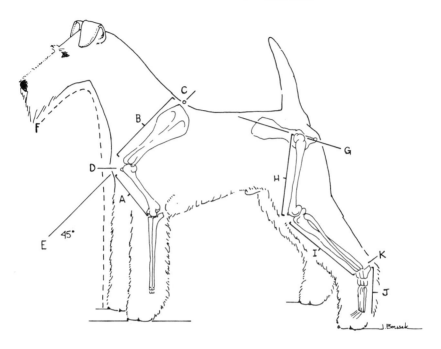

The Front
The straight terrier front (F) is a result of a shortened upper (Humerus) (A), and a lengthened shoulder blade (Scapula) (B). The shoulder should slant from the withers (C) to the point of the shoulder (D) as nearly as possible at a 45× angle to the ground (E).

The Rear
The rear is a result of an elevated pelvic slope (G) creating a level crou and a tail on top and permitting a long first and second thigh (H & I), which should be as near as possible equal in length. The rear pastern is short and perpendicular to the ground (J). The second thigh (I), meeting the rear pastern (J) at the hock joint (K) creates the desired "turn of stifle."

J. A. Butler, when asked what was "the first thing to look for in a Wire," replied "Balance, Balance, and then Balance!" How true! First is the balance of the head, skull to foreface; second, length of head to height at withers (see Weight and Size); while maintaining harmonious proportions, the neck, from base of skull to withers, should equal the length of the head. Third and final balance, as the Standard states, is the length of body from point of shoulder to point of buttocks, which should be NO GREATER, but NO LESS THAN the height at withers. If it is much greater, the dog is said to be "long-cast" or "long in couplings," while a much shorter measurement results in a "leggy" appearance and the dog is said to have "too much daylight under him." (Bitches are allowed to exceed this length to make room for puppies.)

Movement is, indeed, the "crucial test of conformation." A Wire of near perfection conformation may choose to move poorly, but if his conformation is wrong, he cannot move correctly.

The Wire's short back, close couplings, "Terrier Front" (see Fore-quarters) and moderate angulation (see Hindquarters) denote great agility and produces a brisk, businesslike stride, of moderate length. Although of no great extension, the "gait" SHOULD NOT BE MINCING, like a lady in a hobble-skirt. You should not have to line the dog up with a fence post to see if he is moving.

In profile, the action shows flexion of the front pastern occurring as the forefoot leaves the ground—just slightly in advance of the hindfoot, to avoid interference. At full extension—forearm, pastern, and foot form a continuous straight line, which is maintained through the full arc of the downward swing; contact with the ground almost equally divided between toes and heel-pad. In traveling, the object of the foreleg is to reach as far *forward* as possible. At full extension, there is surprisingly little height between foot and ground, therefore any tendency towards the high, prancing action of the Hackney Pony, or the high, stiff "Goosestep" of the W.W. II German military is totally incorrect.

NOTE: Many times a too tight lead will result in too high front action. The judge should instruct the exhibitor to relax the lead before making an evaluation.

At no time do the forelegs pull the body forward! The dog is strictly *rear-drive*. The hindquarter swinging forward contacts the ground at approximately mid-length of the body, the foot strongly pushing back, effectively thrusting the body forward. As the leg moves beyond the line of the body, the foot is quickly lifted, creating the distinctive "snatch of hock" so desirable in Wire movement. It is now, with the lift of the hock, that the greatest degree of angulation is visible.

The gait should be smooth and even, with fore- and rear-quarters working in such perfect harmony that the profile of the moving back appears level. There is nothing worse than a Wire jigging and bouncing around the ring as *first* the fore, and *then* the hind-quarters lift the mass of the body.

The Wire is moderately narrow in front (see Forequarters); when approaching, the outsides of the rear legs are seen beyond the outside edge of the front legs. This is caused by the dog "tracking-true"—the legs, front and

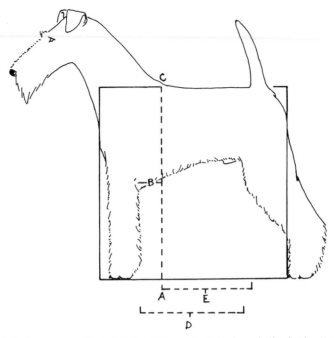

The body fits into a square. The height (A to C) is equally divided, one half to foreleg (A to B), one half to body (B to C). The ground "covered" by the underline (D) exceeds the ground "covered" by the topline (E).

Action

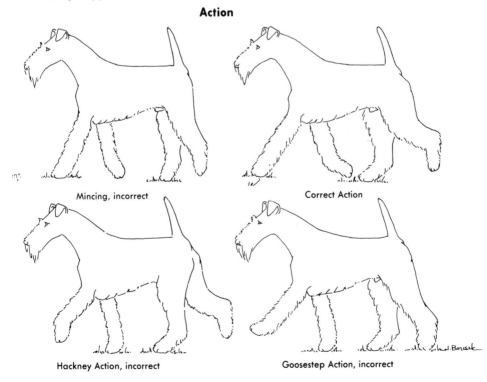

Mincing, incorrect

Correct Action

Hackney Action, incorrect

Goosestep Action, incorrect

rear move straight ahead in travel. Often the lift and fall of the front furnishings (leg hair) make it difficult to determine if movement is correct. Look at the feet—they should be in direct line with the points of the shoulder, creating an H-shaped outline. When the dog is tied at the shoulder (see Forequarters) the legs swing wide apart at the base (feet) to create an A-shaped outline. When the dog is out-at-shoulder (see Forequarters) the outline is V-shaped, the feet having a tendency to move towards each other. This is also true of the dog who is out-at-the-elbow; the elbow turns out, leg and foot turn in toward each other (pigeon-toed) and it is frequently possible to see the bottom of the foot beyond the outside edge of the flexed pastern (sometimes the feet will actually cross). The terms "weave" and "dish" are used to describe this type of faulty "in-and-out" action.

From the rear the dog should be somewhat wider through the hips than he is through the front (see Hindquarters), the hind legs tracking slightly outside of the front legs so that the insides of the front legs are seen between the dog's hind legs when moving or standing. A plumb line dropped from the hip joint should perfectly bisect the rear quarters to the ground, as should a plumb line dropped from the point of the shoulders perfectly bisect the forelegs, in the front.

NOTE: Both fore and rear legs should travel straight through, NO MATTER HOW FAST HE MOVES.

Much has been said and written about "True Type" versus "Soundness." There can be no "versus"! A Wire who conforms to the Standard, as nearly as possible in every respect, IS THE TRUE TYPE, and since THE TRUE TYPE IS "SOUND" HE WILL MOVE CORRECTLY!

Head and Skull

The topline of the skull should be almost flat, sloping slightly and gradually decreasing in width towards the eyes, and should not exceed 3½ inches in diameter at the widest part—measuring with the calipers—in the full-grown dog of correct size, the bitch's skull being proportionately narrower. If this measurement is exceeded the skull is termed "coarse," while a full-grown dog with a much narrower skull is termed "bitchy" in head. The length of the head of a full-grown, well-developed dog of correct size—measured with calipers—from the back of the occipital bone to the nostrils—should be from 7-7¼ inches, the bitch's head being proportionately shorter. Any measurement in excess of this usually indicates an over-sized or long-backed specimen, although occasionally—so rarely as to partake of the nature of a freak—a Terrier of correct size may boast a head 7½ inches in length. In a well-balanced head there should be little apparent difference in length between skull and foreface. If, however, the foreface is noticeably shorter, it amounts to a fault, the head looking weak and "unfinished." On the other hand, when the eyes are set too high up in the skull and too near the ears, it also amounts to a fault, the head being said to have a "foreign appearance." Although the foreface should

The Wire in Profile

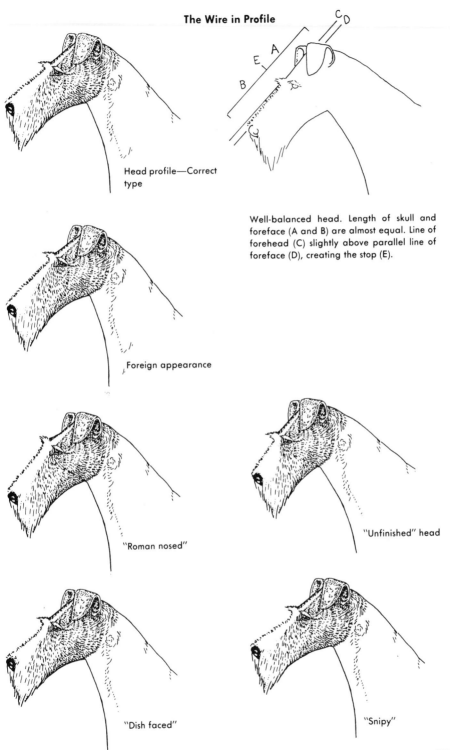

Head profile—Correct type

Well-balanced head. Length of skull and foreface (A and B) are almost equal. Line of forehead (C) slightly above parallel line of foreface (D), creating the stop (E).

Foreign appearance

"Roman nosed"

"Unfinished" head

"Dish faced"

"Snipy"

207

gradually taper from eye to muzzle and should dip slightly at its juncture with the forehead, it should not "dish" or fall away quickly below the eyes, where it should be full and well made up, but relieved from "wedginess" by a little delicate chiseling. While well-developed jawbones, armed with a set of strong, white teeth, impart that appearance of strength to the foreface which is so desirable, an excessive bony or muscular development of the jaws is both unnecessary and unsightly, as it is partly responsible for the full and rounded contour of the cheeks to which the term "cheeky" is applied. should be black.

Amplification

The Standard divides the head into two parts, Skull and Foreface. From the eyes back to the neck, is the Skull; from the eyes forward to the nose, is the Foreface. Skull and Foreface should, as nearly as possible, measure the same.

Length of skull is measured from between the eyes to the back of the occipital bone, and on the ideal head (7¼ inches) should measure 3⅝ inches; the foreface should be equal, but not exceed this length. A too long foreface is as much at fault as one that is too short. THE IDEAL HEAD IS BALANCED.

The width of the ideal skull, only ⅛ inch less than its ideal length, is MODERATELY NARROW. An ultra-narrow skull IS NOT TYPICAL OF THE WIRE and frequently accompanies the objectionable ultra-long head.

From the top, with the ears held back, the widest "flair" of the Zygomatic Arches is exposed (width is measured here). From this "flair" the head, "gradually decreasing in width towards the eyes" continues to gradually decrease in width, tapering to the nose, creating an outline of occiput to nose, that resembles an old-fashioned pine coffin of "Boot Hill" fame. From this angle one can quickly estimate the shape and balance of the head.

Frontal bones should be felt rather than seen, excessive prominence giving a rounded or "apple-domed" shape from the front. This excessive rise of the forehead creates an unsightly down-faced or "Roman-nosed" convex curve to the profile; while a concave depression in the bridge of the nose, just forward of the eye-set, creates the objectionable "dish-face." An excessive buildup of hair on the bridge of the nose is used to disguise both faults.

The top of the eyebrow, aligned with the forehead, should be seen slightly above the parallel line of the foreface in profile, indicating the slight "stop." There should be good depth to the foreface, with nearly 1/3 of this depth seen clearly in the lower jaw, below the corner of the mouth. The depth of the lower jaw, tapering slightly, sweeps forward to form the distinctive "chin" of the Wire. The beard should enhance the appearance of chin, not flatten it. The lower jaw nearly equals the length of the upper.

The strength of the foreface should complement the skull. Where the foreface joins the skull, just below the outer corner of the eye (see Eyes), there should be little apparent difference in width. From here the foreface gradually tapers to the nose. Though strong, the foreface should not be blocky, nor should it be so slender ("snipy") that excessive hair must be grown to make it match the skull. *Hair should complement the shape of the head, not accentuate it unduly.*

The lips should be tight with no appearance of flews.

A brownish hue sometimes afflicts the nose. The exact cause is obscure, but lack of sunlight seems to be a contributing factor, since it is commonly seen during winter months, hence the name "Winter Nose." "Winter Nose" occurring at any time should be ignored as the condition is soon rectified, the nose returning to its customary black.

Wire puppies are born with pink noses. The rapidity of pigmentation varies with the individual. White or white markings upon the foreface may extend through the nose giving a "pied" appearance as pigmentation occurs. In extreme cases complete pigmentation may not occur until full adulthood. Youngsters showing a marked degree of mottling should not be shown until proper pigment is present (see Disqualifications).

NOTE: Small flecks of pink inside the nostrils are permitted in the adult. White or pink, the results of scarring, should not be penalized.

Eyes

Should be dark in color, moderately small, rather deep set, not prominent, and full of fire, life, and intelligence; as nearly as possible circular in shape, and not too far apart. Anything approaching a yellow eye is most objectionable.

Amplification

Extremely important to proper expression is the shape of the eye. Set at the mid-point of the head, the eyes visually divide skull from foreface. The inside corner of the eye (next to the nose) is slightly lower and slightly in advance of the outside corner of the eye (just forward of and above the cheek). When there is too much lift to the outer (outside) corner of the eye, an uncharacteristic oblique (slanted) almond shape results (almond-eye).

The true shape of the eye should never be evaluated from a distance, as trimming will make a too large eye appear smaller, or a small eye appear larger. Dark to blackish hair around the eyes occurs in certain bloodlines, making the eyes appear larger than they are. Close examination reveals the true shape of the eye.

The true circular shape of the eye is often best observed from the side as the depth of eye-set, hair accentuating the fill beneath the eye, plus the eyebrow, combine to create a somewhat oblique look; not to be confused with the undesirable "almond-eye."

Dark eye rims are desirable; however, the degree of early pigmentation depends greatly on the head color. Lighter shades of brown, or dogs having much white about the head (i.e., wide blazes, etc.), or half white to all white heads, may take as much as two years or more to fully pigment.

Eyes set too far apart usually indicate a too broad, or boney development of the skull, while eyes set too close to each other usually accompany the too narrow skull.

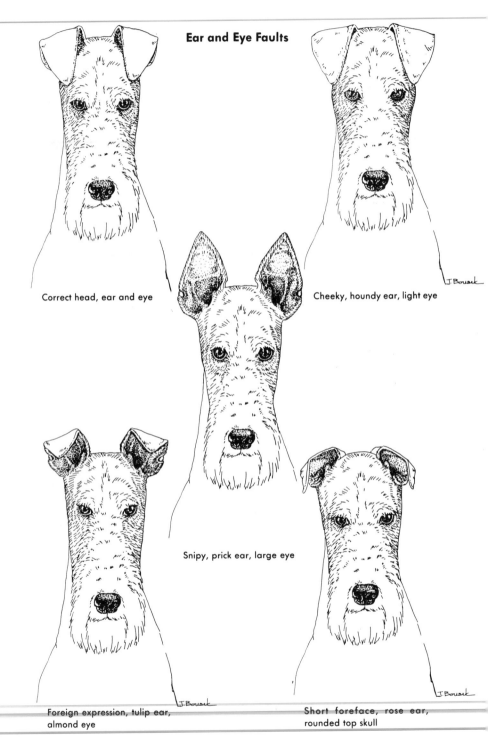

Ear and Eye Faults

Correct head, ear and eye

Cheeky, houndy ear, light eye

Snipy, prick ear, large eye

Foreign expression, tulip ear,
almond eye

Short foreface, rose ear,
rounded top skull

210

Ears

Should be small and V-shaped and of moderate thickness, the flaps neatly folded over and drooping forward close to the cheeks. The top line of the folded ear should be well above the level of the skull. A pendulous ear, hanging dead by the side of the head like a Hound's, is uncharacteristic of the terrier, while an ear which is semi-erect is still more undesirable.

Amplification

Equally important to correct Wire Fox Terrier expression are the ears, which exquisitely frame the face. Their crisp fold rises clearly above the level of the skull. The leather, slightly angled toward the side, falls abruptly; the tips, just below eye level, lie close to the cheeks. The leather should always cover the "flair" of the Zygomatic Arch, enhancing the lean appearance of the skull. When intensely alert, the tips align with the outer corner of the eye.

The ear should be small in relation to the Hound's; V-shaped as opposed to rounded; as if they are to fall, as the Standard requires "CLOSE TO THE CHEEKS," they must be of fair size. The leather should be weighty enough to keep the ears from flying; the tips must touch the skull.

The too high, too thin, too small ear, offering no protection to the ear canal and destroying proper expression, is totally incorrect (see Disqualifications).

NOTE: "Teenage" youngsters must have an ear that appears too large for the head IF THE EAR IS TO BE OF CORRECT SIZE IN ADULTHOOD, as the ear stops growing before the head.

Mouth

Both upper and lower jaws should be strong and muscular, the teeth as nearly as possible level and capable of closing together like a vise—the lower canines locking in front of the upper and the points of the upper incisors slightly overlapping the lower.

Amplification

The term "level bite" used in the Standard describes the smooth joining of the incisors. A finger passing across the line where the upper and lower incisors meet should not feel a protrusion of the upper or lower teeth but, on the contrary, a level or smooth occlusion and alignment in a closed position. alignment in a closed position.

The Standard does not mention dentition, fortunately, for Wires are notorious for breaking off or knocking out a tooth here and there. Therefore, missing teeth should not be penalized except in the most severe cases (see N.B.—Old Scars and Injuries). Nevertheless, breeders must be alert for any sign that their bloodlines are producing less than full dentition.

Neck

Should be clean, muscular, of fair length, free from throatiness and presenting a graceful curve when viewed from the side.

Amplification

The profile of the neck should show a slight crest at the top, then flow smoothly downwards, gradually widening with no break or "dent" into the withers. It must express strength and power, but must not be thick like a workhorse nor thin like a goose. When viewed from the top, the sides should flow smoothly into the shoulders, so that the outline resembles the graceful neck of a French wine bottle, NOT THE BULGY OUTLINE of a jug.

A short neck, or one that is too long (like a swan) is most undesirable; both are detrimental to a Terrier in combat, and if the rest of him is right, then both these necks will look dead wrong.

Since shoulder placement can make a short neck appear longer, or a long neck appear shorter, a truer estimate is derived by glancing at the line from under-jaw to brisket (underside).

The very worst possible neck is one shaped like the ewe (U-shaped).

Forequarters

Shoulders when viewed from the front should slope steeply downwards from their juncture, with the neck towards the points, which should be fine. When viewed from the side they should be long, well laid back, and should slope obliquely backwards from points to withers, which should always be clean-cut. A shoulder well laid back gives the long fore-hand which, in combination with a short back, is so desirable in terrier or hunter. Chest deep and not broad, a too narrow chest being almost as undesirable as a very broad one. Excessive depth of chest and brisket is an impediment to a terrier when going to ground. Viewed from any direction the legs should be straight, the bone of the forelegs strong right down to the feet. The elbows should hang perpendicular to the body, working free of the sides, carried straight through in traveling.

Amplification

Designed for efficient digging, the forequarters of the Wire have a shortened upper arm (humerus). The slightly lengthened shoulder blade (scapula) slants back from the "points," as nearly as possible at a 45° angle, enabling the farthest possible forward reach (an attribute of the "long fore-hand"). Shortening the upper-arm set the foreleg forwards, creating the distinctively straight "Terrier Front."

In profile, little of the brisket shows beyond the leading edge of the upper arm which, angling slightly back from shoulder points, joins the forearm and should never appear to be in advance of the body. The bone of the forearm should be sturdy yet not thick; the muscles, well developed, should not bulge.

A combination of good bone with well-developed muscles gives a rounded appearance to the foreleg.

The tendons should strongly knit into the wrist (carpus), which should be upright, neither slanted back nor bulging over (knuckled-over) the pastern, which should be short and perfectly upright, the bones sturdy enough to match the strength of the upper leg, not "falling away quickly" (narrowing abruptly) below the wrist.

Viewed from the top, shoulders should be clean with no bulging of bone or muscle, the crests set rather close together yet not too close (tied) nor too far apart (out at the shoulder). On the correct sized adult, two slender fingers' width between is about right. The very worst form of shoulder, no matter how well laid back, is short, thick, and wide apart at the crest, causing the front to appear "loaded" and usually accompanies the too short leg.

Any departure from the correct "Terrier Front" is objectionable; the greater the departure the greater the objection.

NOTE: Do not confuse the Standard's use of the term "steeply" with an upright shoulder placement, which is at fault.

Body

The back should be short and level with no appearance of slackness— the loins muscular and very slightly arched. The brisket should be deep, the front ribs moderately arched, and the back ribs deep, and well sprung. The term "slackness" is applied both to the portion of the back immediately behind the withers when it shows any tendency to dip, and also the flanks when there is too much space between the back ribs and hipbone. When there is little space between the ribs and hips, the dog is said to be "short in couplings," "short-coupled," or "well-ribbed-up." A terrier can scarcely be too short in back, provided he has sufficient length of neck and liberty of movement. The bitch may be slightly longer in couplings than the dog.

Amplification

Viewed from above, the foreribs should never be wider, at their widest part, than the forequarters. The "spring" (width) of back ribs should be clearly greater than the foreribs. The loin should not be narrow (wasp-waist) but there should be a slight, yet distinct, difference between its width and the spring of back ribs to indicate a very slight "waist." The hips are nearly as wide, but never wider than the widest spring of the back ribs (see Hindquarters).

In profile, there should be good depth through the loin; the "tuck-up" modest, yet defined. The tuck-up joins the hind leg in a graceful curve. The underline should drop gradually from the tuck-up to the brisket. A too steep drop indicating a too shallow loin, or excessive depth of brisket. The length of the underline, from hind leg to foreleg, is longer than the back (see Size and Weight).

The bottom of the chest (brisket) should align with the point of the elbow. If it is below the elbow the dog looks short on leg, while a chest line that is above is considered "shelly" and gives an uncharacteristic "leggy" appearance.

Forequarters, Standing . . .

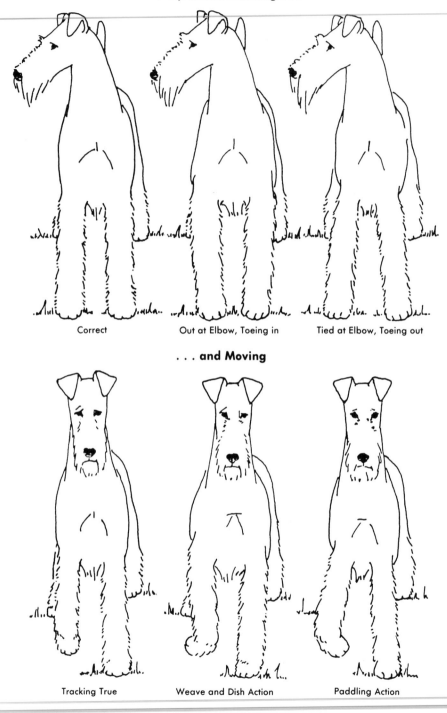

| Correct | Out at Elbow, Toeing in | Tied at Elbow, Toeing out |

. . . and Moving

| Tracking True | Weave and Dish Action | Paddling Action |

The topline of the back should appear level when the dog is standing or moving, the arch over the loin felt rather than seen. There should be no "falling away" in front of the tail (croup); neither should it rise causing the dog to "run downhill." Faults in the level of the back, disguised when the dog is standing, are usually discovered when he moves.

The term "deep," when applied to the ribs, means length. The fore ribs are always deeper than the back ribs and the bottom half should slope well in toward their center allowing room for the moving elbow.

The front ribs should not be too rounded; anything approaching a "barrel chest" would interfere with proper pendulum-like front movement.

NOTE: Immature youngsters may show a lack of depth and spring of rib without prejudice.

The "short back" of the Wire is created by the clearly defined rise of the withers, short couplings, and relatively high set-on tail. The same number of vertebrae are found in the long-backed Dachshund as in the short-backed Wire. Since vertebrae have their own genetic codes, attempting to breed shorter and shorter backs results in shorter and shorter necks, heads, legs, etc. Shortening the whole body, if the legs retain proper length, seriously inhibits movement, plus the whole dog is thrown out of balance. Hence the Standard's warning "provided he has sufficient length of neck and liberty of movement" to which should be appended . . . and length of leg, head, etc. Breeding for extremes destroys the characteristic balance of the Wire.

Hindquarters

Should be strong and muscular, quite free from droop or crouch; the thighs long and powerful; the stifles well curved and turned neither in nor out; the hock joints well bent and near the ground; the hocks perfectly upright and parallel with each other when viewed from behind. The worst possible form of hindquarters consists of a short second-thigh and a straight stifle, a combination which causes the hind legs to act as props rather than instruments of propulsion. The hind legs should be carried straight through in traveling.

Amplification

The terms "droop" and "crouch" are amply illustrated by the profile of the modern German Shepherd. The downwards "drooping" crouch, tail set low enough to drag the ground, and first and second thighs "crouching" at near 90° of angle, is the antithesis of correct Wire Fox Terrier hindquarters. On the Wire, the pelvic slope is elevated, positioning the sacral vertebrae closer to horizontal, creating the level croup, and placing the tail "on top" of the back, well forward of the buttocks. The elevated croup (pelvis) permits a long first and second thigh. The rear pastern is short and perfectly upright when the dog stands in show position. This short pastern places the hock near the ground (hocks well-let-down), and straightens the angle between first and second thigh creating moderate angulation.

Hindquarters, Standing . . .

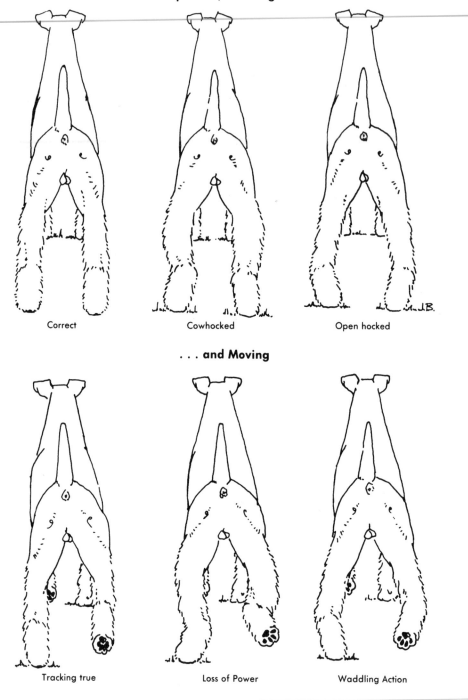

Correct   Cowhocked   Open hocked

. . . and Moving

Tracking true   Loss of Power   Waddling Action

First and second thighs should, as nearly as possible, be of equal length. They join at the stifle, where the second thigh slants backwards to meet the hock joint (tarsus), creating the desired "turn of stifle." The turn of stifle should be, visibly, well below the tuck-up. Over-angulation, occurring when the second thigh is too long, is a weakness, throwing the rear assembly out of natural balance. When extreme, the dog will stand with his foot well in advance of the hock (sickle-hocked) or may stand cow-hocked. Sickle and cow hocks are as objectionable as the too short second thigh, producing the totally devoid of angulation, straight stifled, stilty hocked assembly mentioned in the Standard.

From the rear, the croup is clearly seen to be narrower than the hips, at the joint. The indentation between croup and hip is allowed to fill with hair to form a pleasing line. The hips should be as wide as the full spring of the back ribs, making the dog wider behind than his moderately narrow front (see General Appearance). When the spring of rib and width of hips do not nearly match, either the dog has insufficient spring of rib or his hips are too broad. Comparison is best viewed from the top and it should be remembered that the Wire must be able to fit into a fox's hole.

The muscles of the upper thighs, both inner and outer, show greater development than those of the lower. Nevertheless, the lower thighs should be strongly muscled, with the inside having a little "egg."

In motion the "snatch of hocks" lifts the foot in such a manner that the pads are quickly visible.

Feet

Should be round, compact, and not large—the pads tough and well cushioned, and the toes moderately arched and turned neither in nor out. A terrier with good-shaped forelegs and feet will wear his nails down short by contact with the road surface, the weight of the body being evenly distributed between the toe pads and the heels.

Amplification

The feet should be small, the pads fitting tightly together. Hind feet are never as round as the front.

A foot whose center toes are appreciably longer than the outer, narrowing and flattening the foot (hare-foot) is uncharacteristic of the Wire. Splay feet (toes spread apart) and paper-feet (extremely thin pads) should be faulted. Paper-feet, an inherited defect, is the worst of the two. Excessive hair allowed to build up between the pads is a common cause of splayed feet. The hair should be trimmed from between the pads at regular intervals.

NOTE: Judges should check the correctness of the feet.

Tail

Should be set on rather high and carried gaily but not curled. It should be of good strength and substance and of fair length—a three-quarters dock is about right—since it affords the only safe grip when handling working terriers. A very short tail is suitable neither for work nor show.

Amplification

The characteristic high set of the tail (high set-on) created by an elevated pelvic girdle (see Hindquarters) allows the buttocks to be clearly seen beyond the back of the tail. The tail should be strong and thick at the base, tapering toward the tip, and carried straight up, or just forward of the vertical. It is normally docked so the tip is aligned with the back of the head when the neck is raised.

The tail must not curl forward like a squirrel; nor should it be parallel or lie flat on the back. Youngsters whose bones have not settled may be forgiven a too forward carriage.

The too thin tail, lacking in substance and usually indicating lack of overall bone (pipe-stopper) is undesirable.

Coat

The best coats appear to be broken, the hairs having a tendency to twist, and are of dense, wiry texture—like coconut matting—the hairs growing so closely and strongly together that when parted with the fingers the skin cannot be seen. At the base of these stiff hairs is a shorter growth of finer and softer hair—termed the undercoat. The coat on the sides is never quite so hard as that on the back and quarters. Some of the hardest coats are "crinkly" or slightly waved, but a curly coat is very objectionable. The hair on the upper and lower jaws should be crisp and only sufficiently long to impart an appearance of strength to the foreface. The hair on the forelegs should also be dense and crisp. The coat should average in length from ¾ to 1 inch on shoulders and neck, lengthening to 1½ inches on withers, back, ribs, and quarters. These measurements are given rather as a guide to exhibitors than as an infallible rule, since the length of coat depends on the climate, seasons and individual animal. The judge must form his own opinion as to what constitutes a "sufficient" coat on the day.

Amplification

The outer "jacket" must have a hard (harsh) and "wiry" feel—the harder the better. The best coats, called "pinwire," prickle the fingers. The hard, outer coat is dirt and weather resistant; the undercoat, soft and oily, serves as insulation. This combination of hard, thick, closely-knit hair with dense oily undercoat, sheds water. As the coat tends toward maximum length, color fades, and it softens preparing to "blow" (die). The blown coat is normally "stripped" (plucked) to be replaced by new, hard hair a few weeks later. The newer the coat, the deeper the color and harder the texture. Judges should familiarize themselves with the texture and color changes of varying lengths of coat. Any dog whose color is perfectly even, especially on head, neck, and shoulders (areas most frequently worked) should be checked for foreign substances in the coat. Dogs whose coat is so long or so short—or scanty—that texture cannot be fairly determined, should be penalized; while dogs with soft and silky coats, uncharacteristic of the Wire, should be severely penalized.

Facial hair should complement the head and along with whiskers should never be so full as to make the head appear "blocky" or flared at the nose. Beard hair, longest at the point of the chin, diminishes in length to disappear at the corners of the mouth, to show the strength of the lower jaw. When combed forward, the beard should show beyond the forward line of the whiskers. If the whiskers are longer, or heavier than the beard, the head looks "chopped off" and the underjaw appears weak. In profile whiskers and beard—combed straight forward—must neither overstate nor understate the head length.

Furnishings (leg har), hard and dense, should be trimmed to complement the shape of the legs—fullness achieved through density, not length. The too long, too full furnishing would not last a day in the field. Soft, cottony furnishings usually indicate a softer than desired coat.

NOTE: Judges should make allowance for climatic conditions. No judge would expect full, prime coats on dogs panting in 100° summer weather; neither should they expect dogs living in dry desert-like conditions to grow the same coat as dogs from areas of high humidity. Even during winter months the climate will differ from coast to coast and from border to border.

Color

White should predominate; brindle, red, liver or slaty blue are objectionable. Otherwise, color is of little or no importance.

Amplification

The Wire Fox Terrier must never be mistaken for the fox. In the field, deep hound-like markings with plenty of white quickly identify DOG. Markings, purely cosmetic, often creating an enhancing or detracting optical illusion, should be ignored when making an evaluation.

"Brindle" means distinctly striped, as brown hairs are frequently distributed through the black, with some bloodlines tending towards deep mahogany in adulthood. Ticking and the rare black heads characteristic of certain bloodlines are perfectly permissible.

Weight and Size

Bone and strength in a small compass are essential, but this must not be taken to mean that a terrier should be "cloddy" or in any way coarse—speed and endurance being requisite as well as power. The terrier must on no account be leggy, nor must he be too short on the leg. He should stand like a cleverly-made, short-backed hunter, covering a lot of ground. According to present-day requirements, a full-sized, well-balanced dog should not exceed 15½ inches at the withers—the bitch being proportion-

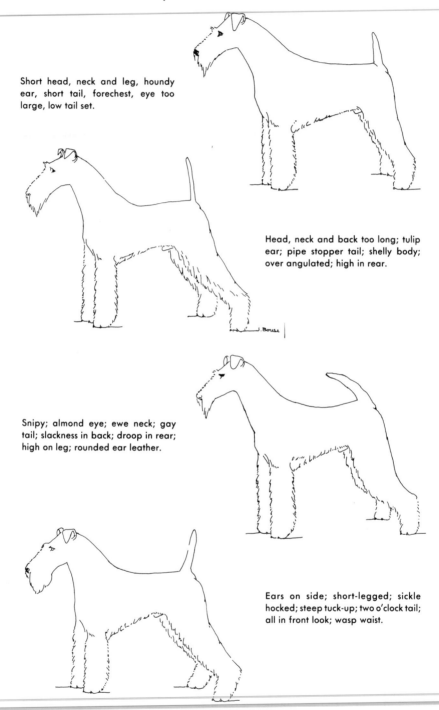

Short head, neck and leg, houndy ear, short tail, forechest, eye too large, low tail set.

Head, neck and back too long; tulip ear; pipe stopper tail; shelly body; over angulated; high in rear.

J. Bouse

Snipy; almond eye; ewe neck; gay tail; slackness in back; droop in rear; high on leg; rounded ear leather.

Ears on side; short-legged; sickle hocked; steep tuck-up; two o'clock tail; all in front look; wasp waist.

ately lower—nor should the length of back from withers to root of tail exceed 12 inches, while to maintain the relative proportions, the head—as before mentioned—should not exceed 7¼ inches or be less than 7 inches. A dog with these measurements should scale 18 pounds in show condition—a bitch weighing some two pounds less—with a margin of one pound either way.

Amplification

The Wire Fox Terrier should have substance, yet be elegant and refined. A good example is the Welsh Terrier, whose weight of 20 pounds on a frame no higher than 15 inches, is two pounds heavier and ½ inch shorter than the Wire. The Welsh is clearly larger boned. This does not mean that the smaller boned Wire lacks strength. A steel cable, no bigger around than a finger, can support the weight of an elephant!

A clear image of the ideal Wire, in profile, is formed when measurements given by the Standard are compared each to the other. It quickly becomes obvious that two maximum lengths of head plus one inch equals his ideal height. Just as it becomes equally obvious that a dog whose head measures 7½ inches must be 16 inches tall to be in balance, while a head measuring 8 inches must belong to a dog 17 inches tall, and so on. Obviously a too long head indicates an over-sized dog or one that must be seriously out-of-balance; both conditions are most objectionable. The bitch should not exceed 15 inches at the withers, nor should the head exceed 7 inches.

As previously mentioned (see General Appearance), length equals height, the ideal being when the body fits into a perfect square. Although the forelegs fit inside the confines of this square, the natural stance (posture) of the Wire places the hind legs outside, with the tip of the toes touching the vertical line drawn from the point of the buttocks. When viewed thusly, two facts become apparent: first, since the Wire must not be too "low on leg" nor "too high," an equal division of height, one-half to foreleg and one-half to body, fulfills the desired proportions. Since the dog is deeper through the body at the chest than at the loin—and his withers, where measured, are higher than his back, loin and croup—the strength displayed by his hindquarters must balance his front, as a dog who looks "all-up-front" is sadly out of balance. Second, the topline of his back—12 inches maximum for this size—is seen to be visibly shorter than the line between foreleg and hindleg (underline). In his natural stance (see above), the area of ground "covered" (between forefeet and hindfeet) far exceeds the area of ground covered by the length of his back, thus obeying the command that he "stand like a cleverly-made" (agile), "short-backed hunter, covering a lot of ground."

The natural posture of the Wire should be evaluated with him STANDING ON THE GROUND! Tables should be used for grooming or for a judge's close examination ONLY. It is vital when judging to OBSERVE THE DOG AS A WHOLE and not as an aggregate of minutiae. Minor faults may and should be forgiven if the whole dog "pleases."

NOTE: Breeders should make every effort to familiarize themselves with their dog's faults. A FAULT UNKNOWN IS SELDOM CORRECTED.

Nose: White, cherry, or spotted to a considerable extent with either of these colors. Ears: prick, tulip, or rose. Mouth: much undershot or much overshot.

Amplification

Nose: "White" is devoid of pigmentation; the same pale pink as the skin, under the white hair.

"Cherry"—weakly pigmented; reddish or reddish-brown, roughly the same color as the skin under the brown hair.

"A Considerable Extent"—should be taken to mean any aggregate area greater than one-third (1/3) the total black.

Ears: "Prick"—perfectly upright from base to tip, like a Scottie.

"Tulip"—stands upright from the base for about one-half to two-thirds of its length; the top half or one-third of the leather bent forward, parallel with, or slightly toward, the head; the tip clearly visible well above the level of the skull. No part of the leather touches the head, i.e., the Collie and Shetland Sheepdog.

"Rose"—folds inward at its back lower edge (outer or outside edge). This fold, maintained with the ears alert, pulls the top edge (inner or inside edge) away from the skull towards the side, exposing the inside of the ear (burr) as in the English Bulldog and Whippet.

Mouth: "Undershot"—the lower jaw exceeds the length of the upper, causing the lower incisors to engage outside of the upper incisors.

"Overshot"—the upper jaw exceeds the length of the lower to such an extent that the upper incisors fit completely over the lower. Upper and lower incisors do not engage their surfaces (not to be confused with the "scissors bite" in which the surfaces of upper and lower incisors must engage).

"Much Under or Overshot"—Should be taken to mean any gap, in excess of 3/16th of an inch, between the engaging surfaces of the incisors.

N.B.: Old scars or injuries, the result of work or accident, should not be allowed to prejudice a terrier's chance in the show ring, unless they interfere with its movement or with its utility for work or stud.

5

Preparing for a Dog Show

ONCE YOU HAVE YOUR BITCH you are ready for the next step, starting her on the road to her show career and, perhaps, if you are lucky, your first champion. If your first puppy is registered when she comes to you, then the choice of a registered name has already been made. But, if you are to be given the privilege of registering your first puppy then you should give serious consideration to your "prefix." Select a prefix that has not been used before. While there is little to prevent anyone from "borrowing" the name of a former or present breeder, the confusion created for posterity is very damaging. In recent years, breeders, both in America and overseas, have usurped a prefix, formerly the mark of a deceased or inactive breeder, for their own use. While "carrying on the name" might have been interpreted as an act of homage, the result is very damaging to the credibility of the knowledge available to students of the two breeds. One idea that has found favor among breeders is an anagram consisting of some rearrangement of the first and last name of the breeder. One word of caution, if you have any future desire to register your prefix with the American Kennel Club, do not use the following words anywhere in your prefix: Smooth, Wire (or any homonyms, i.e., Wyre), Fox, or Terrier. The Kennel Club will not accept any prefix containing those words.

Your new puppy bitch will have one of two AKC registration certificates, an initial registration form which the breeder received when the litter was registered or an individual registration certificate if the puppy has already been named and registered. A puppy may be shown for thirty days with its litter number identification. Once the individual registration has been filed, the puppy may be shown under the name of the new owner "pending transfer." Once a dog is registered, its name and number stay with it for life.

The next step for the fledgling exhibitor is to find out if there is a local all-breed kennel club. You should attend several dog shows, and purchase catalogs. The catalogs will list the address of the Secretary of the show giving club, as well as other Fox Terrier breeders in the area. They will be glad to help you join their clubs. By becoming active, you will be made aware of the canine events that take place in your locale. There are basically three types of conformation contests, Matches (either "A," "B," or Fun) which do not provide any championship points; all-breed events which can offer championship points if the entry qualifies; and Specialty Shows which can offer championship points and may be held alone or in conjunction with an all-breed event. The number of exhibits required for various point levels is indicated on one of the early pages of a catalog of any all-breed show. The major deciding factor that contributes to the weight of a single point is the size of the entries for a breed in a region. Three-, four-and five-point shows are considered "majors" and a championship requires 15 points with at least two "major" wins under two different judges. It is not possible to gain more than five points at any single show. For example, you enter your puppy bitch who is now over six months (minimum age for a point show) and there are five other bitches exhibited in the regular classes. The total entry for regular class competition is six bitches and for the sake of this lesson, let's suppose there are two puppy bitches, and four bitches in the open class. The winner of the puppy class will compete with the winner of the open class for the award "Winners Bitch" which assigns the points from that show to that entry. If your puppy is fortunate to be selected "Winners Bitch" by the judge, then she will receive the bitch "points." Once again, the quantity of points won will vary from region to region of the country so be certain to check the front of the catalog for the scale of points by breed. After the Winners Bitch and the Winners Dog has been selected they will compete against each other along with any champions present for Best of Breed, Best of Opposite Sex to Best of Breed and Best of Winners. If you are fortunate once again and the judge decides that your puppy is the Best of Breed, the award of Best of Winners will automatically be won by your puppy as well. If, on this particular day, there were more dogs than bitches and it was a five-point show for dogs but only a two-pointer for bitches, and your puppy bitch beats the Winners Dog for Best of Winners, then your bitch will pick up the dog points, not to exceed five total points. The award Best of Breed can also swell the point total if the additional competition in the Best of Breed competition, when added to the dog or bitch points, would increase the total but still not exceed five points. If all this sounds confusing, here is how it would work at an actual show. We'll start with this terrific puppy you have entered. She is awarded Winners Bitch for two points. Her dog counterpart, the Winners Dog, earned three points and let's assume that there are two champions competing along with the Winners Dog and Winners Bitch for Best of Breed and the two champions are both dogs. Your entry is awarded Best of Winners and Best of Breed; she would be awarded the extra point for defeating the Winners Dog and, if we are still applying the minimum scale, she would pick up two additional points for defeating the two dog champions. One more clarification is needed. Points, once acquired, are kept. The Winners Dog does not lose the point to your bitch. There is a final point to be explained about POINTS. Supposing that your puppy is the only representative of her breed at the show. Unless disqualified for some severe reason, she will earn Winners Bitch, Best of Winners and Best of Breed by default, but not receive a single point. She will, however, represent her Breed in the Terrier group. If by some good fortune she wins the Terrier group, she will pick up the largest of the points awarded to any of the competing Terrier breeds. So, if your puppy was the only Smooth or Wire, but this particular day there was a five-point show for Cairns, and you won the group, you would be awarded five points. If your puppy was awarded five points in her breed and then goes on to win the group, no additional points can be earned. A championship certificate is awarded by AKC when the required 15 points have been earned including the two major wins.

A good source of dog show information is *Pure-Bred Dogs— American Kennel Gazette,* published by the American Kennel Club. The *Gazette* lists shows and superintendents who will send premium lists. Fill out the entry form, pay the fee, and good luck. Don't get discouraged.

Work with your puppy about 15 to 20 minutes each day. If you selected the right prospect, she will show herself off with a little control and encouragement from you.

Anyone who owns a purebred AKC registered dog that has not been surgically treated or altered can enter a dog in a dog show and exhibit his or her "special friend." The contestant must be at least six months old and possess no disqualifying faults. Chapter 4 describes the disqualifications and an explanation appears in the visual standard. If your Fox Terrier is unaltered and free of disqualifying faults, you may exhibit at any AKC show and at more than 15 regional Fox Terrier Specialty shows. However, it would be better to begin at one of the hundreds of fun and sanctioned matches that take place across the country every weekend. You are probably saying to yourself as you read this, and look at your Fox Terrier that "Mimi" is not a show dog, and you are most probably correct, but you will never know unless you try. All good breeders make decisions about selling or keeping this or that puppy and those decisions are wrong on occasion. You may own someone's most recent error in judgment. If the

Ch. Boarzell Brightest Star with her first litter. Ch. Sirius of Gayterry is in the center.

Ch. Downsbragh Two O'Clock Fox, with Robert Braithwaite, going Best Smooth at the AFTC 91st Specialty, September 22, 1950, in Westbury, Long Island, N.Y.

dog is not shown, it is lost to the breed forever. Thomas Gray wrote, "Full many a gem of purest ray serene, the dark unfathomed caves of oceans bear; full many a flower is born to blush unseen, and waste its sweetness on the desert air." Today, all across this world there are family pets that could be the equal to the greatest "Best in Show" dog. That dog could be yours. You'll never know unless you try, and starting is easy.

Exhibiting dogs began in the middle of the 19th century in England and America. It was and is a sport, a competition to promote improvement in each breed, and to preserve the individuality of each breed. To this end, dog shows serve their purpose. Dog shows also provide opportunities for exhibitors from diverse areas to exchange ideas and compare notes.

The early books on Fox Terriers were written, for the most part, by Smooth people. Lee, Dalziel, Redmond, Bruce, Castles and Marples are examples. However, later scribes were predominantly Wire authorities who wrote about Smooths as an afterthought. I have attempted to strike a more balanced presentation between the two breeds. Silvernail, Williams, Skelly and Ackerman were all Wire exhibitors and their works gave little space to preparing a Smooth for the show ring. Preparation of the Wire received significant attention and today a marvelous booklet prepared by Arden Ross titled *Grooming the Broken Coated Terrier* is available from the Secretary of the American Fox Terrier Club. It provides detailed, illustrated steps that I could not improve upon but I know of no comparable Smooth material. Mrs. Ross has graciously granted me permission to print excerpts from that fine work for this book.

In attempting to provide Smooth grooming information, it seemed propitious to take advantage of the talent and experience of Winnie Stout who has bred, trimmed and exhibited her own Smooths for 25 years.

TRIMMING THE WIRE FOX TERRIER

by Arden M. Ross

"Oh what a miserable mess we make when first we practice to partake." That statement sums up all of the comments and advice I have received about grooming Wires from the most accomplished of Wire handlers!. Whether you wish to compete at the highest level of competition or just want your pet to "look like a Wire," the early learning curve is identical.

STRIP (stripping): Stripping is pulling the hair out completely from the skin surface. The hair is NOT cut, but is pulled out much as a person will pull out those first few gray hairs.

STRIP OUT: This is stripping the animal down to its bare skin, or as nearly so as possible. Here the object is to entirely remove the old coat so a new, fresh coat may grow in its place.

FINE (finely): Designates a very close, short hair. This hair lays flat against the skin and is NOT THICK. It is also completely free from undercoat. Generally it is encouraged to grow by taking some and leaving some. This might also be described as a "thinning process." Fine hair is needed on the skull, the sides of the neck nearest the head, underneath the throat, sometimes the chest and shoulder areas. With the cheeks "very finely" stripped the skin is just barely covered with a fine layer of hair; so close does it lay to the skin, and so short, that it is almost impossible to lift it with your fingers and grasp it.

FINE STRIPPING: I associate the art of "fine stripping" with the use of stripping knives. Here specific areas are stripped down very finely, or close to the skin, but allowing the short hair to remain. There are, of course, varying degrees of fine stripping, and it is all to achieve varying lengths of short, close hair. For example, a good clean shoulder is stripped fairly fine, whereas a heavy or "loaded" shoulder is stripped very fine.

PLUCKING: Essentially plucking is just another word for stripping, but the word "pluck" is so descriptive that I use it to designate pulling small groups of hair. Suppose you are preparing your dog for some weekend shows. In his final "at home" session, if a little clump of hair in the middle of his back persists in sticking up so that the outline is distorted, you reach over, lift up the offending hairs and "pluck" them out! I also associate this word with the use of thumb and forefinger in removing hair. I may "strip" adults, but I invariably "pluck" young puppies. Upon occasion we may "pluck" with the knife . . . usually live hair that our fingers are just not tough enough to remove.

BLENDING: The hair on the Wire in show condition is many different lengths. The fine hair on the skull, the full hair on the muzzle, the short hair on the shoulders, the lush fullness of leg furnishings are just some examples. All this must be "blended" together so that there is no severe line of demarcation. Blending allows longer and shorter hairs to "intermingle." It takes practice, but our object is to have the long and short hair "blend" to form a smooth transition. We don't want "stair steps"!

TRIMMING: Trimming is nothing more than the judicious use of the above methods to achieve a "finished" product . . . a dog ready to be shown! This is not your initial stripping out, but a careful removal of hair designed to produce the symmetry of a well-fitting "jacket." Symmetry is, indeed, the key word. The coat molds itself to the contours of the dog's body . . . the whole to present a smooth, pleasing appearance with no one portion of the coat calling undue attention to itself. Trimming might easily be called "high styling" like a woman's hairstyle. Coat should "complement" a dog, not detract from it.

PUT DOWN: In grooming, preparing the wire coat is "putting the dog down."

IN THE ROUGH: A dog is "in the rough" when his coat is grown out and left in long, shaggy condition. This is the direct opposite of "putting down" a dog.

Having read this far, you no doubt imagine you are ready to start stripping your dog. But No! First you must learn to properly brush and comb him! Why else do you suppose that I listed two brushes and a comb as necessities? Here we deal with the dog "in the rough," as this is how you will start.

With the slicker brush, start brushing your dog. Remember the slicker is very sharp, so care must be taken NOT to allow the wire bristles to come in contact with your dog's skin. This is the only time you will brush the body coat in the wrong direction. Our object now is not to form the coat, but simply to prepare it for pulling. So anything goes! We first brush in the proper direction (as the coat grows), and we brush the dog all over. We hold the brush fairly loose, and rely on repetition rather than strength to brush through. As we brush, the hair comes out in great quantities, mostly the soft undercoat, and our brush very quickly becomes clogged with hair. Remove the hair from the brush frequently, as it cannot do its job with the bristles full. After you are satisfied that you have gotten the coat as well brushed as you can in this manner, go over the whole body again. Always do the leg furnishings last as they are more difficult to do properly. This time brush the "wrong way" of the natural lay of the coat. When brushing the wrong way, use an upward motion. This helps to separate the hair, remove the tangles and prevents the brush from coming in contact with the dog's skin. The skin will be exposed at this time by the backward brushing of the hair. As you come to individual tangles, brush the wrong way for a while and then reverse the process, brushing the right way. You will be surprised at how nicely the slicker removes tangles. Always remember to hold your brush loosely as you are trying to separate this hair; do not "yank" it out with your brush. After you have removed as many mats and tangles as possible, run the coarse end of a comb through the dog's coat where you have brushed, again using a light touch. Unlike the position of the stripping knife, hold the comb at an angle roughly paralleling the dog's body. This prevents the sharp teeth of the comb from cutting the dog. By holding the comb loosely, it can twist out of your hand if you hit a tangle. Our object is not really to drop our comb, and with a little practice you will soon develop the knack of holding it "just tight enough." When you hit the inevitable tangle, change the position of your comb. You will point it at the dog! Here you are using the front tooth (still the coarse end) to separate the tangle. Insert the front tooth of the comb into a few hairs; repeat as often as necessary, working down towards the root of the tangle as you unravel it. When you have the tangle nicely worked out, run the comb through the worked-out tangle area in the usual manner. The comb should pass through the worked-out tangle with little or no pulling. If it does not, you have not worked out the tangle and you must use the front tooth again until you do. When I specify "front tooth," this is the one you will be working with, but the second and possibly the third tooth will more than likely become involved. The important thing is to remove the tangles and mats as painlessly as possible, and with as little loss of hair as possible. You want to be able to control the hair that is pulled; not just tear it out indiscriminately. Occasionally you may revert to the slicker brush to remove little tangles, or to loosen big ones. Use the brush and comb, one after the other to get the coat free of mats and tangles. Now you are ready to start combing and brushing the furnishings.

Furnishings take a very, very long time to grow. When we start out with a puppy, the "puppy" is usually about two years old before it has the proper wealth of furnishings. Much depends upon the texture of the leg hair. The softer the hair . . . the more luxuriant the dog's furnishings . . . BUT, the more it tangles and mats. The harder the hair on the legs, the more difficult it is to attain proper length and fullness. BUT, there is less matting and tangles. The furnishings are encouraged to be softer than the body coat, and indeed, as a general rule they are naturally of a different and less harsh texture. The whiskers, beard and full leg hair are what gives the Wire his distinctive appearance. If it were not for these qualities, he would simply look like a harsh-coated Smooth.

We can, literally, make or break a Wire's appearance by having too little or too much furnishings. We can definitely make our dog look like he is out at the elbow, cow-hocked or toeing-in (or out) by incorrect trimming of his furnishings. It is obvious that the furnishings are a very important part of our dog's coat, and in order to trim them correctly, we need a goodly amount to work with. Whereas you can always take some off, you can never put on hair that is not there. In view of all this, very special care of furnishings must be taken at all times. Combing and brushing this "all important hair" must be done carefully so as to avoid taking out any. There is nothing so heartbreaking as having a hole in your dog's furnishings. Nothing can be done to disguise it, although it is sometimes possible to straighten it out. But here too, we lose much valuable hair in this process, and the dog appears "top-heavy," as taking down one leg necessitates taking down the other.

When handling the furnishings, BE CAREFUL . . . very careful!! Brushing the leg hair is done as on the body coat . . . first the slicker brush is used, but here we do more brushing outward and upward. Hopefully you will never allow your dog's leg hair to become badly matted. If this happens, you must plan on not showing until the hair grows in again. On extremely bad mats, it is sometimes necessary to cut some of the mat to work it out. We do not "cut the mat out"; what we do is to cut through the ends of the mat. This helps to release the hairs so that they may be unraveled.

Hold the slicker brush very lightly. After brushing a few strokes, look at your brush and see how much hair you are getting out. If it is more than a very few hairs, you are using too heavy a hand. Lighten your stroke and try again, rechecking your brush after a few strokes. Brush upward and outward, being extremely careful not to let the wire bristles touch the dog's skin. If you irritate the skin on the legs or feet, the dog will lick and/or chew it, eventually destroying all your efforts. Use the front teeth of your comb with your slickering to remove the tangles. Your object is to thoroughly brush and comb through the furnishings so that a comb may pass through all the furnishings without removing a single hair, or becoming caught in a single tangle while at the same time achieving full, fluffy leg furnishings with no holes in them. After all the tangles have been removed, use a palm brush, and still using a light touch, stroke the hair upward. This is to fluff the furnishings out. Now run your comb lightly downward all around each front leg. Your object is to arrange the hair in the pattern for a show coat. You may now observe how this leg hair lays and determine what needs to come off and what needs to remain . . . and how much of both. The hind legs are done in the same fashion, except that the front legs are somewhat like columns and the hind legs have curves and bends.

NOW YOU ARE READY TO START STRIPPING!

When working the dog's head, underneath his throat and the front of his chest, it is necessary to lift and turn the dog's head into various positions in order to "get at" various areas. This is done by grasping the dog by the muzzle. When doing so, it is extremely important to use a gentle light touch.

The muzzle should be supported by your hand, with any pressure coming from beneath the muzzle, which is the area of the underjaw. The fingers or thumb that wraps around the nasal area just lies there. No pressure should be applied in this area.

It is the dog's eye which separates skull from foreface. When viewing the head from the front, the line of the foreface from its junction with the skull is straight! This line extends from the outer corner of the eye in a straight line to the ends of the whiskers, which are brushed well forward.

The foreface should appear as a rectangle when viewed from any angle.

There are two trouble spots concerning proper lay of whiskers and beard. The stiff "guard whiskers" stand straight out from the side of the nose and front lip. You must cut these whiskers frequently. Part the whisker hair with your fingers until the guard hairs are exposed at their roots. With scissors, cut these hairs as close to the root as possible. BE VERY CAREFUL! Do not cut any of the precious face furnishings.

All alongside the lower lip the hair has a tendency to stick out and be "bunchy," especially where the upper canine tooth overlaps the lower lip. Simply pull out this bunchy hair and the beard will fall in a straight downward line. I've not instructed you to take only the longest hair, and a little at a time when doing the beard. If you have not learned to do that by now you had better start, because your trimming will not be right unless you do. YOU LEARN ONLY BY DOING!

Start stripping the neck area directly adjacent to the head. We are starting where we left off.

Although the illustrations have only one side, your dog has two sides, and this is important. Be sure and work on all sides of your dog, keeping in mind that what comes off one side has to come off the other as well. Like everything else, good grooming involves self discipline. I have formed a "pattern" of stripping that I feel facilitates my doing an even job. The work flows along as one part leads into another, and I don't find myself concentrating on one side only. I like to think of this as good grooming habits, rather than set pattern.

Here is a fairly workable pattern.

When working on the head, leave the area underneath the underjaw and throat until last. This is adjacent to and includes the beard. This can be nicely worked into the upper throat. Then do the top of the neck adjoining the back of the skull; and the sides of the neck in back of and under the ears. Now, take off the top of the neck all the way down to the withers, and do both sides of the neck down to the front of the shoulders. Leave the lower throat area. This is incorporated into the front of the chest (brisket) which is done at the same time as the shoulders and withers.

As you start on the neck you discover the first "cowlicks," also called "crowns," and artfully described as "swirls." Here is where the hair grows in circles and upwards and downwards side by side!

The hair on the side of the upper neck grows down. The hair on the side of the upper throat grows up . . . and the twain must meet! Later we will do some interesting things with these junctions, but right now one of them presents a problem. This is the crown found slightly behind the line of the ear. Where the lower portion of the ear attaches to the dog's head is the "meeting place" of upward and downward growing hair, but about 1/2 to one inch down this line is a spot where the hair grows down from the top of the neck and swirls to meet hair growing, not only up from the throat, but forward towards the head! With a dog "in the rough," this is not much trouble now, but wait until we start our "fine trimming." You must pull the way the hair grows, and I generally wind up pulling this area by hand as I am able to pull against my thumb for the upward parts, and against my finger for the downward areas. For purposes of identification, UP is towards the head, and towards the top of the dog; DOWN is towards the tail, and towards the bottom or feet of the dog.

Strip underneath the jaw and work right into the upper throat area. Hold your dog with his nose pointing up. This is very tiring to the dog, but more so to your arm. I usually wind up with my left hand (supporting the dog's muzzle) in a "Statue of Liberty" position, while kneeling on the floor. Eventually, change position to work on the poll (where the neck joins the skull), coming down behind the ears to meet the sides of the upper throat. Fortunately, the sides of the upper throat can be worked from a standing position. When working on the upper sides of the neck, grasp a large fold of skin on the opposite side, but in the same area of the neck, to hold the skin firm. When working on the poll, stand behind the dog, hold him by the muzzle, and gently pull his nose downward. This tightens the skin at the poll. When working on the side of the upper throat and neck, around the "crown" area, hold the dog's muzzle, and point his nose away from the side you are working on.

As you work down the top of the neck, keep the skin taut by pushing against it, or by grasping a fold of skin. As you work on the lower sides of the neck you may tighten the skin by grasping a fold at the top of the neck. This is also done when stripping the shoulders. Here you grasp skin at the withers.

The lower shoulder should be stripped DOWNWARD. Even though the hair on the shoulders prefers to grow towards the body, by constantly stripping it DOWNWARD, we can train it to grow DOWNWARD so it will blend into the furnishings more readily.

At the front of the chest, or brisket, hair grows in all possible directions at once. The hair grows from the upper throat downward, at the same time it fans out to meet the sides of the upper and lower neck, also the lower shoulders. Where the throat area meets the chest area, this fanlike shape is particularly noticeable. All this hair should be stripped in the direction it grows! In the center, where the brisket hair meets the throat hair, lies another "crown," and leading from this "crown," downwards, is a meeting line where the right and left side grow towards each other. The front of the forelegs has a "crown" on each leg (see illustrations). You can see that when we do our fine trimming we are going to have a devil of a time getting all this to present a smooth unbroken line. Right now you are only interested in removing a long, blown coat. If your dog's coat is thoroughly blown, these trouble areas should not present much of a problem now, as the hair will almost fall out on its own. But if your dog's coat is still rooted firmly, he will suffer some discomfort when you pull these areas. There ARE some tender places here, but if you are successful in pulling the MANY WAYS the hair grows, the discomfort will be kept at a minimum.

To me the hardest part of trimming concerns the head and legs. So let's see what we can do with the legs.

First get the dog to STAND CORRECTLY. As the grooming session progresses in length of time, a dog gets tired and starts letting down. You cannot trim his legs and feet correctly if he is standing down on his pasterns, or all spraddled out, so hoist him up! In doing so, he will, since he's getting tired, probably hang in the loop. Just be sure the loop is not too tight. Many dogs will put up a terrible battle, which is one reason table training should begin in puppyhood. CORRECT TRIMMING NEEDS CORRECT POSTURE, not just for the legs and feet, but for the neck, shoulder area, levelness of the back, and correct underline.

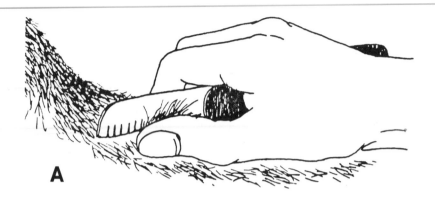

A

This drawing shows how the hair is to be grasped and pulled, using arm and shoulder action rather than twisting the wrist.

B

Hold the the skin firmly, stretching the skin in the opposite direction to the way we are pulling. We want the skin firm and close to the dog's body so that when we pull the hair, it comes out without lifting the dog's skin.

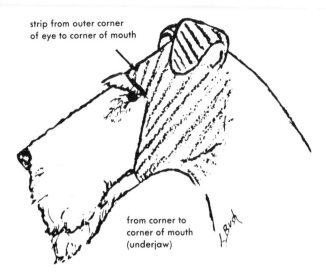

strip from outer corner of eye to corner of mouth

from corner to corner of mouth (underjaw)

". . . strip from outer corner of eye to corner of mouth (shaded area) . . ."

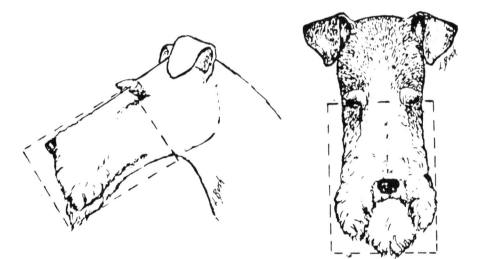

". . . foreface a rectangle viewed from any angle . . ."

235

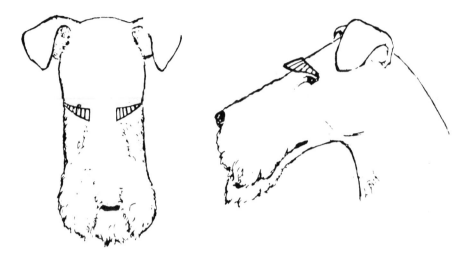

". . . eyebrows—top view and side view . . ."

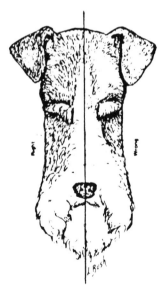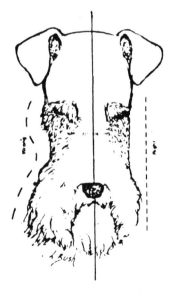

". . . fill in with hair (left) . . . do not hollow out (right) . . ."

". . . the foreface does not pooche out, nor dish in . . ."

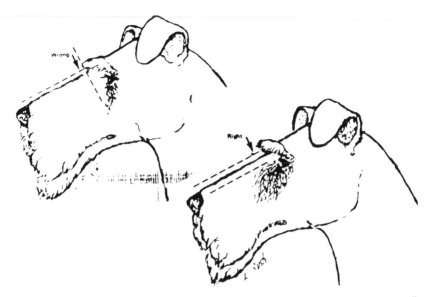

"...the plane of this area is NOT vertical (above) to the horizontal plane of the bridge of the nose..."

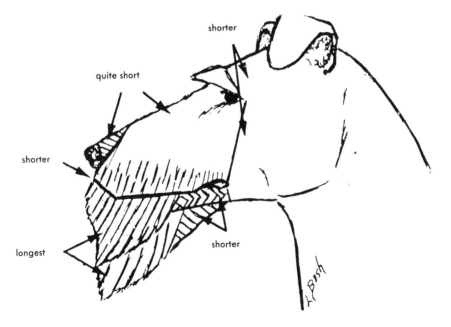

shorter

quite short

shorter

shorter

longest

shorter

"... blend the long and short hairs ..."

237

Now, with your dog standing properly, start at the top and work down. Standing at the side of the dog, gaze upon the line that runs from the point of the shoulder down to the toes. The front of the foreleg, where it joins the body, must never appear to extend beyond the point of the shoulder. Ideally, the Fox Terrier should stand just slightly over his front legs, but many do not generally due to upright shoulders. So we want to produce a comparatively straight line from the point of the shoulder to the toes. If the dog has a well-developed upper forearm, the area where the upper forearm joins the brisket is trimmed very fine and short. But we will not trim it finer nor shorter than the hair of the brisket and lower shoulder. The more your dog's legs extend towards the front of his body, the shorter and closer the hair of the upper forearm must be trimmed. Although you are looking at this line from the side, we are going to work on the upper forearm, so step to the front, please, to trim. You will LIFT the hair, pull a VERY FEW, comb everything back in place, then step to the side to view what you have done. When you have gotten this line to your satisfaction, you progress to yet another imaginary line.

Now step to the front of the dog, and the line will be from the lower shoulder to the toes. To gain the proper perspective, grasp the dog by the muzzle and lift his head. But DON'T crank your dog's head up at an angle that throws him off balance! This makes him crouch down behind, and either spraddle, or turn his elbows out in front.

Because a dog is composed of bone and muscle, there are "hills" and "valleys" all over his body. One of these valleys occurs in the area of the elbow, so that the line from the lower shoulder tucks in where the forearm joins. We don't want a dip in this line, so we fill in with hair. This is a bit tricky as this hair must ultimately be short, but dense. There may be a beautiful line while the dog is standing still, but the moment he starts gaiting, the movement of the leg, back, makes the skin wrinkle, the hair stands out, and our dog looks marvelously "out at the elbow." Now, we must, by repeatedly trimming, arrive at the magic stage of just enough, but not too much.

Trimming the point of the elbow involves holding your dog's foreleg, below the upper front forearm, and pulling it out away from the body, while you twist it slightly so that the point of the elbow faces you. Stand well behind your dog's shoulder, and face the same way he is. If you stand your dog at a bit of an angle (from the left side of the dog, his forelegs towards the right edge of the table, his hindquarters towards the left edge) it helps. Some dogs have more mobility than others. If your dog's legs don't bend that way, you are just going to have to crawl around between them in order to trim in these places, and the more upright in shoulder, the less mobility as a rule. It is an unfortunate fact that the majority of Wires are upright in shoulder. Some to a lesser degree and some to a greater. This causes trouble in attaining the correct look through the brisket and forearm area, but will lend a lovely illusion in other areas.

238

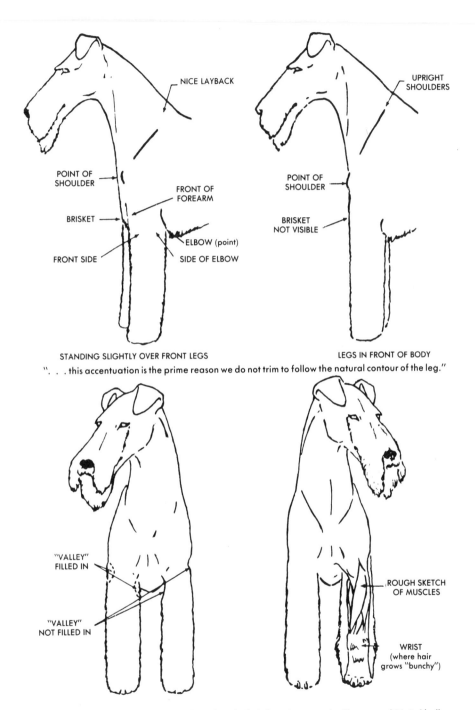

NICE LAYBACK

UPRIGHT SHOULDERS

POINT OF SHOULDER

FRONT OF FOREARM

BRISKET

ELBOW (point)

FRONT SIDE

SIDE OF ELBOW

POINT OF SHOULDER

BRISKET NOT VISIBLE

STANDING SLIGHTLY OVER FRONT LEGS

LEGS IN FRONT OF BODY

". . . this accentuation is the prime reason we do not trim to follow the natural contour of the leg."

"VALLEY" FILLED IN

"VALLEY" NOT FILLED IN

ROUGH SKETCH OF MUSCLES

WRIST (where hair grows "bunchy")

. . . the object is to remove all the long, bunchy hair from between the Plantar and Digital balls, and from around the bottom edges. .

At this time we will trim the point and side of the elbow quite close. If our dog is long in body, we may want a greater wealth of furnishings to shorten him up, but first let's get the proper shape to them.

The side of the elbow should be trimmed so that it has a very faint "tucked in" appearance, from the SIDE only . . . VERY FAINT. This is when the dog is standing still, because when he is moving we don't want this hair making him look out at his elbows, AND, we are attempting to give the legs a rounded, or columnar look. The legs are not rectangular.

Now is the time to practice and experiment. Your dog is not going to a show this weekend, so be brave! Always remember to trim a bit, then stand back and study the overall picture. Be sure when you are doing furnishings to move your dog occasionally on lead, to see how your trimming is affecting his movement. If you do not have someone to move him for you, put him in the run, or anywhere that he will exercise and you can get a good view. When your dog is on the table, take time to step back, and I mean back, away from him in order to see the overall effect of what you have done.

The very first step is trimming the nails. If the nails are already quite short, file them back until just before reaching the quick. We don't want bleeding, unless absolutely necessary; that is, when the nails have been ignored too long. As long as you have the nippers and file out, do all four feet. Nails all neat? Fine! Now trim around the bottom of the feet, and in between the pads, with SCISSORS. Do this by holding the dog's foot and bending it back at the "wrist," so the bottom of the foot is visible. The dog's foot is a variation on the theme of the human hand. He walks on his toes, which structurally are our fingertips. Study the diagrams of the foot so you will know what I am saying. Trim all the hair out from between the plantar ball and the digital balls. DO NOT trim between the individual digital balls. DO trim the long, unsightly hair from AROUND, not between, the digital balls. Trim the hair on the edge of the back of the plantar ball, where the ball joins the skin of the pastern. DO NOT trim too far up. You are just neatening the foot. The object is to remove all the long, bunchy hair from between the plantar and digital balls, and from around the bottom edges of these so that the foot presents a clean, neat appearance. Also, great gobs of hair in this area will spread your dog's feet, and they should be COMPACT!

Comb the hair of the foot so it stands out away from the foot. If this long hair is combed straight down, towards the bottom of the foot, you are going to scissor hair that should NOT be scissored, and you will never get the proper shape to the foot!

Now trim around the outside of the foot . . . front and sides. In trimming this hair, we are still looking at the bottom of the dog's foot. Trim the hair at an angle so that when the foot is on the ground it presents a slight ball appearance, not a flat-footed look. To achieve this angle, the handle of

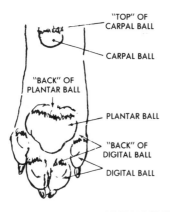

"TOP" OF CARPAL BALL

CARPAL BALL

"BACK" OF PLANTAR BALL

PLANTAR BALL

"BACK" OF DIGITAL BALL

DIGITAL BALL

DIAGRAMS OF FOOT

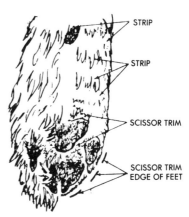

STRIP

STRIP

SCISSOR TRIM

SCISSOR TRIM EDGE OF FEET

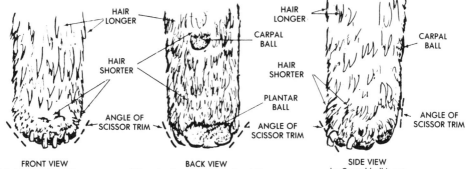

HAIR LONGER

HAIR SHORTER

ANGLE OF SCISSOR TRIM

CARPAL BALL

HAIR SHORTER

PLANTAR BALL

ANGLE OF SCISSOR TRIM

HAIR LONGER

CARPAL BALL

ANGLE OF SCISSOR TRIM

FRONT VIEW
Digital balls not readily seen

BACK VIEW
When dog is on toes, Carpal and Plantar easily seen from back.

SIDE VIEW
he Carpal ball is not seen from the side.

241

the scissors should be over the dog's pads, and blade inclined outward (away from the foot) and slightly downward. Actually, the blades of the scissors can be laid flat, so they are resting on the digital balls; now follow the incline of the digital ball towards its outside edge, and look. Using this angle of scissors, trim all the way around the sides and front of the foot. You have already trimmed the back of the foot when you trimmed the hair on the edge of the plantar ball. The feet are supposed to be ROUND, so trim them to accentuate this.

When the tops of the legs and the bottom of the feet are trimmed, we must now trim everything in between to match.

At this point trim the back of the leg, starting at the elbow where you left off. Trim a nice, straight line down to the carpal ball. Hold the dog's leg in the same position you did to trim the elbows. The hair has a bit of a tendency to swirl out to the side, more so on some dogs than others, so be sure to get a smooth line at the outer side of the back of the leg.

The hair surrounding the carpal ball is trimmed fairly short, especially on good-boned dogs. It is left longer on a smaller-boned dog. You may even want to trim so that the carpal ball is easily seen from the back, shorter at the "top" of the carpal ball, and the hair between the carpal and the plantar is trimmed to have enough "fill" so there is no dishing out in this area. Study the unbroken lines of correctly trimmed legs. THIS IS WHAT YOU ARE STRIVING FOR.

Remember that when you trim the sides of the leg you view it from the front, and you view from the side when trimming the front and back. REMEMBER . . . pull a little . . . brush and comb . . . view your work, and repeat as often as necessary.

The hair grows bunchy at the wrist, so blend this hair into the hair of the toes. In front, when viewed from the side, this bunchy wrist hair makes the dog look "buck kneed." When viewed from the front, when he is moving, this bunchy hair on the inside of the leg makes him look like he is traveling close in front. So we normally trim the hair on the inside of the leg fairly close THROUGH THE WRIST DOWN TO THE GROUND. The hair is left longer as it progresses UPWARD towards the upper forearm, and there is a "valley" where the forearm joins the body. This is filled in, as we are still trimming straight lines from top to bottom.

The body is probably the easiest part to strip, but even here we must also pay attention to what Nature is doing.

We start where we left off, where the withers join the back and where the shoulder blades join the body.

Draw an imaginary line as you reach the dog's chest. This line should start about two inches above the elbow and extend back to the flank area, or more rightly, the area of the tuck-up. Draw the line straight because you will leave the hair below this line so the hair can be blended and shaped to form the correct underline. Continue stripping both sides until you have it

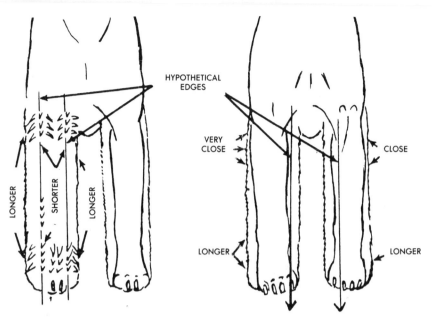

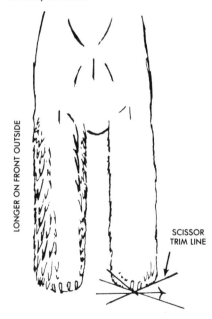

"... on a nice straight leg, your shortest hairs will be on this 'edge,' a trifle longer as you work toward your 'sides.'"

"... the 'toeing-in' dog is really 'pigeon-toed,' some to a greater and some to a lesser extent."

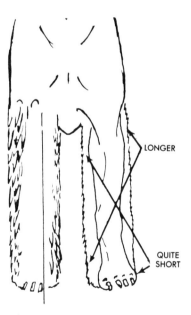

"... if our dog is simply 'moving in,' we need not trim as finely as when he is 'toeing-in' . . ."

"... we have illustrated corrective trimming for the dog that 'toes out.' The exact reverse of what we have just described must be effected."

all stripped even with that portion of the back you have done, and down to your imaginary line.

Now move back to your starting position (behind your dog) and strip the loin in front of the tail and the front of the tail. When stripping the tail, leave what almost amounts to a tassle on the tip of the tail. This looks pretty silly now, with the dog all stripped out, but there is a reason for it. The hair at the tip of the tail is very slow growing, and if you strip it all out, by the time your dog is ready to go into the ring, the tip is not going to have the length of hair it needs to balance the rest of the tail. The tip being narrower than the base, your dog's tail will look like it has been caught in a pencil sharpener . . . very undesirable!

Now do the back of the tail. Move to the side of your dog and stand with your back to his head. The hair on the back of the tail, and also the front, grows from the root up, towards and to the tip, so strip from the root up. Hold the tail gently, but firmly in an upright position, and bending over (sort of mildly standing on your head!) start pulling . . . BUT ONLY A FEW HAIRS AT A TIME! The back root of the tail is a very sensitive spot, and your dog is going to offer some objections. DO NOT allow him to crouch and hand up his tail. He must learn to stand up while you are working on his rear, but since the rear is so sensitive, pull as few hairs at a time as possible. By using the fingertips you will pull far less hair than with a knife. With the hair this long, it shouldn't be a problem at this stage. At the same time, to give your dog a rest, do the top of the hip. You will see that this hair, at the farthest point back, curves around under the back side of the tail. Strip this too, standing in back of your dog, and stripping it close. Strip right down (ONLY in the back) to the point of the buttocks. This is easy to recognize as there is a "crown" there. At this time DO NOT strip the rear end, itself, and although you are stripping the back of the hip area, DO NOT strip the hips themselves in this close manner.

We will now start to blend in two areas . . . the hips and the underline—hips first! The closeness of the stripping in this area will depend on how well developed your dog is. Some dogs are so well developed that this area is stripped as closely as the rest of the body. Others have a tendency to be very slender-hipped, and on these animals leave the hair progressively longer. Study the illustrations as this shows you the approximate area to blend. The hair, of course, is shorter at the top, same as the body coat, and progressively longer as it starts down the leg.

Before we do any more to the rear legs, let's get that underline! Normally, the bottom edge of the back ribs, where the belly starts, is the highest point of the STRAIGHT line that is the correct UNDERLINE. . . the elbow forms the lowest point of this line. I state "normally," as the immature dog, the "leggy" dog, and the "shelly" (bodied) dog, will all have their effect on how much hair to leave where. But let's get this hair off so we can see just how our dog is made.

At the same time we are blending the hips, we will strip the flank and tuck-up area. As we do the tuck-up, we will be forced to remove some hair from the hind leg, where it joins the flank. When working on the tuck-up, you will take a nice fold of skin higher up on the flank and pull the skin taut, as this area IS TENDER. Indeed, the portion where the hind leg joins the flank is only skin . . . a thin fold. The moment you stretch the skin to aid in stripping, you completely destroy the "line" of the "tuck-up." A most pertinent fact . . . remember it . . . as it will come into sad prominence later. At this time, to your amazement, you will find not only have you stripped the "tuck-up," but part of the belly as well. If the coat offers resistance, look for trouble from your dog.

Now get the hair off underneath those back ribs, as this truly starts the underline. As you work, pull straight down toward the floor, and progress toward the elbow, blending the hair left, shorter at the top and underneath toward the back ribs . . . longer at the bottom and toward the front legs. You must comb this hair continuously, lifting UP, pulling DOWN, combing it all back in place. By the time you have it well blended on the side, you should be left with a fringe underneath. Pull this a few hairs at a time with your fingers, your dog standing in a proper position. Start at the highest point of the underline (the back ribs) and pull this fringe, the longest hairs ONLY, progressing toward the front legs. Now comb it all in place, step back and view what you have done. Not proper yet? Pull some more; this underline really takes practice.

To complete this underline, between the front legs, step to the front of the dog, then back to his side, again and again, until the twain DO meet (underline front, underline side) is the best bet. REMEMBER, as your dog moves and shifts positions in the ring this hair between the front legs will be visible to the judge. Therefore, it is important that this line presents an UNBROKEN CONTINUATION of the angle to the very front of the dog.

The correct trim for your individual dog will depend on you. Since you're not vastly experienced, you must experiment with leaving more hair here, less hair there, until you have achieved the best look for YOUR animal. Please note the area between the ankle bones and Achilles tendon consists of little else but skin. Therefore, the hair is extremely slow to grow, and sparser than on the rest of the leg.

Start on the rear, another area where the hair grows in all possible directions at once. You've already trimmed in back of the "hips" down to the point of the buttocks, now take off all the hair in the "center," directly around the anus, and above and around the top of the scrotum. Since I strip my dog's scrotum, I do it too. HOWEVER, all dogs and many people prefer to clip this hair, and you may too. If you choose to clip, this may be left until later. Assume the same position you did to strip the back of the dog's tail, once again holding the tail firmly in an upright position. This holds the skin firm! Start at the area surrounding the scrotum and work up to the anus. As the dog becomes more and more restless, you can strip the inside and back of the first inner thigh. These areas are very tender. But your dog must learn to stand up while it's being done. But do take as few hairs at a time as possible.

The hair from the outside of the leg grows in to meet the hair growing from the inside of the leg. In this case it is very important NOT to allow the hair from the outside to grow too far towards the inside! If you do, this will make the dog look "dumpy" and a bit pear-shaped in the rear—definitely the wrong look. A rather neat trick is, using block chalk, draw a line from the outside edge of the root of the tail, through the center of the "crown" on the point of the buttocks, then extend this line (it's a bit of an angle) to the outside edge of the back of the leg. This, if done correctly, should bring you to the top of the bend caused by the second thigh! Now, still working on the back of the rear leg, remove the hair on that side of the line toward the inside of the leg. All the hair should now be off the rear, inside of the upper thigh, and the back of this portion to the "line."

Now shape the hair on the side of the line toward the outside of the leg, so there is fullness at the outside of the leg and the hair tapers to nothing at the line. Although this pulling is done from in back of the dog, you must step to the side of the leg you're working on, frequently, to be sure you are maintaining the proper outline. You will now come down the back edge of the leg, all the way to the hock. Be extremely careful not to remove too much hair from the outside edge, as this will dish the outline. However, you will discover, by standing at the side of your dog for viewing, that more hair should be removed from the edge of the inside of the leg! Just the edge mind you! These hairs tend to stick out and make the outline messy.

Now take the hair off the inside edge of the "cap" that forms the hock. Clean off an area about the size of the ball of your little finger and at the same time the top of the hock—NOT THE BACK of the hock.

While working on the back of these legs, we also trim on the sides, and this is done while you stand behind your dog. Do the outside first thigh to blend it with the hips, also the inside of the leg all the way down to the foot; start shaping the outside of the second thigh and the outside of the foot. Now is when you'd better have practiced using your left hand, as the outside of the left leg will be partially shaped by your left hand. Remember how I taught you to pull a few hairs by using a "rolling" motion of your thumb against your forefinger? We use this motion again! So your left hand will be using this motion on the left leg of the dog and your right hand will do the same to the right leg. The inside portions of the legs may be done as follows; if you are working on the inside of the left leg, stand on the right side of your dog. Lift the right leg UP. I lift the right leg with my left hand so that my right hand which is more dexterous is left free to strip. It is my earnest hope that during all of this you are combing and brushing these furnishings as you were taught to do on the forelegs. Here the principle

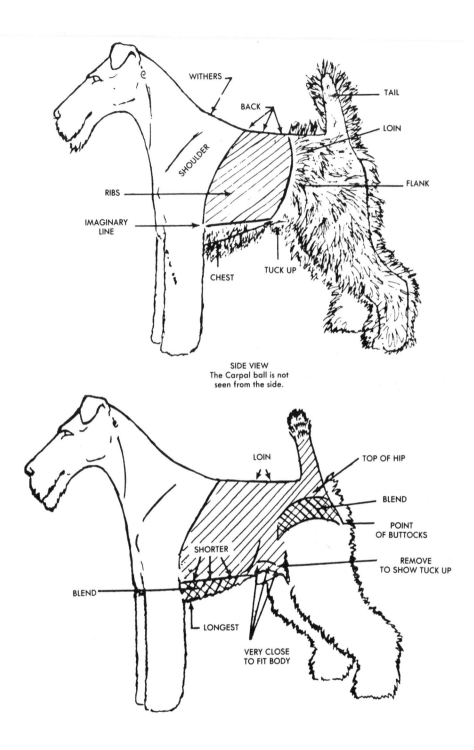

WITHERS

TAIL

BACK

LOIN

SHOULDER

FLANK

RIBS

IMAGINARY
LINE

CHEST

TUCK UP

SIDE VIEW
The Carpal ball is not
seen from the side.

LOIN

TOP OF HIP

BLEND

POINT
OF BUTTOCKS

SHORTER

REMOVE
TO SHOW TUCK UP

BLEND

LONGEST

VERY CLOSE
TO FIT BODY

247

applied is the same as the one we used to trim the inside of the front legs. Again we are looking for a straight vertical line. We even have the ankle joint, which presents the same bunch of hair the wrist joint did. Now, however, since this is the hind leg, we will concentrate our vertical line towards the back of the leg, and extend it from the end of the close-stripped area of the first thigh, to the ground! This is done with a medium or coarse stripping knife. If you have not progressed to mastery of the knife, then stand behind your dog and reaching between his hind legs you will use thumb and forefinger. Your right hand will strip the inside of the left leg and vice versa. Comb or brush the hair so it's standing straight out. Now, pulling only the longest hairs, make your vertical line.

Now you will be left with hair, which originates from the inside of the FRONT of the dog's leg, sticking out and spoiling the overall view of your line. Although this hair is worked on from the back, or the side (with the knife), it should be blended into the whole after shaping is done to the front of the leg.

These excerpts represent some of the useful material found in *Grooming The Broken Coated Terrier*. But there is much, much more. No Wire owner should be without it.

Ch. Sylair Special Edition, owned by Jean Heath and William H. Cosby, Jr., built an outstanding record as one of the top winners of the 1980s. An English import, he was campaigned fearlessly and is shown here winning the Terrier Group at Westminster 1987 under Mr. Glen Sommers, handler Clay Coady.

TRIMMING THE SMOOTH FOX TERRIER

by Winnie Stout

Contrary to public opinion in many quarters, the Smooth Fox Terrier must be trimmed to look its best. There are many ways to achieve the desired result, and this resume is aimed at the novice rather than the expert.

If a Smooth is to be kept strictly as a pet or working terrier, it is necessary only to brush him twice a week and to rake through the coat with a fine-toothed steel comb or stripping knife, or a slicker brush set with fine, angled steel pins that are available in many pet shops. This will keep dead hair from being shed around the house. A hot bath will loosen the coat and enable more hair to be removed if this is desired.

The amount of coat on a Smooth varies considerably in length and thickness, and even smoothness, depending on genetics and environment. The Standard says little about length, but states that the coat should be "smooth, hard, flat, dense and abundant." In practice, the coat is double, with a harsh outer jacket of guard hairs under and within which lies a softer undercoat. In tan marked dogs, this is usually lighter colored. Some Smooths have a very short, slick, double coat, while others carry a coat that is flat but of greater length, with busy breeching on the hindquarters, a plumed tail, and a veritable lion's mane. Such dogs must be kept in heated quarters during the winter and require more frequent grooming to look their best. By contrast, the same animal kept in a warm, dry climate may need little more than a touch-up if being shown regularly.

In order to present a Smooth at his best for show, the dog must be trimmed to enhance his outline. Most exhibitors today begin with a good pair of clippers—I use the Oster A5 or A2 with an 8½, 9 or 10 blade, and a 30 or 40 for the inside or ears and more delicate work. A good pair of barber shears and a pair of thinning shears are essential and should be the best available quality—purchase these at a dog show, pet supply dealer or through a catalog designed for the show exhibitor. They should be carbon steel and not stainless. I also use a Buck Lyons knife to rake the coat. These can be purchased through *Terrier Type*. A Magnet trimmer or a Real brand knife are also excellent for removing undercoat. These knives are used to pull out loose coat and scrape away excess undercoat. Another excellent tool is "The Stone," a black pumice-like substance. The stone can be purchased at the grooming-tool stalls at most shows. It can be used to strip or to sandpaper down the coat to any desired length. This takes a lot of time but is a very safe method as the hair is removed gradually and an attractive natural look is produced.

Position the dog on a grooming table in a well-lighted area and plug in your clippers. Using a medium blade, clean out all the hair under the tuck-up and inside the hind legs above the hocks, clipping any long loose hair away around testicles or vulva. On a male, clip the sheath. You will observe as you face the rear of the dog that there is a thick frill of hair on each quarter which grows inward, with a whorl or cowlick over each pelvic bone. Inside the thighs there is shorter hair which grows upward and outward to meet the exterior frill or breeching. Clip from the anus downward on each leg to a point just inside the hocks, removing only the inward, upward-growing layer. Now, with the dog's muzzle in one hand, clip the throat from a line beginning at the corner of the lip to the base of the ear and down to the breastbone. Clip very closely through the jaw and throat and taper off toward the breastbone for a more natural look. Finally, clip the outer side of the ear going with the lie of the hair. Switch to the 30 or 40 blade and clean out the inside of the ear. (If your dog has tiny ears and you have never trimmed him, do the inside only, leaving the hair on the outside until the effect of weightlessness has been assessed. Removing too much hair from a tiny ear can cause it to "fly.")

Using the straight shears, cut away the downward-growing frill on the neck from ear to shoulder blade. Standing behind the dog, start at the tail and clip a straight line from anus to hock on each quarter. Clip away the long hair at the back of the tail so that it tapers from a thick base to a finer tip. Now, with thinning shears, working with the lie of the hair, thin the hair on the cheeks, sides of neck and shoulders, and hindquarters to taper the cut edge into a smooth blend with the untrimmed portion. Work cautiously until you are familiar with your tools, to avoid gouging the coat. Rake out the cut hair with a comb or pin brush as you work, so you can see what you have accomplished. Shape the hair on the sides of the tail so that it resembles a tapered cone, thickest at the root.

Many Smooths have a thick ruff of hair over the withers and some also over the hips in front of the tail. This may be thinned cautiously with thinning shears. Brush the hair forward with one hand and take a little at a time from underneath until the desired result is achieved. Another method is to pull the hair out with thumb and knife, as you would with a broken-coated terrier, or to sandpaper it down with a stone or real sandpaper. When working with any dog that has a lighter-colored undercoat in an area you must trim, the best results are achieved by stripping. This will result in the area being covered with darker topcoat instead of pale undercoat. The hair on the shoulder blades should be thinned toward the elbow. Finally, go over the whole dog with your Lyon's comb to rake out any dead hair, working with the grain.

Mention must be made of the *bete noir* of Smooth breeders, the rough coat, an old legacy of common ancestry or cross-breeding with the Wire. These coats have heavy ripples from neck to tail. Best results are achieved from a combination of stripping and "stoning," although I know of one exhibitor who clips down the whole dog with a 4 or 7 blade four to six weeks before the show. Trimming then proceeds on a more or less normal course.

To successfully trim a Smooth Fox Terrier, you need (from left) a steel comb, wire slicker brush, electric clipper, barber shears, thinning shears and a selection of stripping knives. Shown here are the Buck Lyons, Magnet and Real models.

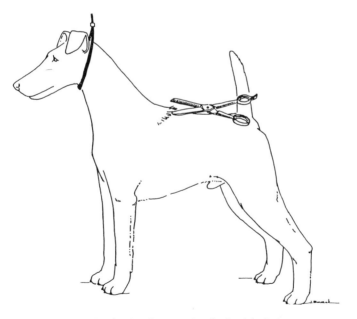

Using thinning shears against the lie of the hair.

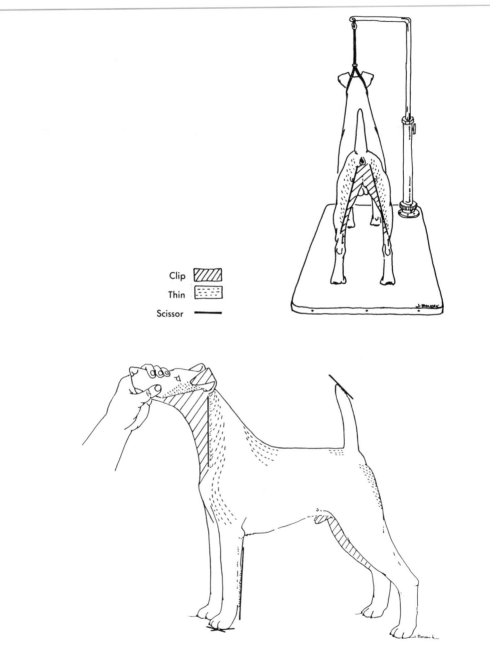

Clip ▨
Thin ⬚
Scissor ▬

Trimming the Smooth

The night before the show, bathe the dog, preferably with a shampoo designed for white coats. Next morning, go over him carefully, combing out dead hair, trimming whiskers, and tidying up the inevitable loose ends. Scissor the back of the front legs into a neat line and trim the hair from the edge of the pads. A dab of Brylcreem rubbed over the palms and then smoothed over the dog makes a nice finishing touch.

A few tips. If your dog has big ears, keeping them very closely trimmed will help. Scissor the hair on the edge of the ear as close as you can, then bevel the edge with a lighted match. Use thinning shears to remove some hair on the top of the skull, around the ears. This will help them to sit higher. Remember that the effect you want to create is that of a short-bodied dog with a level top-line, arched and crested neck and high tailset, flat skull and narrow as well. If your dog has fat, "chipmunk" cheeks, trim the cheeks close, but leave some fullness on the neck behind them to avoid a rounded look. There is a fashion today for trimming the hindquarters down to the skin. If your dog has a great rear end, fine! If he is straight in stifle or low in tailset, you're much better advised to leave some fullness behind the tail.

Before embarking on your trimming debut, do try to visit as many shows and breeders and study some photographs of show dogs. If at all possible, get help from a breeder or handler, and do allow yourself several weeks to get the dog looking right. It's not hard, but it does take practice!

6

Judging—Light a Candle, Don't Curse the Darkness

I AM AN ACTIVE EXHIBITOR with a kind word for judges. The system creates demands that have long ago depleted our resources to adequately fill. The more than 2,500 dog shows each year in the United States must have judges. There are nearly 2,000 all-breed shows annually and about 1,000 specialty shows. If the all-breed events have seven group judges with many of the larger shows requiring breed judges because of the numerical maximum rule, there will be approximately 15,000 judging assignments annually; add to that 1,000 specialty assignments and the total demand approaches 16,500 assignments annually. Breaking it down further to 50 show weeks per year, there are over 350 assignments per week. No need to muddy the water with non-competitive requirements of some breed clubs because the stress on the system is quite obvious.

Now factor into this equation over 100 breeds to be expertly passed upon at these 350 assignments and you begin to imagine the scope of the challenge. Now include a dash of subjectivity since each judge is the product of his or her own experiences, opinions, interpretations, physiology and emergency behavior. Where do these experiences, opinions and interpretations come from? Is it a case of successful breeders continuing to breed, others become judges? Is it that judging is the handler's individual retirement account? Many believe both of these premises to be absolutely true. While most simplistic ideas contain some truth, on balance they wither away in the light of the facts.

Let's start with a given all can agree with. Judges are people. And just as there are no perfect dogs, there are no perfect people. Our talent pool relies upon breeders and handlers. Most judges come from one of those categories. Some were both breeders and professional handlers. Breeders' experiences were limited to their own breed or, in some rare instances, breeds. Mostly, through trial and error they learned what makes a "good one" of their breed. Years of experience, many, many puppies, heartbreak, meager rewards and if the breeder was really fortunate, one or two "flyers" making it worthwhile. But their real earned experience is limited to their breed or breeds.

Handlers today, with rare exceptions, do little serious breeding. Breeding generally is not a revenue producer, so today's handler starts by working with a more experienced handler. There are exceptions, but the exceptions rarely achieve prominence and even more rarely become judges. During apprenticeship they learn grooming, care and conditioning. The neophyte handler gradually develops the skills and contacts needed to go off on his or her own. Their education is centered around conditioning, showmanship, kennel management, ethical trade camouflage and other skills needed to properly prepare and present as many breeds as are in the kennel. But breeding, selecting, the winnowing process is the least of the apprentice's education. There just is no economic justification for developing the skills required to sort out puppies. Besides, a really talented artist can cover most flaws in a coated dog or bitch. Necks and backs can be extended or shortened, set-ons can be created, ears and tails can be "trained," even mouths can be "treated." In that cynical environment why look to breed a good one when it is easier to create one?

Some of the few remaining old-timers had multiple breed experience and also were intimately involved in the planning, rearing and selecting of client's stock, but there are few opportunities for that today. Most of today's handlers' clients are small breeders or small exhibitors. The successful handler up until the end of World War II usually had one or two bread and butter clients who kept large numbers of dogs at the handler's facility. In my short stay at Briar Kennels, the establishment of Len Brumby, Jr., we cared for more than 80 Smooth Fox Terriers. These animals were owned by two clients. Boarding and exhibiting were the main source of income. The owners were interested in breeding competitive stock. Puppies of pet quality were sold off. Usually from six to ten litters of Smooths were bred each year. It was the handler's responsibility to develop quality for the client to show. Occasionally, new blood would be introduced. The handler had a good deal to say about that as well. I do not want to imply or infer that today's handlers are better or worse than some of the prominent handlers of the pre-1950 period, for even then there were a lot of handlers who showed dogs for less affluent clients. The point I am making is that the top handlers had that specific kind of opportunity that has virtually disappeared today. Additionally, many of these people were born into the profession in the British Isles. They knew little else. But more importantly, they were the cream of the British fancy before emigrating to the United States. Few aspiring handlers today have the dog opportunities of their predecessors.

Some of today's top handlers were trained by some of those great people of the past and it shows in their eye for a dog and in their presentation. Here, then, is the talent pool and their experience factors, the successful breeders, the successful handler, but the pool is larger than that. There is the less successful breeder who earns a license. The weekend handler can also become a judge, and the affluent exhibitor who has purchased recognition by commissioning a top handler to acquire top winners also becomes a judge. I am certain that there are other examples of people who become judges but the experience factor is reasonably established as we analyze the judging situation.

Experience is followed by physiology. You may scoff at this observation but I have noticed on balance that very tall judges see a dog's movement differently than very short judges. The angle of vision can alter a judge's perception and perspective. Some judges actually have better eyesight than others. Some have a superior sense of touch. Since this entire chapter on judging is the author's observations and conclusions, I will include in physiological characteristics depth perception, peripheral vision and natural talent. Depth perception and peripheral vision certainly are natural in character but are talent, intelligence and emergency behavior natural or acquired skills? Does it really matter? Judges, like the rest of us, attend school; were they "A" students or somewhat less? Assuming one had a career other than dogs, how did they fare in their chosen profession? All of us bring our life's baggage with us. We cannot leave it behind. Some can see balance and symmetry at once, others have to study and analyze the parts of the whole to come to a conclusion. Others will never master it. There are gifted people whose eye for art and beauty has been there since birth. There are individuals who, by sheer application and determination, can master the gifts described, and unfortunately, there are others who are visually "tone deaf."

Formulating a judgment about the quality of an exhibit in two minutes is difficult. Retaining that judgment and re-evaluating it each time another dog in the class is examined is even more challenging. Keeping score in your head if the class is a large one takes significant retentive power, and finally, assessing all the evaluations in light of experience, interpretation, opinions, physiology and making a reasonably consistent selection within the time constraints is a rare talent.

We breeders take months to assess a puppy. We ask a judge to do it under pressure, in minutes, and to be infallible. One thing is certain—not all judges are created equal. There are judges with more talent, more

Ch. Foxden Bracer.

Ch. Axholme Jimmy Reppin, a prominent Wire stud dog.

257

experience with more breeders, firmer, soundly based opinions, and the mental agility to call upon all these virtues in 120 seconds to arrive at a conclusion consistent with his or her interpretation of the Standard, but there is still one more factor—ego. Will a judge's ego allow for growth, for a mind set that allows for a continuing learning process? A judge who has "arrived" in his or her mind ceases to develop and learn. For all its drain on natural talent, environment and experience, judging dogs, like any other skill, requires constant personal introspection to achieve the level of expertise necessary to be accepted by the fancy as "a judge." A good dog person begins, early on, increasing a sense of awareness of the characteristics of a good Fox Terrier. Each experience raises his or her level of consciousness of the Fox Terrier Standard. If the judge's ego doesn't get in the way, this level of consciousness will carry most people to their ultimate degree of expertise and professionalism. My final statement on this issue to all exhibitors, "Please do not blame the messenger."

Try to assess the quality of your own exhibit. Advance your own knowledge with each new litter, each new dog show. Not every exhibit is a topper. Some will barely complete their title. Others may not make it at all and still others will hold their own in most all-breed shows. A rare few come along in a lifetime, if you are knowledgeable and lucky—lucky to have bred such dogs and knowledgeable to recognize them when they arrive. A good dog will overcome bad judging eventually. Breed and group judging will improve as the quality of the exhibit improves.

When Ruth and I began to exhibit in the Houston area, we rarely saw a Terrier judge. All Terriers were passed upon, for the most part, by good dog people who got their start in another group. A total entry of fifty to sixty Terriers, not just Fox Terriers, but all Terriers was the norm. The all-breed clubs had few members who raised Terriers of any kind. Some of the judging decisions were quite amazing. Most geographic areas contain certain judges who, because of their proximity and popularity with Show Chairmen, seem to receive frequent assignments in that area. As the Fox Terrier activity increased in the Houston area, the judging improved. Did every judge improve? No, but most did and today there are a number of judges who carry out their assignments with credibility and integrity. So the first requisite for good judging is good dogs to judge. So, don't shoot the messenger!

Since most judges are former breeders, former handlers or former exhibitors, they are all products of their past. And they are human beings. Do we, as exhibitors, expect too much? Paraphrase Shylock's words in *The Merchant of Venice*. "I am a Judge. Hath not a Judge eyes? Hath not a Judge hands, organs, dimensions, senses, affections, passions?"

"If you prick us, do we not bleed? If you tickle us, do we not laugh? If you poison us, do we not die? And if you wrong us, shall we not revenge?" Perhaps I am overdramatizing, but can we truly expect a handler turned judge to completely forget those comrades and clients that were such an important part of the previous life? In a relatively equal class, are any of us so insulated, so calculating, that we can totally shut from our minds memories of past kindnesses? I doubt it. This is not a defense of outright cronyism but merely a subtle nuance that even the most sincere and upstanding arbiter can fall victim to on occasion.

If we want to point a finger then point it at the major culprit, the judge who is knowledgeable but easily intimidated. How many times do we see a judge do a creditable job in the classes until the open class? It is then that two or three top handlers enter the ring and the judge literally goes to pieces. No, he or she doesn't break down outwardly but the brain goes blank with fear. I know of one Terrier judge who actually keeps score. There is not a single well-known handler who is not aware of this. The judge actually "takes care" of all the handlers at one time or another. Handlers get paid to win. They sense weakness like jackals trailing an aging wildebeest. It takes great confidence in one's own knowledge and opinion to stand up to the pressure of a successful handler and an impeccably presented exhibit if that knowledge tells you that there is a better dog in the ring on that day. By the same token, a "giant killer" is equally repugnant. That is a judge that takes delight in being different even when knowledge and experience dictate a different decision. He or she is the one who put so-and-so down.

Since most of the previously discussed judging challenges are symptomatic of the human condition, they will always be with us in one degree or another. My greatest frustration stems from those judges who place their opinions above the Standard. The Standard requires that dogs "should not exceed fifteen and a half (15½) inches" and cites no minimum. Certainly anything more than one-half inch in excess is a serious fault. It matters very little if the judge's opinion is that bigger stud dogs are better stud dogs. What does matter is that on the day, the judge is the custodian of the Standard. I do not seek to disqualify larger exhibits, or smaller ones for that matter. Each exhibit must be judged as a whole dog on the day. To put a finer point on the issue, let's suppose in the following example all other things are equal. There is a class of three Specials. Exhibit A is just fifteen and one-half inches but moves a bit close coming at the judge; exhibit B is a good one but is about sixteen and one-half inches; exhibit C is a good one that just makes fifteen inches. You be the judge. Read the Standard and tell me who should be awarded the breed. "C," of course!!

Several years ago I wrote for some information about a prominent stud dog. He was compiling a good record in the ring and his offspring I saw looked quite promising. I knew he was big for a Fox Terrier, easily 16½" and at least 25 pounds. I wrote requesting a pedigree and, also, the weight of the dog. The response came back from the wife. Inscribed on the top of the pedigree was "18-20 lbs." I never bred to the dog.

Nothing sets my teeth on edge more than hearing our most respected judges saying, "I like a great stallion of a stud dog. The bigger stud dogs are better producers." Rot!!! . . . and rubbish!! Mendel would spin in his grave. While our Standard does not place emphasis on exactitude as to size and weight, we must breed functional Fox Terriers. A Fox Terrier is constructed to bolt the badger, foil the fox and to be quick and agile enough to catch and kill mice and rats. Perhaps it would be useful to describe a fox. Many judges of Fox Terriers may have seen hundreds of Fox Terriers but, I wonder, how many are truly acquainted with the Fox Terrier's natural enemy. The typical fox is approximately 36″ long, about 15″ at the withers and weighs from 10 to 15 pounds. A Fox Terrier must be capable of following this adversary into the ground. A dog much over 15½″ and weighing in excess of 20 pounds would be useless. Just picture the size of a tunnel that a three-foot, 15-pound fox can escape into and then examine the Fox Terrier.

A 16½″ or larger dog doesn't get it done. A dog that's over 25 pounds doesn't get it done. The modern history of both breeds contains its share of oversized stud dogs who, because of their "other virtues" became pillars of the breed and successful show dogs. What must be kept in mind is the disparity between what was big in the early days of the breed and our present reference to oversize. Our early working Terriers could be 17 pounds and 15 inches. Rawdon Lee described the early Fox Terrier, "Old Jock 18 pounds, Tartar 17 pounds, Old Trap 17 pounds, Tyrant 18 pounds." In measuring and working 40 Terriers of 1876 Lee attributes the following average to "Mr. Edward Sandell, an excellent judge of terriers, writing under the non de plume of *Caractus*" whose research revealed height 14¾″ and weight 17 to 20 pounds.

Ch. Result, a great early showman, was 14″ high and 16 pounds, and the celebrated bitch, Vesuvienne, was 14½″ and 16¾ pounds. Lee, in summarizing his observations as to height and weight wrote, "I suppose there is little necessity to remind any of my readers, that even if they do possess a Fox Terrier with a head 7½″ in length, that stands 14½″ in height from the ground to the shoulders, and weighs 16 pounds, they do not, of a certainty, own a champion." While the size and weight described by Lee were ideal for 1890, the dog needed more qualities to become a champion. It is important to recall that working Fox Terriers were still being exhibited. It is curious as well that the 7½″ ideal head was for a 14½″ dog of less than 20 pounds. Using those proportions, how big should the head be on a 27-pound, 17″ dog? The original Standard makes no height reference but does offer the following weight reference, "If a dog can gallop and stay, and follow his fox, it matters little what his weight is to a pound or so, though, roughly speaking it may be said he should not scale over 20 pounds in show condition." In the point scale, size, symmetry and character total 20 points. Now we move ahead to 1905 and the Castle-Marple monograph on the Fox Terrier on page 45.

Would "Brat" or "Spot On" fit in the Terrier Man's saddle bag?

I suppose we do our puppies better than yore, but we must look much farther for the cause of oversize—the breeding from over-sized dogs, who themselves are the progeny of dogs admittedly too big to show. This, I fear, will go on until breeders set their faces against 20 and even 22 pound stud dogs, and instead of relegating these to the stud put them in the vine border.

It is quite clear that the early breeders were absolutely certain that while they could live with 18 pounds, 22 pounds was not acceptable and yet size was a problem even then. One major difference was that the Fox Terrier was still used for the hunt on occasion and a dog over 15½″ and 20 pounds had his usefulness impaired. The great dogs of the day were all 20 pounds or under, and 15½ inches or less. And those stud dogs produced good sized, healthy, firm representative Fox Terriers.

Desmond O'Connell writing in 1911 laments the wide disparity in size as follows.

Take the two best dogs in Mr. Redmond's successful kennel at the moment as an illustration of what I write—viz. D'Orsay's Model and Dunleath. If the former is the ideal size, then the latter is far too big, but if Dunleath is the pattern in size, then D'Orsay's Model is too small.

The records will show that D'Orsay's Model was more productive than Dunleath.

However, Mr. O'Connell was the first of our early breeders to expound on the virtues of "big stud dogs." I do not know if the myth began with him but he judged the London Fox Terrier show in 1915 and it must be noted that he was warning against 15 and 16 pound stud dogs. He was concerned about degenerate diminution of the Fox Terrier. What is of even greater interest is the Marples article in *Our Dogs* in 1915 in which he states:

Nearly all our greatest winners on the show bench, dogs and bitches, who, by a concensus of expert opinion, are or were the nearest to the acme of perfection, have been sired by big dogs; in some cases by dogs too big for the show bench. This has always been so. . . .

Again, we see size being presented as a virtue only as it relates to fear of Toy Terriers developing from Smooths and Wires of the day. No one was advocating a big stud dog over 20 pounds.

In response to Theo Marples, Mr. Francis Redmond wrote what I believe to be an astute analysis of the size issue which is just as valid today.

(To the Editor of *Our Dogs*):
Sir—Referring to the article on "Fox Terrier size, etc." which appeared in your issue of the 13th inst. under the signature of Mr. Theo Marples, I must take exception to his statement: "nearly all our greatest winners on the show bench, dogs and bitches, who by a consensus of expert opinion are, or were, the nearest to the acme of perfection, have been sired by big dogs; in some

cases by dogs too big for the show bench. This has always been so." (Mr. Marples has omitted Ch. Venia from the above list—doubtless one of the best and most successful big Terriers as a sire we have had.)

As the owner of the late Ch. D'Orsay, whom Mr. Marples includes in the list, I would advise him that D'Orsay in his best show form never exceeded 17½ pounds. The same weight as his kennel companion, Ch. Dominie, the sire of Ch. Donna Fortuna and several other champions.

One may without difficulty recall a number of small dogs of the correct size who were far more successful than the oversized Terriers he refers to. Take, for instance, Royster (15½ pounds), sire of Chs. Regent, Result, etc. The last named one of the most successful show dogs we ever had only scaled 16 pounds when on the big side, and was sire of Ch. Rachel, Rosemary, Radiance and other good small ones. Ch. Regent, his half brother, was the sire of Reckon (16 pounds) who sired some of the best. Another good small one from whom springs some of our most valued strains was Dickon (16 pounds), sire of Ch. Splinter (16 pounds), sire of Vesuvian, who sired Chs. Venia and Vesuvienne, etc.

In most recent years we have D'Orsay's Double (17 pounds), a good winner, and sire of Ch. Captain Double, winner of more championships than probably any Smooth Terrier we have ever had. Coming to the present time, we have Ch Orkadian, sire of Ch. Kitty Sparks (16½ pounds) and other good ones: Ch. D'Orsay's Model (16½ pounds), sire of Ch. D'Orsay's Donna (16½ pounds), and other good ones: Ch. Collar of Notts (17 pounds), sire of Ch. Wireboy of Paighton, sire of Ch. Wycollar Boy (under 17 pounds).

I submit, if Mr. Marples will compare the above with the stock begotten by the best big ones, he cannot, with any degree of fairness claim that they are nearly as successful at stud, and moreover, cannot support his statement that the small Fox Terriers, being degenerate, they naturally perpetuate their degeneracy. So much from the breeder's point.

Now to take a practical view of Mr. Marple's article, I entirely fail to see this point when one considers the work required of a Fox Terrier—viz. to go to ground, follow and bolt his fox. Now, as a fox weighs anything from 12 to 16 pounds and when hard pressed will go to ground in drain or earth, none but a small Terrier can get to him, and as it is impossible for any terrier of even 22 or 24 pounds weight to live with the hounds when they really run, terriers have to be carried in saddlebag by a hunt servant or brought up by a runner, who not only knows the country, but very often the fox's point. Then why does Mr. Marples advocate the breeding of the 20 pound dog, who cannot keep with the hounds, is too big to be carried in saddlebag, and in many instances too big to get to ground and bolt his fox.

Mr. Redmond continues later in the letter:

I shall be pleased to show Mr. Marples at any time terriers from 15 to 17 pounds that have done their season with hounds, bolted their foxes, and in some instances killed the prey and have stood the hard work and hard fate that fall to the lot of a kennel or huntsman's terrier; and I have no fear of their degenerating to the size of toys or no bigger than white mice; as Mr. Marples put it. Mr. Marples made reference to the Fox Terrier Club's Standard of Points, and refers to 20 pounds as the maximum size. Being one of the subcommittee of the Club for formulating the "Standard Description and Points of the Breeds," the Mss. of which I have before me as I write, I may state the 20 pounds was considered an extreme weight, and many colleagues— among others Messrs. W. Allison (now "our Special Commissioner" of *The Sportsman*), Theo. Bassett, John A. Doyle, Henry Gibson, T. Scott, (all hunting men who knew the Terrier in his work)—only allowed this as the utmost limit, and were unanimous as to the Terrier of 15-17 pounds built on the lines of the Foxhound, the polo pony, or the Hunter, as being the most symmetrical animals of all time, combining both speed and staying power, from this standard has been evolved the Fox Terrier as he exists today, and which Mr. Marples eulogizes as "The gentleman of the Terrier varieties," who has, "in spite of many rivals," mainly owing to his practical use, gameness, and intelligence, remained the most popular terrier for nearly 50 years, and promises to continue, or as long as breeders recognize the size required for work—viz., 15-17 pounds; but once admit the over-sized animal as typical of a Fox Terrier, he is bound to lose favor with the hunting men and sportsman, whom Mr. Marples is pleased to describe as "fossilised old sporting fogies." They have, however, bred and do breed, their terriers for work and gameness, and long may that be the object of all Fox Terrier men. Yours truly, Francis Redmond.

P.S. I may add that having judged Fox Terriers at most of the leading shows in Great Britain and abroad, I have very seldom had to cast an exhibit as being too small or too toyish for work, but on the other hand have had to penalize them for being over-sized. F.R.

Bigness to Redmond, Vicary, The Duchess of Newcastle, Theo Marples, etc., was a dog of 16″ in height and a weight of 20 pounds. They would be shocked and appalled at the dimensions of some of our more recent winners. Going back to Barrington Bridegroom, the Wire penalized for his size at a number of English shows, there has been a procession of champions who were oversize. And there were others who were used extensively who were too big to be shown. Such famous Wires as Gallant Knight of Wildoaks and Smooths as Heir Apparent of Andely and Downsbragh Mickey Finn were just too big to show. Among the Wires and Smooths with great show careers who were big, the most recent were Ch. Sunnybrook Spot On and Ch. Ttarb the Brat.

While a case can be made for both Spot On and the Brat, the fallout resulting from their success is a terrible price to pay. By that I mean lesser dogs with less to offer but equal in size gain acceptance by many judges with limited Fox Terrier exposure so that in addition to the obvious direct impact that a Spot On or a Brat has on a breed, there is considerable fallout that leads to acceptability of oversized dogs of lesser quality both in the ring and at stud. Terriers generally and Fox Terriers more specifically are more frequently misjudged by all-rounders than other groups, especially where the all-rounders have had no real terrier experience. The slight but important differences between the Lakeland and the Welsh are frequently homogenized in the eyes of the all-rounder who has not had terriers of one type or another as a primary breed. Fox Terriers, both Wire and Smooth, are frequently penalized for correct action and rewarded for the reverse. But it is in the judging of size that the all-rounder does the greatest harm. I am not stating that there are no outstanding all-breed judges who began with non-terrier breeds who succeed as terrier judges, but many rely too heavily on the axiom that "A good one is a good one regardless of the breed!" However, the most serious error most are guilty of is confusing size for substance. Judges with working, herding or non-sporting origins are the most common source of Fox Terrier misjudgement. Perhaps size to a half-inch has less significance to them. Or perhaps it is more difficult to train an eye to respond to the challenges created by a 20-pound dog after years of familiar and intimate association with much larger canvasses. The eye becomes trained to accept proportions, symmetry, balance and type but the eye needs a constant mental reminder if it is to program reasonably accurate size into the decision equation.

The early debate on the issue of size between Marples and Redmond took place within the framework of the existing Standard. Marples extolling the virtues of the stud dog weighing 20 pounds and standing approximately 15½ inches and Redmond defending dogs of lesser proportions made a very convincing argument. That argument is totally lost in today's context. Today's discussion is over the merits of a proper-sized dog in relationship to its oversized counterpart. The brilliant 15" representative is left at the starting gate. The early breeders successfully campaigned 14½" dogs who weighed 16 pounds. Ch. Splinter, the great Smooth, and Ch. Collar of Notts, the great Wire, never weighed more than 17 pounds in fighting trim, and they were great producers. Today they would be relegated to pet homes because they would be "undersized." I maintain that the Standard speaks eloquently on the issue of size when it establishes upper limits only, i.e., "According to present day requirement, a full-sized, well-balanced dog *should not exceed 15½ inches at the withers.*" No minimums here, just maximums. And yet, almost without exception, the good 15-inch dog is ignored while his oversized counterpart, of lesser quality, walks off with the ribbons and is bred to the most bitches. Without wishing to be divisive, I believe that the Wire, because of his great popularity as a show dog, has had more struggles, today, with the excessive size problem. So many of the top winning Wire dogs exceeded the Standard by an inch or more, that their legacy is deeply rooted in modern Wire genes.

What to Do

It serves little purpose to ask how we got this way. The question is, "How can corrective action be taken?" It starts with breeders exerting more discipline on the size issue. Judges need to be better informed and the breed club needs to take a firm stand on the size question. Redmond was right!

It is still true. A big stallion of a stud dog is an aberration that will haunt breeders for generations to come. It is now 70 years later and some of our great winning Smooths approach 25 pounds and our Wires even more. The blame falls squarely on the shoulders of the judges who look at large size as a secret virtue known only to them. Oversize is a more serious fault than many others because it negates the dog's ability to successfully work at its original career. Size is difficult to breed out once established. The real shame of judges who reward oversize is that they do it by overlooking the size on the grounds that the dog has so much good to offer but when they see all that soundness, style and type in a correct-sized version many come down on the smaller dog with total disdain. The only conclusion one can draw is that it is not size that is being forgiven but size is being rewarded.

Judges at dog shows have a massive impact on exhibitors' breeding programs. Unfortunately one cannot homogenize genes. If a good big dog is bred to a good small dog, medium-size dogs may not result. If they do, it is as a result of each parent's medium-size genes in their makeup. However, it is a given that size will produce size, if not today then tomorrow. I have tried to determine where this myth comes from that good big dogs are better producers. I can only think of two possible answers. First, many dog fanciers are also horse breeders. Horse people say, "the bigger the better as long as the proportions are right." They look for a great stallion of a horse for speed and stamina. But, horses do not have size and weight as descriptive breed responsibilities and characteristics. Secondly, since many of our top winning dogs were oversized (over 15½") and since there is a tendency for breeders to gravitate toward today's winner, it naturally follows that these large, winning stud dogs would be given more breeding opportunities which would produce more puppies and so their opportunity for success would be greater. So by rewarding size you create a self-fulfilling prophecy that big ones are better producers. Again, rot!!! Rubbish!!!

Another serious error made by many knowledgeable judges is the correct interpretation of movement. Fox Terriers do not and *should not* single track. The amplifications in Chapter 4 clearly describe Fox Terrier action. I have always thought that tall judges ought to crouch somewhat to be able to get a more accurate perspective of the exhibits in motion. Judges whose early experience is not rooted in Terriers need to learn to identify the correct Fox Terrier action. Probably the two most difficult challenges to a budding all-rounder who is non-Terrier rooted are to learn to identify the correct Fox Terrier action and determine the difference between size and substance.

Judging

How should a Fox Terrier be judged? There is an informed way and an uninformed way. The table should be used to examine the exhibit's components: the bite, the shoulders, the firmness of the back, the set-on, the coat, the foot, etc. The next time you attend a show, notice whether or not the judge actually feels coat texture or examines the feet of the dog. Few judges perform this inspection; fewer still know what they should feel or look for. Both Smooth and Wire are double-coated.

The feet are extremely important to a Fox Terrier. They should be small, round and tight with thick, serviceable pads. Both the Smooth and Wire amplification describe the feet in detail.

The most ingenuous error most judges commit and most exhibitors allow is the presentation of the dog to the judge. A Fox Terrier must be alert. I cannot count the number of times I have witnessed a judge stand in one spot and ask an exhibitor to alter the position of an exhibit that was intently staring at some real or imaginary object known only to the dog. The dog was at its best, on the tip-toe of anticipation. All the judge had to do was to walk around the contestant and witness its performance. Instead, the judge asks the exhibitor to alter the dog's position so he or she can get a better look. Well, any terrier worth a damn will not forget whatever it was that attracted it in the first place and will continue to try to follow the progress of its prey. And as the exhibitor exits the ring empty-handed the judge is heard to say, "It's too bad he acted up today, I really liked him." That judge probably came from a non-terrier background. A good terrier judge will take what the exhibit gives and use it. To properly evaluate Fox Terriers, a judge must first understand the breed. So if you are fortunate to be approved to judge Fox Terriers, remember, they should not be overhandled or constantly stacked. A Fox Terrier handler kneeling should be tying a shoelace or praying. The judge should not be concerned about the symmetry of the class but the symmetry of each dog. When it stops moving, its feet should be where they are supposed to be; and if you are fortunate enough to witness a Fox Terrier with its glare fixed upon some object known only to it, and have the dog's tail facing you, put yourself in position to properly evaluate its performance. After all, you are there to judge the dog.

Markings can alter the way a judge sees a dog. Figure A is the same dog with and without the saddle. The saddle breaks into the vision of the top line and distorts the appearance of the tail set-on.

Figure B provides other examples of the effect upon a person's perception that markings cause.

Figure C consists of sketches of the front and hind foot of the Fox Terrier.

C-1 is a side view of a good tight, rounded foot.

A-1 A-2

B-1 B-2

B-3 B-4

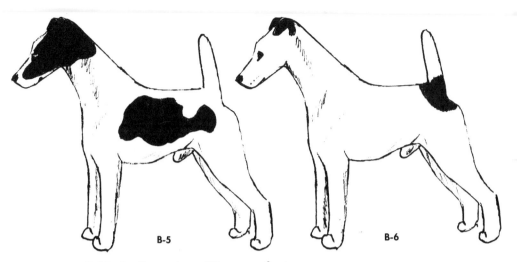

B-5   B-6

C-2 is the front view of the same foot.

C-3 is a foot that is improperly shaped, where the toes do not form a tight, rounded appearance, but instead offer a pointed look. Additionally, the pastern is weak, not upright.

C-4 is a splayed foot where the weight of the dog forces the toes to spread apart.

Anyone who judges Wires or Smooths without paying close attention to feet does the breeds a disservice.

There is this to say for ignorance and incompetence: it shows no favorites. You may be its victim today, but you will be its beneficiary tomorrow. As exhibitors we need to spend less time complaining, selecting and planning campaigns around "Who's judging?" and more time working to improve the conditions.

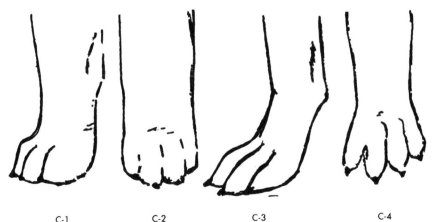

C-1   C-2   C-3   C-4

7

How to Become a Breeder

"**S**OME PEOPLE have it and some people do not. Some people can acquire it while others never will." The "it" referred to in the quote is "an eye"—the ability to sort out a litter of puppies or a ring full of Fox Terriers and select, with consistency, "good, better, best." The decision becomes easier when your candidates are mature adults, but the challenge becomes much greater with puppies that change from day to day, more frequently than the weather.

At least with the weather you can attempt to forecast what tomorrow will bring. With puppies, today's misfit may be tomorrow's star. There is no certain way to select a show quality puppy under the age of one year. Mouths, for example, can go off after that. I have avoided discussing my Foxmoor experiences here because I am too close to the dogs, but am making an exception in this one instance, just to impress the perversity of nature upon the seeker of a potential show dog. The union of Ch. Ttarb the Brat with Ch. Quissex Upsadaisy produced six offspring in two litters; all six became champions. The last breeding produced four puppies, three dogs and one bitch. In Daisy's first litter to Brat, there were two puppies, a dog and a bitch. Of these, all but one was a standout from birth. As I stated earlier, this was an unusual union. But it was the second litter that I feel contains the significant lesson. From the time the four puppies emerged, it was obvious that there were three very attractive dogs and one puny, very ordinary bitch. The dogs fulfilled their promise early and the bitch was relegated to obscurity in the kennel. I couldn't part with her as a pet because this litter would be Daisy's last. So the puppy bitch, Jet, enjoyed a life of frolic, fresh air, food and fondling until her maternal duties were required. At the same time, we were showing a bitch called Foxmoor Forever Amber and she was running into an unusual situation. She had one major and had accumulated over 20 points. The AKC had just increased the major requirements in Texas and at her recent outings we were one bitch shy of a major. I called Tony Giles at the kennel and told him to enter Jet. A couple of days later I got a call from the kennel. It was Tony—"I think you better come out. I've bathed and trimmed Jet and I'm not certain that you will want to take her to the show." My mind immediately conjured up all sorts of problems. I said, "What's wrong with her?" Tony replied, "Nothing, she's gorgeous." She never did develop into a robust bitch but she gained her title with relative ease. At three months, she should have been sold as a pet. At 13 months of age she became Ch. Foxmoor Majorette. The moral of the story is that buying a "show prospect" puppy is, at best, a bad risk. If you truly want a dog to show, buy one that is mature, 18 months is a good age, and have some fun. For those who insist upon purchasing a puppy hoping it will develop into a decent competitor, perhaps the following will reduce the risk a bit.

Whether Wire or Smooth, read and reread the Standard and study the amplifications and illustrations. Attend dog shows and pay particular attention to the breed judging. Hopefully, this experience, plus Standard study will provide the germ of an idea of what a decent Fox Terrier should look like.

When the above experience has been digested, start looking for your puppy. Obtain a list of breeders in your area from the AKC or from the Secretary of the AFTC. Call breeders in your area before you visit to determine if, in fact, puppies are available. Openly state your requirements.

Enough! You say, "How do I buy and select a future Fox Terrier champion?" Contrary to some experts, never ask to see the litter. All puppies are adorable and in a litter of Wires or Smooths one or two will always stand out. But the trap is set if you look at them in a group. You are comparing them to each other and not to the ideal you have in your mind. Ask the breeder to show you one puppy at a time. Look at the puppy in a run or an exercise pen. Observe its demeanor; does it sit and stare off into space or does it head for the perimeter of the run or pen? If it just sits, ask to see another puppy. Remember, you are looking for a show dog; that means one that will show when presented with the opportunity. Many are called but few are chosen. You want a puppy who "makes the most of itself." When you find a candidate that says "here I am," take a good look at its outline. Start with the feet and legs. That is the part most frequently overlooked by expert puppy sorters. If the feet are small and round and the pasterns relatively perpendicular to the ground, keep going. Puppy bone is soft and deceptive. For the most part you can disregard the knobbiness if it exists. A pup with decent bone may have knobby joints. Look at the front.

Are the feet true, neither turning in nor out? Is the distance between the legs the same from the feet to where the legs enter the body? Look at the rear. Do the hocks stare straight back at you, neither turning in nor out and is the rear foot directly under the hock? Lift the puppy gently by the tail and then release the tail. Observe the way the rear "sets itself." From the side, the leg should be perpendicular to the ground and should enter the foot with little or no pastern visible. From the rear, the leg from the hock to the foot should be parallel to the other leg. Study the segment of the visualization on angulation and apply it to the rear of the puppy you are examining.

For me, the most challenging aspect of puppy selection is trying to determine what the head and ears will look like when the puppy is fully matured. Nowhere is bloodline knowledge more important, for the head and ears will follow different development patterns from different lines. For example, it is possible that perfectly placed, small ears on a three-month-old puppy may become erect at eight months, whereas a rather houndy, heavy ear on such a puppy may be perfect at nine months. Before making a decision to buy or reject a specific puppy whose ears are imperfect, I always re-examine the parents and the pedigree. The single exception manifests itself where the puppy at three months has erect or prick ears. Waste no more time with that one. Many of my fellow breeders will "set" ears as a matter of practice. There is nothing illegal or unethical about setting ears. So when visiting a kennel, if you see puppies with their ears set, do not be concerned. Surgically altering ears is an entirely different matter. Anyone who surgically alters ears perpetuates a horrendous hoax upon the purchaser of the altered animal and all the breeders and exhibitors that may some day breed to or purchase a puppy from an altered dog. Do I set ears? I do not believe that it does one bit of good in the long run. The ears will eventually be what nature intended. However, many successful, experienced breeders routinely set ears.

Some things can be fairly apparent early on. A short back may lengthen, but rarely will a long back shorten. A mouth that is overshot or undershot may correct, but the odds are not in favor of that occurring. The bone structure of the skull is fairly constant. A puppy with a flat skull and correct planes to its muzzle will usually retain those virtues. Action or movement will change as the puppy matures and no one has ever been able to impart to me a plan to project the movement of a three-month-old puppy on a two-year-old. I have seen good-moving puppies at three months turn into mincing Mae Wests at a year. I have seen well-let-down, well-angulated puppies at three months become either straight behind or sickle-hocked adults. However, a puppy at three months with a small dark eye will usually retain that lovely feature throughout its life. Of course, the same is true for a large light eye. Level top lines may develop dips, but high rears or uneven top lines rarely improve. Tail sets that are good may deteriorate but poor tail sets will rarely improve. It is almost a waste of time to discuss shoulder analysis in a three-month-old puppy. I have seen decent shoulders go off and what can happen to a puppy with apparently little or no neck. The neck five months later just grew out to a lovely, graceful support for a marvelous headpiece. What does all this mean? It means that if you are really interested in starting to show Fox Terriers, save yourself grief and acquire a young, fully-developed dog or bitch. If your goal is hobby breeding, look for a proven, quality bitch.

Most breeders, from time to time, have bitches whose offspring they wish to keep. Since even the most ambitious breeding program has its numerical limitations, chances are that a good, proven bitch will be available at some point. You may have to contact several kennels before finding exactly what you seek, but persevere; it will be well worth the effort. My advice is, "Do not start any breeding program with a dog, depending on breeding terms to obtain your bitches." The flaw in that plan is that you have no control over the quality of the bitches that will be offered to your dog. If you just want to exhibit without any thought of raising Fox Terriers, then start with a dog rather than a bitch. Because good quality bitches are the backbone of any successful breeding program, a breeder will be less reluctant to part with a top quality male than a female, especially when the breeder is assured that the male FLYER will be shown. A breeder's best advertising is the success of other people with the dogs bearing his or her prefix. Now, back to that proven champion bitch you sought and found. When you and the owner have come to terms, ask for the bitch's breeding history. Who has the offspring of previous litters? How often does she come in season and what was the date of her last cycle? Was she bred the last time she came in season? If so, what were the results? Has she ever missed when she was bred? If so, who was she bred to when she missed? Has the breeder retained a daughter or a son? If the answer is "no" keep looking. Finally, make the transaction subject to an examination by a veterinarian of your choice to make certain that the bitch is in good health and does not have any scars from any previous surgery. The choice of an older proven quality bitch can save a novice years of frustration.

If you are still set on a puppy, then, when you have found the puppy you like, investigate the sire and the dam. Hopefully, you will be as lucky as we were when we returned to Fox Terriers in 1979.

For the first-time buyer interested in a show puppy, remember to observe, study and finally, do business with reputable breeders.

For the first-time Smooth or Wire breeder interested in a "starter kit," the parts of that kit should include:

1. A set of directions and a list of parts. (By doing the homework prescribed earlier, the new hobbyist will develop an idea of what he or she likes in a Fox Terrier—set of directions—and the breeders who breed that type of dog.)

2. Some knowledge of the pedigree of the type of Smooth or Wire that is most admired by the new breeder. (You must, first of all, please yourself.)
3. A knowledge that your first attempt will be imperfect. Neither your purchased puppy nor its offspring will be perfect. (The starter kit must contain its consignment of patience, resiliency, objectivity and tenacity, otherwise don't buy it.)
4. The puppy herself. (A true program cannot start with a dog; it must start with a bitch. Since the owner of a dog cannot select the bitches he receives, the ownership of a dog will eventually require the purchase of a bitch. On the other hand, the owner of a bitch, by merely paying the stud fee, can breed to any dog in the country. And, even more significantly, the bitch owner, in time, can breed to most of the top dogs in the country to the one bitch.)

Once you have secured your starter kit, you are ready for the next step, starting her on the road to her show career. You want her alert and responsive in the ring. At the show, spend a few moments observing the judge. Judges have a set routine for examining and moving the exhibits. When you go into the ring, you will want to know what the judge expects and be ready to follow the judge's directions. You are on your way.

Whether your choice is a Wire or a Smooth, once you become a hobby breeder, parts of your life will never be the same. The metamorphosis from ingenuous novice to unqualified expert varies with the individual, some becoming experts after attending their first dog show, others a week or two longer, and some still do not become authorities until after their first litter. In dogs, as in life, the first sign of wisdom is the recognition of what is not known.

The decision to breed your bitch should not be a flippant choice. A bitch need not be bred to be fulfilled. I could write an entire chapter on the need people seem to have to humanize their dogs. Enjoy Fox Terriers for what they are, fantastic companions and outstanding show dogs, but they are not human. The world will never miss one litter of puppies. Chances are, any litter you raise will cost you time and money. A litter of Fox Terriers ranks below a two-dollar bet on a twenty-to-one shot at the track as a money-making proposition. On the other hand, if you want to raise and exhibit Fox Terriers; if you will enjoy the overwhelming sense of pride experienced by every serious breeder when their efforts bear fruit; if creating a thing of beauty is your secret wish; if all or just one of these experiences appeal to you, then plan to breed your bitch and the sooner the better.

The estrus cycle of a Fox Terrier bitch will vary with the individual. There are two indications that may be useful to the novice. The cycle of the dam of the bitch will frequently be passed on to the offspring, so ask the breeder about the heat cycle of the dam. Secondly, the initial cycle of the bitch may determine her future cycle. A bitch that first cycles at six months will usually cycle in six months. If she matures sexually at nine months, then she will probably cycle every nine months or so. However, do not accept this advice as absolute, but merely as a hint to assist a novice in his or her first experience. It is not uncommon for a puppy bitch to exhibit little or no evidence when she cycles for the first time, especially if it takes place when she is six months or younger. This may mislead the novice who accepts my helpful hint as gospel, since the newcomer may interpret the second cycle as the first and will become confused when the bitch cycles again in six months.

Select the stud dog with care. Believing that bloodlines alone can achieve a desirable result is the most common fault of most new breeders. By all means study the pedigree of the bitch and the stud prospects, but then select the soundest, most beautiful specimen available, not his litter brother or a younger or older brother, but the best representative you can find.

Most Fox Terrier bitches usually come in season at about eight or nine months of age. There has been considerable discussion about the best age to breed a bitch. I do not believe that there is a "best" age. If the bitch is on the large side, say 15½ to 16 inches and about 20 pounds, she can be bred earlier than a smaller bitch. So a good-sized bitch who comes in season at ten months for the first time, can be bred the first time she comes in. It is wise to wait with a smaller bitch until she is past 12 months before breeding her. One of the bromides that seems to impact novice Fox Terrier breeders is the one about not breeding a bitch the first time she comes in season. I have known people who owned a bitch that came in season for the first time at 14 months, and her second season was 10 months later. She was a good-sized bitch and turned out to be a terrific producer. Unfortunately, her seasons were erratic and her productive opportunities limited. Missing that first opportunity was a waste. A bitch that comes in season three times every two years can be bred each time until the age of six or seven, then she can be retired with grace and dignity. My experience has been that puppies of an older bitch are less rugged and, actually, less typey. A brood bitch will produce her best offspring while she is young. Don't waste an opportunity. If a bitch cycles at shorter intervals, then I would arrange it so that she still has three litters every two years until the age of seven.

George Skelly's *All About Fox Terriers* is a tour de force on Fox Terrier lines and families, in-breeding, linebreeding, outcrossing, tail male and tail female lines. While the book is out of print, nonetheless, copies are available to anyone who wants to go to the trouble of running a copy down. Briefly, however, successful breeding programs are impacted by four considerations: genotype, phenotype, environment and luck. And, not necessarily in any particular order of importance. These four parts of any breeding program cannot produce results for anyone if the breeder does not have a point of view and the ability to recognize a result when it presents itself. So, success is really predicated upon two separate and distinct skills; the breeding of good Fox Terriers and the talent to recognize a result when you see it.

In the beginning, you will find people willing to assist you in both areas. The only advice I can offer in this instance is to be certain of your mentor's credentials. In all breeds, there are veteran fanciers who are no further along now than when they started. At the drop of a dog biscuit, they will provide advice and direction to anyone who will listen. They spout pedigrees and bloodlines with great authority, but their greatest contribution is to tear down the latest headliner by regaling their listeners with all the dog's holes and what's been fixed. Or the most common comment, without its big-name handler, the dog would be worthless. One moment of a successful breeder's time is worth hours of conversation with the "Nabobs of Negativism." Ten minutes with a great judge is worth weeks of self-styled experts.

Breeders who concern themselves with genotype only, that is, those who will let the pedigree select the mate, may enjoy some success but a program needs other characteristics. The other extreme ignores the pedigree and just breeds by type. A dog with a good rear is bred to a bitch that is weak in the rear with the hope of getting puppies like the bitch but with improved rears. The result with this system may be the bad rear of the bitch with the faults of the dog. I'm certain that the best programs combine the knowledge of bloodlines and pedigrees with a study of the individual dogs and their offspring.

The accepted genetic formula is that the sire and dam make equal contributions to a litter. That is probably true of the genetic composition of the whelps. However, the bitch also rears the puppies and, therefore, creates the environment for the offspring's first six weeks. Anyone who pooh-poohs the effect that a good brood bitch can have on the personality of a show dog or bitch has never seen a good Fox Terrier bitch in action. A good brood bitch passes on her good qualities and also teaches her brood the doggy facts of life, Fox Terrier version.

The best breeding programs combine the virtues of type compensation, that is, selecting the stud dog likely to overcome the bitch's faults but leaving her good qualities alone, with a matching of antecedents whose general type and productive achievements you admire. The bitch must do the rest after the mating takes place and, of course, you need more than a smattering of luck.

Foxmoor started with a Smooth bitch called Quissex Upsadaisy. She was quite pretty, pleasing enough head and ears, a rather large but dark eye, good front, good shoulders, top line and set-on. She lacked that varminty expression, lacked bone and substance, and while she had good angulation she walked on the outside of the pads of her rear legs. Watching her go away from you, her rear action resembled an inverted wishbone. She was well bred; her sire was Ch. Quissex Sunday Punch by Ch. Quissex Deacon. Deacon is on our list of all-time "great sires." Her dam was Karnilo Completa, a double Chieftan great-granddaughter; Ch. Karnilo Chieftan of Foxden is also a Smooth immortal. Daisy was bred to Eng. and Am. Ch. Burnaun Rascal of Maryholm the first time. He had good bone, substance, and a great rear end. The litter was only marginally successful. The six male puppies were typey and two completed their titles but made no great impact in the breed. We sold them all, but Daisy did give promise of being a producer. On the premise that you breed the best to the best, we then bred Daisy to Ch. Ttarb the Brat. There were two dogs in six generations that appeared in both Brat's and Daisy's pedigrees, Ch. Newmaidley Whistling Jeremy and Ch. Watteau Snuffbox. For Brat they appear on the sire's side in his fourth generation; in Daisy's pedigree in the third and fourth generation on the sire's side. Daisy's dam, Karnilo Completa, was the result of breeding a Chieftan grandson to a Chieftan granddaughter. There are some that would state that Brat-Daisy was linebreeding. If it was, then every Fox Terrier in this country is linebred.

I saw this as breeding the best I had to the best available dog. The result of the match was just two puppies. Ch. Foxmoor One Tuff Cookie and Ch. Foxmoor Macho Macho Man, two really outstanding Fox Terriers. Macho was #1 Smooth in breed competition in 1983 and BB at the AFTC Centenary Show in June, 1985. Most of my friends in the fancy who have seen both Cookie and Macho give a slight edge to Cookie in conformation. Cookie just did not like dog shows, but she is turning out marvelous puppies. We will get to her shortly. A repeat of the Brat-Daisy union produced a litter of four. One of those, Ch. Foxmoor Chief of Staff, was Best in Sweepstakes and Winners Dog at the 1984 Winter Specialty. He repeated those wins several months later at the Maryland Specialty. His litter brother, Ch. Foxmoor Field Marshall, was Reserve Winners Dog at the February Specialty. He went on to finish his championship at nine months of age, is now in England with Vera Goold of Sidewater Kennels, for whom he won the Dog C.C. at Crufts in 1986. The third brother, Ch. Foxmoor Five Star General, is in France with noted Smooth judge and breeder Farkash Wieland and is winning in France and Belgium. The bitch in the litter is Foxmoor Majorette. Her only difficulty is size. She could be bigger. That litter was Daisy's last. Here was an example of breeding the best I had to the best available. It was also an example of extreme good luck.

George Skelly's book *All About Fox Terriers* offers a description of a numerical system that is still utilized by many breeders. Quoting Mr. Skelly,

A typical three-generation pedigree lists two parents, four grandparents, and eight great-grandparents for a total of 14 individual places. A four-generation pedigree includes 16 more places for a total of 62 places. An out-bred ancestry to five generations will carry 62 different names. An ancestry of either in-breeding or line-breeding would have fewer than 62 places with repetitions of certain names filling out the places.

From the foregoing, it is apparent that an extended pedigree is a bit cumbersome to handle readily. A study was made of this problem to develop a shorthand method of describing or stating the line-breeding existing in an extended pedigree. The answer was found in the adoption of an exceedingly simple system of numerical symbols which will be explained here.

Let us review an example of what has been the usual way to describe a good dog's breeding; Ch. Cavalcade of Wildoaks was sired by Ch. Crackley Startler out of Ch. Kemphurst Carnation. Intense half-brother and half-sister breeding was responsible for Cavalcade. Beau Brummel is the sire of both Startler and Carnation, while Simon is the sire of their dam. Cavalcade is exceedingly bred back to Fountain Crusader.

Using the numerical symbols, one would simply say: Ch. Cavalcade of Wildoaks, by Ch. Kemphurst Carnation, was line-bred from Beau Brummel (12.2), Talavera Simon (43.43) and Fountain Crusader (5545.554).

Consider another example together with the explanation. The line-breeding of that great producing matron and Best in Show winner at the Garden in 1946, Ch. Hetherington Model Rhythm, can now be stated clearly in a simple sentence: Sired by Ch. Hetherington Surprise Model out of Hetherington Flash, she was line-bred from Crackley Supreme (4.535), Westbourne Teetotaler (3.5) and Talavera Simon (555.6556).

Each digit of the number in parenthesis stands for one place in the indicated generation, the position at the left of the decimal point indicates top half or male side of the pedigree, the position to the right of the decimal point indicating lower half or female side of the pedigree. Now, reading the number following Crackley Supreme (4.535), the digit 4 at the left of the decimal means that Crackley Supreme appears once on the male side in the fourth generation, the digits 535 at the right of the decimal point mean that Crackley Supreme appears three times on the female side, as once on the third and twice in the fifth generation.

In like manner, the 3.5 following Westbourne Teetotaler indicates his appearance once on the male side in the third generation and once on the female side in the fifth generation.

Now, back to the Brat-Daisy union . . . the offspring of that litter have a brief look at Ch. Watteau Snuff Box (6.6) and Ch. Newmaidley Whistling Jeremy (6.5). Not much to go on if you were out to prove that linebreeding is most productive. It would appear as though the team of "breeding the best to the best" wins that one. But science and genetics require a broader sampling. So we reach out to Australia, the home of the Brat and acquire two bitches, Am. & Aus. Ch. Farleton Fancy Me Too and Am. Ch. Farleton Fine Finish. There is no doubt in anyone's mind which bitch has superior conformation. Me Too had an outstanding show career in Australia and finished in 30 days in the United States winning several

BVs and group placements on the way. I still believe she is one of the best Fox Terrier bitches I have ever seen. She was by Newmaidley Pennyworth out of Farleton Foxglove, a daughter of Aus. Ch. Farleton Don Pedro, one of the great Fox Terriers of this or any other time, according to everyone who ever saw him. Peter Green, Ric Chashoudian, Fred Young and Peter Thomson all declared that this dog was as close to perfection as you can get. He is also .45 maternal line of Brat while a full brother, Aus. Ch. Farleton Felix Flicka, is on the sire's side. Me Too is .34 on the dam's side to Don Pedro and 45. on the sire's side to Whistling Jeremy. The Brat is 6. to Whistling Jeremy. Putting all this in perspective, the offspring are Don Pedro (65.34), Newmaidley Whistling Jeremy (6.65) and Me Too was a fantastic bitch, the Brat a great dog, the best to the best and great linebreeding as well, a match made in heaven that somehow went to the devil. The offspring were sold as pets.

If you are a breeder and if you have decided that a certain course of action will produce well and it doesn't, and if you have a significant amount of money invested in a bitch and your plan and your bitch does not produce, then you have three choices. You can repeat the first disaster. You can sell the bitch and take your loss. You can try to breed her to a different dog. I chose the third alternative—still with the idea that bloodlines notwithstanding, breed the best to the best. One of the outstanding Smooth Fox Terriers of the 1980s or any other time is Ch. Foxden Warspite, a double grandson of Eng. & Am. Ch. Karnilo Chieftain of Foxden (3.3). While the result of this breeding was slightly better than the first, there were two dogs and two bitches, none of the offspring came close to the quality of the sire or the dam. Am. Ch. Farleton Fine Finish breeding was the reverse of Me Too's, but while Me Too could have competed successfully at the highest level of breed competition, Fine Finish could not. She completed her title quickly enough but was not the equal of Me Too. Fine Finish was by Ch. Farleton Don Pedro out of a Newmaidley Pennyworth daughter. Bred to the Brat, the offspring were Ch. Farleton Don Pedro (45.2), Ch. Farleton Felix Flicker, Don Pedro brother (4.4), and Whistling Jeremy (6.6). This breeding produced two lovely dogs, Ch. Foxmoor Painted Pony and Ch. Foxmoor Double Diamond.

If I were judging the three bitches we've discussed thus far, Ch. Quissex Upsadaisy, Ch. Farleton Fancy Me Too, and Ch. Farleton Fine Finish, there is no doubt how they would be placed. Fancy Me Too would be first and the other two a distant second and third. I believe that I would give a slight edge to Daisy for second. The important point of this exercise is that if I were a novice just getting started without the benefit of hindsight, I would purchase Fancy Me Too. As a novice I would be elated by her ring performance, and totally shattered by her performance in the whelping box. If I was a "one bitch" novice breeder, I would be absolutely frustrated. The one really unknown factor is "Will the bitch be a producer?" The fancy learns rather quickly about the productive capacity of a stud dog; you can see his progeny in the ring. A bitch, on the other hand, is usually purchased as a puppy or a young maiden without any previous track record. If you can keep more than one bitch and you want to breed good ones, sell or find homes for those who do not produce. Do not keep trying with matrons and continually produce common puppies. It is heart wrenching to have to make that kind of decision. If you are a small hobby breeder, the odds are not in favor of dramatic success under the best of conditions. With a good producing bitch and a great stud dog you will be rewarded with good, typey Fox Terriers who can compete well. A breeder does not breed for a "Brat" or a "Spot On." Those are accidents. They appear perhaps once in a decade, for no apparent reason. You must look to breed sound, typey Fox Terriers with good temperaments. The great ones will pick their own owners. By starting with a proven bitch, you increase your chances for success considerably.

A major difficulty faced by most small hobby breeders is their loyalty to their brood bitches. Do not misunderstand me. A person can have a good, sound, well-bred bitch that just will not reproduce her good qualities. When this happens there are only a limited number of options. Some breeders will tell you to try three different dogs before giving up on a bitch. Others will tell you to stick with her, blood will finally triumph. My experience has been that just as you have great show dogs that rarely throw a decent puppy, the same is true for a brood bitch. There are producers and non-producers. It is as simple as that. There are some things that the hobby breeder can do to mitigate this risk. There is that proven brood bitch that can be purchased from one of the larger breeders. It is conceivable that even the largest, wealthiest, most successful breeders will have a three- or four-year-old champion bitch for sale, a bitch that has had two or three productive litters but because the breeder desires to retain the offspring, the parent may be available. Before deciding to acquire a bitch in this category you must see the record of the offspring and the offspring themselves. A real pitfall to be wary of is that breeders (I am one of these) will sell a proven bitch who has an outstanding show career but a mediocre record of productivity. The novice is blinded by the show career and tends to lose sight of the real objective. Her show career is shortlived compared to the bitch's impact as a producer. That particular animal may be able to win a few breeds after being acquired, but age creeps up far too swiftly and you are left with a few memories and, where it counts, a very ordinary brood bitch. Geneticists will no doubt provide a differing point of view. I have bred dogs throughout my life, spanning 40 years of hard times and good times. Times when it took all my resources to keep body and mind together, to feed, clothe and shelter my family, and times, later in life, when I could afford to satisfy any dog curiosity or whim. A bitch that throws common, ordinary pet quality puppies should not be kept after a second litter providing the breedings were to two different but suitable proven stud dogs of unquestioned success. Once you have that wonderful bitch who contributes some of her best qualities to every litter, the task gets a bit easier. Your objective of competing well in any company is near. Take a good look at your girl. Where does she excel? Where does she need help? You must develop the ability to see your own shortcomings.

Ch. Quissex Upsadaisy is my housepet. She sleeps at my feet, lives for my arrivals, and looks after my things when I am gone. She (with an assist from Ruth, my wife, who selected her from several photos), was the foundation of Foxmoor Kennel's Smooths. Yet Daisy had her faults and I never stopped seeing them or discussing them openly. She certainly is a lovely bitch and if each litter produced no worse than "All Daisy-quality" puppies, I would consider myself a successful breeder. As I said earlier, I do not believe you can breed for great dogs. A good breeder can strive to continually produce a product of uniform quality and temperament. A good breeder develops a reputation for being competitive every time he or she exhibits. A good breeder does not need to know who is judging. The quality of their program will receive consideration from any competent judge. A good breeder may not always win, but the competition, the spectators, the steward and the judge will know that he or she was there.

Know and admit both the virtues and the faults of your dogs. By the time this book comes out, Ch. Foxmoor Macho Macho Man will be retired from competition. I was fortunate to breed him in my second litter; I could breed 20 more years and not get another as good. He has also proven himself as a producer. His strengths include marvelous head, eyes, ears, expression, neck, shoulders, front action coming at you, side gait and rear angulation. His shortcomings include rear action going away, eye a bit large, a bit light in bone, and short on buttocks. Some might fault him slightly for his feet but I believe a bit heavier bone would have corrected that. Of course, "beauty is in the eye of the beholder." Breeding good dogs is a very private, personal experience but so is judging. Some judges have faulted him for "not being big enough." He is 16 inches and weighs 22 pounds in show condition. Yes, breeding and exhibiting dogs is a very personal, private experience. Before anyone else, you must satisfy yourself.

I was sitting at ringside watching a wonderful Best of Variety class (prior to 1985) at a large, important Specialty on the West Coast. Foxmoor was fortunate to have won WB, so the class had the WB and Macho. There were five BIS winning Smooths among the competitors. An owner of one of the exhibits stood behind me extolling his dog, and no doubt the dog was gorgeous. His major flaw was his shoulders. He was slightly loaded in the shoulders and this caused poor action coming at you. As the dog approached our position at ringside, the owner said, "Look at the front action on that dog. Isn't it great?" Rather than point out the flaw, I simply replied, "If you like your dog's front action you'll be crazy about the way

Macho goes away from you." Neither dog's movement flaws were awful, but they were faults and if you want to breed better dogs you had better know where you need to improve. The other alternative to buying a proven bitch is to acquire a bitch puppy from a top producing bitch. Any chance mating might produce a good one, but that particular good one will be less likely to multiply herself, while bitches who produce consistent quality will usually pass along that capability to their offspring. Therefore, if I have not convinced you to seek out an older bitch then try to buy a puppy from a bitch that has already produced well.

It takes time and study. Go to dog shows. Visit kennels and read, read, read! *Terrier Type* reports on all of the Specialty shows held throughout the country, so does the *AFTC Newsletter* circulated to members. These reports include not only the breed and point winners, but actually duplicate a marked catalog from a standpoint of the placements in each class. For the purpose of acquiring a foundation bitch, examine the results carefully, pay close attention to the dams of the winners; for the moment, block out the sires. If you are fortunate you will see that one litter from one dam (litter brothers and sisters) placed exceptionally well.

If you go to the shows, buy a catalog and study the judging. Mark the class placements and point winners; see if members of the same litter score well. When you have assembled your data over a period of six to twelve months, you should be ready to contact several breeders to request a puppy bitch of the producing bitch or bitches your study has identified. Breeders may not have what you want; they may offer you something else. The only acceptable alternative is a daughter of a full sister, although this increases the risk slightly.

There is something compelling about the need to acquire a dog once you've made up your mind. Many people have written to Foxmoor requesting a "show prospect." We respond by sending photos of the puppies we have available that we believe are show quality, but caution the buyer that until the puppy is five or six months old we do not represent them as show quality. If the puppy is purchased up to three months of age we price it equal to our pet quality puppies. The exception is a serious fault. Therefore, if you want a show quality foundation bitch, have patience or gracefully accept the consequences of impetuosity. One arrangement new breeders should avoid when buying that bitch, either puppy or matron, is to buy it on breeding terms. Do not co-own! Do not buy the bitch if the seller wants to dictate breeding arrangements. In other words, if there are strings attached, I believe that you should not buy the bitch. This is not to say that you won't seek advice from the breeder, but you must begin your effort by being your own person. Some breeders will not sell a quality puppy bitch without a guarantee that the bitch will be campaigned to her championship. While you might want the same result when the bitch is shown, she might not do well in the ring and you have made a commitment that locks you into a long, arduous campaign trying to finish a good bitch that has little or no joy for exhibiting. Just buy the bitch, pay the price and own her without strings. If you are going to make mistakes, let them be yours and not someone else's. Once more, I want to reiterate that you should always seek advice and direction from the breeder from whom you purchased your puppy. So should advice and direction be asked of many people. In the final analysis, trust your own eyes, your hands, your own instincts. There may be more disappointment, but the rewards are so much sweeter.

Before discussing the selection of the stud dog, some direction needs to be offered on when and how often to breed a bitch. Many authorities express the opinion that a bitch should be bred during her second heat cycle, and that she can have two consecutive litters but should be rested by skipping every third cycle. This advice is like generally accepted accounting practices. It sounds fine on paper but it causes confusion in practice. If a bitch comes in season for the first time at six months of age and continues that cycle throughout her productive life, then the traditional advice may be applicable. Breed her for the first time during her second season and again during her third season. Having said that I must share with you some observations. I have had personal, first-hand experience with several top breeders who breed their best bitches each time they come in season, once they are a year old or more. They will continue to do so until the bitch is six or seven and then retire her to the dowager wing of their kennel to live out the rest of her life in happy gossip and occasional tiffs with the other kennel elder statespeople. The bitches seem none the worse for their experience. As for myself, I will breed a bitch her first season if the first season is experienced at 10 months or older and the bitch is a good size. If the bitch cycles every six or seven months, I will skip every third cycle. All of these guidelines pre-suppose that the offspring produced by these ladies are consistent with my objectives; if not, I won't continue to breed them.

Earlier this chapter described the numerical method of expressing the linebred characteristics of a pedigree. We are now ready to put that to use. Study the pedigree of your bitch. Take a good, hard look at her. Try to determine which ancestors are responsible for her various characteristics, good and bad. There is no shortcut to this process; a six-generation pedigree is essential. To demonstrate the approach to breeding that I was taught it is necessary to genetically dissect my favorite Fox Terrier, Ch. Quissex Upsadaisy: head—pleasing enough with the correct proportion of foreface to backskull, good width to backskull, proper strength in lower jaw, planes not quite right, muzzle slopes somewhat away from desired parallel planes, ears beautifully placed and set with correct fold and fall, (they could be a bit smaller), eye dark enough but too large and not set deeply enough, neck, shoulder, really lovely, set-on and buttocks excellent, second thigh solid, bone too light even for a bitch; feet—good, but with better bone would be perfect, front action and extension good, rear extension good, rear action is her major flaw; chest and loin excellent, chest is deep and correct in shape. As long as I write this way about my own dog or dogs, I am on safe ground.

Examine photos, magazines, old yearbooks; observe at shows, visit kennels as the opportunity arises; note those dogs who most please you. Analyze their pedigrees, determine the dominant individuals by the frequency of their appearance in the first six generations, then try to purchase the producing bitch with some common line to your choices. Once you have achieved that goal then breed her to the best representative offspring of your chosen line or lines. Always be alert for that great prepotent sire that manifests himself every ten or 20 years or so. Use him. Work him vigorously into your present program. This advice is not a contradiction. It is called progress. It appears as though two of the greatest winning prepotent Smooth stud dogs were genetic accidents, "Saddler" and "Brat." That is not to say that the Fox Terriers behind those two were not good dogs, they were, but they were the product of outcrosses. Even that description is inaccurate. The sires and dams of Saddler and Brat were outcrosses. In other words, the system that produced those two was breeding the "Best to the Best" or no system at all, just a breeder's hunch or perhaps close proximity of the sire and dam. Whatever the circumstances, I do not believe that anyone can breed that kind of Fox Terrier on a consistent basis. We all try; however, fate is the great unknown; call it the genetic dice box.

One final comment about the productive bitch. The premise that I espouse is distilled from nearly 40 years of observing and breeding. You may ask, "How do you get a top winning bitch from a bitch that I might label as a poor producer?" The scientific answer probably rests in the genotype and phenotype of the individual. There is no sure-fire method. You may purchase a bitch puppy from a good producing bitch that may turn out to be unable to complete her championship and not throw a decent puppy. You may secure a proven bitch that had several champions in each preceding litter and she will give you rubbish. The advice I offer will, however, increase your chances for success and minimize disappointments. Do your best and may "the great dog planner" reward your efforts at least once in your lifetime, and more important, may you recognize it when it happens!

As for your first litter, there is an element of perversity in every litter of puppies. Their features are kaleidoscopic. They change almost as you stare at them. At what age can you tell which puppy is best? How about two years old? Every knowledgeable breeder is haunted by the prospect of selling their one chance for Fox Terrier immortality, and yet it is an economic necessity to make decisions as to which pup or pups are "show quality" and which are not. Even the owner who just wanted his "baby" to experience motherhood will usually decide to keep one of the offspring.

The challenge of litter analysis is more important to the serious fancier, whether the hobby consists of one bitch or several. The selection process must proceed. Most of us cannot keep them all for an indefinite period of time. The interesting aspect to this circumstance is that I know of no common denominator shared by all knowledgeable breeders; each does his or her own thing. Some swear that they decide at birth and stick to that decision while others share the five-day-old theory, and still others when the puppies first stand. Some say, "Make your decision at eight weeks of age and do not look back." The fact is that there is no sure way to predict what a puppy will look like when it matures. Follow the history of sweepstakes winners and see how many go on to outstanding show careers; certainly, some fulfill their early promise, but most do not. A Fox Terrier perfect at ten months will continue to grow. How will it grow? Will it thicken and coarsen as it matures? What will growth do to that marvelous top line? There are no certain answers.

At Foxmoor Kennels we use the winnowing process. We keep them until they eliminate themselves. No decisions are made until the puppies are eight weeks old. At eight weeks we assess our options and rank the puppies and we examine them almost every day. If a mouth begins to go the puppy is offered as a pet. If we go to a match show and the puppy doesn't react positively, it is offered as a pet. A puppy with a gay tail at three months is sold as a pet. Heavy houndy ears and a wide skull will usually get worse after four months. Many breeders say they can tell action at three to four months. I can tell if it's good or bad at that age, but I cannot state that a good mover at four months will be a good-moving adult. Rear action seems to be easier to forecast than front action. The same is true for overall shape. The squarest four-month-old can develop Dachshund tendencies at one year or older. A cobby puppy becomes rangy; an elegant puppy can become a coarse adult.

It is interesting that professional handlers, as a rule, make more competent judges than do breeders. I believe that the reason rests on the handler's way of assessing a dog vs. a breeder's. A breeder focuses on faults and can pick them out with alacrity. Breeders see a dog or a bitch in relationship to their breeding programs and become concerned lest this or that fault be added and, therefore, concentrate and allow the decision to be made on the parts of the contestant. The handler sees the dog as a whole, the sum of its parts. Yes, there are faults but there are virtues as well. It is the picture presented by the sum of all the parts that the handler sees. When you make your decision on which one to keep and which to sell, try to look at the dog in its entirety. You cannot overlook the faults but do not allow the faults to blot out the virtues.

I'm reminded of a story of a gardening enthusiast who sought an azalea bush from a nurseryman. She stated, "I am looking for a very nice azalea for my garden." He picked out an unusually full azalea and offered it to her. She asked, "Is it pink or white?" He stated that it was white. She wanted pink. The man selected another one and said, "Here is a lovely, full plant and it is pink." The gardener proceeded to examine every leaf, every branch and said, "Do you have something a little fresher? This one appears just a bit tired." They walked on a bit more, examining plant after plant, but the gardener found nothing the nurseryman offered to her pleasing enough to make the purchase. Finally, the nurseryman said, "A new shipment just arrived. You wait here and I'll go and get an azalea from the new batch." He returned in a few minutes with a lovely plant still blooming and the lady looked at the plant, examined every leaf, every bud, every branch, sniffed it and even snapped off a lower branch and said, "Don't you have any others?" The man replied, "Madam, an azalea is an azalea. Could you pass such a test?"

For several years I was on the publicity committee for the Houston KC and the Astro-World Series of Dog Shows. One year I succeeded in obtaining several television promotional pieces prior to the first day of the first all-breed show. One of those TV segments was filmed at the Houston Combined Specialties the day before the first all-breed event and if there was time would be aired on the early or late news on KNOU-TV, the CBS station in Houston. The piece consisted of my own special personal dog, Ch. Quissex Upsadaisy, describing the action and the future plans for the weekend as she toured the show areas with a cameraman following close behind. The voice-over was a young lady reporter named Penny Crone, who did marvelous imitations of Joan Rivers. To put the situation in clearer perspective, Daisy is my "special" dog. She was our foundation bitch, a marvelous producer, an eccentrically delightful housepet, the dam of Ch. Foxmoor Macho Macho Man. What more can I say? Additionally, I had been working for three years to get a promotional piece for the dog shows on one of the major TV news shows. We had made several, but they were always pre-empted by more important newsworthy stories. My patient, loving and long-suffering wife was aware of these frustrations and of my continuing efforts on this project. Each year in the past we dutifully watched the early and late news, hoping that our segment would air only to meet with a major fire or one more murder or assorted vice raids, any of which can push our "bit of fluff" into oblivion.

This night as we were glued to our set, what do you know. There was Daisy touring the Astro-Hall!!! There was Daisy commenting on the Dalmatian judging. There was Daisy stopping to chat with an Irish Wolfhound. There was Daisy signing off asking people to come to the "dog show." Ruth jubilantly jumped out of her chair and excitedly said, "Wasn't that great? Wasn't Daisy terrific? Aren't you proud and excited? You did it! You finally made the late news!! Say something, don't just sit there, say something." I said, "She still cannot move going away." And Ruth threw something at me, but I am a breeder and suffer from the same disease. It is

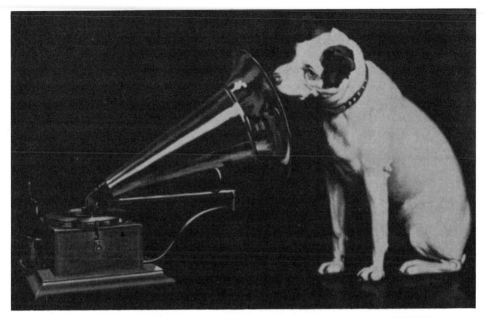

"Nipper," a painting by English artist Francis Barraud, later became the trademark of RCA Victor.

"Pickles," from *Ginger & Pickles* by Beatrix Potter. F. Warne & Co. Publishers, 1909.

287

William Powell and Myrna Loy, stars of "The Thin Man," with the Wire Fox Terrier, Asta. Reproduced by permission of Metro-Goldwyn-Mayer.

Asta's TV successor.

The British film star "Skippy," shown with the immortal Gracie Fields in her film "Keep Smiling," June 1946.

"Jack," a television performer owned and trained by Lisa Sachs.

called "Myopic Imperfection." The only cure is experience and maturity.

While none of us should lower our goals, alter our plans, settle or compromise with quality, we do have a tendency to sit at ringside discussing all the faults of the current top dogs and bitches. The next time you find yourself in a conversation like that, take another look at the dog under discussion and see how discerning you can be about its virtues. And, as your litter matures if you intend to keep one to show or a bitch to breed from later on, then you must learn to identify what is good in a specimen. Most of the greatest ones I have seen had two things wrong with them: 1) I did not breed them, and 2) I did not own them. I believe that those two faults are at the root of the rest of the fault-finding done at ringside and among breeders. If you have bred your bitch so that she has the "fulfillment of motherhood" I hope you come out of it none the worse for the experience. If you are just starting in the hobby and sport of breeding and exhibiting Fox Terriers, I hope this brief segment provides some guidelines. While I cannot see into the future, I am certain of the past and present and there is no better group of people than Fox Terrier people in all of dogdom. I choose to believe that the two Fox Terriers attract only the best of enthusiastic fanciers ready to assist any novice in any way they can.

Another pitfall the novice breeder must be wary of is the current fixation on "ratings." I cannot help but feel concern that people are guided in their breeding programs by the annual results of the various rating systems. As a child, I would visit my dad's place of work and play with a thing called a comptometer which could multiply, divide, add and subtract. I can't recall the exact year, but I was just beginning to struggle with long division at school. One Saturday, I was with my dad on the train to work and he noticed I had my school books with me. Since placing me in such close proximity to my school books at any time was a severe challenge to my parents, this academic interest did not go unnoticed. Dad inquired about my sudden interest in schoolwork, and I told him that I was going to do my entire month's math homework on the comptometer. He made some comments about my brain getting lazy and not being able to take that machine with me wherever I went, but the one comment that stayed with me was that the purpose of learning is to expand your knowledge and train your mind and my father saw the comptometer as an anti-tool. That is how I see the rating systems. In many ways the systems enhance interest in the sport. It is easy for people outside the sport to understand what "Number One" means. The proponents of the ratings state that the systems promote competition and help to improve the sport and the various breeds, but they never say how the rating systems achieve these results. There are several different rating systems but, I believe, all of them were derived from the Phillips System. For many years, Mrs. Irene Castle Phillips compiled statistics annually on every dog or bitch that earned a Group placement or a Best in Show. It was designed to "measure with fairness the difference between a dog show win scored over many dogs and one scored over but a few. This explanation is quoted from the description of the Phillips System as it appeared in the magazine *Popular Dogs*.

Points are awarded for Best in Show, or Group placement wins only.

The Best in Show (BIS) dog earns a point for each dog in actual competition (absentees, miscellaneous and obedience entries are not counted). First in Group (GR1) earns a point for each dog in the Group. Second in Group (GR2) earns a point for each dog in the Group less the total dogs in the breed that was first. And the same applies to the third and fourth placements. Today *Kennel Review* magazine carries on the Phillips System but there are derivations of that original system. For example, the *Terrier Type* System applies similar point weights but counts Terrier Group wins only. Thus a dog or bitch that does well in strong Terrier groups will score better than a multiple Best in Show winner, with firsts in weak Terrier Groups. The Knight System ignores Best in Show and Group victories and just awards points for the Best of Breed wins based upon the number of Smooths or Wires defeated at each show. The *Canine Chronicle* System and Routledge Systems are manifestations of the same theme.

There is one interesting observation that can be made about the ratings as they apply to top bitches. It is a rare top winning, top rated bitch that also becomes a top producer or even a quality producer. And after all is said and done, isn't that the final test of quality?

I have very mixed feelings about the value of ratings. As a Fox Terrier breeder, I am cognizant of the role played by the ratings in the career of Ch. Ttarb the Brat, and that without intelligent handling and aggressive promotion he might not have made so significant a contribution to the breed. As a beneficiary of the Brat's activity, I, therefore, can understand the wonderful recognition that a lesser known breed can gain if it happens to be fortunate enough to come up with the right combination of dog, handler and owner. Such a combination can provide a new, broader base for the breed and create an interest in puppy sales. The rating systems also provide a kind of clearing house for annual achievements in each breed.

Notwithstanding any of the aforementioned achievements of rating systems, I do not believe that they promote competition, nor do they always work for the betterment of individual breeds or the sport as a whole. One glaring example of a negative effect of ratings is the "hit 'em where they ain't school of handling." If two dogs are battling for top honors, they rarely compete head to head. If one is in the East, the other heads South or Midwest where the pickings are a bit easier. Or once certain judges have established their preference, it is not uncommon for the two top rated dogs to be in the same areas on the same weekend and not compete against one another. Say there are two shows in Cleveland and on the same weekend there are two shows in New York. The Saturday judges in Cleveland and the Sunday judges in New York favor Dog A, but the reverse is true for Dog

B; come Saturday night, they will pass each other in the air. How does that promote competition? Winning becomes more important than competing. The same circumstance occurs in the breed competition. If the breed is fortunate enough to have several outstanding representatives at any given time, chances are, with the exception of major events, their handlers will avoid direct competition. Handlers, after all, are being paid to make their client's dog Number One. But, if you can select your judge, avoid your severest competitor, and almost preordain your win, where is the sport? Have we not become the captives of the rating systems, and the Tournament of Champions and all the other promotions that have little to do with improving the breeds?

Another negative of the rating systems is that it creates an artificial superiority of one dog over another. An owner who can afford a top handler and the essential promotional ingredients required to successfully compete for Number One, either in the breed, the group or among all breeds, wittingly, or unwittingly, affects the outcome of many shows. Whether we like it or not, our system of dog shows and judging creates a severe strain on our pool of competent, knowledgeable judges, with one result that some judges are really uncertain about some of the breeds they are approved to pass on. No one wants to make a fool of themselves, least of all, in public. As a consequence, judges are impacted by rating systems and advertising promotions. And, rather than risk derision, many judges will select a "familiar face" at one end of the leash or the other.

Rating systems may be divisive in that they discriminate against less affluent exhibitors. A breeder of average means is motivated to seek a partner "co-owner" if their dog is good enough. While the major cause of co-ownership is the cost of campaigning and promoting a dog, ask yourself, "Why campaign and promote a dog if not to make it Number One?" Ideally, a great example of any breed should be able to be entered in the appropriate class and find its way to the top at most shows with some frequency. However, that is not the case. The combined cost of exhibiting, professional presentation, and promotion makes it almost impossible for the average breeder to successfully exhibit his or her "flyer" without outside assistance of some kind. A recent issue of a popular national dog publication (complimentary copies sent to all AKC licensed judges) revealed that there were 81 pages of advertising for "dog achievements" of which just 20 were breeder/owners.

This may be a heavy load to place on the back of the rating systems, but can anyone doubt that they play their part? Can anyone doubt that the rating systems concentrate attention on the inconsequential immediate aspects of our sport and that they ignore the statistics of significance, the statistics of future impact, the performance of the descendants of the dogs and bitches rated? It is highly possible that the top rated dog and bitch may never produce a single offspring. Or even more probably, the top rated dog or bitch may produce very ordinary, uninspiring offspring. While I agree that this is an unfair burden to place upon our present structure, as long as there is no counter-weight that extolls the virtues and accomplishments of outstanding producers, then the rating systems, to the extent that they focus attention away from breed improvement and on immediate gratification of more fortunate owners and their dogs, must carry its share of the responsibility along with those publications, however necessary and beneficial, that cater to that gratification and by their very existence are an integral part of the myopic focus of the current dog scene.

I am not in favor of eliminating those brilliant and interesting publications that foster the rating systems. I am an avid reader of most of them and an occasional advertiser. I just think that they would be better if they devoted some space to the performance of stud dogs and brood bitches, and developed a rating system for them—perhaps a system based upon the number of bitches bred, the number of puppies produced and the percentage that went on to complete their titles for stud dogs and a similar set of values for brood bitches. Who knows, we are liable to learn something that we would not know otherwise that would help us to breed better Fox Terriers.

8

The Fox Terrier
and Obedience

$\mathbf{F}$OR TOO MANY YEARS, Fox Terrier fans have allowed
other breed supporters to denegrate our wonderful breeds with uninformed
remarks about the intelligence and tractability of Fox Terriers. For years,
most performing dogs were Fox Terriers. Vaudeville and circus acts always
had troupes of Fox Terrier acts that were trained to perform marvelous and
exciting tricks much to the joy and delight of the public.

There is one fact that points out the great appeal that Fox Terriers
have for their owners. I have bred and sold Boxers, Cocker Spaniels,
Whippets, Greyhounds, West Highland White Terriers, and Lakeland
Terriers, but the most loyal owners are owners of Fox Terriers. The breeds
have enjoyed a steady, healthy place in the number of litters each year as a
result of this loyal following, their children and even their children's
children. They have always made superb, well-mannered pets. One of their
greatest virtues is their cleanliness in the house. So it comes as no surprise
to those of us privileged to be a Fox Terrier owner. Obedience, however,
for competition at obedience trials takes a somewhat greater dedication.
What is obedience and how well do Fox Terriers perform? The answer will
be surprising to those boosters of other breeds.

The Purpose of Obedience

The purpose of obedience trials is to demonstrate the usefulness of the
purebred dog as a companion of man, not merely the dog's ability to follow

specified routines in the obedience ring. The basic objective of obedience trials is to promote dogs that have been trained and conditioned always to behave in the home, in public places, and in the presence of other dogs, in a manner that will reflect credit on the sport of obedience. It is also essential that the dog demonstrate willingness and enjoyment of its work, and that smoothness and naturalness on the part of the handler be given precedence over a performance based on military precision and peremptory commands.[1]

"Love me, love my dog" is a very true saying for where is the owner whose heart does not warm to the guest who admires and praises his dog? Yet in spite of all his lovable qualities and intelligence how seldom one sees a Fox Terrier competing in obedience trials. This is most certainly not due to any fault of his, for there is no breed of dog that responds more quickly or repays better any trouble taken in training him. "Always game and lighthearted, always forgiving, never resentful of punishment justly administered, and ever ready to fulfill a task in his master's service."[2]

Breed and Obedience

Can a dog, with his handler, enter conformation competition and, at the same time, undergo the rigors of obedience training? It would be a disservice to encourage the belief that one type of showing plays havoc with the other. As in any undertaking, when done properly pride and pleasure can be derived from both. The question really is can a dog understand and differentiate between two kinds of training at the same time.

Whether it is called obedience training or not, any dog shown in breed must know how to move on a lead, stand for examination, stay, pay attention, and generally behave in a civil manner. Indeed, it would appear basic obedience training is not in opposition to performance in the breed ring. Training will build a dog's self-confidence and improve its concentration; the animal will be more steady and will tolerate distractions such as liver on the floor, loud noises, and crowds. He can be taught to watch his handler's hands and facial expressions. He can even be taught to show himself to great advantage by being trained to react to his handler asking, "Where's the mouse?" or any other effective phrase that keeps him on his toes and tail all a-quiver. How many dogs are gaited as though they are HANGING FROM THE GALLOWS? Basic healing is done briskly and on a loose lead. It's head up because the dog is watching you.

Conversely, breed showing can help in obedience because of the other

---

[1]Obedience Regulations, The American Kennel Club, New York, N.Y., pg. 2.

[2]Pardoe, J. H., *Fox Terriers,* Williams & Norgate Ltd., London, 1949, pg. 107.

dogs' proximity and the many other distractions that tax his concentration. An animal with good conformation will have an easier time in obedience as well, for his gait will be free, he'll be able to retrieve easily if his bite is good and clearing the jumps will be effortless with strong hindquarters.

There are many people who can't handle both kinds of showing simultaneously or simply prefer to accomplish one before the other. Then let's change our original question and switch the words "handler" and "dog" around in the first sentence. If your attitude is yes, we can, then you will and with a great deal of success and satisfaction. Thus, there is no reason that obedience should be viewed as the opposite of breed. Try to think of breed and obedience as different, but related aspects of our very bright little friends' abilities.

There's Obedience and Then There's Obedience

If you are content to have a Fox Terrier who does as he pleases, uses the furniture as though he paid for it, jumps up on all visitors, demands his portion of your dinner and, in general, believes it's very civil of him to allow you to sleep in his bed, then it can be concluded you have no interest in obedience. If, however, you want a civil, well-mannered little friend that can accompany you in public, then some kind of training time must be invested. It needn't be formal, it needn't cost a cent, but it should be a *fait accompli* before that cute puppy becomes a tedious problem, one that can last sixteen or more years.

The days of sprawling, isolated farms when a dog could roam about doing as he pleased are fast disappearing. Fox Terriers are purchased by those who expect the dog to become a respectable member of the family and neighborhood. In our kennels, in our homes, well-mannered animals, with terrier spirit intact, are always welcomed. There is no excuse for not encouraging every single pet owner, along with housetraining and crate training, to teach "NO," "OFF," "COME," "STAY," and "LET'S GO!"

The next level of obedience would be sub-novice training, much of which is just what is expected of a breed dog in the conformation ring; all work is done on lead. Dogs who will follow basic commands learn amusing tricks quite easily. Conversely, a pet who will roll over, give paw, speak, etc., on command would benefit from the mental stimulation of some formal schooling.

Following this is Novice work, which could lead to the degree of Companion Dog. A CD animal is one who has earned your confidence and trust. He can walk with you on a city street or sit on the front seat of your car without interfering with your movements.

If by now you are hooked on this sport and want to continue building the dog/owner relationship, the more sophisticated challenge of Open will fit the bill. At this level, jumping and retrieving are required and all work done is off the lead!

Utility, the canine Ph.D., incorporates several skills already mastered and the new material includes the dog leaving your side and scent discrimination.

How well your dog performs obedience work depends largely on what satisfies you. Fox Terriers are capable of and happy to compete with all comers or provide comic relief at a trial. Your goals become his, for you are part of a team working in unison; the kind of obedience your team performs is a decision you make consciously or otherwise.

Why Obedience?

Why would anyone want to obedience train a Fox Terrier? Just as there are excellent conformation species who are unhappy in the show ring, as in any breed, not all dogs will be candidates for competitive obedience training. There is a small but growing number of Fox Terrier enthusiasts who for various reasons choose to participate in this unique sport.

Who trains whom is up to the handler. More people may be trained by their dogs than would care to admit it. Communication is established and enhanced through training. Obedience training helps to establish a positive rapport whereby the dog is taught to respond in certain ways to particular commands given him by his handler. Many problem dogs, with too much mental and physical energy, have too few acceptable outlets in which to express the same. Obedience training can provide this acceptable outlet. Concurrently, it builds a high level team relationship between trainer and dog. This bond is far stronger than that usually experienced between owner and pet.

The objectivity by which you and your little teammate are judged is an appealing aspect of obedience work. Your team is obviously successful or it obviously isn't at a trial. In a sense, you are your own competition.

Can we teach an older dog new tricks? Obedience training spans all ages, all lifestyles, all economics, and includes both sexes. It stimulates the mind as well as the body. It teaches compassion as well as sportsmanship, strengthens patience and understanding of yourself, your dog, and others around you. It is one aspect of the relationship between dog and man that is slowly gaining much deserved recognition by fanciers of the exceptionally intelligent Fox Terrier.

Puppy Selection

Does it matter which puppy you choose for obedience? Of course it does! Some dogs could never get beyond their CD. Some dogs hate the dumbbell and others aren't sound enough to jump, still others lack motivation, that most essential ingredient in any working dog. A good trainer can provide it, but why bother when there are so many willing dogs waiting for a chance to perform?

The most important factors in selection are temperament, conformation, and suitability. A dog's temperament, his "personality" is his alone. Just as no two people are identical, neither are any two dogs. Experience proves that if you look hard enough and long enough you can find a dog of any breed to suit your purpose. When choosing a pup for obedience, bear in mind that the breed was originally intended to go to ground after vermin. Can you fault a dog who chooses his primary function over his training? It could be quite embarrassing and even aggravating when your "trained" dog breaks the long down to chase a mouse under the bleachers at a trial. You can lose friends that way, too, if his precipitous exit alarms some of the other dogs in your group. Remember, obedience is a *team* sport; even a dead-game dog can look to his handler for a release before pursuing his quarry. This can be an asset in the field, too, as you may not want him going after a particular rat.

While obedience dogs do not need to have close to ideal conformation, soundness does count. A dog with leg or back problems cannot jump. A deaf dog cannot compete, nor can a blind dog, although in theory they can be trained. A dog with a faulty bite will have problems retrieving. Minor cosmetic irregularities should not interfere with a dog's ability to learn. Any sound, healthy dog is able to complete the requirements for a CD.

Suitability is a little harder to define. To me it represents that quality which makes a dog the ideal match for his handler. It combines elements of temperament and conformation. A dog is suitable to his handler if his temperament is complimentary, his appearance acceptable, and if he wishes to learn. A hyperactive dog is not suitable for a little old lady who has severe arthritis. A quiet, sensitive dog does not suit an aggressive, hard-handed handler. Since our breeds offer both, it is important to get the right dog.

There are many ways to assess the obedience potential of a young puppy. Some breeders use early puppy testing wherein the dogs are evaluated by an outsider at six to ten weeks of age. Certain standardized tests are performed and each puppy graded according to his response. There are a variety of methods and each uses its own value system. Remember that these tests are only as good as the tester. The answers are subjective and open to interpretation. What some people find undesirable others may covet.

The best way to get a good obedience prospect is to decide exactly what you want to do with the dog, how far you want to go and if you want breed quality as well. Some breeders will not sell a show puppy to an obedience home. Do you intend to go to class? If not, who will help you with the training? Will the breeder help? If the breeder is knowledgeable in obedience, let him suggest a puppy. Be honest, if you want an OT Ch. *dog* tell him. He probably wishes *he* had one.

When I choose a puppy I look for several things. I like an obedience

Keeping the dog's attention is imperative at all levels.

Retrieve over high jump—Open.

Heeling on a loose lead—Novice.

Broad jump—Open.

Scent discrimination—Utility, leather.

Scent discrimination—Utility, metal.

Show enthusiasm when teaching the recall.

Bar jump in directed jumping—Utility.

Directed retrieve—Utility. Note the keen attention of the dog.

Completing directed retrieve—Utility.

"Ever ready to fulfill a task in his master's service."
Practical Obedience

301

dog who is alert and outgoing. At ten weeks the puppy should be kissing and wagging his tail at me even though he has never seen anybody except his breeder before. He should follow me around the yard without much encouragement. The pup should not cower or act frightened.

Curiosity is of primary importance, but the pup should be responsive. I like to sit down with the pups and play with them. Some of them will wander off to investigate their surroundings. This is fine so long as they pick up their heads and look at me when I call them. Extra points go to the one that comes on that call. What about the pup who clings to you? Very flattering, but not a good prospect for advanced work, some of which is done out of sight. This is not typical breed temperament. A slightly aggressive dog is resilient and could deal better with the distractions at a trial and at work. It is easier to slow down a fast dog than pep up a slow one.

For dual purpose dogs (breed and obedience) I prefer an even *more* outgoing pup, one that is not stubborn or impulsive. These dogs can later be trained to "fix" on something, either bait in your hand or another dog or toy. The pup should be good natured, but independent enough to ignore you when you want him to, so that the judge can see what he looks like. Certain personality quirks may be overlooked in favor of the better-made dog.

Retrieving is important in obedience. Take the puppies individually to a quiet room. Play with a puppy with a toy, sock, or even a piece of paper. Wave it around. Let him grab it a few times. Make sure his attention is on the toy and toss it gently a few feet away. Sit back and observe his response. He must go after the toy and pick it up. Pat the ground gently to get his attention and encourage him to carry the toy to you. If he does this on the first try. . . BUY HIM! If he goes to the toy, mouths it, then picks it up but doesn't bring it back, try again. He may have seen something more interesting. If he continues to respond similarly I would have second thoughts about training him to do anything without a lot of firm handling. Reject the one which ignores the toss, also the one that won't pick up the toy. Be leary of the one that lies down and chews on the toy, a common problem with obedience dogs. As dumbbell work is hard enough, I see no reason to make it harder with a dog who has demonstrated a lack of natural ability in this test. A dog who cannot or will not retrieve is stuck forever in Novice.

The ideal obedience prospect is an alert pup. He should listen to you when you talk. He should not be afraid to make eye contact frequently. This need not be aggressive, merely interested. Caution is *admirable, cowardice is unacceptable.* He should not fear you or other people without reason. He should respond to encouragement when in a strange situation. A young pup may cower for an instant when a truck backfires, but he must stand right back up to watch the passing traffic. He should ignore the next truck. The ideal pup will look in the direction of the noise, decide that it was

It can be done! Ch. Harbor View Heather, CDX, shown winning first place in Open competition for her third leg. "Jellybean" was first in Open A competition two out of three times, defeating 37 other dogs.

A Smooth performing the broad jump—Open.

harmless and return to what he was doing. When older he will merely look to you to see if you react.

Be wary of the following traits. Some dogs sulk; this can be controlled to an extent by proper handling. You will meet the occasional Fox Terrier who seems not to care. These impervious dogs are not ill-tempered, they really don't relate to people at all. You might just as well be part of the scenery. The shy dog, a rarity in this breed, never makes a truly reliable performer. Every breed has its quota of really nasty dogs. Fortunately for Fox Terrier people, we get very few. All of these dogs are not for the novice handler. Some are not for anybody.

So if you want a Fox Terrier for obedience, get a dog that will do the work. Pick a friendly pup who likes to retrieve. Make sure he isn't spooky or very stubborn, observe the pup in a variety of situations before you buy. Be sure to get a pup with a personality that complements your own family's and NEVER, as a novice, choose one because he will be a "challenge" or because you feel sorry for him. Obedience is hard enough—there's no need to make it harder.

Dog vs. Bitch

There are generalized, natural differences in temperament between males and females of the same breed. Obedience people have long acknowledged this fact and used it to their advantage when selecting a dog. First decide what type of obedience you intend to pursue, then make your decision.

Females are steadier and more reliable. They are much less easily distracted. Conversely, they tend to be more independent. A bitch is also far less likely to pick a fight with a passing dog or to mix in an existing one. Bitches do come into season once every six or seven months. This can really upset your show plans as they are not permitted to compete in obedience trials while in heat. You can always spay her as long as you're not showing her in breed, too. Bitches, while not prone to starting fights, are harder to break out of one. Some bitches are truly "silent but deadly," never giving warning except in their body pounce.

Dogs are flashier. They can put on quite a show. Some dogs will select a dog in the group which they dislike for some reason and jump him at any opportunity. This behavior can be controlled by proper handling. Some dogs will give the performance of the century one day and fail even the stand on the next. Dogs may be more showy, which nets high scores on the day, but to insure that style while adding a bit more consistency some handlers neuter them. A dog that has been used at stud a few times is the hardest to control. Seasoned studs seem much more relaxed. Dogs are more affectionate than bitches. Take your pick or take two, it's more fun that way.

Successful Practice

"Practice makes perfect," but what if the practice isn't perfect? The best results would probably be gained by being in class where the instructor respects and likes Fox Terriers. Only the very basic facts can be learned from obedience manuals. Each and every handler/trainer is as individual as is his dog. If you rely on a training manual alone, there is often a dead end when a problem arises and, with no qualified person about to assist, frustration can set in. An experienced trainer can usually offer a solution. What works in one situation may be wrong for another. However, the suggestions in the following section should be effective with most Fox Terriers and may indeed prevent problems encountered while practicing. Good practice makes the difference between a dog that progresses and one that does not. Happy Heeling!

At the very outset of training, dog attention is imperative! The more attentive your dog, the better the practice. Never begin any exercise unless Foxie is looking at you. This is a learned skill and one which isn't found in many obedience books but should be included in sub-novice work. Before heeling, for example, with the dog in correct heel position, say his name. If he looks at you—great, start heeling. If he doesn't, repeat his name. If the lights are on, but nobody's home, get his attention by tapping head (his), snapping lead, whistling, making noises or whatever it takes for him to make eye contact with you. When he finally does—praise! Proceed with the exercise. Indeed, attention could be taught as a separate exercise. You need his attention in all training, and taking the time to develop it in the very beginning will pay off. Watch for this attention at trials in the top performers.

As an aid to learning, always say the dog's name first, just before giving a command involving a moving exercise. It's "FOXIE, heel." Do not use his name when doing an exercise that requires no motion such as "DOWN" or "STAY." Integrate hand signals with early novice training. If you do decide to go on through Utility, you'll both be at a great advantage. Hand signals, once learned, can be occasionally used in place of verbal commands for variety.

While practicing, there are a number of additional points to remember if you have decided to train a Fox Terrier for obedience competition. Make certain *YOU* understand what is required for the satisfactory execution of a particular exercise—be it the simple "sit-stay" or a more complex task such as retrieve over the high jump. There are standards by which the performance will be judged. Understand the requirements thoroughly before attempting to teach the exercise.

A Fox Terrier must respect his master, so never give a command unless you intend to enforce it. If you tell the dog to stay and he gets up—correct him. This also carries over into everyday living. You will only

Correcting the front.

Correcting for a straight front.

Obedience exercises modeled by Lynne Bockelman with her Fortune's Hickory Daquiri Doc.

Praising while in motion.

The correct attentive attitude.

Awaiting recall.

307

create confusion if you enforce selectively. For instance, if it's really not that important that Foxie remains where you tell him because you don't intend to correct him if he does get up, then PLEASE use another term such as "rest," or "park it." The formal command must be respected by the biped and quadruped alike.

Give just one command. If you get into the very poor habit of repeating commands, Foxie will learn he needn't listen until you finally do decide to make him. By giving only one command, Foxie learns you are sincere. If he chooses not to listen, a correction must follow. Anyway, why on earth would he suddenly listen to your third command, if he didn't listen to the first one? BE CONSISTENT! Consistency is imperative! The proper heel position is dog sitting at your left side so that he is parallel to you and not more than six inches away. Your toes and his should be even. If this is what you demand on Monday, then it's also what you demand on Thursday, and whenever you work. This simple consistency helps to eliminate confusion. As time goes on, your dog will gain security because of it.

Work briskly and happily. YOU set the pace. Don't train if you're not in the mood to do a good job. Training is meant to build a relationship, not destroy one. Your voice needs to be firm, but never threatening. Foxie's performance will reflect your frame of mind . . . he constantly reads you. If you enjoy practice, so will he. Should you be tired or disgusted or bored, Foxie will be, too. Never take out your frustrations on the dog. Hopefully, on a bad day, training will be a real "pick-me-up." If it's not, then skip it.

Fox Terriers are bright—you needn't practice every day. Sometimes three or even two weekly sessions will do. The length of a session will also vary. Fifteen minutes? Forty minutes? This depends on what you wish to accomplish. Routine can also be boring to Foxie; vary the order of the sessions. Perhaps you don't need to do a "sit-stay" every time. Practice in different locations to hold Foxie's interest. Work on establishing a sense of timing. This comes with experience. Practice footwork without a dog. The way you do an "about turn" can either throw the animal off, or help him. The same goes for all exercises. After all, your feet are what the dog sees most when not making eye contact.

The best practice sessions are those which involve an element of proofing. Proofing simply means setting up situations and distractions that create a challenge to the dog in obeying a command. We don't live in a vacuum. The fact that under ideal conditions (no distractions) Foxie drops immediately is no guarantee he'll do the same should a car come roaring down the road. This lifesaving skill is one of the many practical applications of obedience training. Proofing builds reliability. Instead of a quiet place to practice, bring a portable radio or ask a friend to stand between Foxie and you as you do a recall. Place a treat several feet from the dog when he is on a down stay. If he makes a mistake, simply correct. Reward him with the treat after he's successful. Be creative with distractions. Use them AFTER your dog knows the exercise. This will build confidence in both of you. Be generous and genuine with your praise. The amount of praise, as well as your tone of voice, will vary. Why should Foxie always come trotting and wagging on a recall if you stand there like a post? Cheer him on. Let him know how proud you are of him. Fox Terriers can sometimes be too exuberant . . . then a quiet "good boy" or "nice work" will do very well. Other times require real cheering and applause. Make him feel proud and happy he's done so well.

Teach a release word to be used, such as "OK" when the dog's work is momentarily over. Sound happy; it lets him know you are pleased with him. If he's been working hard, giving you attention, and really trying, this could be the time for a brief break. Give him a treat or let him chase a ball until it's time to work again.

Corrections are an integral part of practice. There must be an understanding as to why a dog fails to respond to a command. Determine why the animal isn't responding, then use the appropriate method of solving the problem. If the dog is confused, then a firm correction would be uncalled for as well as ineffective. Set up situations where the dog cannot make a mistake. Break the task down into simple steps. Repeat it several times and use lots of praise.

Have you ever known a Fox Terrier that ignored you? Then it's up to you to show him that you mean business. We can all love and tolerate the independent nature of the breed, but not at all times. Certainly obedience practice is one of the times Foxie needs to listen. He must learn that obeying a command has its reward. Why else would he ever listen to you at any time? The rewards are the praise and petting you lavish on him. He must also learn that deciding not to listen is to his disadvantage. If Foxie is distracted, easily, then you need to practice, always on lead, with distractions. Inject surprise and variations. Keep him interested, but don't let him con you. Praise must follow each correction. If a "backlash" occurs, perhaps you are in error in judging the reason for the animal not obeying in the first place. Always watch for Foxie's body language . . . his eyes, ears, tail carriage, and posture. Confusion is not refusal and vice versa. You are the dog's trainer. What he knows, you have taught him and so if he makes a mistake you must assume it's your fault. Dogs learn at different rates— some days will be better than others. Dogs also learn with repeated, consistent corrections and praise. Never become discouraged. Your second and third dogs will be better than your first. With every problem you face, you are learning even if you don't realize it at the time. That first leg towards that first CD is like a BB over Specials. That first CD an owner-handled championship!! Be patient, you will be rewarded!

Novice Exercises and Scores for the Degree of Companion Dog

1. Heel on Leash   35 points
2. Stand for Examination   30 points
3. Heel Free   45 points
4. Recall   30 points
5. Long Sit   30 points
6. Long Down   30 points

Maximum Total Score . . . 200 points

Open Exercises and Scores for the Degree of Companion Dog Excellent

1. Heel Free   40 points
2. Drop on Recall   30 points
3. Retrieve on Flat   25 points
4. Retrieve over High Jump   35 points
5. Broad Jump   20 points
6. Long Sit   25 points
7. Long Down   25 points

Maximum Total Score . . . 200 points

Utility Exercises and Scores for the Degree of Utility Dog

1. Scent Discrimination—Art. No. 1   30 points
2. Scent Discrimination—Art. No. 1   30 points
3. Directed Retrieve   30 points
4. Signal Exercise   35 points
5. Directed Jumping   40 points
6. Group Examination   35 points

Maximum Total Score . . . 200 points

Complete obedience regulations may be obtained by writing to the American Kennel Club in New York, N.Y.

9

The Fox Terrier Legends

HAVE YOU EVER NOTICED how some minor incident or happenstance can have a dramatic impact upon your life? Perhaps, the chance meeting that led to love, marriage, and family, or some insignificant encounter that altered your career. Two events, not totally unrelated, may have firmly molded the future of the Wire Fox Terrier in America from the late 19th century to the present.

The first resulted from the early dispute among Wire exhibitors whether to trim or not to trim. The "Au Naturelle" forces were championed by Francis Redmond who exhibited and won with a Wire aptly, though unimaginatively, called The Untrimmed. The bitch was exhibited in 1888 and, at one show, the judge strictly applied the rules and totally ignored the dressed exhibits in favor of Redmond's undressed The Untrimmed. The controversy continued until The Kennel Club arrived at a compromise that permitted the removal of hair with brush, comb or fingers but by no other means. Since the exhibit arrives at a show prepared to compete, who is to know how a result is arrived at. That ruling forever cast the Wire as a "man made" show dog. Because of the unique qualities of coat and color, a clever trimmer can hide a Wire's faults and enhance its virtues more than with any other terrier.

The second situation revolved around the burning desire of Major G. M. Carnochan to be *top dog* in Wires. The Major not only imported the best of England's Wires but he brought over the leading kennel man of the day, George Porter, who was the manager of Sam Hill's Meersbrook Kennels. The Major must have realized, at that early date, that the best dogs required the best conditioning and presentation. By 1897, Carnochan's Cairnsmuir Wires were, perhaps, the best in the world. So the two incidents, separate but not totally unrelated, gave birth to the environment so conducive to reliance on the expertise of professional kennel managers and professional handlers. The Kennel Club ruling which allowed trimming and the success of the Carnochan-Porter Team established the need for expert handling and presenting in Wires forever more.

No book on the history and development of these two breeds would be complete without some reference to the Fox Terrier legends. The people I've selected have, on the contrary, selected themselves by virtue of available information. For the most part, they were working men of poor to modest beginnings, so there are no permanent trophies offered in their names. While the passing of those now gone was duly recorded in the periodicals, the obituaries usually concerned themselves with their age and most important wins. And yet these men played a major role in the history of the two breeds, and it is to all of them that this chapter is dedicated.

George Steadman Thomas

If George Thomas was not the first professional handler, he certainly takes his place as one of the most prominent. Arriving in the United States in Boston around 1890, the 25-year-old Thomas went right to work for a Massachusetts banker, Charles N. Symonds, who had imported Yorkshire Terriers from Thomas' brother-in-law, Richard Toon. It wasn't long before Thomas and Toon were running a canine ferry service from England to the U.S.A. While still employed by Symonds, Thomas branched out to exhibiting and importing for others. In 1899, he made Wire history when he acquired Meersbrook Bristles for Charles W. Keyes. Thomas not only imported, sold and exhibited dogs, but he was a major force in bringing interested others into the Fox Terrier fold, including Mrs. A. V. Crawford and her nephew, Charles Perrin, who started the Vickery Kennels near Chicago. George Thomas supplied the plans for the kennel, the blood stock, and the kennel manager, in this case, Eland Hadfield. Hadfield was one of the first mentors of Percy Roberts.

Alf Delmont and Harry Hardcastle were among the first terrier men brought over by George Steadman Thomas. His great skill as an organizer and his growing reputation on both sides of the Atlantic as a fine and astute judge of dogs made it possible for Thomas to maintain two kennels, one in the United States and one in England which he staffed with the best terrier men he could find. The scope of his activities was prodigious. On one boat, in 1919, Thomas brough over 97 dogs. During this period of his career, he imported and sold approximately 2,500 dogs for a total sum in excess of $2,000,000.00.

By the mid-1920s Thomas became more active as a judge and advisor to kennels. His judging assignments took him all over the world, and in 1933 The American Kennel Club granted him an all-rounder's license. Some of the better-known imports of Thomas in addition to Bristles were Ridgeway Result, who became Sabine Result, Ch. Wireboy of Paington, Pendley Calling, along with 37 other dog breeds. He imported several toy breeds, never exhibited in the United States prior to Thomas introducing them. One of his last judging assignments was the BIS at the 1952 Morris and Essex, and he chose the Wire Ch. Wyretex Wyns Traveler of Trucote as his top dog. On April 2, 1955, at the age of 90, George Steadman Thomas died. He was our great purebred dog pioneer. He did everything well with dignity and integrity.

George Raper

In the late 19th century and the early years of the 20th century, if you did not get your stock from George Thomas then it came from George Raper. Raper was born in 1846 into a dog environment. Tom Raper, George's father, was famous in racing Greyhounds, so George came by his interest early in life. He became active in Fox Terriers in 1861 and, over the next 60 years, became generally recognized as the finest breed judge of his time. Raper bred Fox Terriers under three different prefixes—Raby, Richmond and Runswick. Irving Ackerman had a long and rewarding friendship with George Raper, and in his book, *The Complete Fox Terrier,* Ackerman provides the following personal insight.

> When a youth, George became a draper's assistant, but his love for dogs, coupled with his born ability to spot the "good uns," led him gradually into the then somewhat unusual trade of buying, selling, exhibiting and judging dogs.

In 1899, there were 90 dog shows recorded in the Fox Terrier Club Stud Book and Show Record, and Raper judged 20 of them.

But even the mightiest among us receives our left-handed compliments. Rawdon Lee, in his 1893 book, *The Fox Terrier,* wrote of Raper,

> Mr. G. Raper (near Sheffield, Yorkshire), one of our very best judges, has time after time taken leading prizes in the ring; the bitch Richmond Olive he exported to America being, about five year ago, the best of her sex before the public. Just lately Mr. Raper appears to have got into an indifferent strain, some of his best dogs being coarse and inclined to be Bull Terrier-like at the cheeks, whilst the bitches, as a rule, have been light of bone and stilty and stiff in their action.

OUCH!!!!
Back to the more loving account of Ackerman:

> Raper judged dog shows in almost every country on the globe. He is said to have bought and sold more Fox Terriers during his active years than any dozen other fanciers combined, and it is a certainty that he realized more

George Steadman Thomas, the founder of the system.

Percy Roberts, one of the world's greatest dog men.

George Raper: Breeder, handler, exhibitor, raconteur and one of the first international judges.

money for the Wires he sold to wealthy Americans than any other English dealer before or since.

Ackerman offers the following account of an after dinner speech of Raper's at a San Francisco affair in 1908.

> Upon the occasion of a banquet given some 30 years ago, when he was judging a show in San Francisco, Raper remarked to his hearers that he not only possessed terriers but Bulldogs as well that would "go to ground."
> When asked to explain how a Bulldog could "go to ground," he told of how he was continually "putting into the ground" numerous of his Bulldog purchases which turned out to be duffers. Raper was at times a most erratic buyer; however, when it came to judging, "the irrepressible," as he was lovingly dubbed by the canine world, knew them probably better than any man living or dead.

It was George Raper who guided Major Carnochan and his Cairnsmuir Wires. He had a marked influence upon George Porter's decision to come to work for the Major and was no less responsible for the arrival in the United States of Barkby Ben and many other famous early Wires. George Raper was active until his demise in 1924. The two Georges, Raper in England and Thomas in the United States, were all the assistance the Fox Terrier needed to steal America's heart.

Percy Roberts

Attempting to piece together a biography of Percy Roberts was a difficult task. Once his daughter declined to provide any information, the task became even more challenging. To begin with, some readers might ask who Percy Roberts is, or was. Well, Percy Roberts was probably the most formidable combination of promoter-salesman-handler who ever held a leash, and, depending upon whom you speak to, he was either a brilliant judge of dogs or an absolutely charming charlatan. Suffice to say that Percy Roberts brough wit, excitement, interest and talent to the sport we all love. Earlier in this work I wrote of Vickery Kennels, which was established in 1912 with the help of George Thomas. Thomas not only provided the English Wires but also was instrumental in bringing some fine Terrier men, Eland Hadfield and Walter Reeves, to Vickery as well. When Walter Reeves arrived, he hired a young Welshman, Percy Roberts, who was about sixteen at the time. His slender, dark appearance earned him the nickname of "The Gypsy"; there are still some people who claim that Percy Roberts was a gypsy. Either way, it is reasonably certain that he came to America around 1914, at the age of sixteen and began his career as kennel helper at Vickery.

As a handler, Percy abhorred having his clients visit the "tack area" while he was preparing the dogs to enter the ring. When they would, on occasion, wander over, Percy Roberts would say in his most condescending tone, "A lady or a gentleman never comes back to this area. They belong at ringside. It just isn't done." And he could pull it off. Throughout the '20s and '30s, Roberts exhibited for Stanley Halle's Halleston Wires, for whom he won two Westminster top awards. In 1926 with Ch. Signal Circuit of Halleston, and in 1937, Percy Roberts showed the all-white Champion Flornell Spicy Piece of Halleston to a Westminster Best. He began his judging career about 1949 and continued actively until his death.

Mac Silver

Another interesting character emerged from the Merchant Marines after World War I, and his story would make a terrific movie. Imagine this scenario. The scene opens on a merchant ship making home port after an extensive voyage. The first mate and a seaman leave the ship together and spend their free time carousing and generally doing those things that sailors on liberty do. As they return to their ship for another voyage you have to come to the conclusion that the first mate and the seaman are close friends. The night before they return to the ship, some bully picks on the first mate and his seaman friend comes to his aid and flattens the bully. "Where did you learn to fight like that?" asks the mate. "Oh, I was an amateur light-heavyweight," replies the seaman. As they approach the ship, there is a chauffeur-driven car at the pier. "Who do you think that is?" asks the seaman. "I don't know, but now with the war over we can carry passengers again," the mate answers. The ship sails with the wealthy passenger and his wife aboard. The passengers are named Mr. and Mrs. Richard C. Bondy; he is president of General Cigar Company. Mr. Bondy takes a liking to the mate and offers him a shore job helping to run his estate, called Wildoaks, in Goldens Bridge, New York. The mate accepts and tells the seaman that if he ever gets tired of the sea to look him up. About a year later, say 1921 or 1922, the seaman, Mac Silver, comes to visit the mate to see if the offer is still good. Silver is put on as a general handyman around the Bondy home.

Now, the story really gets interesting. The Bondys had a Wire Fox Terrier who really was a terror. No one but Mr. or Mrs. Bondy could approach the dog. But something magical happens, and the dog follows Silver wherever he goes. The two are inseparable. Richard Bondy is so impressed by this seemingly mysterious turn of events that when he decides to begin to raise and exhibit Wires, he puts Mac Silver in charge of the kennel. In 1923 and again in 1924, Silver is sent to England to spend time with the world's most celebrated Wire Fox Terrier man, J. R. "Bobby" Barlow. Barlow teaches Silver the art of trimming and presenting Wires to their best advantage, and Silver is an apt and willing pupil. The combination of Bondy, Silver and Barlow build Wildoaks into the most successful Wire kennel the breed has ever known or probably will ever know. The Wildoaks influence is present today in most Wires, both in

America and in England. Wildoaks Wires, with Silver in America and Barlow in England, competed successfully at the highest levels of competition. The relationship of Silver with the Bondy family lasted for nearly 40 years. After Wildoaks dispersed, Mac Silver struck out on his own. He handled for some prominent Wire exhibitors and bred a few Wires under the Revlis prefix. He died in November of 1980, one of those remarkable individuals who contributed to the Golden Age of Wires.

J. R. "Bobby" Barlow

I believe that our British friends are more appreciative of the efforts of their great handlers through the years. Perhaps we still have a bit to learn about sportsmanship and the appreciation of the real priorities of the sport of exhibiting dogs. When I decided to include this chapter in this work, I had no idea there would be so little material available about the early handlers who were so important to the development of the Fox Terrier in America. The chapter would not be complete without some reference to J. R. "Bobby" Barlow, the Crackley Wizard. I was concerned that if my task turned out to be more difficult than the research required for the American handlers, the book would never get done. But fortunately, the British came to my rescue. *My Pal the Fox Terrier,* by MacDonald Daly, and the wonderful Penda Lady, Elsie Williams' fine book, *The Fox Terrier Wire and Smooth* provide the required data on Bobby Barlow. First, the Daly account.

> Bob Barlow, the man whose Crackley Wire Fox Terriers have been the world's most famous strain in modern times, benched his pre-1914 champions in partnership with Mr. H. Sellars. When he went off for war service in Egypt, it was with the feeling that the best dog he had yet produced was one named Crackley Security, which was the first of the modern stamp of quality terrier to which we are now used. His long, lean head, full of expression, caused a stir among contemporary breeders.
>
> It is worthwhile pausing for a moment to speak of Bob Barlow, for he was probably the most successful terrier man that ever lived.
>
> Barlow bought his first Wire champion for £4 12s 6d. This was a dog named Antiseptic, and he was third of three in the Maiden class at Nuneston one day in 1911. The owner wanted £5 for him.
>
> "Harry Sellars and I couldn't afford it," said Bob. "I was just a shop assistant in the gent's tailoring, at 30/ a week. So I told the owner that I could only give the fiver if he paid the license—which meant the price was £4 12s 6d."
>
> Antiseptic came out at Birmingham show a month later, and to the amazement and joy of the partners "it seemed a miracle to us" he beat the great Ch. Collarbone of Notts, winner of 19 challenge certificates for the championship.
>
> Barlow went off in 1915, as I have said, to fight in Egypt. He came back in the '20s to breed, buy, handle and own the most famous Wires of the Golden Age. He provided the best All Breeds at Boston, Massachusetts, where the

Frank Brumby handling Tilwall Triumph to Best in Show at an AFTC Specialty in the mid 1940s. Pictured with Frank Brumby, from left to right, are: E. Coe Kerr, Charles P. Scott and the judge, W. L. Lewis.

Ch. Crackley Startler,
a Barlow Wire.

prize was $1,000 in gold, five times in succession. He won prime honors at every great show on both sides of the Atlantic.

Elsie Williams says of Barlow,

> Ch. Crackley Startler I particularly remember, having seen him shown by the greatest professional handler the Wire ring has ever known, Mr. J. R. Barlow. Bob Barlow was known as Mr. Fox Terrier!

It is sad that, with the exception of Ackerman's account of George Steadman Thomas, little is known about the early American Barlows. I hope in some small way that this chapter balances the scale a little.

The Brumbys

The Brumby brothers were born into a terrier family. Their father, William Brumby, owned the Briar prefix and under that name sent several Wires to America, among the most notable were Briar Cackler and Briar Sportsman who went to the States around 1904. Ten years later Leonard and Frank came to America to seek their fortune. From 1914 through 1919 the two men were in and out of dogs, supplementing their dog income with various jobs. They started out working together, but, as with many families, they did not see eye to eye and so went their separate ways.

Leonard Brumby is best remembered as the handler of the great Champion Nornay Saddler and one of the founders of The Professional Handlers Association. The P.H.A. brought standards of ethics and performance to the occupation of dog handling. A member of the P.H.A. had to have served an apprenticeship with a P.H.A. member, required character references and had to have adequate kennel facilities. It required licensing of professional handlers by the American Kennel Club. Leonard Brumby will always be remembered for Saddler and the P.H.A.

Frank Brumby's greatest contribution to the dog game was as a teacher to many aspiring terrier handlers. Among them, Jake Terhune and the wonderful dog man whose career is highlighted next in this segment, Tommy Gately.

Thomas M. Gately

When I decided to include a chapter on the prominent handlers who were instrumental in the development of Fox Terriers, I never realized how scarce information about their origins and background is. Most have long since left us. However, as I was writing this book, Tommy Gately, an outstanding representative of those wonderful terrier men, was still active as a judge. I contacted him and he was kind enough to provide me with the following brief autobiography.

"I was born in Reading, Pennsylvania, and while I was very young my father ventured into the timber business in the Blue Mountains about 20 to

25 miles north of Reading, along the Berks and Schuylkill County lines. I loved being outdoors and close to nature. Undoubtedly I would have taken over my father's business if I had been a little older when he passed on. No, my family could hardly be classified as 'dog people,' but they always had dogs, usually farm or hunting breeds. I acquired the first dog of my very own, a Beagle, when I was about 11 years old. My father also owned many horses and as I was growing up, it was touch and go, whether I would go dogs or horses. I have had a love affair with both all my life, and Kay and I still breed and race harness horses.

"One day I wandered into a news store and spied a copy of *The Dog Fancier* on the shelves. *The Dog Fancier* was a monthly publication that went out of existence many years ago, but I read each issue from cover to cover. Inspired by the show reports in the magazine, I decided to spend my hard earned savings to purchase an Irish Terrier. Terry and I began our show careers together, and he became my first champion. He was still alive when I married Kay, and our kennel name resulted from combining the first syllable of our name, Gately, with the name of our Irish Terrier, Terry; the result—Gayterry.

"I became known around the shows as the kid with the Irish Terrier. I badgered all the better handlers with constant questions. They seemed to like me and were very kind and helpful. When I made the decision to become a handler I wanted to learn under the very best, so I found employment with Frank Brumby. Frank was considered one of the tops of that era, and I learned much from him over the years. One day I received a special delivery letter from Mr. Alex Stuart of Chicago. He wrote,

> I have been informed that you are a most promising young dogman, and I am writing this letter asking you to go to work for me.

He then went on to tell me about salary, working conditions and opportunities. I told one of the handlers who had befriended me, and he urged me to take it. I really didn't like to leave Frank and finally decided to just tell him about it. He simply could not have been nicer. He said, 'Go ahead and take it, lad (he nearly always called me lad); if you need a friend any time out there, look up Jimmy Sullivan, tell him that you are a friend of mine, and if you don't make out alright there is always a job waiting for you here.' Alex Stuart was a very well-known breeder and exhibitor of Bulldogs, Airedales, Scotties, and Wire Fox Terriers. He was a wealthy man and, for many years, President of the Chicago Kennel Club, the predecessor of the present-day International. He owned the first Bulldog to win Best in Show at Westminster as well as BIS dogs in each of the other breeds. I learned a great deal there, but matters changed due to the tragic death of Mrs. Stuart, and I went back to Frank Brumby. While in Chicago I did get to know Jimmy Sullivan, and both Frank and Jimmy were my close friends as long as they lived. During my tenure with Frank, one of his

Kay and Tom Gately with two of their interets, Wires and horses.

Richard M. Chashoudian earning one of the more than 500 all-breed Bests of his fine career, this time with the Wire Ch. Falstaff Lady Fayre, under judge R. A. Cross at the Idaho Capitol City KC, 1963.

321

top clients was Richard C. Bondy, who was just starting with some very good imported Wires. In fact, when he built his Wildoaks Kennels at Goldens Bridge, New York, he hired one of his laborers, Mac Silver, to manage the kennel and sent him down to Frank Brumby for training. The job with Frank ended when one of his clients, George Sloan, who had Brookemeade Kennels of Schnauzers, made Frank an offer that he could not refuse, to go private with him. I then spent some time with another talented handler, Abe Swartz, who also became a lifelong friend. To gain all-breed experience, I spent some time with Lew Worden before striking out on my own.

"After a whirlwind courtship, July 24th to September 1st, I married Kay, who took to the dog game like a duckling to a mill pond.

"Early in my career I decided that in order to succeed one must have the best dogs, and I worked hard in persuading my clients to have me buy top dogs for them. This led to importing, which brought me into contact with England's greatest dog minds who added considerably to my knowledge and experience. When Joy Swann of Boarzell moved to this country, her English handler, Vernon Hirst, convinced her to have me handle her dogs in the States, and, as a result, I did some fine winning with Eng., Am. Ch. Boarzell Brilliance. When Mrs. Swann decided to go into Collies, Kay and I purchased Ch. Boarzell Brightest Star, whose show career really did a lot to put the relatively unknown Gatelys on the map. Kay and I refused some fabulous offers for her and never regretted it. We have always considered her one of the greatest ever. She was the start of our line, and the two champion bitches that we still own as our beloved pets go back to her.

"I don't really know how many Bests in Show we won with Wires, or with how many different Wires, but one of our biggest winners was Eng., Am. Ch. Travella Superman, imported for Mrs. Harold Florsheim. He won 25 Bests, a record for any Wire at the time. While that record may have been broken, one record I believe still stands is making a champion winning three straight Specialties in one week. This I did with Ch. Stocksmoor Slogan, a dog I purchased in England for James T. Boyle of Chicago.

"Other BIS Wires were Chs. Brookly Call Boy, Dogberry Rio Grande, Boarzell Brilliance, Boarzell Brightest Star, Sirius of Gayterry, Chief Barmaid, Travella Suredo, Cudhill Calypso, Stocksmoor Snowdrift, Gayterry Little Cherry and finally, a dog whom I consider to be one of the all time greats, Eng., Am. Ch. Wintor Caracus Call Boy. Call Boy died while still quite young but still sired 22 champions. Ch. Gayterry Little Cherry won permanent possession of the Baywood Trophy by winning it in three straight Specialty Shows. I know there are others, but these are the ones that come to mind at this writing.

"During our career, we had the honor and pleasure of handling for some wonderful people. There was one family for which we handled for three generations; Mrs. Joseph Sailor, her daughter and granddaughter were clients of ours over a 30-year period. Other wonderful sportspeople were the Florsheims and J. R. T. Alford. It was for Mr. Alfrod that we imported Call Boy, and, in the fall of 1969, I told Mr. Alford that I would finish out the year and then retire. His response was, 'When you quit, I quit. I would never be satisfied with second best.' This was a tremendous compliment, but was also very sad."

Kay and Tom Gately still are actively judging, and it is fortunate that they could share their experiences.

Richard M. Chashoudian

Another fine terrier man, although of a more current generation, is Ric Chashoudian. However, Ric was one of the very last to learn his craft from the British terrier men. He will be the first to tell you the importance of Ben Brown and Harold Duffy to his career. In doing research for this book, I taped a two-hour interview with Chashoudian, and one of the more interesting perspectives on this topic of the impact of handlers on the dog game was offered by Ric. He tells of "coming East" from California every year in the '50s and '60s and getting his "tail whipped" by the specialists. Ric shared with me that he thought he was pretty good until his first trip East. There he went head to head with "the specialists." These were handlers who had one wealthy client capable of sustaining their exclusive attention. There were people like Pop Sayres in Kerries; Len Brumby, Jr. in Smooths; Phil Prentice, thanks to the support of the Winants, could devote the bulk of his time to their Scotties, and several other specialists. When all you have to do is one breed, you can become extremely hard to beat. Ric recalls coming to Westminster in the late '50s with several different terrier breeds, only to be out-trimmed, out-groomed, out-handled and out-classed by the specialists. (Of course, times have changed, but it appears to me, having witnessed the transition from specialist in one terrier breed to terrier generalist, the difference could be that the old timers were coat cultivators while the modern handlers are sculptors. Is it possible that today the dog is less important than what it can be made to look like? The reason I raise the issue is that there are so few people alive today, breeders and judges, who understand coat or place any significance on coat and its condition. So why should anyone do more than is required to win?)

Ric Chashoudian fell in love with Wire Fox Terriers at age nine. He saw a litter of Wires in a pet shop in Hollywood and was smitten for life. While he has handled most of the terrier breeds, when he sees a good Wire, he becomes possessed. His first dog, however, was not a Wire but an Airedale. Ric's dad was an outstanding musician and Ric had a fine musical education. It was taken for granted that Ric would follow in Marshall's footsteps until the dogs took hold.

Mac Silver showing Ch. Striking Example of Wildoaks to Best in Show at Devon, 1945. The judge is Lewis H. Marks.

By the time Ric was 17 he had begun to master the "trimmers trade" under the tutelage of Harold Duffy. I was bemused by Ric's account of his first full-time position in the dog game. He worked at Kerryland Kennels owned by Floyd Pierce. He scrubbed the kennels and groomed and fed the Kerries 6½ days per week for $35.00 per week. I performed similar tasks for Len Brumby, Jr. for $80.00 per month on the East Coast while Chashoudian was working on the West Coast.

In 1954, Ric started Bonnie Briar Kennels, and within a few years he was winning many of the shows on the West Coast. Four dogs in Ric's career amassed more than 250 all breed BIS. They were the Wire, Ch. Miss Skylight; the Kerry, Ch. Melbee's Chances Are; the Lakeland, Ch. Jo-Ni's Red Baron of Crofton; and, of course, Ch. Ttarb the Brat, the Smooth. In all, Ric Chashoudian had more than 500 all breed BIS wins.

With Ric Chashoudian's retirement, only George Ward remains active from the era that was known for its great dog men. Perhaps our present group of active handlers still contains a Chashoudian, a Roberts, a Gately, a Brumby; let us hope so, because the dog game in general, and Fox Terriers in particular, desperately need them.

10

Back Through Time: Pedigrees

THIS LAST CHAPTER is devoted to a simplistic roadmap that should allow each of us to examine our own pedigrees and follow them back to Old Tip for Wires and Old Foiler for Smooths.

Smooths

As for Belgrave Joe, the reader recalls that while he was the Adam of the breed, his male descendants disappeared by the 1950s, leaving Old Foiler's offspring and their progeny to carry on through the dog, Ch. Splinter. Pedigree S-1, Fox Smooth One, therefore, must be Foiler's, born in 1871. Foiler sired Hognaston Willie, and his son Hognaston Dick sired Dickon, who, in turn, was Splinter's sire. Figure S-2 starts with Splinter in 1883, and through a continuing line of sires brings us to the start of World War I.

However, an examination of the pedigree of Venio (S-3), Splinter's grandson, reveals more than a smattering of Belgrave Joe in the bitches' lines. In the early days of the kennel club the role of the dam was greatly underestimated with the result that the dam's pedigree was given short shrift. Figure S-3 reveals that Splinter sired Vesuvian, who, in turn, sired Venio. What most historians ignore is that Vesuvian's dam, Koh-i-noor, was a Belgrave Joe granddaughter and great-great-granddaughter. Venio's pedigree is offered as an in-depth starting point in the Smooths' journey to the present day. Ch. Oxonian's pedigree (S-4) reveals a direct line down the top of the pedigree (sometimes referred to as "tail male") from Visto, a grandson of Vesuvian, and a son of Venio. High on anyone's list of important Smooths is Cromwell Ochre (S-5). And a truly significant sire, but one who has had little recognition in previous manuscripts, was Kidder Karzan (S-6). His sons, Ch. Little Aristocrat (S-7) and Watteau Battleshaft (S-24), formed the "A" and "B" lines of the modern Smooth respectively. These, together with the "S" line progeny of Southboro Sandman (S-8), comprise a link between the modern Smooth and Old Foiler.

The bitches played their role in maintaining and enhancing the quality of the modern Smooth.

The Reverend Rosslyn Bruce was the first to make reference to lines and families—the lines are dog descendants and the families are the descendants of bitches. Miss E. Lindley Wood, Hampole Smooths, wrote of the lines and families in her book *Smooth Fox Terriers,* published in 1960. The pedigrees of the foundation dogs are readily available and are reproduced in this chapter, but the origins of some of the foundation bitches are obscured by time. It is better left to Miss Wood to explain the families.

> Family 1 springs from a bitch called Juddy, born about 1868 and bred by the famous Rev. Jack Russell, who was one of the old-fashioned sporting parsons. Here it is worth mentioning that you may hear people talking about "Jack Russell" terriers as being a distinct strain or offshoot from Fox Terriers from Fox Terriers proper; this is incorrect and to make it quite clear I quote the late Rev. Doctor Bruce, who besides being largely responsible for all the research necessary to trace out the various tap-root dogs' lines and the tap-root bitches' families, did so much by his writings and labours for our Fox terriers today. He wrote in 1941 as follows: "In answer to a correspondent about Jack Russell terriers, we are lately all astonished to read, 'Here and there in the West County of England one may meet with specimens, but they are scarce. Captain B claims to have a strain.'
>
> "The Rev. Jack Russell had numbers of terriers from his undergraduate days on, but one of his best was Juddy (not Judy, but called after a certain Mr. Juddy)."

A descendant of Juddy's, Avon May, proved an outstanding brood bitch and was the ancestress of some two dozen or more champions, among them being such famous bitches as Ch. Dame Fortune (S-9), Ch. Donna Fortuna, Ch. Avon Musc, Ch. Farleton Suzette (S-10), and Ch. Maryholm Sweetmeat (S-11).

To go back to Doctor Bruce's article about Jack Russell terriers, this is what he has to say: "We could undertake to find in any pedigree of a pure-bred smooth fox terrier, which extends say for ten generations, not one, but ten strains of Jack Russell blood. In most we should find more. It is true that the type, which Parson Russell strove for, has been improved beyond all knowing, but the length of leg, quality of skull, and thick hard dense smooth coat were all as much joy to the old Parson's eye as they are to ours today. His model is our model; and one could find today a team of modern Smooth Fox Terriers that would make his dear old eyes twinkle again. It is curious how once a great name is used to bolster up a modern fallacy; and one wonders when people say Parson Jack Russell terriers are smaller than our Smooth Fox Terriers what evidence they think they have. Here, at any rate, is a fact for younger breeders to hang on to. In November 1897 Parson Jack Russell said, 'An ideal fox terrier should be over seventeen and under twenty pounds and a rough haired Terrier is best the same size.'"

Family 2. The tap-root bitch of this remarkable family was Venom who was born about 1866. She was bought by the Marquis of Huntley from Morgan, Huntsman of the Grove Hounds, with whom she ran for two seasons. Her descendants have produced many, many champions and continue to do so today. From 1946 to 1957 this family has produced no less than 34 dogs and 29 bitch champions, a remarkable record indeed. A few more notable bitches of this family are Avon Secret (S-12), dam of Ch. Bowden Whisper, and Secret's three sisters, two of whom each bred a champion, and the third, who was the dam of champions Avon Fanfare and Avon Vagabond, Brockenhurst Waif, grandmother of that pillar of the breed, Ch. Avon Oxonian, Brooklands Queen Bee, dam of two champions and grandmother of Ch. Watteau Songstress (S-13), dam of Ch. Watteau Chorister (S-14), who is the sire of that very famous bitch Ch. Watteau Sonata; Crystal Lady, dam of Ch. Hermon Palmist and Ch. Hermon Rebel. Tidser Tranquil, dam of the twin champions Hampole Tinkler (S-15) and Hampole Tinkle; Hampole Chat, dam of champions Hampole Housemaster and Hampole Housewife, and Housewife is the dam of Ch. Hampole Fidelity and Ch. (U.S.A.) Hampole Sincerity, Ch. Farleton Fuchia, dam of champions Farleton Florette and Farina, and Amber Solitaire, dam of Ch. Hermon Parthings Loyal Lad (S-16) and Ch. Parthings Land Girl.

Family 3. The famous bitch Grove Nettle was the founder of this family, she was born in 1862, and was by Grove Tarter ex the Rev. W. Handley's bitch named Sting.

Miss Wood goes on to describe Nettle, but her unique role as the only great-grandmother Foiler has insured her place in our Fox Terrier montage.

Picking up Miss Wood's narrative on Family 3, she states:

She (Nettle) had three daughters: Nectar, Ruby and Tricksey, who between them were the direct female ancestors up to 1940, of some forty champion dogs and bitches, and since then, up to 1957 the family has produced sixteen more champions.

Some of the more famous winner-producing bitches of this illustrious Family 3 were Ch. Sutton Veda, dam of Ch. Splinter, founder of the old A, B, O, and S lines; Malva, the dam of Ch. Wrose Indelible (S-17), and three Ch. bitches, Cromwell Miss Legacy, Dunsting and Mint. Mint was the grandmother of Ch. Cromwell Superb's Replica who sired the famous bitch Ch. Choicest Donna of Notts (S-18), whelped in 1927. Cromwell Ochrette, litter sister to Cromwell Ochre's Legacy, by Cromwell Ochre ex Cromwell Stella proved a most excellent brood bitch. She was the dam of Ch. Chosen of Notts and Ch. Cromwell Dark Girl.

> Ch. Chosen Damsel of Notts, whelped in 1922, was the dam of Ch. Corrector of Notts, who also proved a great sire of this Family 3, which is further represented by such excellent terriers as Ch. Chosen Dinah of Notts, whelped in 1948, and Ch. Laurel Wreath (S-19) whelped in 1946, who sired six champion dogs but only one champion bitch.

> Family 4 was founded by a bitch called White Fairy 1 born about 1869. She had a daughter called Arnold's Nettle; not the same Nettle as Grove Nettle, founder of Family 3. This name Nettle has led to many difficulties in tracing the various bitch families, as it was found to have been given to some thirty or more pedigreed bitches.

Some of the more prominent bitches in this family are Ch. Dusky Dinah, Cromwell Tan Girl, Ch. Miss Watteau, Ch. Danesgate Diana, Ch. Avon Snowflake, Ch. Harkaway Lilli and Ch. Burmar Dawn.

The remaining family that needs mention is known as Family 6. The root bitch was called Vic, whelped in 1872. It is noted for the dogs it produced: Ch. Selecta Ideal, Ch. Farleton Flavian (S-20) and Ch. Nornay Saddler. But there were a few really important bitches as well: Ch. Worksop Flair, Ch. Avon Bondette and Cream of Andely.

Modern Smooth breeders, "modern" defined as post-World War II, would be hard pressed to find any Smooth whose pedigree avoids two English war babies who were among the first postwar champions—Lionel Wilson's Ch. Lethal Weapon and Dr. Miller's Ch. Boreham Belsire (S-21 and S-22). Snuff Box, Chieftain, Deacon, Brat, Extra Smoth, Fireflash, Ebony Box Bonanza, Breeze Away, Sammy Sayres and Solus Soloist all trace their origins back to Lethal Weapon or Belsire. Prewar studies show Little Aristocrat and Ch. Corrector of Notts (S-23) as the two stud dogs most likely to appear in the modern pedigree by virtue of their respective influence upon Belsire and Lethal Weapon. And finally, through Oxonian to Splinter, there is a clear case that it was Belgrave Joe and his offspring that first popularized the breed.

Departing from Ms. Wood's account of Smooth lines and families, the study of the Smooth must include dogs of the present and recent past whose progeny have enjoyed important successes at today's exhibitions.

The most dominant Smooth of the past 45 years is, without question, Ch. Ttarb The Brat (S-34). Brat's ancestry can be divided into two parts, recent English (i.e., the Brooklands and the Watteau) and the early English in the dog Eng. Ch. Levenside Luke. The latter is behind much of present-day Australian home-bred lines.

Following Brat, but by no means secondary to him as an important

Smooth influence, is Eng. & Am. Ch. Karnilo Chieftain of Foxden (S-29). It would be difficult to find an active Smooth breeder in 1986 who does not have at least one line to Chieftain.

Ch. Quissex Deacon (S-20), Eng. & Am. Ch. Higrola Horatio of Britlea (S-32) and Ch. Waybroke Extra Smooth are the most frequently found dogs in American Smooth pedigrees in 1985.

Two new names that probably will become important future figures in Smooth annals are the line-bred Chieftain, son of Ch. Foxden Warpaint, Ch. Foxden Warspite and Brat's most important son to date, Ch. Foxmoor Macho Macho Man. Macho represents the marriage of Brat with a Deacon-Chieftain bitch.

While most of the Fox Terrier background in the United States had English origins, the effect of Ch. Ttarb the Brat on the American Smooth necessitates a look at Fox Terrier activity in Australia if this chapter is to properly present an accurate roadmap for those who wish to journey into their puppy's past. Serious breeders may also find the summary of pedigrees useful, but first a brief glimpse at Australian Smooth Fox Terrier activity.

Ch. Ttarb the Brat's arrival in America focused American attention on Australia, a country about the same size as the United States with less than 10% of the population, thereby compounding and intensifying the problems of communication and making an Australian overview a bit sketchy. The space and distances make it difficult to present an Australian perspective since most early activity took place in individually isolated pockets of interest throughout the expanse.

However, Fox Terrier activity in Australia dates back to 1872 when an English-bred Smooth won a gold medal. With history so rich in age and tradition, this book would be incomplete without an attempt to present Fox Terrier activity "down under."

One of the early importers of Smooths was a Mr. M. Moses of Sydney, who imported Raper- and Vicary-bred Smooths (Richmond is a Raper prefix and "V" dogs were Vicary's), among them Vano, Eggesfor Foiler, Vedette, Vainglorious, Richmond Fixen and Validity. New South Wales KC held its first show in 1895 with a small entry of Smooths. Other breeders followed the same pattern established by Mr. Moses, so it is accurate to state that the Australian Smooths share common roots with English and American counterparts in that Foiler, Belgrave Joe, and Splinter were the foundation of Australian activity.

One of the challenges to reporting Australian Fox Terrier history is the unique Australian characteristic of having separate registries for each state. As a result, a dog registered with the governing kennel council of New South Wales may have no history with the Queensland KC. Elsewhere in this book, I present the pedigree of Ch. Ttarb the Brat. I obtained the information from the appropriate kennel council, but they had no record of several ancestors because they were from a different territory.

Bob Comley of New South Wales imported an outstanding English Smooth in 1913, Ch. Levenside Luke. Luke was less successful as a sire than as a show dog in England but he had a profound effect on Australian Smooths. Nearly every Smooth in Australia today not directly descended from the more recent imports goes back to Ch. Levenside Luke.

England continued to supply a steady stream of Smooths to the enthusiastic Aussies. The Selwor Kennels of John and Glenys Rowles were founded in 1912 by an earlier family member. He imported Floorcloth, a 12-month-old daughter of Ch. Cromwell Ochre's Legacy. Since Luke and Ochre went directly back to Oxonian, Floorcloth was bred to Levenside Luke with the resulting offspring forming the base for the Selwor Smooth line that is still producing good ones today.

During the 1930s, Bowden Decision, Ch. Bowden Mascot, Netswell Refrain, Southboro Symbol, Solus Tan Boy, Molten Mikado and many others made the long ocean voyage from England. (One interesting sidelight to the Australian Smooth story was the effect that Smooth mascots of the early ships' crews had on the early Smooth activity. A number of these early records confirm that a certain bitch was bred to the Smooth dog belonging to this or that ship's crew or captain. That was the only identification.) A most important Smooth of this period was a home-bred, Jerry Ideal, owned and bred by Bill Polley. He was whelped in 1930 and won his last CC in 1939. Along the way he won 60 BIS including successive Bests at the 1932, 1933 and 1934 Sydney Royal.

After World War II, Cam Milward won a BIS with Douglas of Clarence. I could find no earlier reference to the notable Mr. Milward, so Douglas of Clarence may have been the start of the Grenpark Smooths. Certainly Mr. Milward is to Australian Smooths what the Farrells are to the American effort and Mary Blake is to England's picture. It would be difficult to find an Australian Smooth pedigree without a Grenpark influence somewhere. The Brat, on his dam's side, has Aus. Ch. Grenpark Beauty Girl, Aus. Ch. Grenpark Miraculous, Grenpark Present and Grenpark Amethyst. Cam Milward is respected throughout the Fox Terrier world as an outstanding breeder and judge.

The 1950s was affected by three more imports, Brooklands Present, Brooklands Black Ace and Watteau Wellwisher. Joining these fine English Smooths was the American-bred Top Score of Beverly.

The 1960s and 1970s were distinguished by two Australian-bred Smooths, Mrs. Wapshott's Ch. Garrleigh Golden Sands, winner of the 1969 Melbourne, and Ch. Farleton Don Pedro, owned and bred by Allan Bailey. The story goes that Mr. Bailey was offered a very handsome price by several top American handlers for Don Pedro but refused them all.

Another author with a different perspective might see a different group of dogs, but the 34 Smooth pedigrees that follow should enable the owner of any Smooth puppy to track the history of that dog back to Foiler.

Index of Smooth Lineage

	Dog or Bitch	Date of Birth
S-1	Foiler	1871
S-2	Ch. Splinter	12/12/82
S-3	Venio	1889
S-4	Ch. Oxonian	12/06/02
S-5	Cromwell Ochre (from Oxonian)	1915
S-6	Kidder Karzan	1919
S-7	Ch. Little Aristocrat (from Cromwell Ochre)	11/01/22
S-8	Southboro Sandman	08/15/12
S-9	Ch. Dame Fortune	01/12/94
S-10	Ch. Farleton Suzette	06/14/32
S-11	Ch. Maryholm Sweetmeat	03/24/54
S-12	Avon Secret	09/27/25
S-13	Ch. Watteau Songstress	01/24/51
S-14	Ch. Watteau Chorister	11/02/54
S-15	Ch. Hampole Tinkler	03/15/46
S-16	Ch. Hermon Parthing's Loyal Lad	06/21/57
S-17	Ch. Wrose Indelible	07/05/21
S-18	Ch. Choicest Donna of Notts	10/02/27
S-19	Ch. Laurel Wreath	02/26/46
S-20	Ch. Farleton Flavian	03/20/28
S-21	Lethal Weapon	07/02/43
S-22	Boreham Belsire	10/20/43
S-22A	Boreham Beavron	03/01/34
S-23	Ch. Corrector of Notts	11/03/29
S-24	Watteau Battleshaft	1925
S-25	Ch. Watteau Midas	01/23/48
S-26	Ch. Watteau Snuff Box	02/02/62
S-27	Ch. Von Nassau's Ter-a-Cycloon	01/01/64
S-28	Ch. Laurel Drive	01/01/69
S-29	Ch. Karnilo Chieftain of Foxden	01/03/71
S-30	Ch. Quissex Deacon	12/12/71
S-31	Ch. Waybroke Extra Smooth	08/15/74
S-32	Ch. Higrola Horatio of Britlea	03/06/78
S-33	Ch. Riber Ramsey	10/23/72
S-34	Ch. Ttarb the Brat	12/23/78

```
                    Grove Tartar                              Visto (by Venio)
          Grove Willie                             Vibo
                    Grove Nettle                              Eggesford Dora
      Grip                                    Eton Blue
                    Grove Tartar                              Ch. Donnington
          Grove Vixen                              Ch. Hester Sorrel
                    Grove Nettle                              Dinah Morris
S-1: Foiler, 1871                             Dark Blue
                    Grove Tartar                              Hunton Bridegroom
          Grove Willie                             Daddy
                    Grove Nettle                              Beacon Tartaress
      Juddy                                   Brocken Hurst Waif
                    Grove Tartar                              St. Ledger
          Grove Vixen                              Struck Out
                    Grove Nettle                              Absence
                                              S-4: Ch. Oxonian, 12/6/02
                                                              Ch. Dominie
                                                    Ch. Kibworth Baron
                                                              Cowley Palm
          Willie (by Foiler)                        Rowton Baron
      Hognaston Dick                                         Belmont Warrior
          Needle                                   Rowton Vivandiere
Dickon                                                        Merford Nellie
          Belgrave Joe                        Overture
      Nettle II                                         Ch. Dominie
          Lady II                             Ch. Donnington
S-2: Ch. Splinter, 12/12/1882                           Divorcee
          Tweezers                            Charlton Guinea Gold
      Tackler                                           Devereux
          Baby                                Guinea Gold
Sutton Veda                                             Old Gold
          Pickle II
      Gradele
          Gaudy
```

S-3: Venio, 1889				
Vesuvian	Splinter	Dickon	Hognaston Dick	Hognaston Willie / Hognaston Needle
			Nettle II	Belgrave Joe / Lady II
		Sutton Veda	Tackler	Tweezers / Baby (A)
			Gradely	Pickle II / Gandy
	Koh-I-Noor	Dugdale Joe	Belgrave Joe	Belvoir Joe / White Vic
			Nell II	Honest Joe / Needle
		Diamond Dust	Pickle II	Tyrant IV / Olive
			Dusty	Old Foiler / Diamond
Venilla	Veni	Vedette	Buff	Buffet / Swan
			Chips	Bolus / Testy
		Village Belle	Volo	Pickle II / Vashti
			Beauty	Artful Joe / Busy
	Valetta	Vedette	Buff	Buffet / Swan
			Chips	Bolus / Testy
		Vehement	Brockenhurst Joe	Belgrave Joe / Tricksey
			Busy	Bitters / Damsel

Ch. Oxonian
Ch. Orkney
Domino Blanc
Ch. Orkadian
Crumbo
Faye
Lady Claudia
S-5: **Ch. Cromwell Ochre,** 1915
Baby Ruler
Trinity Princess
Broadgate Queen

Orkadian
Ch. Cromwell Ochre
Trinity Princess
Cromwell Ochre's Legacy
Yeovil Don
Cromwell Stella
Rowton Stellata
Cromwell Raw Umber
Little Marcon
Tan
Tuckwell
Ch. Cromwell Tan Girl
Ch. Waterman
Southland Duchess
Cobridge Peggy
S-6: **Kidder Karzan,** 1919
Orkadian
Ch. Cromwell Ochre
Trinity Princess
Cromwell Ochre's Legacy
Yeovil Don
Cromwell Stella
Rowton Stellata
Dunstable Princess
Dusky Collar
Dusky D'Orsay
Ch. Dorsay's Donna
Lady Claudia
Ch. Darrel
Darrel's Dame
Camp Winning Woman

New Forest
Belmont Ranger
Brockenhurst Banquet
Ch. Despoiler
Reckon
Stipendiary
Shindy
Belmont Cherry
Belmont Oliver
S-9: **Ch. Dame Fortune,** 1/12/1894
Reckon
Stipendiary
Shindy
D'Orsay
Rutty
Dame D'Orsay
Director
Directress
Dominissa

Ch. Cromwell Ochre
Cromwell Ochre's Legacy
Cromwell Stella
Cromwell Raw Umber
Tan
Ch. Cromwell Tan Girl
Southland Duchess
Kidder Karzan
Ch. Cromwell Ochre
Cromwell Ochre's Legacy
Cromwell Stella
Dunstable Princess
Dusky D'Orsay
Lady Claudia
Darwell's Dame
S-7: **Ch. Little Aristocrat,** 11/1/22
Ch. Defacer
Ch. D'Orsay's Model
Dulcinia
Digby
Camp White Woman
Kidder Kisobel
Dusky Collar (Wire)
Dusky D'Orsay
Ch. D'Orsay's Donna
Avon Bondette
Beau Queen

Ch. Oxonian
Ch. Orkney
Domino Blanc
Ch. Orkadian
Crumbo
Fay
Dusky D'Orsay
Lady Claudia
Darrel's Dame
S-8: **Southboro Sandman,** 8/15/12
Ch. Avon Oxendale
Ormidale
Domino Blanc
Pit A Pat
Elton Mixture
Hibernico
Bonnie Bouche

Kidder Karzan
Watteau Battershaft
Parade Rose
Ch. Farleton Flavian
Ch. Brockford Dandy
Ch. Watteau Nanette
Brownhill Duchess
S-10: **Ch. Farleton Suzette,** 6/14/32
Ch. Wrose Indelible
First Monceux
Ch. Hermon Bequest
Lady Jessamine
Ch. Avon Mainstay
Hells Bells
Nedwob Krispette

333

```
        Molten Moonlighter
    Rory of Doury
        Danesgate Gwenny
Ch. Farleton O'Hill Bahram
        Ch. Boreham Belsire
    Abberdale Prim
        Abberdale Charm
S-11: Ch. Maryholm Sweetmeat, 3/24/54
        Call Up of Notts
    Solus Congress
        Wild Rose
Maryholm Sweet Bit
        Gaylord of Sker
    Maryholm Sweetbriar
        Travelling On Time
```

```
        Kidder Karzan
    Ch. Little Aristocrat
        Kidder Kisobel (unregistered)
Ch. Selecta Ideal
        Unknown
    Berried Holly (unregistered)
        Unknown
S-12: Avon Secret, 9/27/25
        Ch. Kinver
    Ch. Arrogant Albino
        Ashbrook Alma
Avon Russett
        Ch. Myrtus
    Avon Mavis
        Avon Marie
```

```
        Ch. Lethal Weapon
    Ch. Laurel Wreath
        Parthings Lassie
Ch. Lavish Warpaint
        Ch. Boreham Belsire
    Boreham Bequile
        Boreham Beginner
S-13: Ch. Watteau Songstress, 4/24/51
        Ch. Laurel Wreath
    Ch. Watteau Midas
        Brooklands Ebony Belle
Wildflower
        Molten Mainmast
    Brooklands Queen Bee
        Brooklands Chic
```

```
        Abberdale Admiral
    Boreham Bedad
        Boreham Berberis
Ch. Boreham Belsire
        Boreham Bisrah
    Boreham Belmalva
        Boreham Bellona
S-15: Ch. Hampole Tinkler, 3/15/46
        Bowden Hamish
    Touchwood Town Guard
        Touchwood Bess
Tidser Tranquil
        Watteau Cherrio
    Tidser Taffeta
        Tidser Trinket
```

```
                                                   Ch. Lethal Weapon
                          Ch. Laurel Wreath        Parthings Lassie
     Ch. Watteau Midas                             Molten Mainmast
                          Brooklands Ebony Belle    Brooklands Chic
  Ch. Brooklands Black Prince                       Democrat of Sker
                          Wychway Fanfare           Wychway Cousin
     Ch. Brooklands Black Narcissus                 Molten Mainmast
                          Brooklands Queen Bee      Brooklands Chic
                                                    Travelling Sample
  Ch. Brooklands Lucky Wishbone    Lybian Warrior   Lady Wayward
                                                    Lethean Waters
     Burham Bencher          Pleezmoor Demoiselle   Lady Wayward
                                                    Boreham Bedad
  Burham Bint                Ch. Boreham Belsire     Boreham Belmalva
                                                    Ch. Abberdale Admiral
     Cathwill Cassandra      Abberdale Cyder        Abberdale Brandy

S-14: Ch. Watteau Chorister, 11/2/54                Lethean Waters
                             Ch. Lethal Weapon      Smeatonwood Girlie
     Ch. Laurel Wreath                              Armaine Brigadier
                             Parthings Lassie       Danesgate Decima
  Ch. Lavish Warpaint                               Boreham Bedad
                             Ch. Boreham Belsire     Boreham Belmalva
     Boreham Beguile                                Colland Reynard
                             Boreham Beginner       Boreham Becamaster
  Ch. Watteau Songstress                            Ch. Lethal Weapon
                             Ch. Laurel Wreath      Parthings Lassie
     Ch. Watteau Midas                              Molten Mainmast
                             Brooklands Ebony Belle  Brooklands Chic
  Wild Flower                                       Molten Mainstay
                             Molten Mainmast        Molten Marion
        Brooklands Queen Bee                        Farleton First Flight
                             Brooklands Chic        Watteau Kathleen
```

Ch. Cromwell Ochre
Trinity Princess
Cromwell Ochre's Legacy
Yeovil Don
Cromwell Stella
Rowton Stellata
S-17: **Ch. Wrose Indelible,** 7/5/21
Wellesley Duke
Ch. Levenside Luke
Levenside Lisbeth
Malva
Mallow
Modesty
Mayblossom

Danesgate Demijohn
Leathean Waters
Danesgate Dream
Ch. Lethal Weapon
Golden Spur of Sker
Smeatonwood Girlie
Leprechaun Wealth
Parthings Laddie
Ch. Buckland
Armaine Brigadier
Armaine Stirling Maid
Parthings Lassie
Danesgate Demijohn
Danesgate Decima
Boreham Benzine
S-16: **Ch. Hermon Parthings Loyal Lad,** 6/21/51
Boreham Bedad
Ch. Boreham Belsire
Boreham Belmalva
Boreham Belucky
Sweet Cygnet
Amber Solitaire
Ch. Aire Ideal
Ch. Electric Real Amber
Nosbor Really Sweet
Amber Susan
Danesgate Cynthia

Danesgate Dean
Danesgate Demijohn
Danesgate Dahlia
Lethean Waters
Danesgate Dream
Ch. Lethal Weapon
Golden Spur of Sker
Smeaton Wood Girlie
Leprechaun Wealth
S-19: **Ch. Laurel Wreath,** 2/26/46
Ch. Buckland
Armaine Brigadier
Armaine Stirling Maid
Parthings Lassie
Danesgate Dean
Danesgate Demijohn
Danesgate Dahlia
Danesgate Decima
Boreham Benzine

Ch. Little Aristocrat
Cromwell Superb
Berried Holly
Ch. Cromwell Superb's Replica
Ch. Brockford Dandy
Cromwell Dainty
Ch. Mint
S-18: **Ch. Choicest Donna of Notts,** 10/2/27
Cromwell Ochre's Legacy
Cromwell Raw Umber
Ch. Cromwell Tan Girl
Ch. Chosen Damsel of Notts
Ch. Cromwell Ochre
Cromwell Ochrette
Cromwell Stella

Cromwell Raw Umber
Kidder Karzan
Dunstable Princess
Watteau Battleshaft
Ch. Wrose Indelible
Parade Rose
Active Lassie
S-20: **Ch. Farleton Flavian,** 3/20/28
Southboro Sandman
Ch. Brockford Dandy
Arden Sting
Ch. Watteau Nanette
Ch. Warbreck Spero
Brownhills Duchess
Lady Bunty

Pedigree of Eng. Ch. Corrector of Notts (charted dog: Clanish of Notts)

- **Clanish of Notts**
  - **Bowden Hamish** (sire)
    - **Eng. Ch. Brockford Dandy**
      - Dandifino
        - Southboro Sandman
          - Eng. Ch. Orkadian
            - Eng. Ch. Orkney
            - Fay
          - Pit a Pat
            - Ormidale
            - Hibernico
        - Arden Sting
          - Eng. Ch. Dandyford
            - Wattoford
            - Gedling Dolly (unregistered)
          - Arden Gipsy
      - Avon Marie
        - Legacy Lad
          - Cromwell Ochre's Legacy
            - Eng. Ch. Cromwell Ochre
            - Cromwell Stella
          - Krismas Karol
            - Eng. Ch. Orkadian
            - Krismas Number
        - Avon Rosary
          - Octavius
            - Eng. Ch. Orkadian
            - Marceda
          - Avon Muffett
            - Eng. Ch. Defacer
            - Avon Marigold
    - **Eng. Ch. Warbreck Spero**
      - Musa
        - Eng. Ch. Darell
          - Ordnance
            - Brancote Carbine
            - Eng. Ch. Miss Watteau
          - Brinsop
            - Standard Reformer
            - Ver Quiz
        - Cymbeline
          - Eng. Ch. Levenside Luke
            - Wellesley Duke
            - Levenside Lisbeth
          - Nanette (unregistered)
      - Maurandia
        - Cromwell Ochre's Legacy
          - Eng. Ch. Cromwell Ochre
            - Eng. Ch. Orkadian
            - Trinity Princess
          - Cromwell Stella
            - Yeovil Don
            - Rowton Stellata
        - Malva
          - Eng. Ch. Levenside Luke
            - Wellesley Duke
            - Levenside Lisbeth
          - Modesty
  - **Bowden She's Charming** (dam)
    - **Eng. Ch. Brockford Dandy**
      - Dandifino
        - Southboro Sandman
          - Eng. Ch. Orkadian
            - Eng. Ch. Oxonian
            - Domino Blanc
          - Pit a Pat
            - Crumbo
            - Lady Claudia
        - Arden Sting
          - Eng. Ch. Dandyford
            - Eng. Ch. Avon Oxendale
            - Domino Blanc
          - Arden Gipsy
            - Elton Mixture
            - Bonne Bouche
      - Avon Marie
        - Legacy Lad
          - Cromwell Ochre's Legacy
            - Oppidan
            - Watteau Lily
          - Krismas Karol
            - Gedling Roger
            - Gedling Sceptre
        - Avon Rosary
          - Octavius
          - Avon Muffett
    - **Avon Marie**
      - Legacy Lad
        - Cromwell Ochre's Legacy
          - Eng. Ch. Cromwell Ochre
            - Eng. Ch. Orkadian
            - Trinity Princess
          - Cromwell Stella
            - Yeovil Don
            - Rowton Stellata
        - Krismas Karol
          - Eng. Ch. Orkadian
            - Eng. Ch. Orkney
            - Fay
          - Krismas Number
      - Avon Rosary
        - Octavius
          - Eng. Ch. Orkadian
            - Eng. Ch. Orkney
            - Fay
          - Marceda
        - Avon Muffett
          - Eng. Ch. Defacer
            - Eng. Ch. Doncaster Dodger
            - Burton Nellie
          - Avon Marigold
            - Eng. Ch. Oxonian
            - Eng. Ch. Doralice

Chosen Dame of Notts

- Cromwell Desmond
  - Eng. Ch. Brockford Dandy
    - Southboro Sandman
      - Eng. Ch. Orkadian
        - Eng. Ch. Orkney
          - Eng. Ch. Oxonian
          - Domino Blanc
        - Fay
          - Crumbo
          - Lady Claudia
      - Pit a Pat
        - Ormidale
          - Eng. Ch. Avon Oxendale
          - Domino Blanc
        - Hibernico
          - Elton Mixture
          - Bonne Bouche
    - Arden Sting
      - Eng. Ch. Dandyford
        - Wattoford
          - Oppidan
          - Watteau Lily
        - Gedling Dolly (unregistered)
          - Gedling Roger
          - Gedling Sceptre
      - Arden Gipsy
  - Eng. Ch. Mint
    - Cromwell Ochre's Legacy
      - Eng. Ch. Cromwell Ochre
        - Eng. Ch. Orkadian
          - Eng. Ch. Orkney
          - Fay
        - Trinity Princess
          - Raby Ruler
          - Broadgate Queen
      - Cromwell Stella
        - Yeovil Don
          - Bramcote Carbine
          - Yeovil Kitty
        - Rowton Stellata
          - Rowton Roy
          - Dally (unregistered)
    - Malva
      - Eng. Ch. Levenside Luke
        - Wellesley Duke
          - Oppidan
          - Nitram Chance
        - Levenside Lisbeth
          - Warren Variety
          - Levenside Lady
      - Modesty

- Eng. Ch. Chosen Damsel of Notts
  - Cromwell Raw Umber
    - Cromwell Ochre's Legacy
      - Eng. Ch. Cromwell Ochre
        - Eng. Ch. Orkadian
          - Eng. Ch. Orkney
          - Fay
        - Trinity Princess
          - Raby Ruler
          - Broadgate Queen
      - Cromwell Stella
        - Yeovil Don
          - Bramcote Carbine
          - Yeovil Kitty
        - Rowton Stellata
          - Rowton Toy
          - Dally (unregistered)
    - Cromwell Tangirl
      - Tan
        - Little Marcon
          - Marcon
          - Waldonna
        - Tuckwell
          - Cyllene
          - Tut Tut
      - Southlands Duchess
        - Eng. Ch. Waterman
          - Billy Willan
          - Little Fairy
        - Cobridge Peggy
  - Cromwell Ochrette
    - Eng. Ch. Cromwell Ochre
      - Eng. Ch. Orkadian
        - Eng. Ch. Orkney
          - Eng. Ch. Oxonian
          - Domino Blanc
        - Fay
          - Crumbo
          - Lady Claudia
      - Trinity Princess
        - Raby Ruler
          - Sabine Ruler (unregistered)
          - Sabine Fay (unregistered)
        - Broadgate Queen
          - Fullerton Valuator
          - Queen
    - Cromwell Stella
      - Yeovil Don
        - Bramcote Carbine
          - Eng. Ch. Defacer
          - Gyp (unregistered)
        - Yeovil Kitty
          - The President
          - Yeovil Treasure
      - Rowton Stellata
        - Rowton Roy
          - Breamore Fillip
          - Outline
        - Dally (unregistered)

337

S-24: Watteau Battleshaft, 1925

- **Kidder Karzan**
  - Cromwell Raw Umber
    - Cromwell Ochre's Legacy
      - Ch. Cromwell Ochre
        - Ch. Orkadian
          - Ch. Orkney
            - Ch. Oxonian
              - Dark Blue Overture
            - Domino Blanc
          - Fay
            - Crumbo
            - Lady Claudia
        - Cromwell Stella
          - Yeovil Don
          - Rowton Stellata
    - Ch. Cromwell Tangirl
      - Tan
      - Southlands Duchess
  - Dunstable Princess
    - Lady Claudia
      - Cromwell Ochre's Legacy
        - Ch. Cromwell Ochre
          - Ch. Orkadian
          - Trinity Princess
        - Cromwell Stella
          - Yeovil Don
          - Rowton Stellata
      - Claudemon
        - Demon
        - Claudienne
    - Lady Babbie
      - Dreadnought Tiny
      - Watcombe Tiny

Ch. Orkadian

Trinity Princess

Yeovil Don

Rowton Stellata

Wellesley Duke

Levenside Lisbeth

Mallow

Mayblossom

Ordinance

Brinksop

Ch. Levenside Luke

Nanette (unregistered)

Ch. Cromwell Ochre

Cromwell Stella

Ch. Levenside Luke

Modesty

Ch. Darell

Cymbeline

Castelton Diver

Dandy

Cromwell Ochre's Legacy

Malva

Ch. Warbreck Spero

Floss (unregistered)

Ch. Wrose Indelible

Parade Rose

Active Lassie

339

Ch. Avon Vagabond
Avon Springtime
Farleton Fullcry
Ch. Farleton Fusilier
Abberdale Admiral
Farleton Fox Glove
Ch. Farleton Fair Maid
Ch. Farleton Fox Earth
Farleton Fortuna
Watteau Cheerio
Ch. Farleton Suzette
Scofton Showman
Boreham Belmalva
Ch. Farleton Forethought
Haven Memory
Ch. Farleton Flavian
Ch. Electric Real Amber
Ch. Aire Ideal
Aire Winnie
Ch. Paddock Premium
Boreham Berberis
Nosbor Really Sweet
Nosbor Real Lace
Ch. Avon Pedler
Boreham Bevy
Ch. Avon Vagabond
Avon Springtime
Boreham Belton
Boreham Beavron
Boreham Beave

S-22A: Ch. Boreham Belsire, 10/20/43

Caravan Qui Vive
Avon Rufus
Caravan Rufus
Tissot
Ch. Selecta Ideal
Boreham Bisrah
Avon Secret
Avon Russet
Cromwell Raw Umber
Boreham Bis
Last of Umber
Cromwell Ochrette
Mirabilis
Boreham Bedad
From Illa
Cromwell Ochrette
Cromwell Raw Umber
Ch. Little Aristocrat
Kidder Karzan
Dunstable Princess
Digby
Boreham Bellona
Kidder Kisabel
Avon Bronette
Diving Jack
Morna
Jack The Diver
Lady Sands
Cromwell Ochrettes Legacy
Maurandia
Malva

Danesgate Dean
Danesgate Demijohn
Danesgate Dahlia
Ch. Watteau Midas
Lethean Waters
Eng. & Am. Ch. Brookland's Black Prince (of Horham)
Ch. Corrector of Notts
Eng. Ch. Brookland's Black Narcissus
Danesgate Dream
Eng. Ch. Brookland's Lucky Wishbone
Balgair
Burham Bencher
S-21: Ch. Lethal Weapon, 7/2/43
Burham Bint
Ch. Electric Real Amber
Cathwell Cassandra
Golden Spur of Sker
Ch. Newmaidley Jason
Danesgate Olive
Eng. Ch. Brookland's Lucky Wishbone
Smeatonwood Girlie
Ch. Watteau Chorister
Ch. Travelling Fox
Eng. Ch. Watteau Songstress
Leprechaun Wealth
Newmaidley Destiny
Aragon Shining Gold
Eng. Ch. Maryholm Spun Gold
Newmaidley Tuppence
Newmaidley Farthing

S-27: Am. & Can. Ch. Von Nassau's Ter-A-Cycloon, 1/1/64
Eng. Ch. Hermon Parthing's Loyal Lad
Hiya Hector
Hiya Hedda
Ch. Corrector of Notts
Am. Can. Dutch Ch. Barbed Wire What's This
Boreham Bismark
Newmaidley Happy Day
Boreham Bis
Newmaidley Gold
Boreham Belton
Hieover Lovely
Boreham Bellona
Von Nassau's Ter-A-Countess
S-22B: Boreham Beavron, 3/1/34
Ch. Assault of Andely
Ch. Ochre of Notts
Ch. Taldora's Newscaster
Boreham Beave
Taldora's Wickland Camille
Ch. Little Aristocrat
Taldora's Patrice
Boreham Beryl
Taldora's Simfield Sonny
Last of Umber
Ch. Taldora's Wylam Ardiel
Boreham Bijou
Ch. Foxden Frill of Andely
Fromilla

S-25: **Ch. Watteau Midas,** 1/21/48

- Ch. Laurel Wreath
  - Ch. Lethal Weapon
    - Lethean Waters
      - Danesgate Demijohn
        - Danesgate Dean
        - Danesgate Dahlia
      - Danesgate Dream
        - Ch. Corrector of Notts
        - Balgair
    - Smeatonwood Girlie
      - Golden Spur of Sker
        - Ch. Electric Real Amber
        - Danesgate Olive
      - Leprechaun Wealth
        - Ch. Travelling Fox
        - Aragon Shining Gold
  - Parthings Lassie
    - Armaine Brigadier
      - Ch. Buckland
        - Ch. Corrector of Notts
        - Balgair
      - Armaine Stirling Maid
        - Ch. Avon Stirling
        - Almaine Donetta
    - Danesgate Decima
      - Danesgate Demijohn
        - Danesgate Dean
        - Danesgate Dahlia
      - Boreham Benzine
        - Coxland Cobbles
        - Boreham Begam
- Brooklands Ebony Belle
  - Molten Mainmast
    - Molten Mainstay
      - Bowden Blarney
        - Bowden Hamish
        - Ch. Boreham Whisper
      - Molten Minella
        - Danesgate Dickon
        - Ch. Flanchford Finella
    - Molten Marion
      - Danesgate Dean
        - Ch. Corrector of Notts
        - Molten Janet
      - Dunton Reine
        - Avon Rufus
        - Ch. Raine Rarity
  - Brooklands Chic
    - Farleton First Flight
      - Ch. Farleton Fusilier
        - Ch. Farleton Flavian
        - Cutian Countess
      - Umber Girl
        - George Umber
        - Choice Line
    - Watteau Kathleen
      - Watteau Cheerio
        - Ch. Farleton Foxearth
        - Ch. Farleton Suzette
      - Watteau Wild Rose
        - Watteau Cheerio
        - Ch. Farleton Forethought

S-26: **Ch. Watteau Snuff Box,** 2/2/62

- Watteau Sculpture
  - Brooklands Decorator
    - Ch. Brooklands Black Ace
      - Ch. Brooklands Lucky Wishbone
        - Ch. Brooklands Black Prince
        - Burham Bint
      - Brooklands Black Tulip
        - Ch. Watteau Midas
        - Brooklands Ebonetta
    - Andersley Relsah Reward
      - Ch. Brooklands Black Mask
        - Ch. Brooklands Black Prince
        - Brooklands Milady
      - Watteau Whimsical
        - Brooklands Jolly Tar
        - Misty Morn
  - Watteau Loyal Lass
    - Ch. Hermon Parthings Loyal Lad
      - Parthings Laddie
        - Ch. Lethal Weapon
        - Parthings Lassie
      - Amber Solitaire
        - Boreham Belucky
        - Amber Susan
    - Watteau Choirgirl
      - Ch. Watteau Chorister
        - Ch. Brooklands Lucky Wishbone
        - Ch. Watteau Songstress
      - Watteau Marylyn
        - Ch. Hampole Tinkler
        - Brooklands Milady
- Beech Bank Olive
  - Ch. Watteau Chorister
    - Ch. Brooklands Lucky Wishbone
      - Ch. Brooklands Black Prince
        - Ch. Watteau Midas
        - Ch. Brooklands Black Narcissus
      - Burham Bint
        - Burham Bencher
        - Cathwill Cassandra
    - Ch. Watteau Songstress
      - Ch. Lavish Warpaint
        - Ch. Laurel Wreath
        - Boreham Beguile
      - Wild Flower
        - Ch. Watteau Midas
        - Brooklands Queen Bee
  - Beech Bank Flower Girl
    - Ch. Lanneau Jerod
      - Lanneau Hayespark Topnotcher
        - Hayespark Phone Call
        - Hayespark Callous
      - Kenlucky Teddibar Ailleen
        - Kenlucky Renown
        - Mullantean Beauty
    - Lanneau Jenta
      - Ch. Brooklands Lucky Wishbone
        - Ch. Brooklands Black Prince
        - Burham Bint
      - Lanneau Jayne
        - Ch. Black Andrew
        - Ch. Lanneau Jewel

Ch. Brooklands Lucky Wishbone
Ch. Watteau Chorister
Ch. Watteau Songstress
Ch. Watteau Madrigal
Ch. Hampole Tinkler
Watteau Marylyn
Brooklands Milady
S-28: **Laurel Drive,** 1/1/69
Lanneau Jepcot
Ch. Lanneau Jevron
Lanneau Jeminy
Lanneau Jexas
Ch. Watteau Madrigal
Ch. Lanneau Jessie
Lanneau Jezebel

Ch. Watteau Chorister
Ch. Watteau Madrigal
Watteau Marylyn
Ch. Laurel Drive
Lanneau Jevron
Lanneau Jexas
Lanneau Jessie
S-29: **Ch. Karnilo Chieftain,** 1/3/71
Watteau Sculpture
Ch. Watteau Snuff Box
Beechbank Olive
Ch. Karnilo Cavalena
Ch. Maryholm Sureline
Maryholm Special Line
Maryholm Silver Heiress

Watteau Sculpture
Eng. Ch. Watteau Snuff Box
Beechbank Olive
Ch. Viscum Voracity
Eng. Ch. Hermon Parthings Loyal Lad
Eng. Ch. Hampole Hero
Eng. Ch. Hampole Housewife
S-30: **Ch. Quissex Deacon,** 12/12/71
Ch. Watteau Snifter
Ch. Quissex De Quincey
Lindow Quissex Forest
Quissex Nixie
Quissex Vladimir
Ch. Quissex Matilda
Foxformee Charlotte

Eng. Ch. Watteau Snuffbox
Eng. Ch. Harkaway Lancashire Lad
Harkaway Mandy
Eng. Ch. Burmar Ted
Eng. Ch. Burman Warrior
Eng. Ch. Burman Snocat
Eng. Ch. Harkaway Emma
Riber Rockafella
Eng. Ch. Hampole Tinkler
Eng. Ch. Hampole Housemaster
Hampole Home Chat
Riber Pineapple Poll
Eng. Ch. Hermon Parthings Loyal Lad
Riber Regalia
Hayespark Lily Ways
S-33: **Eng. Ch. Riber Ramsey,** 10/23/72
Eng. Ch. Hampole Housemaster
Hampole Householder
Eng. Ch. Hampole Fidelity
Rampole Craftsman
Hampole Tatler
Hampole Housecraft
Eng. Ch. Hampole Housewife
Riber Side Saddle
Eng. Ch. Hampole Tinkler
Eng. Ch. Hampole Housemaster
Hampole Home Chat
Riber Pineapple Poll
Eng. Ch. Parthings Loyal Lad
Riber Regalia
Hayespark Lily Ways

Eng. Ch. Riber Rockafella
Eng. Ch. Riber Ramsey
Riber Sidesaddle
Eng. Ch. Mosvalley Marksman
Eng. Ch. Burmar Ted
Mosvalley Magpie
Sprotboro Spring Day
S-32: **Higrola Horatio of Britlea,** 3/6/78
Teesford Tartan
Teesford Tartar
Teesford Tara
Teesford Teaser
Watteau Pittlea Cherokee
Teesford Twink
Teesford Tara

S-31: **Ch. Waybroke Extra Smooth,** 8/15/74

Ch. Waybroke Red Lobster

    Ch. Stoney Meadows Neptune

        Ch. Stoney Meadows Mainbrace

            Eng. Ch. Watteau Snifter

                Eng. Ch. Watteau Snuff Box

                Watteau Cantata

            Battle Cry Carry On

                Ch. Stoney Meadows Bouy

                Ch. Hampole Sincerity

        Spice of Stoney Meadows

            Ch. Stoney Meadows Bouy

                Ch. Stoney Meadows Intrepid

                Glenhaven's Counterpoint

            Downsbragh Orange Bounce

                Downsbragh O'Malley

                Midstar Mandy

    Ch. Waybroke's Whistling Oyster

        Ch. Foxden Leprechaun

            Eng. & Am. Ch. Watteau Last Word of Foxden

                Ch. Watteau Snufsed of Cragcrest

                Lingrove Linnet

            Irish & Am. Ch. Parkgrove Camphill Golden Fairy

                Clondara Coach

                Camphill Bonny Girl

        Ch. Foxden Titania

            Eng. & Am. Ch. Foremark Ebony Box of Foxden

                Eng. Ch. Watteau Snuff Box

                Watteau Gaybird

            Irish & Am. Ch. Parkgrove Camphill Golden Fairy

                Clondara Coach

                Camphill Bonny Girl

Ch. Waybroke Smooth As Silk

    Ch. Watteau Musical Box

        Watteau Sculpture

            Brooklands Decorator

                Eng. Ch. Brooklands Black Ace

                Andersley Relsah Reward

            Watteau Loyal Lass

                Eng. Ch. Hermon Parthings Loyal Lad

                Watteau Choir Girl

        Beechbank Olive

            Eng. Ch. Watteau Chorister

                Eng. Ch. Brooklands Lucky Wishbone

                Eng. Ch. Watteau Songstress

            Beechbank Flower Girl

                Eng. Ch. Lanneau Jerod

                Lanneau Jenda

    Ch. Foxden Titania

        Eng. & Am. Ch. Foremark Ebony Box of Foxden

            Eng. Ch. Watteau Snuff Box

                Watteau Sculpture

                Beechbank Olive

            Watteau Gaybird

                Eng. Ch. Brooklands Happy Wish

                Watteau Skylark

        Irish & Am. Ch. Parkgrove Camphill Golden Fairy

            Clondara Coach

                Eng. Ch. Watteau Chorister

                Capella

            Camphill Bonny Girl

                Debough

                Wynnor's Fancy

S-34: Ch. Ttarb the Brat, 12/23/78

- **Ch. Farleton Capt. Sandy**
  - Ch. Newmaidley Pennyworth
    - Ch. Newmaidley Soap Box
      - Ch. Watteau Snuff Box
        - Watteau Sculpture
          - Brooklands Decorator
          - Watteau Loyal Lass
        - Beechbank Olive
          - Ch. Watteau Chorister
          - Beechbank Flower Girl
      - Newmaidley Anthea
        - Ch. Newmaidley Whistling Jeremy
          - Ch. Newmaidley Vodka
          - Newmaidley Dew
        - Newmaidley Echo
          - Ch. Newmaidley Vodka
          - Newmaidley Leira
    - Newmaidley New Penny
      - Ch. Newmaidley Whistling Jeremy
        - Newmaidley Vodka
          - Ch. Watteau Snuff Box
          - Newmaidley Destiny
        - Newmaidley Dew
          - Ch. Newmaidley Joshua
          - Newmaidley Destiny
      - Newmaidley Leira
        - Ch. Watteau Chorister
          - Ch. Brooklands Lucky Wishbone
          - Ch. Watteau Songstress
        - Newmaidley Tuppence
          - Ch. Maryholm Spun Gold
          - Ch. Newmaidley Farthing
  - Farleton Hi Society
    - Ch. Farleton Felix Flicker
      - Ch. Gothic Grandgem
        - Grange Rogue
          - Lingfield Fame
          - Grange Duenna
        - Gothic Gleaming
          - Ch. Gothic Gems Legacy
          - Gothic Galathea
      - Redyan La Ronde
        - Aus. Ch. Kenwood On Top
          - Ch. Grange Top Line
          - Grange Georgina
        - Redvian Rhea
          - Milda Morpheus
          - Redding Lynette
    - Farleton Frolic
      - Gothic Gallant Fox
        - Gothic Gandhi
          - Elgar Royal
          - Gothic Galsborough
        - Diadcam Bambi
          - Marco Polo Duplicate
          - Diadcam Destiny
      - Gothic Black Tulip
        - Ch. Gothic Gems Legacy
          - Perocliff Beau Brummel
          - Gothic Gem
        - Gothic Galathea
          - Wattle Brae Saddle
          - Gothic Gorgeous

- **Ch. Ttarb Teena**
  - Ch. Warkita Watta Lad
    - Ch. Ttarb the Klinka
      - Ch. Farleton Don Pedro
        - Aus. Ch. Gothic Grand Gem
          - Grange Rogue
          - Gothic Gleaming
        - Redvan La Ronde
          - Ch. Kenwood On Top
          - Redvian Rhea
      - Grenpark Amethyst
        - Aus. Ch. Grenpark Miraculous
          - Ch. Doric Oscar
          - Grenpark Greta
        - Grenpark Present
          - Ch. Doric Oscar
          - Grenpark Stardust
    - Ch. Grenpark Beauty Girl
      - Grenpark Miraculous
        - Aus. Ch. Doric Oscar
          - Ch. Brooklands Sailor Lad
          - Doric Eula
        - Grenpark Greta
          - Kavon Hasluck
          - Grenpark Firefly
      - Grenpark Present
        - Aus. Ch. Doric Oscar
          - Ch. Brooklands Sailor Lad
          - Ch. Doric Eula
        - Grenpark Stardust
          - Grenpark Surprise
          - Ch. Grenpark Real Charm
  - Ttarb Tuppence
    - Ch. Farleton Don Pedro
      - Gothic Grand Gem
        - Grange Rogue
          - Lingfield Flame
          - Grange Duenna
        - Gothic Gleaming
          - Ch. Gothic Gems Legacy
          - Gothic Galathea
      - Redvan La Ronde
        - Aus. Ch. Kenwood On Top
          - Ch. Grange Top Line
          - Grange Georgina
        - Redvan Rhea
          - Milda Morpheus
          - Redding Lynette
    - Grenpark Amethyst
      - Grenpark Miraculous
        - Aus. Ch. Doric Oscar
          - Ch. Brooklands Sailor Lad
          - Ch. Doric Eula
        - Grenpark Geta
          - Kavon Hasluck
          - Grenpark Firefly
      - Grenpark Present
        - Aus. Ch. Doric Oscar
          - Ch. Brooklands Sailor Lad
          - Ch. Doric Eula
        - Grenpark Stardust
          - Ch. Grenpark Surprise
          - Ch. Grenpark Real Charm

Wires

The early Wire went through a period of evolution and development lasting about twelve generations, starting with the Bristles double-grandson, Ch. Barkby Ben (W-1), and climaxing with Comedian of Notts in 1906. So, from Kendall's Old Tip, whelped in 1872, to Comedian in 1906, there is a straight, unerring line through Cackler of Notts in 1898. However, unlike the Smooths, the Wire history does not lend itself well to lines and families. Ch. Comedian of Notts had three significant sons, Ch. Collar of Notts (1907), Ch. Chunky of Notts (1908) and Olcliffe Captain (1923), and a case could be made that these three were responsible for nearly all the present top-winning Wires. But, Barrington Bridegroom was out of a bitch called Sarsgrove Molly, who was a daughter of Ch. Chunky of Notts. Just to further reinforce the point, Bridegroom's great descendant, Ch. Gallant Fox of Wildoaks (W-2), was out of a marvelous bitch, Ch. Gains Great Surprise, a great-granddaughter of Olcliffe Captain.

In 1949, J. H. Pardoe wrote a small but important book called *Fox Terriers*. It contains a lineage diagram of the great Wires from Ch. Cackler of Notts in 1898 through the first post-World War II Wire champions (W-3A, B, C, D). Since many of our American Wires were imports, the fact that the dogs listed are all British should not detract from the chart's value. Although the chart stops in 1946, I have attempted to update it to bridge the gap from immediate post-war English Wires to present-day American Wires. Additionally, Wires, like their Smooth cousins, suffered from the effects of World War II in that there were no championship shows in England, and, therefore, no champions. The net effect was to partially obscure the facts relating to the wartime activity so as to make it difficult for the casual or less determined student to trace the pedigree of his or her favorite back to its roots.

The chart has been extended to Eng. & Am. Ch. Harwire Hetman of Whinlatter (W-4), Eng. & Am. Ch. Maltman Country Life of Whinlatter (W-5), Ch. Deko Druid (W-6), Eng. Ch. Zeloy Endeavour (W-7—sire of Eng. Ch. Zeloy Emperor and Eng. & Am. Ch. Wintor Caracus Call Boy), Eng. Ch. Townville Tally'O (W-8—sire of Spot On), Eng. Ch. Kirmoor Speculation (W-9—sire of Ch. Gosmore Kirkmoor Craftsman), Eng. Ch. Worsbro Betoken Again (W-10—sire of Ch. Axholme Jimmy Reppin), Ch. Wintor Statesman (W-11), Ch. Mac's Revelation (W-12), Eng. & Am. Ch. Wyretex Wyns Traveller of Trucote (W-13), Eng. & Am. Ch. Wyretex Wyns Jupiter of Glynhir (W-14), Ch. Wyrequest's Pay Dirt (W-15), Ch. Bowyre Contender (W-16) and Ch. Wintor Caracus Call Boy (W-17). The inclusion of the extended pedigree of these important Wire stud dogs should make it possible for anyone with a three-generation pedigree of their Wire to trace it back to Barkby Ben, as well as provide a handy reference for use by the serious breeder.

The Wire history in Australia parallels the Wire history in England and the United States in that they arrived later but differ in that they never really overtook the Smooth. Perhaps the trimming talent was less available. Surely the call to America was a sweeter call than the call to Australia for talented trimmers of England. However, the first Wire to be shown in Australia was bred by Parson Jack Russell and imported by a Doctor Le Febre. The major early breeders were E. D. Davis (Heathcote), R. E. Twopenny (Edenthorpe), A. D. McMichael (Abbotsford) and H. Bartlett (Oxford).

Wires began their rise to prominence thanks mainly to an English emigre, Len Latchford, who while still a resident of England, sent Mysia Pickup to Australia. Mr. Latchford brought the art of trimming with him when he arrived in Australia and for the next forty years was one of Australia's most noteworthy canine journalists and all-round judges. Prior to Latchford's arrival the Wires were exhibited untrimmed. Just prior to World War I, Raby Holdfast, Wheatshead Duchess and Wyche King were imported by H. Bartlett.

Just after World War I, the get of Fountain Crusader, Wycollar Boy and Olcliffe Captain began arriving in Australia. The Selwor Kennels' Wires were descended from imports arriving in the early years of the 1920s. In the 1930s the offspring of Talavera Simon and Gallant Fox of Wildoaks joined the Wire ranks. Such familiar prefixes as Ryburn and Crackley were seen around the dog shows of that period. Some of the top winners of the time were Letcombe Leander, owned by Ted Forehan, who topped the Melbourne Royal in 1934 and the Sydney Royal in 1935. Dunure Sunset, imported by Tom Manning, was Best in Show at Sydney in 1938 and Flornell Conquest completed the dominance by imports by winning Brisbane in 1940.

After World War II, the flood of imports resumed with Zeloy Caramea, Geddling's Nimbus and Wrose Showgirl, just to cite a few.

The 1960s saw Penda Pied Piper and Penda Polly Perkins bring the fine hand of Elsie Williams to Australia. Roundway Patsy Ann was imported in whelp to Eng. Ch. Roundway Bell Boy and Eng. Ch. Roundway Shanlaw Guardsman also added to the bloodlines of the Wire in Australia.

In 1962, Leo Wilson awarded Foxwyre Flash Gem the Best in Show sash at Sydney. Leo Wilson was the outstanding English Smooth breeder whose program produced Lethal Weapon and Laurel Wreath. Today's Wire breeders include John and Glenys Rowels (Selwor), Marj. Clark (Cooniwire), Liz Imlay and Adrian Walmsley, who recently imported Eng. Ch. Sarabel Second Chance of Granemore. Selwor recently imported Am. Ch. Aldees Poncharelo of Ana-Dare. Through the years, in Australia, as in the United States, the top Wires were always made in England.

If you meet an Aussie he will tell you that the best Fox Terriers in the world are in Australia and if he or she is still actively breeding, theirs will be the best of the best. Aussies are marvelous friends. They are just not prone to underestimate.

Index of Wire Lineage

	Dog or Bitch	*Date of Birth*
W-1	Ch. Barkby Ben	1900
W-2	Ch. Gallant Fox of Wildoaks	12/23/29
W-3	From 1898 to 1946	
W-4	Ch. Harwire Hetman of Whinlatter	10/16/74
W-5	Ch. Maltman Country Life of Whinlatter	09/12/82
W-6	Ch. Deko Druid	07/25/60
W-7	Ch. Zeloy Endevour	08/21/56
W-8	Ch. Townville Tally'O	06/04/67
W-9	Ch. Kirkmoor Speculation	05/01/66
W-10	Ch. Worsbro Betoken Again	05/25/66
W-11	Ch. Wintor Statesman	08/10/64
W-12	Ch. Mac's Revelation	09/28/56
W-13	Ch. Wyretex Wyns Traveller of Trucote	10/15/48
W-14	Ch. Wyretex Wyns Jupiter of Glynhir	09/06/48
W-15	Ch. Wyrequest's Pay Dirt	11/21/72
W-16	Ch. Bowyre Contender	11/05/70
W-17	Ch. Wintor Caracus Call Boy	05/18/64
W-18	Ch. Sunnybrook Spot On	10/04/69
W-19	Ch. Zeloy Emperor	03/10/60
W-20	Ch. Evewire You Better Believe It	07/05/75
W-21	Ch. Brownstone's Mac Broom	11/13/67
W-22	Ch. Raylu Recharge	09/08/76
W-23	Ch. Galsul Excellence	05/03/83
W-24	Ch. Sylair Special Edition	07/14/83

	Meersbrook Ben	Meersbrook Bristles
		Meersbrook Norma
W-1: Ch. Barkby Ben, 1900		
	Barkby Vixen	Meersbrook Bristles
		Tormentella

347

W.-2: **Ch. Gallant Fox of Wildoaks,** 12/23/29

Int. Ch. Crackley Supreme of Wildoaks
- Int. Ch. Crackley Sensational
  - Int. Ch. Crackley Sensation
    - Int. Ch. Welwire Barrington Bridegroom
      - Barrington Fearnought
        - Barrington Cracker
        - Barrington Brisk
      - Sarsgrove Molly
        - Eng. Ch. Chunky of Notts
        - Sarsgrove Pansy
    - Love Bird
      - Eng. Ch. Wharfeside Wiseacre
        - Bolton Dandy
        - Olcliffe Becky
      - Stourbridge Swank
        - Barrington Fearnought
        - Seabreese Salome
  - Keresley Pandy
    - Pedro Toff
      - Barrington Fearnought
        - Barrington Cracker
        - Barrington Brisk
      - Stoke Sue
        - Eng. Ch. Southboro Salex
        - Larkspur
    - Roman Wire Girl
      - Epping Epicure
        - Fighting Action
        - Olcliffe Rose Bloom
      - Roman Lass
        - Medhurst Nut
        - Medhurst Queen
- Eng. Ch. Eden Bridesmaid of Thorndale
  - Int. Ch. Welwire Barrington Bridegroom
    - Barrington Fearnought
      - Barrington Cracker
        - Eng. Ch. Corker of Notts
        - Barrington Crack 'em
      - Barrington Brisk
        - Comedian of Notts
        - Gileston Prospect
    - Sarsgrove Molly
      - Eng. Ch. Chunky of Notts
        - Comedian of Notts
        - Cobnut of Notts
      - Sarsgrove Pansy
        - Bishops Selected
        - Sarsgrove Gamester's Model
  - Treviac Tartlett
    - Gaffer of Gretna
      - Watteau Warrior
        - Int. Ch. Wireboy of Paignton
        - Watteau Crest
      - Amron Wire Girl
        - Melton President
        - Sweet Clonmelody
    - Coffee of Notts
      - Eng. Ch. Chunky of Notts
        - Comedian of Notts
        - Cobnut of Notts
      - Eng. Ch. Cocoatina of Notts
        - Cocoanut of Notts
        - Lucky Omen (of Notts)

Int. Ch. Gains Great Surprise of Wildoaks
- Eng. Ch. Talavera Simon
  - Eng. Ch. Fountain Crusader
    - Olcliffe Captain
      - Comedian of Notts
        - Catch 'Em of Notts
        - Cobweb of Notts
      - Olcliffe Jess
        - Barrington Banker
        - Olcliffe Louie
    - Merton Popay
      - Mannville Wireboy
        - Int. Ch. Wireboy of Paignton
        - Crystal Star
      - Odsal Nell
        - Eng. Ch. Briar Cackler
        - Peggy
  - Kingsthorp Donah
    - Int. Ch. Welwire Barrington Bridegroom
      - Barrington Fearnought
        - Barrington Cracker
        - Barrington Brisk
      - Sarsgrove Molly
        - Eng. Ch. Chunky of Notts
        - Sarsgrove Pansy
    - Eng. Ch. Indecision
      - Bishops Selected
        - Exon Eclipson
        - Bishops Hull Sally
      - Clove Hitch
        - Bishops Selected
        - Karamea Tiny Biddy
- New Town Bella Donna
  - Eng. Ch. Wycollar Trail
    - Consulter of Notts
      - Wincanton Rufus
        - Eng. Ch. Collarbone of Notts
        - Wincanton Bessie
      - Wincanton Spoof-Off
        - Int. Ch. Vickery Short Circuit
        - Wincanton Snip
    - Wycollar Queen
      - Int. Ch. Conejo Wycollar Boy
        - Int. Ch. Wireboy of Paignton
        - Queen Collar
      - Queen Collar
        - Lodge Mickey
        - Gipsy
  - Miss Harvest Time
    - Eng. Ch. Epping Emblem
      - Eng. Ch. Brakesmere Benedict
        - Watteau Warrior
        - Romping Girl
      - Eng. Ch. Indecision
        - Bishops Selected
        - Clove Hitch
    - Miss Bendigo
      - Lashbrook Bendigo
        - Round Up
        - Gradeley Girl
      - Marsh Lady
        - Barrington Fearnought
        - Corn Exchange Sadie

348

Part I

W-3: From 1898 to 1946
Ch. Barrington Bridegroom

Ch. Cackler of Notts 1898

Ch. Briar Cackler

Ch. Dusky Cackler 1900

Ch. Dusky Cracker

Ch. Sylvan Result 1902

Ch. Raby Coastguard

Kilmore

Ch. Gladiator 1906

Ch. Short Circuit 1909

Morden Blusterer 1902

Ch. Southboro Salex

Ch. West Point Result

Catch 'em of Notts 1904

Comedian of Notts 1906

Ch. Guycroft Salex 1910

Ch. Collar of Notts 1922

Ch. Corker of Notts 1911

Barrington Cracker

Olcliffe Captain 1912
ex Olcliffe Jess by Barrington Banker

Ch. Fountain Crusader 1919

Barrington Fearnought

Ch. Barrington Bridegroom 1919

Ch. Let's Go

ex Sarsgrove Molly by Ch. Chunky of Notts

Ch. Commodore of Notts

Ch. Captain of Notts

Ch. Common Scamp of Notts

Ch. Chunky of Notts 1908

Ch. Wireboy of Paignton 1912

Ch. Signal Wire

Watteau Warrior 1915

Ch. Brakesmere Benedict 1917

Ch. Epping Emblem

Ch. Wycollar Boy

Wyche Warrant 1914

Ch. Wyche Wallet 1921

Ch. Wyche Workman 1917

Ch. Wyche Wrangler

Brynhir Captain

Brynhir Burner

Ch. Thet Fusilier

Ch. Deykin Wireboy

Ch. Speedy Ball

Ch. Aman Fox Trot

349

Part II   Ch. Barrington Bridegroom

Ch. Gang Warily 1921
Ch. Stockamoor Storm 1923
Ch. Chantry Cinnamon

Ch. Wyche Warm

Ch. Crackley Sensation 1922
Ch. Crackley Sensational 1923
Ch. Crackley Supreme 1925
Ch. Kingsthorpe Sunstorm

Ch. Barry Brigadier 1921
Ch. Epping Extreme

Ch. Roboro Playboy 1921

Ch. Crackley Supremacy 1927
Ch. Grandon Masterpiece 1929

Ch. Gallant Fox of Wildoaks 1929
Ch. Bobby Burns of Wildoaks 1928
Ch. Cornwell Cyclone

ex Ch. Gains Great Suprise by Ch. Talavera Simon
1927

Ch. Langtoun Lancelot 1935
Ch. Weltons Exemplar 1936
Ch. Cawthorne Full Cry 1935
Ch. Bowes Barham 1935

Ch. Ravelly Radiance 1934
Ch. Cynosure of Certosa 1936

Ch. Crackley Supreme Again 1934
Ch. Stocksmoor Sportsman 1933
Ch. Castlecroft Contender 1935
Ch. Tanyard Thriller 1933
Whitecastle Games
Ch. Whitecastle Warrior 1937

Ch. Crackley Striking 1937
Ch. Crackley Straightaway 1941
Ch. Miltona Mahmoud 1936
Copleydene Lucky Strike
Harley Fulgent

Mahmoud's Double
Ch. Burtona Bonanza 1937
Travella Sensation
Hotel Traveller

Ch. Wynstead What's Wanted 1943
Burtona Beacon
Ch. Travella Strike 1946
Ch. Casfala Copyright 1945

Ch. Tornadic Burtona Bonanza Again

Part III

Ch. Fountain Crusader

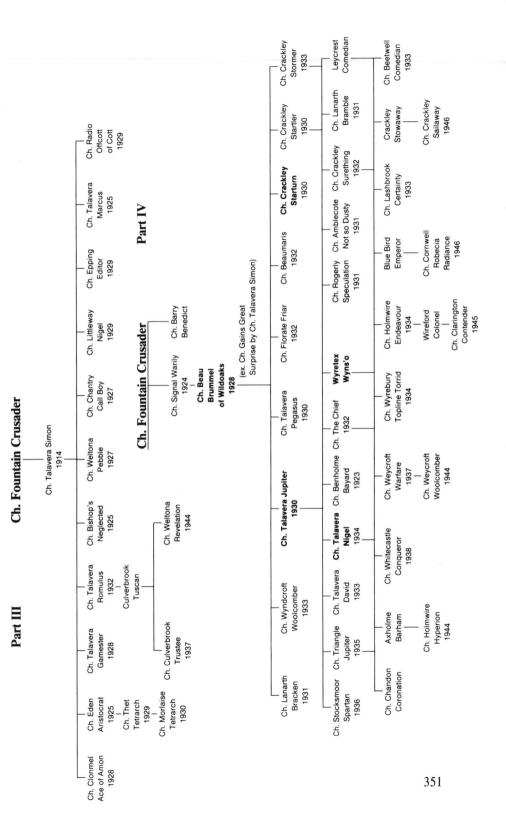

Part IV

Ch. Fountain Crusader

351

W-4: Eng. & Am. Ch. Harwire Hetman of Whinlatter, 10/16/74

- **Eng. & Am. Ch. Townville Tobias** (sire)
  - Eng. Ch. Wintor Statesman
    - Eng. Ch. Wintor Townville
      - Townville Traveller
        - Eng. Ch. Zeloy End
          - Eng. Ch. Wyretex Wyn's Wun Dar
            - Eng. Ch. Wyretex Wyns Tuscan
            - Eng. Ch. Wyrebury Penda Quicksilver
          - Supremacy's Smart Girl
            - Zeloy Supremacy
            - Simon's Little Lady
        - Townville True Love
          - Townhill Masterpiece
            - Eng. Ch. Burtona Betoken
            - Cawthorne Carnation
          - Cheview Candida
            - Steetonian Sortie
            - Townville Twilight
      - Townville Trinket
        - Albion Monotype
          - Eng. Ch. Wyrevale Monotype
            - Eng. Ch. Cornwell Robecia Radiance
            - Wyrevale Marguerite
          - Roman Susan
            - Cornwell Cert
            - Surprise Melody
        - Townville True Love
          - Townhill Masterpiece
            - Eng. Ch. Burtona Betoken
            - Cawthorne Carnation
          - Cheview Candida
            - Steetonian Sortie
            - Townville Twilight
    - Wintor Twilight
      - Eng. Ch. Lyngarth Scout
        - Eng. Ch. Zeloy Crusader
          - Eng. Ch. Zeloy Endevour
            - Eng. Ch. Wyretex Wyn's Wun Dar
            - Supremacy's Smart Girl
          - Zeloy Cinderella
            - Ryburn Romeo
            - Ryburn Glenside Eve
        - Eng. Ch. Lyngarth Social Call
          - Eng. Ch. Axholme Double Strike
            - Eng. Ch. Travella Strike
            - Axholme Miss Miranda
          - Lyngarth Serenade
            - Eden Autocrat
            - Lyngarth Precision
      - Lyngarth True Call
        - Eng. Ch. Zeloy Crusader
          - Eng. Ch. Zeloy Endevour
            - Eng. Ch. Wyretex Wyn's Wun Dar
            - Supremacy's Smart Girl
          - Zeloy Cinderella
            - Ryburn Romeo
            - Ryburn Glenside Eve
        - Lyngarth Chance Call
          - Lyngarth Limberhill
            - Eng. Ch. Cawthorne Climax
            - Lyngarth Soubrette
          - Eng. Ch. Lyngarth Social Call
            - Eng. Ch. Axholme Double Strike
            - Lyngarth Serenade
  - Eng. Ch. Worsbro Betoken Again
    - Anfield Betoken
      - Eng. Ch. Burtona Betoken
        - Burtona Bosun
          - Burtona Beacon
          - Burtona Brimful
        - Torkard Countess
          - Eng. Ch. Crackley Sailaway
          - Newmaidley Eve
      - Windlehurst Pretty Piece
        - Eng. Ch. Cawthorne Climax
          - Eng. Ch. Burtona Betoken
          - Cawthorne Twynstar Actionette
        - Twynstar Pretty Piece
          - Twynstar Selection
          - Eng. Ch. Cawthorne Climax
    - Cawthorne Comfrey
      - FCI Ch. Sideron Cawthorne
        - Cawthorne Cracker
          - (sire not legible)
          - Cawthorne Ready Maid
        - Steelholm Sally
          - Eng. Ch. Burtona Betoken
          - Clifton Pandora
      - Cawthorne Ready Maid
        - Florate Frontpiece
          - Eng. Ch. Travella Skyflyer
          - Florate Felicia of Freams
        - Warm Welcome
          - Castlecroft Cleanaway
          - Lucky Legend
- **Townville Tamlyn** (dam)
  - Townville Top Form
    - Eng. Ch. Burtona Betoken
      - Burtona Bosun
        - Burtona Beacon
        - Burtona Brimful
      - Torkard Countess
        - Eng. Ch. Crackley Sailaway
        - Newmaidley Eve
    - Townville Tingaling
      - Eng. Ch. Caradochouse Spruce of Trucote
        - Drakehall Ardour Advocate
        - Caradochouse Ramblerrose
      - Tollhill Treacle
        - Eng. Ch. Axholme Double Strike
        - Barklyhill Patricia
  - Townville Tiara
    - Tollhill Masterpiece
      - Eng. Ch. Burtona Betoken
        - Burtona Bosun
        - Torkard Countess
      - Cawthorne Carnation
        - Cawthorne Coalite
        - Cawthorne Cornflake
    - Cheview Candida
      - Steetonian Sortie
        - Eng. Ch. Wyretex Wyn's Wun Dar
        - Steetonian Suntan
      - Townville Twilight
        - Int. Ch. Caradochouse Spruce
        - Tollhill Treacle

352

- **Eng. Ch. Harwire Hallmark**
  - Eng. Ch. Seedfield Meritor Super Flash
    - Eng. Ch. Zeloy Emperor
      - Eng. Ch. Zeloy Endevour
        - Eng. Ch. Wyretex Wyn's Wun
          - Eng. Ch. Wyretex Wyns Tuscan
            - Culverbrook Tuscan
            - Wyretex Wyns Thralia
          - Eng. Ch. Wyrebury Penda Quicksilver
            - Eng. Ch. Penda Blackwell Revelation
            - Eng. Ch. Penda Hoover Warrior
        - Supremacy's Smart Girl
          - Zeloy Supremacy
            - Eng. Ch. Kirkmoore Cobbler
            - Zeloy Lucky Patch
          - Simon's Little Lady
            - Tescot Steetonian Simon
            - My Choice
      - Zeloy Rhapsody
        - Zeloy Carouso
          - Eng. Ch. Maryholm Mighty Good
            - Eng. Ch. Knollbrook Keyman
            - Fair Pretender
          - Zeloy Tarantella
            - Tescot Steetonian Simon
            - Zeloy Roseta
        - Zeloy Roseta
          - Tescot Majestic
            - Copleydene Supafox
            - Stoneycrag Sparkler
          - Soundman's Result
            - Steetonian Soundman
            - Daughter of Delegate
    - Maryholm Wintersweet
      - Eng. Ch. Extreal Realization
        - Extreal Revelation
          - Thistleton Dandy
            - Colonel of Allanville
            - Thistledown Serenade
          - Extreal Queen
            - Eng. Ch. Maryholm Northern Monarch
            - Spray Pauleen
        - Crawley Countess
          - Eng. Ch. Emprise Sensational
            - Eng. Ch. Cawthorne Climax
            - Twynstar Authoress
          - Extreal Regent
            - Thistleton Dandy
            - Extreal Queen
      - Maryholm Winning Way
        - Eng. Ch. Anfield Contender
          - Eng. Ch. Weltona What's This
            - Eng. Ch. Wyretex Wyns Tuscan
            - Fulldress of the Forces
          - Anfield Striking
            - Wyrecliff Travella Strikelike
            - Christyline Lady
        - Maryholm Whynot
          - Eng. Ch. Maryholm Northern Monarch
            - Eng. Ch. Knollbrook Keyman
            - Newtown Spitfire
          - Bankside Gay Girl
            - Eng. Ch. Burtona Betoken
            - Roylan Summer Breeze
  - Harwire Hellina
    - Harwire Hero
      - Harwire Headway
        - Eng. Ch. Gosmore Harwire
          - Eng. Ch. Wyrecliffe Statellite of Senganel
            - Exelwyre Mooroak Aristocrat
            - Smart Biddy of Senganel
          - Maltmans Sunrise
            - Eng. Ch. Axholme Double Strike
            - Wagon Girl
        - Harwire Honeybee
          - Wyrecroft Warrior
            - Rhythmic Remus
            - Roundway Matchmaker
          - Wicklewood Twilight
            - Eng. Ch. Travella Starshine
            - Toplight Titbit
      - Harwire Humorist
        - Eng. Ch. Penda Peerless
          - Eng. Ch. Penda Cawthorne Cobnut
            - Eng. Ch. Cawthorne Climax
            - Cawthorne Ready Maid
          - Eng. Ch. Wyrebury Penda Quicksilver
            - Eng. Ch. Penda Blackwell Revelation
            - Eng. Ch. Penda Hoover Warrior
        - Harwire Honeybee
          - Wyrecroft Warrior
            - Rhythmic Remus
            - Roundway Matchmaker
          - Wicklewood Twilight
            - Eng. Ch. Travella Starshine
            - Toplight Titbit
    - Harwire Hazel
      - Eng. Ch. Weltona Has It
        - Eng. Ch. Holmwire Roxville
          - Holmwire Paul Tudor
            - Eng. Ch. Zeloy Endevour
            - Holmwire Evening Sunset
          - Roxville Mooremaides Moment
            - Eng. Ch. Zeloy Emperor
            - Mooremaides Cha-Cha-Cha
        - Eng. Ch. Weltona Plalla Dainty Princess
          - Eng. Ch. Anfield Contender
            - Eng. Ch. Weltona What's This
            - Anfield Striking
          - Mac's Model Wire
            - Meritor Moorcrest Mac
            - Miss Dusty
      - Shoemans Mooremaide Meg
        - Eng. Ch. Wintor Statesman
          - Eng. Ch. Wintor Townville Tuscan
            - Townville Traveller
            - Townville Trinket
          - Wintor Twilight
            - Eng. Ch. Lyngarth Scout
            - Lyngarth True Call
        - Mooremaides Newire Magpie
          - Eng. Ch. Zeloy Crusader
            - Eng. Ch. Zeloy Endevour
            - Zeloy Cinderella
          - Newire Lyngarth Tannette
            - Mitre Advocate
            - Lyngarth Soubrette

W-6: Ch. Deko Druid, 7/25/60

- Sire: Eng. Ch. Travella Strike
  - Travella Sensation
    - Copleydene Lucky Strike
      - Eng. Ch. Castlecroft Contender
        - Int. Ch. Gallant Fox of Wildoaks
          - Int. Ch. Crackley Supreme
          - Int. Ch. Gains Great Surprise
        - Eng. Ch. Castlecroft Content
          - Int. Ch. Beau Brummel of Wildoaks
          - Castlecroft Countess
      - Greenside Lassie
        - Eng. Ch. Crackley Supreme Again
          - Int. Ch. Gallant Fox of Wildoaks
          - Eng. Ch. Crackley Society
        - Eng. Ch. Lanarth Zenia
          - Eng. Ch. Lanarth Bramble
          - Janellin
    - Greenside Lassie
      - Eng. Ch. Talavera Nigel
        - Eng. Ch. Talavera Jupiter
          - Int. Ch. Beau Brummel of Wildoaks
          - Talavera Pauline
        - Talavera Cleopatra
          - Eng. Ch. Talavera Simon
          - Talavera Patchwork
      - Sylvia of Copleydene
        - Eng. Ch. Chandon Cornation
          - Eng. Ch. Triangle Jupiter
          - Standard Indecision
        - Copleydene Carefree
          - Eng. Ch. Talavera Romulus
          - Copleydene Graceful Bride
  - Travella Gloria
    - Eng. Ch. Crackley Straightaway
      - Eng. Ch. Crackley Supreme Again
        - Int. Ch. Gallant Fox of Wildoaks
          - Int. Ch. Crackley Supreme
          - Eng. Ch. Gains Great Surprise
        - Eng. Ch. Crackley Society
          - Eng. Ch. Crackley Surething
          - Crackley Sequence
      - Crackley Sequel
        - Eng. Ch. Crackley Stormer
          - Int. Ch. Beau Brummel of Wildoaks
          - Eckersley Editress
        - Eng. Ch. Crackley Social
          - Eng. Ch. Crackley Surething
          - Crackley Sequence
    - Lady Contender of Laracor
      - Eng. Ch. Castlecroft Contender
        - Int. Ch. Gallant Fox of Wildoaks
          - Int. Ch. Crackley Supreme
          - Int. Ch. Gains Great Surprise
        - Eng. Ch. Castlecroft Content
          - Int. Ch. Beau Brummel of Wildoaks
          - Castlecroft Countess
      - Lady Ruth of Laracor
        - Eng. Ch. Talavera Simon
          - Eng. Ch. Fountain Crusader
          - Kingsthorp Donah
        - Ruth of Laracor
          - Int. Ch. Beau Brummel of Wildoaks
          - Ruby of Laracor
- Dam: Vingos Verve
  - Hunsull Fulgent
    - Eng. Ch. Travella Skyflyer
      - Eng. Ch. Travella Strike
        - Travella Sensation
          - Copleydene Lucky Strike
          - Copleydene Fashion Pride
        - Travella Gloria
          - Eng. Ch. Crackley Straightaway
          - Lady Contender of Laracor
      - Travella Mannequin
        - Travella Bridegroom
          - Eng. Ch. Castlecroft Contender
          - Lady Ruth of Laracor
        - Travella Peach
          - Newmaidley Rex
          - Chillie Sauce
    - Robroy Sunshine
      - Eng. Ch. Wynstead Whats Wanted
        - Mahmouds Double
          - Eng. Ch. Miltona Mahmoud
          - Castlecroft Compact
        - Nigel's Sunshine
          - Tangos Double
          - Nigels Lassie
      - Bluebird Wants It
        - Bluebird Emperor
          - Wynetex Wyns O
          - Firefly of the Forces
        - Bluebird Sunstream
          - Eng. Ch. Crackley Straightaway
          - Culverbrook Tonia
  - Vingos Vivacity
    - Travella Sensation
      - Copleydene Lucky Strike
        - Eng. Ch. Castlecroft Contender
          - Int. Ch. Gallant Fox of Wildoaks
          - Eng. Ch. Castlecroft Content
        - Greenside Lassie
          - Eng. Ch. Crackley Supreme Again
          - Eng. Ch. Lanarth Zenia
      - Copleydene Fashion Pride
        - Eng. Ch. Talavera Nigel
          - Eng. Ch. Talavera Jupiter
          - Talavera Cleopatra
        - Sylvia of Copleydene
          - Eng. Ch. Chandon Cornation
          - Copleydene Carefree
    - Vingos Fashion
      - Eng. Ch. Travella Strike
        - Travella Sensation
          - Copleydene Lucky Strike
          - Copleydene Fashion Pride
        - Travella Gloria
          - Eng. Ch. Crackley Straightaway
          - Lady Contender of Laracor
      - Vingos Megan
        - Super Duper
          - Ebbw Sir Nigel
          - Ebbw Swell Tulle
        - Caldicote Eleanor Ann
          - Foxdenton Withdare
          - Caldicot Ann Penelope

Eng. Ch. Burtona Betoken

Burtona Bosun
- Burtona Beacon
  - Eng. Ch. Burtona Bonanza
    - Eng. Ch. Miltona Mahmoud
      - Eng. Ch. Castlecroft Contender
      - Wakeful Susan
    - Elmwood Emblem
      - Truwire Technique
      - Elmwood Empress (unregistered)
  - Elmwood Emulous
    - Truwire Technique
      - Eng. Ch. Beetwell Comedian
      - Sparken Solstice
    - Truwire Tempest
      - Eng. Ch. Gedling Safeguard
      - Truwire Tantrums
- Burtona Brimful
  - Burtona Weycroft Wireboy
    - Eng. Ch. Weycroft Warfare
      - Eng. Ch. Talavera Nigel
      - Greenmoor Glitter
    - Weycroft Sparkler
      - Eng. Ch. Castlecroft Contender
      - Allwire Sunflower
  - Burtona Baroness
    - Burtona Beacon
      - Eng. Ch. Burtona Bonanza
      - Elmwood Emulous
    - Burtona Bellona
      - Gamco Chevalier
      - Elmwood Emulous

Torkard Countess
- Eng. Ch. Crackley Sailaway
  - Crackley Stowaway
    - Eng. Ch. Crackley Surething
      - Eng. Ch. Crackley Startler
      - Dagshai Dhu
    - Crackley Swanmaiden
      - Int. Ch. Gallant Fox of Wildoaks
      - Crackley Sequence
  - Straightlace Susan
    - Crackley Searchlight
      - Eng. Ch. Crackley Striking
      - Crackley Sequel
    - Crackley Straightlace
      - Eng. Ch. Crackley Straightaway
      - Crackley Sportsgirl
- Newmaidley Eve
  - Newmaidley George
    - Eng. Ch. Castlecroft Contender
      - Int. Ch. Gallant Fox of Wildoaks
      - Eng. Ch. Castlecroft Content
    - Newmaidley Leading Lady
      - Cawthorne Comedian
      - Talavera Sparkle
  - Newmaidley Zeal
    - Newmaidley Quoodle
      - New Maidley Rex
      - Newmaidley Ethyl
    - Newmaidley Sonnet
      - Newmaidley Knave
      - Newmaidley Bubbles

Rumsam Duskie

Eng. Ch. Arley Topper
- Polo Prince
  - Polo Spotlight
    - Castlecroft Cleanaway
      - Eng. Ch. Crackley Sailaway
      - Castlecroft Cover Girl
    - Polo Peach
      - Copleydene Lucky Strike
      - Polo Spinaway
  - Polo Gay Lady
    - Eng. Ch. Crackley Sailaway
      - Crackley Stowaway
      - Straightlace Susan
    - Polo Picture
      - Weycroft Woolcomer
      - Polo Minted
- Polo Skylark
  - Stoneycrag Stayfast
    - Wireford Colonel
      - Eng. Ch. Holmwire Endeavor
      - Cocksure Countess
    - Grenville Countess
      - Clarington Chief
      - Blackthorn Queen
  - Polo Spinaway
    - Eng. Ch. Crackley Straightaway
      - Eng. Ch. Crackley Supreme Again
      - Crackley Sequel
    - Polo Minted
      - Eng. Ch. Castlecroft Contender
      - Polo Great Surprise

Bobetty Trehaverne Sapphire
- Bluebird Emperor
  - Wyretex Wyns O
    - Eng. Ch. Talavera Jupiter
      - Int. Ch. Beau Brummel of Wildoaks
      - Talavera Pauline
    - Wyretex Wynsnina
      - Cawthorne Comedian
      - Wyretex Wynsmaid
  - Firefly of the Forces
    - Eng. Ch. Talavera Jupiter
      - Int. Ch. Beau Brummel of Wildoaks
      - Talavera Pauline
    - Talavera Olive
      - Eng. Ch. Talavera Simon
      - Talavera Patchwork
- Milbourne Amethyst
  - Wyretex Wynstock
    - Eng. Ch. Talavera Romulus
      - Eng. Ch. Talavera Simon
      - Talavera Sparkle
    - Wyretex Wynsunshine
      - Eng. Ch. Miltona Mahmoud
      - Wyretex Wynsnina
  - Flawless of the Forces
    - Eng. Ch. Talavera Jupiter
      - Int. Ch. Beau Brummel of Wildoaks
      - Talavera Pauline
    - Talavera Olive
      - Eng. Ch. Talavera Simon
      - Talavera Patchwork

Eng. Ch. Zeloy Endevour

- Eng. Ch. Wyretex Wyn's Wun Dar
  - Eng. Ch. Wyretex Wyns Tuscan
    - Culverbrook Tuscan
      - Eng. Ch. Talavera Romulus
        - Eng. Ch. Talavera Simon
          - Eng. Ch. Fountain Crusader
            - Olcliffe Captain
            - Merton Topsy (unregistered)
          - Kingsthorp Donah
            - Eng. Ch. Barrington Bridegroom
            - Eng. Ch. Indecision
        - Talavera Sparkle
          - Oakdene Courtier
            - Talavera Paul
            - Oakdene Comedienne
          - Talavera Prudence
            - Eng. Ch. Talavera Simon
            - Coronal of Fistral
      - Culverbrook Trophy
        - Eng. Ch. Crackley Startum
          - Int. Ch. Beau Brummel of Wildoaks
            - Signal Warily
            - Int. Ch. Gains Great Surprise
          - Derkath Little Wonder
            - Eng. Ch. Talavera Simon
            - Lady Pyrnimon
        - Tydraw Dairymaid
          - Bictons Limit
            - Citadel Speed Limit
            - Chelston Frolic
          - Keystar Bellatrix
            - Hirwain Collar On
            - Liewnur Lila
    - Wyretex Wyns Thralia
      - Wyretex Wynso
        - Eng. Ch. Talavera Jupiter
          - Int. Ch. Beau Brummel of Wildoaks
            - Signal Warily
            - Int. Ch. Gains Great Surprise
          - Talavera Pauline
            - Eng. Ch. Talavera Simon
            - Talavera Toothache
        - Wyretex Wynsnina
          - Cawthorne Comedian
            - Int. Ch. Gallant Fox of Wildoaks
            - Oakdene Trixie
          - Wyretex Wynsmaid
            - Eng. Ch. Crackley Surething
            - Weltona Spring Fashion
      - Talavera Tansy
        - Eng. Ch. Talavera Romulus
          - Eng. Ch. Talavera Simon
            - Eng. Ch. Fountain Crusader
            - Kingsthorp Donah
          - Talavera Sparkle
            - Oakdene Courtier
            - Talavera Prudence
        - Talavera Crocus
          - Eng. Ch. Talavera Jupiter
            - Int. Ch. Beau Brummel of Wildoaks
            - Talavera Pauline
          - Talavera Cleopatra
            - Eng. Ch. Talavera Simon
            - Talavera Patchwork
- Eng. Ch. Wyrebury Penda Quicksilver
  - Eng. Ch. Penda Blackwell Revelation
    - Eng. Ch. Weltona
      - Eng. Ch. Talavera Romulus
        - Culverbrook Trophy
          - Eng. Ch. Crackley Startum
            - Eng. Ch. Talavera Simon
            - Talavera Sparkle
          - Hornby Knockout
            - Eng. Ch. Crackley Startum
            - Tydraw Dairymaid
        - Culverbrook Trophy
          - Snootie (unregistered)
            - Eng. Ch. Whitecastle Conqueror
            - Barnslo Lady Gay
      - Myddleton Major
        - Express Boy
          - Wonlock Bracken
          - Wonlock Springtime
        - Betty of Whitefoot
          - Boy
          - Betty
    - Edenholme Elfreida
      - Rickerby Wren
        - Eden Commander
          - Eden Smasher
          - Eng. Ch. Eden Serenade
        - Eden Cinderella
          - Eden Commander
          - Eden Juliet
  - Eng. Ch. Penda Hieover
    - Penda Pompilius
      - Eng. Ch. Talavera Romulus
        - Eng. Ch. Talavera Simon
          - Eng. Ch. Fountain Crusader
          - Kingsthorp Donah
        - Talavera Sparkle
          - Oakdene Courtier
          - Talavera Prudence
      - Wyretex Wynsdainty
        - Wynstead Warrior
          - Eng. Ch. Stocksmoor Sportsman
          - Highview Lady
        - Brummels Bride
          - Int. Ch. Gallant Fox of Wildoaks
          - Courtcroft Beau Queen (unregistered)
    - Hieover Music
      - Wyretex Wynstock
        - Eng. Ch. Talavera Romulus
          - Eng. Ch. Talavera Simon
          - Talavera Sparkle
        - Wyretex Wynssunshine
          - Eng. Ch. Miltona Mahmoud
          - Wyretex Wynsnina
      - Shine Princess
        - Hotel Traveller
          - Wycote Fulgent
          - Hotel Girl
        - Newmaidley Wanda
          - Newmaidley Rex
          - Newmaidley Leading Lady

356

Pedigree chart:

Gen 1	Gen 2	Gen 3	Gen 4	Gen 5
Eng. Ch. Kirkmoor Cobbler	Copleydene Dante	Copleydene Lucky Strike	Eng. Ch. Castlecroft Contender	Int. Ch. Gallant Fox of Wildoaks
				Eng. Ch. Castlecroft Content
			Greenside Lassie	Eng. Ch. Crackley Supreme Again
				Eng. Ch. Lanarth Zenia
		Allwire Cynthia	Truwire Target	Truwire Technique
				Truwire Tempest
			Allwire Rosebud	Eng. Ch. Miltona Mahmoud
				Allwire Nanette
	Kingsbridge Selected	Eng. Ch. Weltona Revelation	Culverbrook Tuscan	Eng. Ch. Talavera Romulus
				Culverbrook Trophy
			Hoddlesden Lady	Hornby Knockout
				Snootie (unregistered)
		Coppwood Confidence	Coppwood Gay Cockade	Eng. Ch. Miltona Mahmoud
				Elmwood Emulous
			Eng. Ch. Coppwood Gay Camille	Eng. Ch. Cawthorne Full Cry
				Summers Sapphire
Zeloy Supremacy	Rendale Repeater	Eng. Ch. Holmwire Endeavour	Eng. Ch. The Chief	Eng. Ch. Talavera Jupiter
				Jane Frylls
			Holmwire Impudence	Eng. Ch. Grandon Masterpiece
				Holmwire Dainty
		Rendale Rythmn	Bentonville Siren	Eng. Ch. Whitecastle Warrior
				Epping Epina
			Bentonville Surething	Eng. Ch. Talavera Nigel
				Bentonville Sweetness
Zeloy Lucky Patch	Zeloy Emperess	Foxdenton Wundayre	Eng. Ch. Talavera Romulus	Eng. Ch. Talavera Simon
				Talavera Sparkle
			Duchess of Copleydene	Eng. Ch. Talavera Nigel
				Manxland Melody
		Marionette	Printer's Boy	Steetonian Supreme
				Steetonian Serena
			Sinbad's Daughter	Steetonian Sinbad
				Miss Prim
Tescot Steetonian Simon	Foxdenton Wundayre	Eng. Ch. Talavera Romulus	Eng. Ch. Talavera Simon	Eng. Ch. Fountain Crusader
				Kingsthorp Donah
			Talavera Sparkle	Oakdene Courtier
				Talavera Prudence
		Duchess of Copleydene	Eng. Ch. Talavera Nigel	Eng. Ch. Talavera Jupiter
				Talavera Cleopatra
			Manxland Melody	Eng. Ch. Castlecroft Contender
				Manxland Marchioness
	Steetonian Sylvia	Wycote Fulgent	Harley Gulgent	Eng. Ch. Castlecroft Contender
				Florate Fifi
			Hotel Girl	Eng. Ch. Cawthorne Full Cry
				Remember Me (unregistered)
		Steetonian Stella	Steetonian Supreme	Eng. Ch. Stocksmoor Sportsman
				Flashing Win
			Steetonian Pride	Crackley Supremacy
				Shoemakers Pride
My Choice	Printer's Boy	Steetonian Supreme	Eng. Ch. Stocksmoor Sportsman	Int. Ch. Gallant Fox of Wildoaks
				Lady Ha Ha
			Flashing Win	Fountain Colorado
				Shoemakers Pride
		Steetonian Serena	Eng. Ch. Fourwents Rocket	Dogberry Barbed Wire
				Rickettswood Judy
			Shoemakers Pride	Flashby Orman
				Elmsley Wiregirl
	Steetonian Spicey-Bit	Flornell Saloon	Eng. Ch. Talavera Simon	Eng. Ch. Fountain Crusader
				Kingsthorp Donah
			Oakbrook Rose Bud	Stocksmoor Storm
				Parkhurst Radiance
		Steetonian Pride	Crackley Supremacy	Eng. Ch. Crackley Supreme
				Keresley Pandy
			Shoemakers Pride	Flashby Orman
				Elmsley Wiregirl

Supremacy's Smart Girl

Simon's Little Lady

357

W-8: Eng. Ch. Townville Tally'O, 6/4/67

- **Eng. Ch. Wintor Townville Tuscan**
  - Townville Traveller
    - Eng. Ch. Zeloy Endevour
      - Eng. Ch. Wyretex Wyn's Wun Dar
        - Eng. Ch. Wyretex Wyns Tuscan
          - Culverbrook Tuscan
          - Wyretex Wyns Thralia
        - Eng. Ch. Wyrebury Penda Quicksilver
          - Eng. Ch. Penda Blackwell Revelation
          - Eng. Ch. Penda Hieover Warrior
      - Supremacy's Smart Girl
        - Zeloy Supremacy
          - Eng. Ch. Kirkmoor Cobbler
          - Tescot Steetonian Simon
        - Simon's Little Lady
          - Zeloy Lucky Patch
          - My Choice
    - Townville True Love
      - Tollhill Masterpiece
        - Eng. Ch. Burtona Betoken
          - Burtona Bosun
          - Torkard Countess
        - Cawthorne Carnation
          - Cawthorne Coalite
          - Cawthorne Cornflake
      - Cheview Candida
        - Steetonian Sortie
          - Eng. Ch. Wyretex Wyns Wun-Dar
          - Steetonian Suntan
        - Townville Twilight
          - Int. Ch. Caradochouse Spruce
          - Tollhill Treacle
  - Townville Trinket
    - Albion Monotype
      - Eng. Ch. Wyrevale Monotype
        - Eng. Ch. Cornwell Rebecia Radiance
          - Bluebird Emperor
          - Robecia Streamlined
        - Wyrevale Marguerite
          - Eng. Ch. Weycroft Woolcomber
          - Penda Paragon
      - Roman Susan
        - Cornwell Cert
          - Eng. Ch. Castlecroft Contender Again
          - Eng. Ch. Westroad Lucky Charm
        - Surprise Melody
          - Eng. Ch. Wyrevale Monotype
          - Cornwell Dorine
    - Townville True Love
      - Tollhill Masterpiece
        - Eng. Ch. Burtona Betoken
          - Burtona Bosun
          - Torkard Countess
        - Cawthorne Carnation
          - Cawthorne Coalite
          - Cawthorne Cornflake
      - Cheview Candida
        - Steetonian Sortie
          - Eng. Ch. Wyretex Wyns Wun-Dar
          - Steetonian Suntan
        - Townville Twilight
          - Int. Ch. Caradochouse Spruce
          - Tollhill Treacle

- **Wintor Twilight**
  - Eng. Ch. Wintor Statesman
    - Eng. Ch. Lyngarth Scout
      - Eng. Ch. Zeloy Crusader
        - Eng. Ch. Zeloy Endevour
          - Eng. Ch. Wyretex Wyn's Wun Dar
          - Supremacy's Smart Girl
        - Zeloy Cinderella
          - Ryburn Romeo
          - Ryburn Glenside Eve
      - Eng. Ch. Lyngarth Social Call
        - Eng. Ch. Axholme Double Strike
          - Eng. Ch. Travella Strike
          - Axholme Miss Miranda
        - Lyngarth Serenade
          - Eden Autocrat
          - Lyngarth Precision
    - Lyngarth True Call
      - Eng. Ch. Zeloy Crusader
        - Eng. Ch. Zeloy Endevour
          - Eng. Ch. Wyretex Wyn's Wun Dar
          - Supremacy's Smart Girl
        - Zeloy Cinderella
          - Ryburn Romeo
          - Ryburn Glenside Eve
      - Lyngarth Chance Call
        - Eng. Ch. Cawthorne Climax
          - Eng. Ch. Burtona Betoken
          - Lyngarth Soubrette
        - Lyngarth Limberhill
          - Eng. Ch. Axholme Double Strike
          - Lyngarth Serenade

Burtona Bosun
Torkard Countess
Cawthorne Coalite
Cawthorne Cornflake
Eng. Ch. Wyretex Wyns Wun-Dar
Steetonian Suntan
Int. Ch. Caradochouse Spruce
Tollhill Treacle
Eng. Ch. Wyretex Wyns Tuscan
Eng. Ch. Wyrebury Penda Quicksilver
Zeloy Supremacy
Simon's Little Lady
Moorcrest Modeller
Rybun Candy
Tollhill Topsail
Goldswood Lady o'Quality
Travella Sensation
Travella Gloria
Eng. Ch. Weltona Revelation
Axholme Miss Sunstream
Wyretex Wynstock
Eden Copycat
Lyngarth Legacy
Penhill Precision
Eng. Ch. Wyretex Wyns Tuscan
Eng. Ch. Wyrebury Penda Quicksilver
Zeloy Supremacy
Simon's Little Lady
Moorcrest Modeller
Rybun Candy
Tollhill Topsail
Goldswood Lady o'Quality
Eng. Ch. Burtona Betoken
Cawthorne Twynstar Actionette
Eng. Ch. Axholme Double Strike
Lyngarth Serenade
Eng. Ch. Travella Strike
Axholme Miss Miranda
Eden Autocrat
Lyngarth Precision

358

Pedigree of **Townville Teresa**

- **Townville Teresa**
  - **Townville Traveller**
    - Eng. Ch. Zeloy Endevour
      - Eng. Ch. Wyretex Wyn's Wun Dar
        - Eng. Ch. Wyretex Wyns Tuscan
          - Culverbrook Tuscan
            - Eng. Ch. Talavera Romulus
            - Culverbrook Trophy
          - Wyretex Wyns Thralia
            - Wyretex Wynso
            - Talavera Tansy
        - Eng. Ch. Wyrebury Penda Quicksilver
          - Eng. Ch. Penda Blackwell Revelation
            - Eng. Ch. Weltona Revelation
            - Edenholme Elfreida
          - Eng. Ch. Penda Hieover Warrior
            - Penda Pompilius
            - Hieover Music
      - Supremacy's Smart Girl
        - Zeloy Supremacy
          - Eng. Ch. Kirkmoor Cobbler
            - Copleydene Dante
            - Kingsbridge Selected
          - Zeloy Lucky Patch
            - Rendale Repeater
            - Zeloy Empress
        - Simon's Little Lady
          - Tescot Steetonian Simon
            - Foxdenton Wundayre
            - Steetonian Sylvia
          - My Choice
            - Printers Boy
            - Steetonian Spicey-Bit
    - Townville True Love
      - Tollhill Masterpiece
        - Eng. Ch. Burtona Betoken
          - Burtona Bosun
            - Burtona Beacon
            - Burtona Brimful
          - Torkard Countess
            - Eng. Ch. Crackley Sailaway
            - Newmaidley Eve
        - Cawthorne Carnation
          - Cawthorne Coalite
            - Kirkfield Trumpeter
            - Kirkfield Thrift
          - Cawthorne Cornflake
            - Copleydene Dante
            - Copleydene Valentine
      - Cheview Candida
        - Steetonian Sortie
          - Eng. Ch. Wyretex Wyns Wun Dar
            - Eng. Ch. Wyretex Wyns Tuscan
            - Eng. Ch. Wyrebury Penda Quicksilver
          - Steetonian Suntan
            - Eng. Ch. Carefree Captain
            - Steetonian Starlight
        - Townville Twilight
          - Int. Ch. Caradochouse Spruce
            - Drakehall Ardoch Advocate
            - Caradochouse Ramblerrose
          - Tollhill Treacle
            - Eng. Ch. Axholme Double Strike
            - Barklyhill Patricia
  - **Townville Trinket**
    - Albion Monotype
      - Eng. Ch. Wyrevale Monotype
        - Eng. Ch. Cornwell Robecia Radiance
          - Bluebird Emperor
            - Wyretex Wynso
            - Firefly of the Forces
          - Robecia Streamlined
            - Eng. Ch. Castlecroft Contender
            - Robecia Silver
        - Wyrevale Marguerite
          - Eng. Ch. Weycroft Woolcomber
            - Eng. Ch. Weycroft Warfare
            - Grendon Success
          - Penda Paragon
            - Eng. Ch. Crackley Supreme Again
            - Wyretex Wynssunshine
      - Roman Susan
        - Cornwell Cert
          - Eng. Ch. Castlecroft Contender Again
            - Castlecroft Cleanaway
            - Castlecroft Cleancut
          - Eng. Ch. Westroad Lucky Charm
            - Eng. Ch. Cornwell Robecia Radiance
            - Wyretex Wyns Dream Girl
        - Surprise Melody
          - Eng. Ch. Wyrevale Monotype
            - Eng. Ch. Cornwell Robecia Radiance
            - Wyrevale Marguerite
          - Cornwell Dorine
            - Eng. Ch. Travella Skyflyer
            - Cornwell Freda
    - Townville True Love
      - Tollhill Masterpiece
        - Eng. Ch. Burtona Betoken
          - Burtona Bosun
            - Burtona Beacon
            - Burtona Brimful
          - Torkard Countess
            - Eng. Ch. Crackley Sailaway
            - Newmaidley Eve
        - Cawthorne Carnation
          - Cawthorne Coalite
            - Kirkfield Trumpeter
            - Kirkfield Thrift
          - Cawthorne Cornflake
            - Copleydene Dante
            - Copleydene Valentine
      - Cheview Candida
        - Steetonian Sortie
          - Eng. Ch. Wyretex Wyns Wun Dar
            - Eng. Ch. Wyretex Wyns Tuscan
            - Eng. Ch. Wyrebury Penda Quicksilver
          - Steetonian Suntan
            - Eng. Ch. Carefree Captain
            - Steetonian Starlight
        - Townville Twilight
          - Int. Ch. Caradochouse Spruce
            - Drakehall Ardoch Advocate
            - Caradochouse Ramblerrose
          - Tollhill Treacle
            - Eng. Ch. Axholme Double Strike
            - Barklyhill Patricia

W-9: Eng. Ch. Kirkmoor Speculation, 5/1/66

- Holmwire Contender
  - Holmwire Tudorclassic
    - Eng. Ch. Zeloy Endevour
      - Eng. Ch. Wyretex Wyn's Wun Dar
        - Eng. Ch. Wyretex Wyns Tuscan
          - Culverbrook Tuscan
            - Eng. Ch. Talavera Romulus
            - Culverbrook Trophy
          - Wyretex Wyns Thralia
            - Wyretex Wynso
            - Talavera Tansy
        - Eng. Ch. Wyrebury Penda Quicksilver
          - Eng. Ch. Penda Blackwell Revelation
            - Eng. Ch. Weltona Revelation
            - Edenholme Elfreida
          - Eng. Ch. Penda Hieover Warrior
            - Penda Pompilius
            - Hieover Music
      - Supremacy's Smart Girl
        - Zeloy Supremacy
          - Eng. Ch. Kirkmoor Cobbler
            - Copleydene Dante
            - Kingsbridge Selected
          - Zeloy Lucky Patch
            - Rendale Repeater
            - Zeloy Empress
        - Simon's Little Lady
          - Tescot Steetonian Simon
            - Foxdenton Wundayre
            - Steetonian Sylvia
          - My Choice
            - Printers Boy
            - Steetonian Spicey-Bit
    - Holmwire Evening Sunset
      - Eng. Ch. Anfield Contender
        - Eng. Ch. Weltona What's This
          - Eng. Ch. Wyretex Wyns Tuscan
            - Culverbrook Tuscan
            - Wyretex Wyns Thralia
          - Fulldress of the Forces
            - Wireford Colonel
            - Flyhigh of the Forces
        - Anfield Striking
          - Wyrecliff Travella Strikelike
            - Eng. Ch. Travella Starshine
            - Travella Sunmaid
          - Christylene Lady
            - Copleydene Peacemaker
            - Cristina of Copleydene
      - Macs Model Wire
        - Meritor Moorcrest Mac
          - Moorcrest Modeller
            - Eng. Ch. Weltona Exelwyre Dustynight
            - Eng. Ch. Eden Kirkmoor Sunset
          - Moorcrest Madcap
            - Eng. Ch. Weltona Revelation
            - Eng. Ch. Eden Kirkmoor Sunset
        - Miss Dusty
          - Jescar Dustymorn
            - Eng. Ch. Weltona Exelwyre Dustynight
            - Jescar Wynette
          - Marsden Mannequin
            - Holmpark Masterpiece
            - The Stick Girl
  - Burbeck Bali Hai
    - Platta Starturn
      - Eng. Ch. Steetonian Skipper
        - Eng. Ch. Wyretex Wyns Wun Dar
          - Eng. Ch. Wyretex Wyns Tuscan
            - Culverbrook Tuscan
            - Wyretex Wyns Thralia
          - Eng. Ch. Wyrebury Penda Quicksilver
            - Eng. Ch. Penda Blackwell Revelation
            - Eng. Ch. Penda Hieover Warrior
        - Steetonian Suntan
          - Eng. Ch. Karefree Captain
            - Whitwyre Mubarak
            - Kebser Konstellation
          - Steetonian Starlight
            - Steetonian Dante
            - Susan of Maristow
      - Macs Model Wire
        - Meritor Moorcrest Mac
          - Moorcrest Modeller
            - Eng. Ch. Weltona Exelwyre Dustynight
            - Eng. Ch. Eden Kirkmoor Sunset
          - Moorcrest Madcap
            - Eng. Ch. Weltona Revelation
            - Eng. Ch. Eden Kirkmoor Sunset
        - Miss Dusty
          - Jescar Dustymorn
            - Eng. Ch. Weltona Exelwyre Dustynight
            - Jescar Wynette
          - Marsden Mannequin
            - Holmpark Masterpiece
            - The Stick Girl
    - Holmwire Morningstar
      - Holmwire Talysman
        - Kenward Nizefella
          - Eng. Ch. Sunnybrook Special Choice
            - Eng. Ch. Taravella Wildcroft Superb
            - Sunnybrook Starrymodel
          - Kenward Carnation
            - Eng. Ch. Weltona Exelwyre Dustynight
            - Kenward Coronation
        - Holmwire Morning Mist
          - Eng. Ch. Weltona Exelwyre Dustynight
            - Middleforth Tuscan
            - Juliette of Exelwyre
          - Kenward Coronation
            - Winstan Wish
            - Eng. Ch. Winstan Wishwell
      - Holmwire Evening Sunset
        - Eng. Ch. Anfield Contender
          - Eng. Ch. Weltona What's This
            - Eng. Ch. Wyretex Wyns Tuscan
            - Fulldress of the Forces
          - Anfield Striking
            - Wyrecliff Travella Strikelike
            - Christyline Lady
        - Macs Model Wire
          - Meritor Moorcrest Mac
            - Moorcrest Modeller
            - Moorcrest Madcap
          - Miss Dusty
            - Jescar Dustymorn
            - Marsden Mannequin

Platta Star Princess

Mac's Model Wire

Miss Dusty

Eng. Ch. Anfield Contender

Anfield Striking

Meritor Moorcrest Mac

Eng. Ch. Weltona What's This

Fulldress of the Forces

Wyrecliff Travella Strikelike

Christyline Lady

Moorcrest Modeller

Moorcrest Madcap

Jescar Dustymorn

Marsden Mannequin

Eng. Ch. Wyretex Wyns Tuscan

Wyretex Wyns Thralia

Wireford Colonel

Flyhigh of the Forces

Eng. Ch. Travella Starshine

Travella Sunmaid

Copleydene Peacemaker

Cristina of Copleydene

Eng. Ch. Weltona Exelwyre Dustynight

Eng. Ch. Eden Kirkmoor Sunset

Eng. Ch. Weltona Revelation

Eng. Ch. Eden Kirkmoor Sunset

Eng. Ch. Weltona Exelwyre Dustynight

Jescar Wynette

The Stick Girl

Culverbrook Tuscan
Culverbrook Trophy
Wyretex Wynso
Talavera Tansy
Eng. Ch. Holmwire Endevour
Cocksure Countess
Wyretex Wynstock
Firefly of the Forces
Eng. Ch. Travella Strike
Travella Crystal
Eng. Ch. Travella Quick Decision
Travella Jasmine
Eng. Ch. Talavera Nigel
Sylvia of Copleydene
Copleydene Dante
Milady of Copleydene
Middleforth Tuscan
Juliette of Exelwyre
Eng. Ch. Holmwire Hyperion
My Model Miss
Culverbrook Tuscan
Hoddlesden Lady
Eng. Ch. Holmwire Hyperion
My Model Miss
Middleforth Tuscan
Juliette of Exelwyre
Eng. Ch. Weltona Revelation
Exelwyre Jewel
Eng. Ch. Weycroft Woolcomber
Holmpark Carefree
Poolstock Stormer
Mayken Mannequin

Eng. Ch. Talavera Simon
Talavera Sparkle
Eng. Ch. Crackley Starturn
Tydraw Dairymaid
Wyretex Wynsnina
Eng. Ch. Talavera Romulus
Talavera Crocus
Eng. Ch. The Chief
Holmwire Impudence
Cawthorne Cocksure
Wyrebury Wisdom
Eng. Ch. Talavera Romulus
Wyretex Wynssunshine
Eng. Ch. Talavera Jupiter
Talavera Olive
Travella Sensation
Travella Gloria
Eng. Ch. Travella Strike
Travella Sunshine
Travella Sensation
Travella Rosebud
Eng. Ch. Travella Sizzler
Travella Caress
Eng. Ch. Talavera Jupiter
Talavera Cleopatra
Eng. Ch. Chandon Cornation
Copleydene Carefree
Copleydene Lucky Strike
Allwire Cynthia
Eng. Ch. Talavera Nigel
Copleydene Lucky Dame
Culverbrook Tuscan
New Lane Peggy
Exelwyre Diplomat
Xelwyre Jewel
Weltona Axholme Bahram
Woodstead Wish
Culverbrook Tuscan
Moorcrest Mischief
Eng. Ch. Talavera Romulus
Culverbrook Trophy
Hornby Knockout
Snootie (unregistered)
Weltona Axholme Bahram
Woodstead Wish
Culverbrook Tuscan
Moorcrest Mischief
Culverbrook Tuscan
New Lane Peggy
Exelwyre Diplomat
Xelwyre Jewel
Culverbrook Tuscan
Hoddlesden Lady
Wyretex Wyns-o
Wyretex Wynsdainty
Int. Ch. Beau Brummel of Wildoaks
Florale Fairy
Kirkmoor Creation
Holmpark Wishful
Eng. Ch. Crackley Straightaway
Irish Ch. Coronetta
Thet Searchlight
Aman Sparkle

361

W-10: Eng. Ch. Worsbro Betoken Again, 5/25/66

- **Anfield Betoken**
  - Eng. Ch. Burtona Betoken
    - Burtona Bosun
      - Burtona Beacon
        - Eng. Ch. Miltona Mahmoud
          - Eng. Ch. Castlecroft Contender
          - Wakeful Susan
        - Elmwood Emblem
          - Truwire Technique
          - Elmwood Empress (unregistered)
      - Elmwood Emulous
        - Truwire Technique
          - Eng. Ch. Beetwell Comedian
          - Sparken Solstice
        - Truwire Tempest
          - Eng. Ch. Gedling Safeguard
          - Truwire Tantrums
    - Burtona Brimful
      - Burtona Weycroft Wireboy
        - Eng. Ch. Weycroft Warfare
          - Eng. Ch. Talavera Nigel
          - Greenmoor Glitter
        - Weycroft Sparkler
          - Eng. Ch. Castlecroft Contender
          - Allwire Sunflower
      - Burtona Baroness
        - Burtona Beacon
          - Eng. Ch. Burtona Bonanza
          - Gamco Chevalier
        - Burtona Bellona
          - Elmwood Emulous
          - Eng. Ch. Crackley Starler
  - Torkard Countess
    - Eng. Ch. Crackley Sailaway
      - Crackley Stowaway
        - Eng. Ch. Crackley Surething
          - Dagshai Dhu
          - Int. Ch. Gallant Fox of Wildoaks
        - Crackley Swanmaiden
          - Crackley Sequence
          - Eng. Ch. Crackley Striking
      - Straightface Susan
        - Crackley Searchlight
          - Crackley Sequel
          - Eng. Ch. Crackley Straightaway
        - Crackley Straightlace
          - Crackley Sportsgirl
          - Int. Ch. Gallant Fox of Wildoaks
    - Newmaidley Eve
      - Newmaidley George
        - Eng. Ch. Castlecroft Contender
          - Eng. Ch. Castlecroft Content
          - Cawthorne Comedian
        - Newmaidley Leading Lady
          - Talavera Sparkle
          - Newmaidley Rex
      - Newmaidley Zeal
        - Newmaidley Quoodle
          - Newmaidley Ethyl
          - Newmaidley Knave
        - Newmaidley Sonnet
          - Newmaidley Bubbles
          - Eng. Ch. Burtona Bonanza
- **Windlehurst Pretty Piece**
  - Eng. Ch. Cawthorne Climax
    - Eng. Ch. Burtona Betoken
      - Burtona Bosun
        - Burtona Beacon
          - Elmwood Emulous
          - Burtona Weycroft Wireboy
        - Burtona Brimful
          - Burtona Baroness
          - Crackley Stowaway
      - Torkard Countess
        - Eng. Ch. Crackley Sailaway
          - Straightface Susan
          - Newmaidley George
        - Newmaidley Eve
          - Newmaidley Zeal
          - Eden Smasher
    - Cawthorne Twynstar
      - Eng. Ch. Twynstar Accurist
        - Eden Commander
          - Eng. Ch. Eden Serenade
          - Eden Supreme
        - Twynstar Typist
          - Twynstar Active
          - Eng. Ch. Talavera Nigel
      - Wayside Winsum
        - Walcross President
          - Walcross Wartime
          - Thet Searchlight
        - Wayside Wedding Gown
          - Gem
          - Eden Smasher
  - Twynstar Pretty Piece
    - Twynstar Selection
      - Eng. Ch. Twynstar Accurist
        - Eden Commander
          - Eng. Ch. Eden Serenade
          - Eden Supreme
        - Twynstar Typist
          - Twynstar Active
          - Eng. Ch. Talavera Jupiter
      - Mount Pleasant Girl
        - Twynstar Action
          - Radio Active
          - Wharton Lad
        - Sweet Nell
          - Sweet Salute
          - Miltona Minstrel
    - Twynstar Primrose
      - Eng. Ch. Miltona Master Gunner
        - Miltona Marmaduke
          - Miltona Miss May
          - Miltona Matador
        - Miltona Miss Maud
          - Eng. Ch. Miltona Miss Martha
          - Eden Commander
      - Twynstar Accurette
        - Eng. Ch. Twynstar Accurist
          - Twynstar Typist
          - Eng. Ch. Crackley Straightaway
        - Ridgecroft Primrose
          - Ebbw Swell Rose

Pedigree chart

Subject: FCI Ch. Sideron Cawthorne Crackshot

2nd generation (parents):
- Cawthorne Comrey
- Cawthorne Ready Maid

3rd generation:
- Cawthorne Cracker
- Steelholm Sally
- Florate Frontpiece
- Warm Welcome

4th generation:
- Eng. Ch. Cawthorne Climax
- Cawthorne Ready Maid
- Eng. Ch. Burtona Betoken
- Clifton Pandora
- Eng. Ch. Travella Skyflyer
- Florate Felicia of Freams
- Castlecroft Cleanaway
- Lucky Legend

5th generation:
- Eng. Ch. Burtona Betoken
- Cawthorne Twynstar Actionette
- Florate Frontpiece
- Warm Welcome
- Burtona Bosun
- Torkard Countess
- Quayside Cawthorne Coalite
- Kirkfield Nan
- Eng. Ch. Travella Strike
- Travella Mannequin
- Florate Friarspun
- Florate Farrinette
- Eng. Ch. Crackley Sallaway
- Castlecroft Cover Girl
- Bedlam Wynstead Woolsack
- Keystock Prelude

6th generation:
- Burtona Bosun
- Torkard Countess
- Eng. Ch. Twynstar Accurist
- Wayside Winsum
- Eng. Ch. Travella Skyflyer
- Florate Felicia of Freams
- Castlecroft Cleanaway
- Lucky Legend
- Burtona Beacon
- Burtona Brimful
- Eng. Ch. Crackley Sallaway
- Newmaidley Eve
- Kirkfield Trumpeter
- Kirkfield Thrift
- Copleydene Dante
- Kirkfield Victory
- Travella Sensation
- Travella Gloria
- Travella Bridegroom
- Travella Peach
- Am. Ch. Florate Cwmbath Combine
- Am. Ch. Hallwyre Homespun
- Am. Ch. Florate Cwmbath Combine
- Florate Farina
- Crackley Stowaway
- Straightlace Susan
- Castlecroft Cracker
- Castlecroft Camille
- Wynstead War Bonus
- Perihart Picardian
- Losco Bingo
- Losco Letago

7th generation:
- Burtona Beacon
- Burtona Brimful
- Eng. Ch. Crackley Sallaway
- Newmaidley Eve
- Eden Commander
- Twynstar Typist
- Walcross President
- Wayside Wedding Gown
- Eng. Ch. Travella Strike
- Travella Mannequin
- Florate Friarspun
- Florate Farrinette
- Eng. Ch. Crackley Sallaway
- Castlecroft Cover Girl
- Bedlam Wynstead Woolsack
- Keystone Prelude
- Eng. Ch. Burtona Bonanza
- Burtona Weycroft Wireboy
- Burtona Baroness
- Crackley Stowaway
- Straightlace Susan
- Newmaidley George
- Newmaidley Zeal
- Castlecroft Cleanaway
- Kirkfield Blossom
- Copleydene Lucky Strike
- Kirkfield Blossom
- Copleydene Lucky Strike
- Allwire Cynthia
- Hotel Traveller
- Kirkfield Fancy
- Copleydene Lucky Strike
- Copleydene Fashion Pride
- Eng. Ch. Crackley Straightaway
- Lady Contender of Laracor
- Eng. Ch. Castlecroft Contender
- Lady Ruth of Laracor
- Newmaidley Rex
- Chillie Sauce
- Empire's Double
- Florate Festival
- Eng. Ch. Florate Friar
- Am. Ch. Hallwyre Halo
- Empire's Double
- Florate Festival
- Eng. Ch. Triangle Jupiter
- Florate Festival
- Eng. Ch. Crackley Surething
- Crackley Swanmaiden
- Crackley Searchlight
- Crackley Straightlace
- Int. Ch. Gallant Fox of Wildoaks
- Castlecroft Countess
- Eng. Ch. Castlecroft Contender
- Ravelly Renown
- Foxyard Bonanza
- Edna's Tess
- Eng. Ch. Weycroft Warfare
- Perihart Pixie
- Gamco Chevalier
- Elmwood Emulous
- Gamco Chevalier
- Losco Ballito

Eng. Ch. Wintor Townville Tuscan

- Townville Traveller
  - Eng. Ch. Zeloy Endevour
    - Eng. Ch. Wyretex Wyn's Wun Dar
      - Eng. Ch. Wyretex Wyns Tuscan
        - Culverbrook Tuscan
          - Eng. Ch. Talavera Romulus
          - Culverbrook Trophy
        - Wyretex Wyns Thralia
          - Wyretex Wynso
          - Talavera Tansy
      - Eng. Ch. Wyrebury Penda Quicksilver
        - Eng. Ch. Penda Blackwell Revelation
          - Eng. Ch. Weltona Revelation
          - Edenholme Elfreida
        - Eng. Ch. Penda Hieover Warrior
          - Penda Pompilius
          - Hieover Music
    - Supremacy's Smart Girl
      - Zeloy Supremacy
        - Eng. Ch. Kirkmoor Cobbler
          - Copleydene Dante
          - Kingsbridge Selected
        - Zeloy Lucky Patch
          - Rendale Repeater
          - Zeloy Empress
      - Simon's Little Lady
        - Tescot Steetonian Simon
          - Foxdenton Wundayre
          - Steetonian Sylvia
        - My Choice
          - Printer's Boy
          - Steetonian Spicey-Bit
  - Townville True Love
    - Tollhill Masterpiece
      - Eng. Ch. Burtona Betoken
        - Burtona Bosun
          - Burtona Beacon
          - Burtona Brimful
        - Torkard Countess
          - Eng. Ch. Crackley Sailaway
          - Newmaidley Eve
      - Cawthorne Carnation
        - Cawthorne Coalite
          - Kirkfield Trumpeter
          - Kirkfield Thrift
        - Cawthorne Cornflake
          - Copleydene Dante
          - Copleydene Valentine
    - Cheview Candida
      - Steetonian Sortie
        - Eng. Ch. Wyretex Wyn's Wun Dar
          - Eng. Ch. Wyretex Wyns Tuscan
          - Eng. Ch. Wyrebury Penda Quicksilver
        - Steetonian Suntan
          - Eng. Ch. Carefree Captain
          - Steetonian Starlight
      - Townville Twilight
        - Int. Ch. Caradochouse Spruce
          - Drakehall Ardoch Advocate
          - Caradochouse Ramblerrose
        - Tollhill Treacle
          - Eng. Ch. Axholme Double Strike
          - Barklyhill Patricia
- Townville Trinket
  - Albion Monotype
    - Eng. Ch. Wyrevale Monotype
      - Eng. Ch. Cornwell Robecia Radiance
        - Bluebird Emperor
          - Wyretex Wyns-o
          - Firefly of the Forces
        - Robecia Streamlined
          - Eng. Ch. Castlecroft Contender
          - Robecia Silver
      - Wyrevale Marguerite
        - Eng. Ch. Weycroft Woolcomber
          - Eng. Ch. Weycroft Warfare
          - Grendon Success
        - Penda Paragon
          - Eng. Ch. Crackley Supreme Again
          - Wyretex Wynssunshine
    - Roman Susan
      - Cornwell Cert
        - Eng. Ch. Castlecroft Contender Again
          - Castlecroft Cleanaway
          - Castlecroft Cleancut
        - Eng. Ch. Westroad Lucky Charm
          - Eng. Ch. Cornwell Robecia Radiance
          - Wyretex Wyns Dream Girl
      - Surprise Melody
        - Eng. Ch. Wyrevale Monotype
          - Eng. Ch. Cornwell Robecia Radiance
          - Wyrevale Marguerite
        - Cornwell Dorine
          - Eng. Ch. Travella Skyflyer
          - Cornwell Freda
  - Townville True Love
    - Tollhill Masterpiece
      - Eng. Ch. Burtona Betoken
        - Burtona Bosun
          - Burtona Beacon
          - Burtona Brimful
        - Torkard Countess
          - Eng. Ch. Crackley Sailaway
          - Newmaidley Eve
      - Cawthorne Carnation
        - Cawthorne Coalite
          - Kirkfield Trumpeter
          - Kirkfield Thrift
        - Cawthorne Cornflake
          - Copleydene Dante
          - Copleydene Valentine
    - Cheview Candida
      - Steetonian Sortie
        - Eng. Ch. Wyretex Wyn's Wun Dar
          - Eng. Ch. Wyretex Wyns Tuscan
          - Eng. Ch. Wyrebury Penda Quicksilver
        - Steetonian Suntan
          - Eng. Ch. Carefree Captain
          - Steetonian Starlight
      - Townville Twilight
        - Int. Ch. Caradochouse Spruce
          - Drakehall Ardoch Advocate
          - Caradochouse Ramblerrose
        - Tollhill Treacle
          - Eng. Ch. Axholme Double Strike
          - Barklyhill Patricia

Wintor Twilight

Eng. Ch. Zeloy Crusader

Eng. Ch. Lyngarth Scout

Eng. Ch. Lyngarth Social Call

Eng. Ch. Zeloy Crusader

Lyngarth Chance Call

Lyngarth True Call

Eng. Ch. Zeloy Endevour

Zeloy Cinderella

Eng. Ch. Axholme Double Strike

Lyngarth Serenade

Eng. Ch. Zeloy Endevour

Zeloy Cinderella

Eng. Ch. Cawthorne Climax

Lyngarth Limberhill

Eng. Ch. Lyngarth Social Call

Eng. Ch. Wyretex Wyn's Wun Dar

Supremacy's Smart Girl

Ryburn Romeo

Ryburn Glenside Eve

Eng. Ch. Travella Strike

Axholme Miss Miranda

Eden Autocrat

Lyngarth Precision

Eng. Ch. Wyretex Wyn's Wun Dar

Supremacy's Smart Girl

Ryburn Romeo

Ryburn Glenside Eve

Eng. Ch. Cawthorne Climax

Lyngarth Soubrette

Eng. Ch. Axholme Double Strike

Lyngarth Serenade

Eng. Ch. Wyretex Wyns Tuscan

Eng. Ch. Wyrebury Penda Quicksilver

Zeloy Supremacy

Simon's Little Lady

Moorcrest Modeller

Ryburn Candy

Tollhill Topsail

Goldswood Lady o'Quality

Travella Sensation

Travella Gloria

Eng. Ch. Weltona Revelation

Axholme Miss Sunstream

Wyretex Wynstock

Eden Copycat

Lyngarth Legacy

Penhill Precision

Eng. Ch. Wyretex Wyns Tuscan

Eng. Ch. Wyrebury Penda Quicksilver

Zeloy Supremacy

Simon's Little Lady

Moorcrest Modeller

Ryburn Candy

Tollhill Topsail

Goldswood Lady o'Quality

Eng. Ch. Burtona Betoken

Cawthorne Twynstar Actionette

Eng. Ch. Axholme Double Strike

Lyngarth Serenade

Eng. Ch. Travella Strike

Axholme Miss Miranda

Eden Aristocrat

Lyngarth Precision

Culverbrook Tuscan
Wyretex Wyns Thralia
Eng. Ch. Penda Blackwell Revelation
Eng. Ch. Penda Hieover Warrior
Zeloy Lucky Patch
Texcot Steetonian Simon
My Choice
Eng. Ch. Weltona Exelwyre Dustynight
Eng. Ch. Eden Kirkmoor Sunset
Meritor Moorcrest
Ryburn Romantic
Eng. Ch. Castala Kepple Nobleman
Tollhill Topsy Turvy
Golden Emblem
Copleydene Sunstroke
Copleydene Lucky Strike
Copleydene Fashion Pride
Lady Contender of Laracor
Culverbrook Tuscan
Hoddlesden Lady
Copleydene Lucky Strike
Axholme Friars Lass
Eng. Ch. Talavera Romulus
Wyretex Wynssunshine
Eden Commander
Eden Juliet
Gedling Warrior Fox
Copleydene Sequin
Wyretex Wyns-o'
Hillmur Hummer
Culverbrook Tuscan
Wyretex Wyns Thralia
Eng. Ch. Penda Blackwell Revelation
Eng. Ch. Penda Hieover Warrior
Zeloy Lucky Patch
Texcot Steetonian Simon
My Choice
Eng. Ch. Weltona Exelwyre Dustynight
Eng. Ch. Eden Kirkmoor Sunset
Meritor Moorcrest
Ryburn Romantic
Eng. Ch. Castala Kepple Nobleman
Tollhill Topsy Turvy
Golden Emblem
Copleydene Sunstroke
Burtona Bosun
Torkard Countess
Eng. Ch. Twynstar Accurist
Wayside Winsum
Eng. Ch. Travella Strike
Axholme Miss Miranda
Eden Autocrat
Lyngarth Precision
Travella Sensation
Travella Gloria
Eng. Ch. Weltona Revelation
Axholme Miss Sunstream
Wyretex Wynstock
Eden Copycat
Lyngarth Legacy
Penhill Precision

W-12: Ch. Mac's Revelation, 9/28/56

Eng. Ch. Weltona Exelwyre Dustynight						
Middleforth Tuscan	Culverbrook Tuscan	Eng. Ch. Talavera Romulus	Eng. Ch. Talavera Simon	Eng. Ch. Fountain Crusader	Olcliffe Captain	
					Merton Topsy (unregistered)	
				Kingsthorp Donah	Eng. Ch. Barrington Bridegroom	
					Eng. Ch. Indecision	
			Talavera Sparkle	Oakdene Courtier	Talavera Paul	
					Oakdene Comedienne	
				Talavera Prudence	Eng. Ch. Talavera Simon	
					Coronal of Fistral	
		Culverbrook Trophy	Eng. Ch. Crackley Starturn	Int. Ch. Beau Brummel of Wildoaks	Signal Warily	
					Int. Ch. Gains Great Surprise	
				Derkath Little Wonder	Eng. Ch. Talavera Simon	
					Lady Plynlimon	
			Tydraw Dairymaid	Bictons Limit	Citadel Speed Limit	
					Chelston Frolic	
				Keystar Bellatrix	Hirwain Collar On	
					Llewnu Lula	
	New Lane Peggy	Stoneycrag Solario	Wycote Critic	Eng. Ch. Talavera Jupiter	Int. Ch. Beau Brummel of Wildoaks	
					Talavera Pauline	
				Talavera Cleopatra	Eng. Ch. Talavera Simon	
					Talavera Patchwork	
			Winkley Society	Eng. Ch. Crackley Surething	Eng. Ch. Crackley Startler	
					Dagshai Dhu	
				Nutcrackley Sally	Eng. Ch. Crackley Startler	
					Crackley Sunmaid	
		Emblem of Copleydene	Eng. Ch. Talavera Nigel	Eng. Ch. Talavera Jupiter	Int. Ch. Beau Brummel of Wildoaks	
					Talavera Pauline	
				Talavera Cleopatra	Eng. Ch. Talavera Simon	
					Talavera Patchwork	
			Fairbourne Frizette	Eng. Ch. Croyland Compactom	Crackley Selection	
					Croyland Crocus	
				Crestona Tetina	Crestona Gay Knight	
					Netherside Gingerette	
Juliette of Exelwyre	Exelwyre Diplomat	Lyneve Jovial Jove	Eng. Ch. Talavera Jupiter	Int. Ch. Beau Brummel of Wildoaks	Signal Warily	
					Int. Ch. Gains Great Surprise	
				Talavera Pauline	Eng. Ch. Talavera Simon	
					Trevlac Toothache	
			Wyretex Wynsnina	Cawthorne Comedian	Int. Ch. Gallant Fox of Wildoaks	
					Oakdene Trixie	
				Wyretex Wynsmaid	Eng. Ch. Crackley Surething	
					Weltona Spring Fashion	
		Lyneve Jasmine	Eng. Ch. Talavera Jupiter	Int. Ch. Beau Brummel of Wildoaks	Signal Warily	
					Int. Ch. Gains Great Surprise	
				Talavera Pauline	Eng. Ch. Talavera Simon	
					Trevlac Toothache	
			Lyneve Koringa	Lyneve Chiefton	Eng. Ch. The Chief	
					Lyneve Blazette	
				Lyneve Dainty	Grandon Masterpiece	
					Hunting Belle	
	Exelwyre Jewel	Wyretex Wyns-o'	Eng. Ch. Talavera Jupiter	Int. Ch. Beau Brummel of Wildoaks	Signal Warily	
					Int. Ch. Gains Great Surprise	
				Talavera Pauline	Eng. Ch. Talavera Simon	
					Trevlac Toothache	
			Wyretex Wynsnina	Cawthorne Comedian	Int. Ch. Gallant Fox of Wildoaks	
					Oakdene Trixie	
				Wyretex Wynsmaid	Eng. Ch. Crackley Surething	
					Weltona Spring Fashion	
		Wyretex Wynsdainty	Wynstead Warrior	Eng. Ch. Stocksmoor Sportsman	Int. Ch. Gallant Fox of Wildoaks	
					Lady Ha Ha	
				Highview Lady	Int. Ch. Gallant Fox of Wildoaks	
					Arley Lady	
			Brummels Bride	Int. Ch. Gallant Fox of Wildoaks	Eng. Ch. Crackley Supreme	
					Int. Ch. Gains Great Surprise	
				Courtcroft Beau Queen (unregistered)		

Moorcrest Modeller

Eng. Ch. Weltona Exelwyre Dustynight
   Middleforth Tuscan
      Culverbrook Tuscan
         Eng. Ch. Talavera Romulus
         Culverbrook Trophy
      New Lane Peggy
         Stoneycrag Solario
         Emblem of Copleydene
   Juliette of Exelwyre
      Exelwyre Diplomat
         Lyneve Jovial Jove
         Lyneve Jasmine
      Exelwyre Jewel
         Wyretex Wyns-o'
         Wyretex Wynsdainty

Meritor Moorcrest Mac

Eng. Ch. Eden Kirkmoor Sunset
   Eng. Ch. Holmwire Hyperion
      Weltona Axholme Bahram
         Eng. Ch. Triangle Jupiter
         Axholme Friars Lass
      Woodstead Wish
         Miltona Matador
         Woodstead Warlan
   My Model Miss
      Culverbrook Tuscan
         Eng. Ch. Talavera Romulus
         Culverbrook Trophy
      Moorcrest Mischief
         Eng. Ch. Weycroft Warfare
         Wyrebury Warragal

Eng. Ch. Weltona Revelation
   Culverbrook Tuscan
      Culverbrook Tuscan
         Eng. Ch. Talavera Simon
         Talavera Sparkle
      Eng. Ch. Talavera Romulus
         Eng. Ch. Crackley Starturn
         Tydraw Dairymaid
   Hoddlesden Lady
      Culverbrook Trophy
         Eng. Ch. Whitecastle Conqueror
         Barnsilo Lady Gay
      Hornby Knockout
      Snootie (unregistered)

Moorcrest Madcap

Eng. Ch. Eden Kirkmoor Sunset
   Eng. Ch. Holmwire Hyperion
      Weltona Axholme Bahram
         Eng. Ch. Triangle Jupiter
         Axholme Friars Lass
      Woodstead Wish
         Miltona Matador
         Woodstead Warlan
   My Model Miss
      Culverbrook Tuscan
         Eng. Ch. Talavera Romulus
         Culverbrook Trophy
      Moorcrest Mischief
         Eng. Ch. Weycroft Warfare
         Wyrebury Warragel

Mac's Model Wire

Eng. Ch. Weltona Exelwyre
   Middleforth Tuscan
      Culverbrook Tuscan
         Eng. Ch. Talavera Romulus
         Culverbrook Trophy
      New Lane Peggy
         Stoneycrag Solario
         Emblem of Copleydene
   Juliette of Exelwyre
      Exelwyre Diplomat
         Lyneve Jovial Jove
         Lyneve Jasmine
      Exelwyre Jewel
         Wyretex Wyns-o'
         Wyretex Wynsdainty

Jescar Dustymorn

Jescar Wynette
   Eng. Ch. Weltona Revelation
      Culverbrook Tuscan
         Eng. Ch. Talavera Romulus
         Culverbrook Trophy
      Hoddlesden Lady
         Hornby Knockout
         Snootie (unregistered)
   Exelwyre Jewel
      Wyretex Wyns-o'
         Eng. Ch. Talavera Jupiter
         Wyretex Wynsnina
      Wyretex Wynsdainty
         Wynstead Warrior
         Brummels Bride

Miss Dusty

Holmpark Masterpiece
   Eng. Ch. Weycroft Woolcomber
      Int. Ch. Beau Brummel of Wildoaks
         Signal Warily
         Int. Ch. Gains Great Surprise
      Florate Fairy
         Eng. Ch. Chantry Call Boy
         Florate Sweet Snowflake
   Holmpark Carefree
      Kirkmoor Creation
         Miltona Matador
         Kirkmoor Carefree
      Holmpark Wishful
         Eng. Ch. Holmwire Endeavour
         Trade Wind

Marsden Mannequin

The Stick Girl
   Poolstock Stormer
      Eng. Ch. Crackley Straightaway
         Eng. Ch. Crackley Supreme Again
         Crackley Sequel
      Irish Ch. Coronetta (unreg. in England)
   Mayken Mannequin
      Thet Searchlight
         Eng. Ch. Burtona Bonanza
         Thet Torchlight
      Aman Sparkle
         Eng. Ch. Whitecastle Warrior
         Snowcloud of Shepp

Eng. Ch. Wyretex Wyns Tuscan

- **Culverbrook Tuscan**
  - **Eng. Ch. Talavera Romulus**
    - **Eng. Ch. Talavera Simon**
      - Eng. Ch. Fountain Crusader
        - Olcliffe Captain
          - Comedian of Notts
          - Olcliffe Jess
        - Merton Topsy
          - Mannville Wire Boy
          - Odsal Nell
      - Kingsthorp Donah
        - Eng. Ch. Barrington Bridegroom
          - Barrington Fearnought
          - Sarsgrove Molly
        - Eng. Ch. Indecision
          - Bishop's Selected
          - Clove Hitch
    - **Talavera Sparkle**
      - Oakdene Courtier
        - Talavera Paul
          - Eng. Ch. Talavera Simon
          - Treviac Toothache
        - Oakdene Comedienne
          - Eng. Ch. Aman Comedian
          - Oakdene Vivacity
      - Talavera Prudence
        - Eng. Ch. Talavera Simon
          - Eng. Ch. Fountain Crusader
          - Kingsthorp Donah
        - Coronal of Fistral
          - Kemphurst Corporal
          - Tiptoe of Fistral
  - **Culverbrook Trophy**
    - **Eng. Ch. Crackley Startum**
      - Int. Ch. Beau Brummel of Wildoaks
        - Signal Warily
          - Eng. Ch. Signal Circuit
          - Hampden Queen
        - Int. Ch. Gains Great Surprise
          - Eng. Ch. Talavera Simon
          - New Town Bella Donna
      - Derkath Little Wonder
        - Eng. Ch. Talavera Simon
          - Eng. Ch. Fountain Crusader
          - Kingsthorp Donah
        - Lady Plynlimon
          - Eng. Ch. Crackley Sensational
          - Plynlimon Dairymaid
    - **Tydraw Dairymaid**
      - Bictons Limit
        - Citadel Speed Limit
          - Chelston Crack
          - Chunkyite
        - Chelston Frolic
          - Eng. Ch. Gedling Safeguard
          - Hirwain Wire Girl
      - Keystar Bellatrix
        - Hirwain Collar On
          - Morlais Comedian
          - Sweet Swan
        - Llewnur Lila
          - Eng. Ch. Signal Circuit
          - Hampden Queen

- **Wyretex Wyns Thralia**
  - **Wyretex Wyns-o'**
    - **Eng. Ch. Talavera Jupiter**
      - Int. Ch. Beau Brummel of Wildoaks
        - Signal Warily
          - Eng. Ch. Talavera Simon
          - New Town Bella Donna
        - Int. Ch. Gains Great Surprise
          - Eng. Ch. Fountain Crusader
          - Kingsthorp Donah
      - Talavera Pauline
        - Eng. Ch. Talavera Simon
          - Eng. Ch. Barry Benedict
          - Lisvane Folly (unregistered)
        - Treviac Toothache
          - Int. Ch. Crackley Supreme
          - Int. Ch. Gains Great Surprise
    - **Wyretex Wynsnina**
      - Cawthorne Comedian
        - Int. Ch. Gallant Fox of Wildoaks
          - Eng. Ch. Lanarth Bramble
          - Oakdene Comedienne
        - Oakdene Trixie
          - Int. Ch. Crackley Starter
          - Dagshai Dhu
      - Wyretex Wynsmaid
        - Eng. Ch. Crackley Surething
          - Flornell Sovereign
          - Weltona Spagirl
        - Weltona Spring Fashion
          - Olcliffe Captain
          - Merton Topsy
  - **Talavera Tansy**
    - **Eng. Ch. Talavera Romulus**
      - Eng. Ch. Talavera Simon
        - Kingsthorp Donah
          - Eng. Ch. Barrington Bridegroom
          - Eng. Ch. Indecision
        - Oakdene Courtier
          - Talavera Paul
          - Oakdene Comedienne
      - Talavera Sparkle
        - Talavera Prudence
          - Eng. Ch. Talavera Simon
          - Coronal of Fistral
    - **Talavera Crocus**
      - Eng. Ch. Talavera Jupiter
        - Int. Ch. Beau Brummel of Wildoaks
          - Talavera Pauline
            - Signal Warily
            - Int. Ch. Gains Great Surprise
      - Talavera Cleopatra
        - Eng. Ch. Talavera Simon
          - Eng. Ch. Talavera Simon
          - Treviac Toothache
        - Talavera Patchwork
          - Eng. Ch. Fountain Crusader
          - Kingsthorp Donah
        - Eng. Ch. Crackley Sensational
        - Nona of Rusthall

Pedigree of **Wyretex Wyns Treasure**

- Wyretex Wynstock
  - Eng. Ch. Talavera Romulus
    - Eng. Ch. Talavera Simon
      - Eng. Ch. Fountain Crusader
        - Olcliffe Captain
          - Comedian of Notts
          - Olcliffe Jess
        - Merton Topsy
          - Mannville Wire Boy
          - Odsal Nell
      - Kingsthorp Donah
        - Eng. Ch. Barrington Bridegroom
          - Barrington Fearnought
          - Sargrove Molly
        - Eng. Ch. Indecision
          - Bishop's Selected
          - Clove Hitch
    - Talavera Sparkle
      - Oakdene Courtier
        - Talavera Paul
          - Eng. Ch. Talavera Simon
          - Talavera Toothache
        - Oakdene Comedienne
          - Eng. Ch. Aman Comedian
          - Oakdene Vivacity
      - Talavera Prudence
        - Eng. Ch. Talavera Simon
          - Eng. Ch. Fountain Crusader
          - Kingsthorp Donah
        - Coronal of Fistral
          - Kemphurst Corporal
          - Tiptoe of Fistral
  - Wyretex Wynsunshine
    - Eng. Ch. Miltona Mahmoud
      - Eng. Ch. Castlecroft Contender
        - Int. Ch. Gallant Fox of Wildoaks
          - Int. Ch. Crackley Supreme
          - Int. Ch. Gains Great Surprise
        - Eng. Ch. Castlecroft Content
          - Int. Ch. Beau Brummel of Wildoaks
          - Castlecroft Countess
      - Wakeful Susan
        - Eng. Ch. Littleway Nigel
          - Eng. Ch. Talavera Simon
          - My Luck
        - Eng. Ch. Wakeful Dairymaid
          - Int. Ch. Beau Brummel of Wildoaks
          - Brilliant Sunshine
    - Wyretex Wynsnina
      - Cawthorne Comedian
        - Int. Ch. Gallant Fox of Wildoaks
          - Int. Ch. Crackley Supreme
          - Int. Ch. Gains Great Surprise
        - Oakdene Trixie
          - Eng. Ch. Lanarth Bramble
          - Oakdene Comedienne
      - Wyretex Wynsmaid
        - Eng. Ch. Crackley Surething
          - Int. Ch. Crackley Starter
          - Dagshai Dhu
        - Weltona Spring Fashion
          - Flornell Sovereign
          - Weltona Spagirl
- Cawthorne Confection
  - Eng. Ch. Weltona Exemplar
    - Eng. Ch. Cawthorne Full Cry
      - Int. Ch. Gallant Fox of Wildoaks
        - Int. Ch. Crackley Supreme
          - Eng. Ch. Crackley Sensational
          - Eng. Ch. Eden Bridesmaid
        - Int. Ch. Gains Great Surprise
          - Eng. Ch. Talavera Simon
          - New Town Bella Donna
      - Langtoun Lady Luck
        - Int. Ch. Crackley Starter
          - Int. Ch. Beau Brummel of Wildoaks
          - Pettico Prudence
        - Langtoun Laurentic
          - Eden Knockout
          - Langtoun Light
    - Goystock Winfrieda
      - Eng. Ch. The Chief
        - Eng. Ch. Talavera Jupiter
          - Int. Ch. Beau Brummel of Wildoaks
          - Talavera Pauline
        - Jane Frylls
          - Int. Ch. Talavera Simon
          - Molly Frylls
      - Dainty Simmie
        - Eng. Ch. Talavera Simon
          - Eng. Ch. Fountain Crusader
          - Kingsthorpe Donah
        - Roberto's Girl
          - Watteau Roberto
          - Jess
  - Cawthorne Consolation
    - Eng. Ch. Cawthorne Full Cry
      - Int. Ch. Gallant Fox of Wildoaks
        - Int. Ch. Crackley Supreme
          - Eng. Ch. Crackley Sensational
          - Eng. Ch. Eden Bridesmaid
        - Int. Ch. Gains Great Surprise
          - Eng. Ch. Talavera Simon
          - New Town Bella Donna
      - Langtoun Lady Luck
        - Int. Ch. Crackley Starter
          - Int. Ch. Beau Brummel of Wildoaks
          - Pettico Prudence
        - Langtoun Laurentic
          - Eden Knockout
          - Langtoun Light
    - Cawthorne Confidence
      - Eng. Ch. Talavera Romulus
        - Eng. Ch. Talavera Simon
          - Eng. Ch. Fountain Crusader
          - Kingsthorpe Donah
        - Talavera Sparkle
          - Oakdene Courtier
          - Talavera Prudence
      - Stapenhill Barmaid
        - Eng. Ch. Crackley Sportsman
          - Knockout Radium
          - Trail's Lady
        - Dainty Simmie
          - Eng. Ch. Talavera Simon
          - Roberto's Girl

Eng. & Am. Ch. Wyretex Wyns Jupiter of Glynhir, 9/6/48

- **Eng. Ch. Wyretex Wyns Royalist**
  - Culverbrook Tuscan
    - Eng. Ch. Talavera Romulus
      - Eng. Ch. Talavera Simon
        - Eng. Ch. Fountain Crusader
          - Comedian of Notts
          - Olcliffe Jess
        - Kingsthorp Donah
          - Mannville Wire Boy
          - Odsal Nell
      - Talavera Sparkle
        - Oakdene Courtier
          - Eng. Ch. Barrington Bridegroom
          - Eng. Ch. Indecision
            - Bishop's Selected
            - Clove Hitch
        - Talavera Prudence
          - Talavera Paul
            - Eng. Ch. Talavera Simon
            - Trevlac Toothache
          - Oakdene Comedienne
            - Eng. Ch. Aman Comedian
            - Oakdene Vivacity
    - Culverbrook Trophy
      - Eng. Ch. Crackley Starturn
        - Int. Ch. Beau Brummel of Wildoaks
          - Eng. Ch. Talavera Simon
            - Eng. Ch. Fountain Crusader
            - Kingsthorp Donah
          - Coronal of Fistral
            - Kemphurst Corporal
            - Tiptoe of Fistral
        - Derkath Little Wonder
          - Signal Warily
            - Eng. Ch. Signal Circuit
            - Hampden Queen
          - Eng. Ch. Talavera Simon
            - Eng. Ch. Talavera Simon
            - New Town Bella Donna
      - Tydraw Dairymaid
        - Bictons Limit
          - Citadel Speed Limit
            - Eng. Ch. Fountain Crusader
            - Kingsthorp Donah
          - Chelston Frolic
            - Eng. Ch. Crackley Sensational
            - Plynlimon Dairymaid
        - Keystar Bellatrix
          - Hirwain Collar On
            - Chelston Crack
            - Chunkyite
          - Llewnur Lila
            - Eng. Ch. Gedling Safeguard
            - Hirwain Wire Girl
  - Wyretex Wynstock
    - Eng. Ch. Talavera Romulus
      - Eng. Ch. Talavera Simon
        - Eng. Ch. Fountain Crusader
          - Morlais Comedian
          - Sweet Swan
        - Kingsthorp Donah
          - Olcliffe Captain
          - Merton Topsy
      - Talavera Sparkle
        - Oakdene Courtier
          - Eng. Ch. Barrington Bridegroom
          - Eng. Ch. Indecision
        - Talavera Prudence
          - Talavera Paul
          - Oakdene Comedienne
    - Wyretex Wynssunshine
      - Eng. Ch. Miltona Mahmoud
        - Eng. Ch. Castlecroft Contender
          - Eng. Ch. Talavera Simon
          - Coronal of Fistral
        - Wakeful Susan
          - Int. Ch. Gallant Fox of Wildoaks
          - Eng. Ch. Castlecroft Content
      - Wyretex Wynsnina
        - Cawthorne Comedian
          - Eng. Ch. Littleway Nigel
          - Eng. Ch. Wakeful Dairymaid
        - Wyretex Wynsmaid
          - Int. Ch. Gallant Fox of Wildoaks
          - Oakdene Trixie
- **Eng. Ch. Wyretex Wyns Princess**
  - Wyretex Wynsdainty
    - Wynstead Warrior
      - Eng. Ch. Stocksmoor Sportsman
        - Int. Ch. Gallant Fox of Wildoaks
          - Eng. Ch. Crackley Surething
          - Weltona Spring Fashion
        - Lady Ha Ha
          - Int. Ch. Crackley Supreme
          - Int. Ch. Gains Great Surprise
      - Highview Lady
        - Int. Ch. Gallant Fox of Wildoaks
          - Eng. Ch. Gedling Safeguard
          - Lady of Marquis
        - Arley Lady
          - Int. Ch. Crackley Supreme
          - Int. Ch. Gains Great Surprise
    - Brummels Pride
      - Int. Ch. Crackley Supreme
        - Crackley Sally
      - Int. Ch. Gains Great Surprise
        - Eng. Ch. Crackley Sensational
          - Eng. Ch. Talavera Simon
          - New Town Bella Donna
        - Eng. Ch. Eden Bridesmaid
  - Courtcroft Beau Queen (unregistered)

Wyretex Wynstock

- Eng. Ch. Talavera Romulus
  - Eng. Ch. Talavera Simon
    - Eng. Ch. Fountain Crusader
      - Olcliffe Captain
        - Comedian of Notts
        - Olcliffe Jess
      - Merton Topsy
        - Mannville Wire Boy
        - Odsal Nell
    - Kingsthorp Donah
      - Eng. Ch. Barrington Bridegroom
        - Barrington Fearnought
        - Sargrove Molly
      - Eng. Ch. Indecision
        - Bishop's Selected
        - Clove Hitch
  - Talavera Sparkle
    - Oakdene Courtier
      - Talavera Paul
        - Eng. Ch. Talavera Simon
        - Treviac Toothache
      - Oakdene Comedienne
        - Eng. Ch. Aman Comedian
        - Oakdene Vivacity
    - Talavera Prudence
      - Eng. Ch. Talavera Simon
        - Eng. Ch. Fountain Crusader
        - Kingsthorp Donah
      - Coronal of Fistral
        - Kemphurst Corporal
        - Tiptoe of Fistral

- Wyretex Wynssunshine
  - Eng. Ch. Miltona Mahmoud
    - Eng. Ch. Castlecroft Contender
      - Int. Ch. Gallant Fox of Wildoaks
        - Int. Ch. Crackley Supreme
        - Int. Ch. Gains Great Surprise
      - Eng. Ch. Castlecroft Content
        - Int. Ch. Beau Brummel of Wildoaks
        - Castlecroft Countess
    - Wakeful Susan
      - Eng. Ch. Littleway Nigel
        - Eng. Ch. Talavera Simon
        - My Luck
      - Eng. Ch. Wakeful Dairymaid
        - Int. Ch. Beau Brummel of Wildoaks
        - Brilliant Sunshine
  - Wyretex Wynsnina
    - Cawthorne Comedian
      - Int. Ch. Gallant Fox of Wildoaks
        - Int. Ch. Crackley Supreme
        - Int. Ch. Gains Great Surprise
      - Oakdene Trixie
        - Eng. Ch. Lanath Branhbie
        - Oakdene Comedienne
    - Wyretex Wynsmaid
      - Eng. Ch. Crackley Surething
        - Eng. Ch. Crackley Starter
        - Dagshai Dhu
      - Weltona Spring Fashion
        - Flornell Sovereign
        - Weltona Spagirl

Wyretex Wyns Unity

- Ch. Talavera Jupiter
  - Int. Ch. Beau Brummel of Wildoaks
    - Signal Warily
      - Eng. Ch. Signal Circuit
        - Eng. Ch. Fountain Crusader
        - Peri
      - Hampden Queen
        - Eng. Ch. Gang Warily
        - Quality Wire Girl
    - Int. Ch. Gains Great Surprise
      - Eng. Ch. Talavera Simon
        - Eng. Ch. Fountain Crusader
        - Kingsthorp Donah
      - New Town Bella Donna
        - Eng. Ch. Wycollar Trail
        - Miss Harvest Time
  - Talavera Pauline
    - Eng. Ch. Talavera Simon
      - Eng. Ch. Fountain Crusader
        - Olcliffe Captain
        - Merton To sy
      - Kingsthorp Donah
        - Eng. Ch. Barrington Bridegroom
        - Eng. Ch. Indecision
    - Treviac Toothache
      - Eng. Ch. Barry Benedict
        - Eng. Ch. Fountain Crusader
        - Sweet Song
      - Lisvane Folly (unregistered)

Wyretex Wynsvenus

- Wynstead Warrior
  - Eng. Ch. Stocksmoor Sportsman
    - Int. Ch. Gallant Fox of Wildoaks
      - Int. Ch. Crackley Supreme
      - Int. Ch. Gains Great Surprise
    - Lady Ha Ha
      - Eng. Ch. Gedling Safeguard
      - Lady of Marquis
  - Highview Lady
    - Int. Ch. Gallant Fox of Wildoaks
      - Int. Ch. Crackley Supreme
      - Int. Ch. Gains Great Surprise
    - Arley Lady
      - Int. Ch. Beau Brummel of Wildoaks
      - Crackley Sally
- Wyretex Wynsdainty
  - Talavera Pauline
    - Int. Ch. Crackley Supreme
      - Eng. Ch. Crackley Sensational
      - Eng. Ch. Eden Bridesmaid
    - Int. Ch. Gains Great Surprise
      - Eng. Ch. Talavera Simon
      - New Town Bella Donna
  - Brummels Pride
    - Int. Ch. Gallant Fox of Wildoaks
    - Courtcroft Beau Queen (unregistered)

371

Ch. Wyrequest's Pay Dirt

- **Eng. & Am. Ch. Bengal Ryburn Regent**
  - Eng. Ch. Zeloy Endevour
    - Eng. Ch. Wyretex Wyn's Wun Dar
      - Eng. Ch. Wyretex Wyns Tuscan
        - Culverbrook Tuscan
          - Eng. Ch. Talavera Romulus
          - Culverbrook Trophy
        - Wyretex Wyns Thralia
          - Wyretex Wyns O
          - Talavera Tansy
      - Eng. Ch. Wyrebury Penda Quicksilver
        - Eng. Ch. Penda Blackwell Revelation
          - Eng. Ch. Weltona Revelation
          - Edenholme Elfreida
        - Eng. Ch. Penda Hieover Warrior
          - Penda Pompilius
          - Hieover Music
    - Supremacy's Smart Girl
      - Zeloy Supremacy
        - Eng. Ch. Kirkmoor Cobbler
          - Copleydene Dante
          - Kingsbridge Selected
        - Zeloy Lucky Patch
          - Rendale Repeater
          - Zeloy Empress
      - Simon's Little Lady
        - Tescot Steetonian Simon
          - Foxdenton Wundayre
          - Steetonian Sylvia
        - My Choice
          - Printer's Boy
          - Steetonian Spicey-Bit
  - Ryburn Radiance
    - Eng. Ch. Penda Peerless
      - Eng. Ch. Penda Cawthorne Cobnut
        - Eng. Ch. Cawthorne Climax
          - Eng. Ch. Burtona Betoken
          - Cawthorne Twynstar Actionette
        - Cawthorne Ready Maid
          - Florate Frontpiece
          - Warm Welcome
      - Eng. Ch. Wyrebury Penda Quicksilver
        - Eng. Ch. Penda Blackwell Revelation
          - Eng. Ch. Weltona Revelation
          - Edenholme Elfreida
        - Eng. Ch. Penda Hieover Warrior
          - Penda Pompilius
          - Hieover Music
    - Ryburn Glenside Eve
      - Tollhill Topsail
        - Eng. Ch. Casfala Kepple Noobleman
          - Eng. Ch. Casfala Copyright
          - Drakehall Deluxe
        - Tollhill Topsy Turvy
          - Tollhill Toreador
          - Faithful Belita
      - Goldswood Lady O'Quality
        - Golden Emblem
          - Copleydene Dante
          - Brinbella Charlebelle
        - Copleydene Sunstroke
          - Copleydene Nigels Double
          - Mossfield Miranda
- **Can. & Am. Ch. Nugrade Regent**
  - Eng. Ch. Zeloy Emperor
    - Zeloy Carouso
      - Eng. Ch. Wyretex Wyn's Wun Dar
        - Eng. Ch. Wyretex Wyns Tuscan
          - Culverbrook Tuscan
          - Wyretex Wyns Thralia
        - Eng. Ch. Wyrebury Penda Quicksilver
          - Eng. Ch. Penda Blackwell Revelation
          - Eng. Ch. Penda Hieover Warrior
      - Supremacy's Smart Girl
        - Zeloy Supremacy
          - Eng. Ch. Kirkmoor Cobbler
          - Zeloy Lucky Patch
        - Simon's Little Lady
          - Tescot Steetonian Simon
          - My Choice
    - Zeloy Rhapsody
      - Zeloy Roseta
        - Eng. Ch. Maryholm Mighty Good
          - Eng. Ch. Knollbrook Keyman
          - Fair Pretender
        - Zeloy Tarantella
          - Tescot Steetonian Simon
          - Zeloy Roseta
      - Tescot Majestic
          - Copleydene Supafox
          - Stoneycrag Sparkler
        - Soundman's Result
          - Steetonian Soundman
          - Daughter of Delegate
  - Nugrade Nena
    - Nugrade Nemo
      - Nugrade Nonstop
        - Eng. Ch. Caradochouse Spruce of Trucote
          - Drakehall Ardoch Advocate
          - Caradochouse Ramblerrose
        - Nugrade Nuflame
          - Nugrade Torkard Bangaway
          - Nugrade Nublue
      - Nugrade Nadene
        - Nugrade Torkard Bangaway
          - Torkard Trade Mark
          - Eng. Ch. Torkard Susan
        - Nugrade Nimosa
          - Bruntland Speciality
          - Nugrade Nublue
    - Nugrade Bridget
      - Nugrade Nonnicer
        - Drakehall Ardoch Advocate
          - Eng. Ch. Weltona Exelwyre Dustynight
          - Ardoch Enchantress
        - Caradochouse Ramblerrose
          - Bruntland Speciality
          - Eng. Ch. Caradochouse Foxglove
      - Nugrade Nuflame
        - Nugrade Tockard Bangaway
          - Torkard Trade Mark
          - Eng. Ch. Torkard Susan
        - Nugrade Nublue
          - Nugrade Cavalier
          - Baysgarth Park

Pedigree of **Can. & Am. Ch. Nugrade Countess**

- **Can. & Am. Ch. Nugrade Countess**
  - Eng. Ch. Wintor Statesman
    - Eng. Ch. Wintor Townville Tuscan
      - Townville Traveller
        - Eng. Ch. Zeloy Endevour
          - Eng. Ch. Wyretex Wyn's Wun Dar
            - Eng. Ch. Wyretex Wyns Tuscan
            - Eng. Ch. Wyrebury Penda Quicksilver
          - Supremacy's Smart Girl
            - Zeloy Supremacy
            - Simon's Little Lady
        - Townville True Love
          - Townhill Masterpiece
            - Eng. Ch. Burtona Betoken
            - Cawthorne Carnation
          - Cheview Candida
            - Steetonian Sortie
            - Townville Twilight
      - ...wnville Trinket
        - Albion Monotype
          - Eng. Ch. Wyrevale Monotype
            - Eng. Ch. Cornwell Robecia Radiance
            - Wyrevale Marguerite
          - Roman Susan
            - Cornwell Cert
            - Surprise Melody
        - Townville True Love
          - Townhill Masterpiece
            - Eng. Ch. Burtona Betoken
            - Cawthorne Carnation
          - Cheview Candida
            - Steetonian Sortie
            - Townville Twilight
    - Eng. Ch. Lyngarth Scout
      - Wintor Twilight
        - Eng. Ch. Zeloy Crusader
          - Eng. Ch. Zeloy Endevour
            - Eng. Ch. Wyretex Wyn's Wun Dar
            - Supremacy's Smart Girl
          - Zeloy Cinderella
            - Ryburn Romeo
            - Ryburn Glenside Eve
        - Eng. Ch. Lyngarth Social Call
          - Eng. Ch. Axholme Double Strike
            - Eng. Ch. Travella Strike
            - Axholme Miss Miranda
          - Lyngarth Serenade
            - Eden Autocrat
            - Lyngarth Precision
      - Lyngarth True Call
        - Eng. Ch. Zeloy Crusader
          - Eng. Ch. Zeloy Endevour
            - Eng. Ch. Wyretex Wyn's Wun Dar
            - Supremacy's Smart Girl
          - Zeloy Cinderella
            - Ryburn Romeo
            - Ryburn Glenside Eve
        - Lyngarth Chance Call
          - Lyngarth Limberhill
            - Eng. Ch. Cawthorne Climax
            - Lyngarth Soubrette
          - Eng. Ch. Lyngarth Social Call
            - Eng. Ch. Axholme Double Strike
            - Lyngarth Serenade
  - Nugrade Bridget
    - Eng. Ch. Zeloy Emperor
      - Eng. Ch. Zeloy Endevour
        - Eng. Ch. Wyretex Wyn's Wun Dar
          - Eng. Ch. Wyretex Wyns Tuscan
            - Culverbrook Tuscan
            - Wyretex Wyns Thralia
          - Eng. Ch. Wyrebury Penda Quicksilver
            - Eng. Ch. Penda Blackwell Revelation
            - Eng. Ch. Penda Hieover Warrior
        - Supremacy's Smart Girl
          - Zeloy Supremacy
            - Eng. Ch. Kirkmoor Cobbler
            - Zeloy Lucky Patch
          - Simon's Little Lady
            - Tescot Steetonian Simon
            - My Choice
      - Zeloy Rhapsody
        - Zeloy Carouso
          - Eng. Ch. Maryholm Mighty Good
            - Eng. Ch. Knollbrook Keyman
            - Fair Pretender
          - Zeloy Tarantella
            - Tescot Steetonian Simon
            - Zeloy Roseta
        - Zeloy Roseta
          - Tescot Majestic
            - Copleydene Supafox
            - Stoneycrag Sparkler
          - Soundman's Result
            - Steetonian Soundman
            - Daughter of Delegate
    - Nugrade Nena
      - Nugrade Nemo
        - Nugrade Nonstop
          - Eng. Ch. Caradochouse Spruce of Trucote
            - Drakehall Ardoch Advocate
            - Caradochouse Ramblerrose
          - Nugrade Nuflame
            - Nugrade Torkard Bangaway
            - Nugrade Nublue
        - Nugrade Nadene
          - Nugrade Torkard Bangaway
            - Torkard Trade Mark
            - Eng. Ch. Torkard Susan
          - Nugrade Nimosa
            - Bruntland Speciality
            - Nugrade Nublue
      - Nugrade Nonnicer
        - Eng. Ch. Caradochouse Spruce of Trucote
          - Drakehall Ardoch Advocate
            - Eng. Ch. Weltona Exelwyre Dustynight
            - Ardoch Enchantress
          - Caradochouse Ramblerrose
            - Bruntland Speciality
            - Eng. Ch. Caradochouse Foxglove
        - Nugrade Nuflame
          - Nugrade Torkard Bangaway
            - Torkard Trade Mark
            - Eng. Ch. Torkard Susan
          - Nugrade Nublue
            - Nugrade Cavalier
            - Baysgarth Park

373

Mitre Advocate

- Int. Ch. Caradochouse Spruce of Trucote
  - Drakehall Ardoch Advocate
    - Eng. Ch. Weltona Exelwyre Dustynight
      - Middleforth Tuscan
        - Culverbrook Tuscan
        - New Lane Peggy
      - Juliette of Exelwyre
        - Exelwyre Diplomat
        - Exelwyre Jewel
    - Ardoch Enchantress
      - Eng. Ch. Weltona Revelation
        - Culverbrook Tuscan
        - Hoddlesden Lady
      - Ardoch Excellence
        - Eng. Ch. Crackley Straightaway
        - Ardoch Astute
  - Caradochouse Ramblerrose
    - Bruntland Speciality
      - Bruntland Stormer
        - Crackley Solution
        - Bruntland Sublime
      - Bruntland Sports Girl
        - Bruntland Sportsman
        - Bruntland Society
    - Eng. Ch. Caradochouse Foxglove
      - Eng. Ch. Bedlam Beau Ideal
        - Bedlam Wynstead Woolsack
        - Bedlam Guda
      - Crowcroft Mermaid
        - Bedlam Wynstead Warrant
        - Crowcroft Rebelmaid

- Mitre Miss Molyneux
  - Eng. Ch. Travella Strike
    - Travella Sensation
      - Copleydene Lucky Strike
        - Eng. Ch. Castlecroft Contender
        - Greenside Lassie
      - Copleydene Fashion Pride
        - Eng. Ch. Talavera Nigel
        - Sylvia of Copleydene
    - Travella Gloria
      - Eng. Ch. Crackley Straightaway
        - Eng. Ch. Crackley Supreme Again
        - Crackley Sequel
      - Lady Contender of Laracor
        - Eng. Ch. Castlecroft Contender
        - Lady Ruth of Laracor
  - Mitre Miss Mavourneen
    - Eng. Ch. Castlecroft Cleanaway
      - Eng. Ch. Crackley Sailaway
        - Crackley Stowaway
        - Straightface Susan
      - Castlecroft Cover Girl
        - Castlecroft Cracker
        - Castlecroft Camille
    - Mitre Miss Maida
      - Eng. Ch. Crackley Sailaway
        - Crackley Stowaway
        - Straightface Susan
      - Mitre Miss Mabel
        - Bluebird Tipper
        - Castlecroft Cover Girl

Eng. & Am. Ch. Whitwyre Money Market

- Eng. & Ire. Ch. Whitwyre Field Marshal
  - Eng. Ch. Striking of Laracor
    - Eng. Ch. Travella Strike
      - Travella Sensation
        - Copleydene Lucky Strike
        - Copleydene Fashion Pride
      - Travella Gloria
        - Eng. Ch. Crackley Straightaway
        - Lady Contender of Laracor
    - Gloria of Laracor
      - Castlecroft Cleanaway
        - Eng. Ch. Crackley Sailaway
        - Castlecroft Cover Girl
      - Lady Contender of Laracor
        - Eng. Ch. Castlecroft Contender
        - Lady Ruth of Laracor
  - Flyagain of the Forces
    - Bluebird Emperor
      - Wyretex Wyns O
        - Eng. Ch. Talavera Jupiter
        - Wyretex Wynsnna
      - Firefly of the Forces
        - Eng. Ch. Talavera Jupiter
        - Talavera Olive
    - Footprints of the Forces
      - Eng. Ch. Travella Strike
        - Travella Sensation
        - Travella Gloria
      - Flyaway of the Forces
        - Eng. Ch. Crackley Straightaway
        - Firefly of the Forces

- Eng. Ch. Whitwyre Even Money
  - Eng. Ch. Travella Strike
    - Travella Sensation
      - Copleydene Lucky Strike
        - Eng. Ch. Castlecroft Contender
        - Greenside Lassie
      - Copleydene Fashion Pride
        - Eng. Ch. Talavera Nigel
        - Sylvia of Copleydene
    - Travella Gloria
      - Eng. Ch. Crackley Straightaway
        - Eng. Ch. Crackley Supreme Again
        - Crackley Sequel
      - Lady Contender of Laracor
        - Eng. Ch. Castlecroft Contender
        - Lady Ruth of Laracor
  - Whitwyre Maunday Mouney
    - Whitwyre Memento
      - Eng. Ch. Weycroft Woolcomber
        - Int. Ch. Beau Brummel of Wildoaks
        - Florate Fairy
      - Whitwyre Memory
        - Whitwyre Monsoon
        - Whitwyre Moll Mahal
    - Whitwyre Magenta
      - Whitwyre Mahatma
        - Eng. Ch. Castlecroft Contender
        - Dogberry Queenly
      - Whitwyre Misty Morn
        - Whitwyre Monsoon
        - Whitwyre Mantilla

Pedigree chart (read left to right):

Generation 1
- Eng. Ch. Holmwire Roxville Revision
- Am. Ch. Rancourt Platta Charmer
- Platta Susan's Princess

Generation 2
- Holmwire Paul Tudor
- Roxville Mooremaides Moment
- Eng. Ch. Anfield Contender
- Macs Model Wire

Generation 3
- Eng. Ch. Zeloy Endevour
- Holmwire Evening Sunset
- Eng. Ch. Zeloy Emperor
- Mooremaides Cha-Cha-Cha
- Eng. Ch. Weltona What's This
- Anfield Striking
- Meritor Moorcrest Mac
- Miss Dusty

Generation 4
- Eng. Ch. Wyretex Wyn's Wun Dar
- Supremacy's Smart Girl
- Eng. Ch. Anfield Contender
- Mac's Model Wire
- Eng. Ch. Wyretex Wyn's Wun Dar
- Supremacy's Smart Girl
- Eng. Ch. Zeloy Endevour
- Mooremaides Foxhill Fandancer
- Eng. Ch. Wyretex Wyns Tuscan
- Fulldress of the Forces
- Wyrecliff Travella
- Christylene Lady
- Moorcrest Modeller
- Moorcrest Madcap
- Jescar Dustymorn
- Marsden Mannequin

Generation 5
- Eng. Ch. Wyretex Wyns Tuscan
- Eng. Ch. Wyrebury Penda Quicksilver
- Zeloy Supremacy
- Simon's Little Lady
- Eng. Ch. Weltona What's This
- Anfield Striking
- Meritor Moorcrest Mac
- Miss Dusty
- Eng. Ch. Wyretex Wyns Tuscan
- Eng. Ch. Wyrebury Penda Quicksilver
- Zeloy Supremacy
- Simon's Little Lady
- Eng. Ch. Wyretex Wyn's Wun Dar
- Supremacy's Smart Girl
- Burtona Beau Ideal
- Axholme Miss Saucy
- Culverbrook Tuscan
- Wyretex Wyns Thralia
- Wireford Colonel
- Flyhigh of the Forces
- Eng. Ch. Travella Starshine
- Travella Sunmaid
- Copleydene Peacemaker
- Cristina of Copleydene
- Eng. Ch. Weltona Exelwyre Dustynight
- Eng. Ch. Eden Kirkmoor Sunset
- Eng. Ch. Weltona Revelation
- Eng. Ch. Eden Kirkmoor Sunset
- Eng. Ch. Weltona Exelwyre Dustynight
- Jescar Wynette
- Holmpark Masterpiece
- The Stick Girl

Generation 6
- Culverbrook Tuscan
- Wyretex Wyns Thralia
- Eng. Ch. Penda Blackwell Revelation
- Eng. Ch. Penda Hieover Warrior
- Eng. Ch. Kirkmoor Cobbler
- Zeloy Lucky Patch
- Tescot Steetonian Simon
- My Choice
- Eng. Ch. Wyretex Wyns Tuscan
- Fulldress of the Forces
- Wyrecliff Travella Strikelike
- Christylene Lady
- Moorcrest Modeller
- Moorcrest Madcap
- Jescar Dustymorn
- Marsden Mannequin
- Culverbrook Tuscan
- Wyretex Wyns Thralia
- Eng. Ch. Penda Blackwell Revelation
- Eng. Ch. Penda Hieover Warrior
- Eng. Ch. Kirkmoor Cobbler
- Zeloy Lucky Patch
- Tescot Steetonian Simon
- My Choice
- Eng. Ch. Wyretex Wyns Tuscan
- Eng. Ch. Wyrebury Penda Quicksilver
- Zeloy Supremacy
- Simon's Little Lady
- Eng. Ch. Castlecroft Contender Again
- Burtona Brunette
- Danygraig Caiach Have-a-Go
- Axholme Miss Sunstream
- Eng. Ch. Talavera Romulus
- Culverbrook Trophy
- Wyretex Wyns O
- Talavera Tansy
- Eng. Ch. Holmwire Endevour
- Cocksure Countess
- Wyretex Wynstock
- Firefly of the Forces
- Eng. Ch. Travella Strike
- Travella Crystal
- Eng. Ch. Travella Quick Decision
- Travella Jasmine
- Eng. Ch. Talavera Nigel
- Sylvia of Copleydene
- Copleydene Dante
- Milady of Copleydene
- Middleforth Tuscan
- Juliette of Exelwyre
- Eng. Ch. Holmwire Hyperion
- My Model Miss
- Culverbrook Tuscan
- Hoddlesden Lady
- Eng. Ch. Holmwire Hyperion
- My Model Miss
- Middleforth Tuscan
- Juliette of Exelwyre
- Exelwyre Jewel
- Eng. Ch. Weycroft Woolcomber
- Holmpark Carefree
- Poolstock Stormer
- Mayken Mannequin

375

W.-17: **Ch. Wintor Caracus Call Boy**, 5/18/64

- **Eng. Ch. Zeloy Crusader**
  - Eng. Ch. Zeloy Endevour
    - Eng. Ch. Wyretex Wyn's Wun Dar
      - Eng. Ch. Wyretex Wyns Wyn Tuscan
        - Culverbrook Tuscan
          - Eng. Ch. Talavera Romulus
            - Eng. Ch. Talavera Simon
            - Talavera Sparkle
          - Culverbrook Trophy
            - Eng. Ch. Crackley Starturn
            - Tydraw Dairymaid
        - Wyretex Wyns Thralia
          - Wyretex Wyns O
            - Eng. Ch. Talavera Jupiter
            - Wyretex Wynsnina
          - Talavera Tansy
            - Eng. Ch. Talavera Romulus
            - Talavera Crocus
      - Eng. Ch. Wyrebury Penda Quicksilver
        - Eng. Ch. Penda Blackwell Revelation
          - Eng. Ch. Weltona Revelation
            - Culverbrook Tuscan
            - Hoddlesden Lady
          - Edenholme Elfreida
            - Myddleton Major
            - Rickerby Wren
        - Eng. Ch. Penda Hieover Warrior
          - Penda Pompilius
            - Eng. Ch. Talavera Romulus
            - Wyretex Wynsdainty
          - Hieover Music
            - Wyretex Wynstock
            - Shine Princess
    - Supremacy's Smart Girl
      - Zeloy Supremacy
        - Eng. Ch. Kirkmoor Cobbler
          - Copleydene Dante
            - Copleydene Lucky Strike
            - Allwire Cynthia
          - Kingsbridge Selected
            - Eng. Ch. Weltona Revelation
            - Coppwood Confidence
        - Zeloy Lucky Patch
          - Rendale Repeater
            - Eng. Ch. Holmwire Endevour
            - Rendale Rhythm
          - Zeloy Empress
            - Foxdenton Wundayre
            - Marionette
      - Simon's Little Lady
        - Tescot Steetonian Simon
          - Foxdenton Wundayre
            - Eng. Ch. Talavera Romulus
            - Duchess of Copleydene
          - Steetonian Sylvia
            - Wycote Fulgent
            - Steetonian Stella
        - My Choice
          - Printer's Boy
            - Steetonian Supreme
            - Steetonian Serena
          - Steetonian Spicey-Bit
            - Flornell Saloon
            - Steetonian Pride
  - Zeloy Cinderella
    - Ryburn Romeo
      - Moorcrest Modeller
        - Eng. Ch. Weltona Exelwyre Dustynight
          - Middleforth Tuscan
            - Culverbrook Tuscan
            - New Lane Peggy
          - Juliette of Exelwyre
            - Exelwyre Diplomat
            - Xelwyre Jewel
        - Eng. Ch. Eden Kirkmoor Sunset
          - Eng. Ch. Holmwire Hyperion
            - Weltona Axholme Bahram
            - Woodstead Wish
          - My Model Miss
            - Culverbrook Tuscan
            - Moorcrest Mischief
      - Ryburn Candy
        - Meritor Moorcrest Mac
          - Moorcrest Modeller
            - Eng. Ch. Weltona Exelwyre Dustynight
            - Eng. Ch. Eden Kirkmoor Sunset
          - Moorcrest Madcap
            - Eng. Ch. Weltona Revelation
            - Eng. Ch. Eden Kirkmoor Sunset
        - Ryburn Romantic
          - Kirkmoor Connoisseur
            - Eng. Ch. Weltona Revelation
            - Eng. Ch. Kirkmoor Carefree
          - Ryburn Romance
            - Whitecastle Crusader
            - Judy
    - Ryburn Glenside Eve
      - Tophill Topsail
        - Eng. Ch. Casfala Kepple Nobleman
          - Eng. Ch. Casfala Copyright
            - Hotel Traveller
            - Cawthorne Copyright
          - Drakehall Deluxe
            - Drakehall Debonair
            - Bedlam Christabelle
        - Tophill Topsy Turvy
          - Tollhill Toreador
            - Florate Cwmbath Combine
            - Hallwyre Homespun
          - Faithful Belitta
            - Faithful Gayspark
            - Mons Leo Lucky Charm
      - Goldswood Lady O'Quality
        - Golden Emblem
          - Copleydene Dante
            - Copleydene Lucky Strike
            - Allwire Cynthia
          - Brinbella Chariebelle
            - Miltona Mikado
            - Brinbella Acquisition
        - Copleydene Sunstroke
          - Copleydene Nigels Double
            - Eng. Ch. Talavera Nigel
            - Talavera Ditty
          - Moosfield Miranda
            - Eng. Ch. Talavera Romulus
            - Mossfield Marjorie

St. Erme Nugrade Nupeer

- Eng. Ch. Penda Peerless
  - Eng. Ch. Penda Cawthorne Cobnut
    - Eng. Ch. Cawthorne Climax
      - Eng. Ch. Burtona Betoken
        - Burtona Bosun
        - Torkard Countess
      - Cawthorne Twynstar Actionette
        - Eng. Ch. Twynstar Accurist
        - Wayside Winsum
    - Cawthorne Ready Maid
      - Florate Frontpiece
        - Eng. Ch. Travella Skyflyer
        - Florate Felicia of Freams
      - Warm Welcome
        - Eng. Ch. Castlecroft Cleanaway
        - Lucky Legend
  - Eng. Ch. Wyrebury Penda Quicksilver
    - Eng. Ch. Penda Blackwell Revelation
      - Eng. Ch. Weltona Revelation
        - Culverbrook Tuscan
        - Hoddlesden Lady
      - Edenholme Elfreida
        - Myddleton Major
        - Rickerby Wren
    - Eng. Ch. Penda Hieover Warrior
      - Penda Pompilius
        - Eng. Ch. Talavera Romulus
        - Wyretex Wynsdainty
      - Hieover Music
        - Wyretex Wynstock
        - Shine Princess

Nugrade Nena

- Nugrade Nemo
  - Nugrade Nonstop
    - Eng. Ch. Caradochouse Spruce of Trucote
      - Drakehall Ardoch Advocate
      - Caradochouse Ramblerrose
    - Nugrade Nuflame
      - Nugrade Torkard Bangaway
      - Nugrade Nublue
  - Nugrade Nadene
    - Nugrade Torkard Bangaway
      - Torkard Trade Mark
      - Eng. Ch. Torkard Susan
    - Nugrade Nimosa
      - Bruntland Speciality
      - Nugrade Nublue
- Nugrade Nonnicer
  - Eng. Ch. Caradochouse Spruce of Trucote
    - Drakehall Ardoch Advocate
      - Eng. Ch. Weltona Exelwyre Dustynight
      - Ardoch Enchantress
    - Caradochouse Ramblerrose
      - Bruntland Speciality
      - Eng. Ch. Caradochouse Foxglove
  - Nugrade Nuflame
    - Nugrade Tockard Bangaway
      - Torkard Trade Mark
      - Eng. Ch. Torkard Susan
    - Nugrade Nublue
      - Nugrade Cavalier
      - Baysgarth Park

Nugrade Nesta

- Nugrade Torkard Bangaway
  - Eng. Ch. Castlecroft Contender Again
    - Eng. Ch. Castlecroft Cleanaway
      - Eng. Ch. Crackley Sailaway
      - Castlecroft Cover Girl
    - Castlecroft Cleancut
      - Castlecroft Courier
      - Castlecroft Cover Girl
  - Torkard Trade Mark
    - Newmaidley George
      - Eng. Ch. Castlecroft Contender
      - Newmaidley Leading Lady
    - Newmaidley Zeal
      - Newmaidley Quoodle
      - Newmaidley Sonnet
- Eng. Ch. Torkard Susan
  - Eng. Ch. Castlecroft Cleanaway
    - Eng. Ch. Crackley Sailaway
      - Crackley Stowaway
      - Straightlace Susan
    - Castlecroft Cover Girl
      - Castlecroft Cracker
      - Castlecroft Camille
  - Newmaidley Eve
    - Newmaidley George
      - Eng. Ch. Castlecroft Contender
      - Newmaidley Leading Lady
    - Newmaidley Zeal
      - Newmaidley Quoodle
      - Newmaidley Sonnet

Jewel of Nuncar

- Eng. Ch. Bedlam Beau Ideal
  - Bedlam Wynstead Woolsack
    - Wynstead War Bonus
      - Foxyard Bonanza
      - Edna's Tess
    - Perihart Placid
      - Weycroft Wyldfox
      - Perihart Picardian
  - Bedlam Guda
    - Eng. Ch. Holmwire Hyperion
      - Weltona Airchime Bahram
      - Woodstead Wish
    - Bedlam Camelia
      - Miltona Matador
      - Woodstead Warfan
- Nugrade Nylon
  - Nugrade Cavalier
    - Gamco Chevalier
      - Chandon Coronet
      - Gamston Spark
    - Toppa Fulady
      - Harley Fulgent
      - Breaston Jess
  - Nugrade Nublue
    - Baysgarth Park
      - Wycote Fulgent
        - Eng. Ch. Castlecroft Contender
        - Florate Fi Fi
      - Flanders Poppy
        - Kincraig Lad
        - Westfield Peg

377

W-5: Eng. & Am. Ch. Maltman Country Life of Whinlatter, 9/12/82

SIRE: **Eng. Ch. Harwire Halyard of Whinlatter**
- **Eng. Ch. Townville Tradition**
  - Townville Tillie
    - **Eng. Ch. Townville Trail**
      - **Eng. Ch. Seedfield Meritor Super Flash**
        - Eng. Ch. Zeloy Emperor
        - Maryholm Wintersweet
      - Townville Traveeda
        - Eng. Ch. Townville Tally'O
        - Townville Trudy
    - **Eng. Ch. Harwire Hallmark**
      - **Eng. Ch. Seedfield Meritor Super Flash**
        - Eng. Ch. Zeloy Emperor
        - Maryholm Wintersweet
      - Harwire Hazel
        - Harwire Hero
        - Harwire Hellina
  - **Eng. Ch. Harrowhill Huntsman**
    - Townville Tarik
      - **Eng. Ch. Seedfield Meritor Super Flash**
        - Eng. Ch. Zeloy Emperor
        - Maryholm Wintersweet
      - Townville Traveeda
        - Eng. Ch. Townville Tally'O
        - Townville Trudy
    - Townville Tamlyn
      - Eng. Ch. Zeloy Emperor
        - Eng. Ch. Zeloy Endevour
        - Zeloy Rhapsody
      - Townville Tiara
        - Townville Top Form
        - Townville True Love
- **Eng. Ch. Penda Precision**
  - **Eng. Ch. Penda Pretty Perfect**
    - **Eng. Ch. Townville Tally'O**
      - Eng. Ch. Wintor Statesman
        - Eng. Ch. Wintor Townville Tuscan
        - Wintor Twilight
      - Townville Teresa
        - Wintor Townville Traveller
        - Townville Trinket
    - Harrowhill Happy Talk
      - Harrowhill Happy Day
        - Eng. Ch. Whitwyre Market Day
        - Harrowhill Happy Birthday
      - Harrowhill Twiggy
        - Harrowhill Golden Legend
        - Harrowhill Sally
  - **Eng. Ch. Penda Worsbro Weasel**
    - **Eng. Ch. Worsbro Betoken**
      - Anfield Betoken
        - Eng. Ch. Burtona Betoken
        - Windlehurst Pretty Piece
      - Cawthorne Comfrey
        - Eng. FCI Ch. Sideron Cawthorne Crackshot
        - Cawthorne Ready Maid
    - **Eng. Ch. Worsbro Oladar Royal**
      - Cawthorne Contender
        - Cawthorne Coconut
        - Cawthorne Conquest
      - Cawthorne Comfrey
        - Eng. FCI Ch. Sideron Cawthorne Crackshot
        - Cawthorne Ready Maid

DAM: **Eng. Ch. Maltman Sunny Smile**
- Worsbro Wide Awake
  - Maltman Pride
    - **Eng. Ch. Sunnybrook Spot On**
      - Eng. Ch. Townville Tally'O
        - Eng. Ch. Winter Statesman
        - Townville Teresa
      - Sunnybrook Gosmore Photogenic
        - Gosmore Kirkmoor Clinker
        - Gosmore Meritor Springtime
    - Brookewire Wonderful
      - Worsbro Wayfarer
        - Eng. Ch. Zeloy Emperor
        - Cawthorne Comfrey
      - Brookewire Royal Bloom
        - Eng. Ch. Worsbro Betoken Again
        - Eng. Ch. Worsbro Oladar Royal Maid
  - Maltman Waggon Girl
    - **Eng. Ch. Seedfield Meritor Super Flash**
      - Eng. Ch. Zeloy Emperor
        - Eng. Ch. Zeloy Endevour
        - Zeloy Rhapsody
      - Maryholm Wintersweet
        - Eng. Ch. Extreal Realization
        - Maryholm Winning Way
    - Maltman Dainty Girl
      - Eng. Ch. Weltona Has It
        - Eng. Ch. Holmwire Roxville Revision
        - Eng. Ch. Weltona Platta Dainty Princess
      - Maltman Even-Money
        - Eng. Ch. Zeloy Crusader
        - Maltman Larkspur
- Maltman Sunshine
  - **Eng. Ch. Townville Trail**
    - **Eng. Ch. Seedfield Meritor Super Flash**
      - Eng. Ch. Zeloy Emperor
        - Eng. Ch. Zeloy Endevour
        - Zeloy Rhapsody
      - Maryholm Wintersweet
        - Eng. Ch. Extreal Realization
        - Maryholm Winning Way
    - Townville Traveeda
      - Eng. Ch. Townville Tally'O
        - Eng. Ch. Wintor Statesman
        - Townville Teresa
      - Townville Trudy
        - Eng. Ch. Zeloy Emperor
        - Townville Teresa
  - Maltman Pride
    - **Eng. Ch. Seedfield Meritor Super Flash**
      - Eng. Ch. Zeloy Emperor
        - Eng. Ch. Zeloy Endevour
        - Zeloy Rhapsody
      - Maryholm Wintersweet
        - Eng. Ch. Extreal Realization
        - Maryholm Winning Way
    - Maltman Dainty Girl
      - Eng. Ch. Weltona Has It
        - Eng. Ch. Holmwire Roxville Revision
        - Eng. Ch. Weltona Platta Dainty Princess
      - Maltman Even-Money
        - Eng. Ch. Zeloy Crusader
        - Maltman Larkspur

W-18: Eng. & Am. Ch. Sunnybrook Spot On, 10/4/69

- Eng. Ch. Townville Tally'O
  - Ch. Wintor Statesman
    - Ch. Wintor Toonville Tuscan
    - Wintor Twilight
  - Wintor Townville Traveller
    - Townville Teresa
    - Townville Trinket
- Sunnybrook Gosmore Photogenic
  - Gosmore Kirkmoor Clinker
    - Ch. Zeloy Emperor
    - Brigston Carousel Miss Fonda
  - Gaymore Meritor Springtime
    - Extreal Realization
    - Nedwar Madonna

W-19: Ch. Zeloy Emperor, 3/10/60

- Ch. Zeloy Endeavor
  - Ch. Wyretex Wyns Wundar
    - Ch. Wyretex Wyns Tuscan
      - Culverbrook Tuscan
      - Wyretex Wyns Thralia
    - Ch. Wyrebury Penda Quicksilver
      - Ch. Penda Revelation
      - Ch. Kirkmoor Cooler
  - Supremacy's Smart Girl
    - Zeloy Supremacy
      - Zeloy Lucky Patch
      - Tescot Streetonian Simon
    - Simon's Smart Girl
      - My Choice
- Zeloy Rhapsody
  - Zeloy Carouso
    - Ch. Maryholm Mighty Good
    - Zeloy Tarantella
  - Zeloy Rosetta
    - Tescot Mavestil
    - Soundmans Result

W-20: Ch. Evewire You Better Believe It, 7/5/75

- Ch. Evewire Evening Jacket
  - Ch. Evewire Evening Edition
    - Ch. Evewire Druid Dynamic
      - Ch. Deko Druid
      - Ch. Evewire Dyna-Mite
    - Ch. Evewire Espirit
      - Ch. Evewire Extra Edition
      - Evewire Exchantress
  - Ch. Evewire Early Copy
    - Ch. Winmore Christar
      - Ch. Liscoole Star
      - Ch. Winmor's Christar Electra
    - Ch. Evewire Early Edition
      - Ch. Evewire Extra Edition
      - Ch. Little Bits Sassy Bit
- Evewire Vickey Jane
  - Ch. Evewire Exemplar
    - Ch. Evewire Druid Dynamic
      - Ch. Deko Druid
      - Ch. Evewire Dyna-Mite
    - Ch. Evewire Evenstart
      - Ch. Mac's Revelation
      - Evewire Even Exchange
  - Ch. Penda Helenstowe Priscilla
    - Ch. Wyrecroft Penda Popular
      - Eng. Ch. Penda Peerless
      - Eng. Ch. Penda Purbeck Deborah
    - Helenstowe Charm
      - Helenstowe Culswood Cresta
      - Helenstowe Portrait

- **Eng. Ch. Harwire Hallmark**
  - Eng. Ch. Harwire Helmsman of Whinlatter
    - Eng. Ch. Seedfield Meritor Super Flash
      - Eng. Ch. Zeloy Emperor
        - Eng. Ch. Zeloy Endevour
          - Eng. Ch. Wyretex Wyn's Wun Dar
            - Eng. Ch. Wyretex Wyns Tuscan
            - Eng. Ch. Wyrebury Penda Quicksilver
          - Supremacy's Smart Girl
            - Zeloy Supremacy
            - Simon's Little Lady
        - Zeloy Rhapsody
          - Zeloy Carouso
            - Eng. Ch. Maryholm Mighty Good
            - Zeloy Tarantella
          - Zeloy Roseta
            - Tescot Majestic
            - Soundman's Result
      - Maryholm Wintersweet
        - Eng. Ch. Extreal Realization
          - Extreal Ervelation
            - Thistleton Dandy
            - Extreal Queen
          - Crawley Countess
            - Eng. Ch. Emprise Sensational
            - Extreal Regent
        - Maryholm Wining Way
          - Eng. Ch. Anfield Contender
            - Eng. Ch. Weltona What's This
            - Anfield Striking
          - Maryholm Whynot
            - Eng. Ch. Maryholm Northern Monarch
            - Bankside Gay Girl
    - Townville Trudy
      - Eng. Ch. Townville Tally O
        - Eng. Ch. Wintor Statesman
          - Eng. Ch. Wintor Townville Tuscan
            - Townville Traveller
            - Townville Trinket
          - Wintor Twilight
            - Eng. Ch. Lyngarth Scout
            - Lyngarth True Call
        - Townville Teresa
          - Wintor Townville Traveller
            - Eng. Ch. Zeloy Endevour
            - Townville True Love
          - Townville Trinket
            - Albion Monotype
            - Townville True Love
      - Townville Traveeda
        - Eng. Ch. Townville Trail
          - Eng. Ch. Zeloy Emperor
            - Eng. Ch. Zeloy Endevour
              - Eng. Ch. Wyretex Wyn's Wun Dar
              - Supremacy's Smart Girl
            - Zeloy Rhapsody
              - Zeloy Carouso
              - Zeloy Roseta
        - Townville Teresa
          - Wintor Townville Traveller
            - Eng. Ch. Zeloy Endevour
            - Townville True Love
          - Townville Trinket
            - Townville True Love
            - Townville Trinket

- **Harwire Hazel**
  - Harwire Hero
    - Harwire Headway
      - Eng. Ch. Gosmore Harwire Heyday
        - Eng. Ch. Wyrecliffe Satellite of Senganel
        - Mallmans Sunrise
      - Harwire Honeybee
        - Wyrecroft Warrior
        - Wicklewood Twilight
    - Harwire Humorist
      - Eng. Ch. Penda Peerless
        - Eng. Ch. Penda Cawthorne Cobnut
        - Eng. Ch. Wyrebury Penda Quicksilver
      - Harwire Honeybee
        - Wyrecroft Warrior
        - Wicklewood Twilight
  - Harwire Hellina
    - Weltona Has It
      - Eng. Ch. Holmwire Roxville Revision
        - Holmwire Paul Tudor
        - Roxville Mooremaides Moment
      - Eng. Ch. Weltona Platta Dainty Princess
        - Eng. Ch. Anfield Contender
        - Mac's Model Wire
    - Shoemans Mooremaides Meg
      - Eng. Ch. Wintor Statesman
        - Eng. Ch. Wintor Townville Tuscan
        - Wintor Twilight
      - Mooremaides Newire Magpie
        - Eng. Ch. Zeloy Crusader
        - Newire Lyngarth Tannette

Exelwyre Jason

- Bengal Crispy Brigadier
  - Eng. Ch. Cripsey Townville T'Other'Un
    - Eng. Ch. Townville Tally'O
    - Townville Tamlyn
  - Eng. Ch. Cripsey Nedwar Miss Mathilda
    - Eng. Ch. Seedfield Meritor Super Flash
    - Eng. Ch. Nedwar Misslyn
- Exelwyre Emily
  - Exelwyre Gold Dust
    - Eng. Ch. Townville Tally'O
      - Eng. Ch. Wintor Statesman
      - Townville Teresa
    - Eng. Ch. Kirkmoor Carousel
      - Eng. Ch. Worsbro Betoken Again
      - Townville Tiara
  - Exelwyre Golden Circle
    - Exelwyre Mooroak
      - Eng. Ch. Zeloy Emperor
      - Maryholm Wintersweet
    - Sparkle of Senganel
      - Eng. Ch. Zeloy Emperor
      - Miss Delightful

Galsul Pacesetter

Galsul Marjie

- Eng. Ch. Exelwyre Excelence of Jokyl
  - ⁼xelwyre Gold Dust
    - Eng. Ch. Townville Tally'O
      - Eng. Ch. Wintor Statesman
      - Townville Teresa
    - Eng. Ch. Kirkmoor Carousel
      - Eng. Ch. Kirkmoor Speculation
      - Eng. Ch. Rancourt Kirkmoor Cowslip
  - ..lwyre Golden Circle
    - Exelwyre Mooroak Aristocrat
      - Crackerjack of Cranmore
      - Eden Sunshine
    - Sparkle of Senganel
      - Eng. Ch. Wyrecliff Satelite of Senganel
      - Sentina of Senganel
- Exelwyre Kate
  - Littleway Whitwyre Stock Market
    - Eng. Ch. Whitwyre Market Day
      - Eng. Ch. Wintor Statesman
      - Townville Teresa
    - Whitwyre Mighty Cute
      - Eng. Ch. Kirkmoor Speculation
      - Eng. Ch. Rancourt Kirkmoor Cowslip
  - Exelwyre Golden Circle
    - Exelwyre Mooroak Aristocrat
      - Crackerjack of Cranmore
      - Eden Sunshine
    - Sparkle of Senganel
      - Eng. Ch. Wyrecliff Satelite of Senganel
      - Sentina of Senganel

Galsul Institution

- Eng. Ch. Emprise Exterminator
  - Exelwyre Gold Dust
    - Eng. Ch. Townville Tally'O
      - Eng. & Am. Ch. Whitwyre Money Market
      - Whitwyre Miss Elegance
    - Eng. Ch. Kirkmoor Carousel
      - Crindu Thunderball
      - Whitwyre Marshaline
  - Exelwyre Golden Circle
    - Exelwyre Mooroak Aristocrat
      - Crackerjack of Cranmore
      - Eden Sunshine
    - Sparkle of Senganel
      - Eng. Ch. Wyrecliff Satelite of Senganel
      - Sentina of Senganel

Eng. Ch. Emprise Extremist

- Exelwyre Margaret
  - Eng. Ch. Townville Tally'O
    - Eng. Ch. Winter Statesman
      - Eng. Ch. Wintor Statesman
      - Townville Teresa
    - Townville Teresa
      - Eng. Ch. Kirkmoor Speculation
      - Eng. Ch. Rancourt Kirkmoor Cowslip
  - Eng. Ch. Kirkmoor Carousel
    - Eng. Ch. Kirkmoor Speculation
      - Crackerjack of Cranmore
      - Eden Sunshine
    - Eng. Ch. Rancourt Kirkmoor Cowslip
      - Eng. Ch. Wyrecliff Satelite of Senganel
      - Sentina of Senganel

Galsul Wendy Tusan

- Eng. Ch. Exelwyre Excelence of Jokyl
  - Exelwyre Gold Dust
    - Eng. Ch. Townville Tally'O
      - Eng. Ch. Wintor Townville Tuscan
      - Wintor Twilight
    - Eng. Ch. Kirkmoor Carousel
      - Wintor Townville Traveller
      - Townville Trinket
  - Exelwyre Mooroak Aristocrat
    - Holmwire Contender
    - Platta Star Princess
  - Sparkle of Senganel
    - Eng. Ch. Zeloy Emperor
    - Kirkmoor Cygnet

Galsul Marjie

- Exelwyre Kate
  - Littleway Whitwyre Stock Market
    - Eng. Ch. Whitwyre Market Day
      - Eng. Ch. Wintor Statesman
      - Townville Teresa
    - Whitwyre Mighty Cute
      - Eng. Ch. Kirkmoor Speculation
      - Eng. Ch. Rancourt Kirkmoor Cowslip
  - Exelwyre Golden Circle
    - Exelwyre Mooroak Aristocrat
      - Crackerjack of Cranmore
      - Eden Sunshine
    - Sparkle of Senganel
      - Eng. Ch. Wyrecliff Satelite of Senganel
      - Sentina of Senganel

For Galsul Wendy Tusan line (far right continued):
- Eng. Ch. Wintor Statesman
- Townville Teresa
- Eng. Ch. Kirkmoor Speculation
- Eng. Ch. Rancourt Kirkmoor Cowslip
- Crackerjack of Cranmore
- Eden Sunshine
- Eng. Ch. Wyrecliff Satelite of Senganel
- Sentina of Senganel
- Eng. & Am. Ch. Whitwyre Money Market
- Whitwyre Miss Elegance
- Crindu Thunderball
- Whitwyre Marshaline
- Crackerjack of Cranmore
- Eden Sunshine
- Eng. Ch. Wyrecliff Satelite of Senganel
- Sentina of Senganel

381

Eng. Ch. Sylair Star Leader

- **Eng. Ch. Harrowhill Hunter's Moon**
  - **Eng. Ch. Harrowhill Huntsman**
    - Eng. Ch. Townville Tally'O
      - Eng. Ch. Wintor Statesman
        - Eng. Ch. Wintor Townville Tuscan
          - Townville Traveller
          - Townville Trinket
        - Wintor Twilight
          - Eng. Ch. Lyngarth Scout
          - Lyngarth True Call
      - Townville Teresa
        - Wintor Townville Traveller
          - Eng. Ch. Zeloy Endevour
          - Townville True Love
        - Townville Trinket
          - Albion Monotype
          - Townville True Love
    - Harrowhill Happy Talk
      - Harrowhill Happy Day
        - Eng. Ch. Whitwyre Market Bay
          - Eng. & Am. Ch. Whitwyre Money Market
          - Whitwyre Miss Elegance
        - Harrowhill Happy Birthday
          - Weltona Has It
          - Harrowhill Gina
      - Harrowhill Twiggy
        - Harrowhill Golden Legend
          - Eng. Ch. Zeloy Crusader
          - Harrowhill Golden Treasure
        - Harrowhill Sally
          - Harrowhill Nortwyre Strike at Dawn
          - Harrowhill Golden Jewel
  - **Eng. Ch. Harrowhill Golden Aureole**
    - Harrowhill Happy Day
      - Eng. Ch. Whitwyre Market Day
        - Mitre Advocate
        - Eng. Ch. Whitwyre Even Money
      - Harrowhill Happy Birthday
        - Eng. Ch. Karefree Captain
        - Whitwyre Moth
    - Harrowhill Golden Aura
      - Eng. Ch. Wintor Statesman
        - Eng. Ch. Wintor Townville Tuscan
          - Townville Traveller
          - Townville Trinket
        - Wintor Twilight
          - Eng. Ch. Lyngarth Scout
          - Lyngarth True Call
      - Harrowhill Golden Jewel
        - Eng. Ch. Crackley Cawthorne Compensation
          - Cawthorne Coconut
          - Cawthorne Conquest
        - Harrowhill Hidden Jewel
          - Eng. Ch. Harrowhill Strike Again
          - Harrowhill Gilt Edge
- **Conock Clarissa**
  - **Eng. Can. & Am. Ch. Townville Tristanian**
    - Eng. Ch. Harwire Halyard of Whinlatter
      - Eng. Ch. Townville Trail
        - Eng. Ch. Seedfield Meritor Super Flash
          - Eng. Ch. Zeloy Emperor
          - Maryholm Wintersweet
        - Townville Traveeda
          - Eng. Ch. Townville Tally'O
          - Townville Trudy
      - Eng. Ch. Harwire Hallmark
        - Eng. Ch. Seedfield Meritor Super Flash
          - Eng. Ch. Zeloy Emperor
          - Maryholm Wintersweet
        - Harwire Hazel
          - Harwire Hero
          - Harwire Hellina
    - Cubhunter of Hendell
      - Int. Ch. Axholme Townville Tarik
        - Eng. Ch. Seedfield Meritor Super Flash
          - Eng. Ch. Zeloy Emperor
          - Maryholm Wintersweet
        - Townville Traveeda
          - Eng. Ch. Townville Tally'O
          - Townville Trudy
      - Townville Tamlyn
        - Eng. Ch. Worsbro Betoken Again
          - Anfield Betoken
          - Cawthorne Comfrey
        - Townville Tiara
          - Townville Top Form
          - Townville True Love
  - **Eng. Ch. Conock Carousel**
    - Eng. Ch. Harrowhill Huntsman
      - Eng. Ch. Townville Tally'O
        - Eng. Ch. Wintor Statesman
          - Eng. Ch. Wintor Townville Tuscan
          - Wintor Twilight
        - Townville Teresa
          - Wintor Townville Traveller
          - Townville Trinket
      - Harrowhill Happy Talk
        - Harrowhill Happy Day
          - Eng. Ch. Whitwyre Market Day
          - Harrowhill Happy Birthday
        - Harrowhill Twiggy
          - Harrowhill Golden Legend
          - Harrowhill Sally
    - Conock Holmwire Tudor Vicki
      - Zeloy Majestic
        - Eng. Ch. Zeloy Emperor
          - Eng. Ch. Zeloy Endevour
          - Zeloy Rhapsody
        - Holmwire Tudor Radiance
          - Eng. Ch. Holmwire Tudor Renown
          - Seuchad Girl
      - (dam)
        - Eng. Ch. Seedfield Meritor Super Flash
          - Eng. Ch. Zeloy Emperor
          - Maryholm Wintersweet
        - Holmwire Tudor Rita
          - Eng. Ch. Holmwire Tudor Renown
          - Seuchad Girl

Fairwyre Knockwellan Tina

Int. Ch. Talisman de la Noe Aux Loups

Eng. & Am. Ch. Littleway Haranwal Barrister

Eng. & Am. Ch. Sandwyre Mr. Softy of Jokyl

Eng. Ch. Sandwyre Lulu of Wilwyre

Eng. & Am. Ch. Trucote Admiral

Eng. & Am. Ch. Sunnybrook Spot On

Eng. Ch. Helenstowe Pearly Queen of Jokyl

Eng. Ch. Holmwire Tudor Regent

Helenstowe Parasol

Eng. Ch. Sandwyre Spindrift of Jokyl

Int. Ch. Talisman de la Noe Aux Loups

Eng. Ch. Sandwyre Sportsman of Littleway

Eng. Ch. Sandwyre Mr. Softy of Littleway

Sandwyre Sugar Puff

Eng. Ch. Sandwyre Lulu of Wilwyre

Jokyl Spunsugar

Eng. & Am. Ch. Littleway Haranwal Barrister	Eng. Ch. Wintor Statesman	Eng. Ch. Wintor Townville Tuscan
	Sandwyre Roxville Revue	Wintor Twilight
		Roxville Snowflake
		Roxville Rapture
Madam Fleur	Eng. Ch. Penda Worsbro Whistler	Eng. Ch. Worsbro Betoken Again
		Eng. Ch. Worsbro Oladar Royal Maid
	Winter Gift	Eng. Ch. Crackley Cawthorne Compensation
		Brooklands Giftie
Bengal Cripsey Brigadier	Eng. Ch. Cripsey Townville T'Other'Un	Eng. Ch. Townville Tally'O
		Townville Tamlyn
	Eng. Ch. Cripsey Nedwar Miss Mathilda	Eng. Ch. Seedfield Meritor Super Flash
		Eng. Ch. Nedwar Misslyn
Sandwyre Sugar Puff	Eng. Ch. Wintor Statesman	Eng. Ch. Wintor Townville Tuscan
		Wintor Twilight
	Sandwyre Roxville Revue	Roxville Snowflake
		Roxville Rapture
Eng. Ch. Townville Tally'O	Townville Teresa	Eng. Ch. Wintor Townville Tuscan
		Wintor Twilight
		Wintor Townville Traveller
		Townville Trinket
Sunnybrook Gosmore Photogenic	Gosmore Kirkmoor Clinker	Eng. Ch. Zeloy Emperor
		Brigston Carosel Miss Fonda
	Gosmore Meritor Springtime	Eng. Ch. Extreal Realization
		Nedwar Madonna
Eng. Ch. Holmwire Tudor Regent	Eng. Ch. Zeloy Emperor	Eng. Ch. Zeloy Endevour
		Zeloy Rhapsody
	Holmwire Suntan	Eng. Ch. Holmwire Roxville Revision
		Meritor Spicey Piece
Helenstowe Portrait	Eng. Ch. Helenstowe Pied Piper	Eng. Ch. Wyretex Wyns Wun Dar
		Helenstowe Pamela
	Tuxdene Tealeaf	Tuxdene Timothy of Cranmore
		Tuxdene Tansy
Int. Ch. Talisman de la Noe Aux Loups	Eng. & Am. Ch. Littleway Haranwal Barrister	Eng. Ch. Wintor Statesman
		Sandwyre Roxville Revue
	Madam Fleur	Eng. Ch. Penda Worsbro Whistler
		Winter Gift
Eng. Ch. Sandwyre Mr. Softy of Littleway	Bengal Cripsey Brigadier	Eng. Ch. Cripsey Townville T'Other'Un
		Eng. Ch. Cripsey Nedwar Miss Mathilda
	Sandwyre Sugar Puff	Eng. Ch. Wintor Statesman
		Sandwyre Roxville Revue
Eng. Ch. Sandwyre Lulu of Wilwyre	Eng. Ch. Wintor Townville Tuscan	Townville Traveller
		Townville Trinket
	Wintor Twilight	Eng. Ch. Lyngarth Scout
		Lyngarth True Call
	Roxville Snowflake	Penda Silver Model
		Roxville Mooremaides Moments
	Roxville Rapture	Holmwire Paultudor
		Roxville Mooremaides Moments
Eng. Ch. Wintor Statesman	Eng. Ch. Wintor Townville Tuscan	Eng. Ch. Wintor Townville Tuscan
		Wintor Twilight
	Wintor Twilight	Roxville Snowflake
		Roxville Rapture
Sandwyre Roxville Revue	Roxville Snowflake	Eng. Ch. Worsbro Betoken Again
		Eng. Ch. Worsbro Oladar Royal Maid
	Roxville Rapture	Eng. Ch. Crackley Cawthorne Compensation
		Brooklands Giftie
Bengal Cripsey Brigadier	Eng. Ch. Wintor Statesman	Eng. Ch. Townville Tally'O
		Townville Tamlyn
	Sandwyre Roxville Revue	Eng. Ch. Seedfield Meritor Super Flash
		Eng. Ch. Nedwar Misslyn
Sandwyre Sugar Puff	Eng. Ch. Wintor Townville Tuscan	Eng. Ch. Wintor Townville Tuscan
		Wintor Twilight
	Wintor Twilight	Roxville Snowflake
		Roxville Rapture

383

W-21: Ch. Brownstone's Mac Broom, 11/13/67

- Eng. Ch. Gosmore Kirkmoor Craftsman
  - Ch. Kirkmoor Speculation
    - Holmwire Contender
      - Holmwire Tudorclassic
      - Burbeck Bali Hai
    - Platta Star Princess
      - Ch. Anfield Contender
      - Mac's Model Wire
  - Kirkmoor Cygnet
    - Ch. Kirkmoor Coachman
      - Exelwyre Mooroak Aristocrat
      - Tescot Penda Prunella
    - Excelwyre Luella
      - Exelwyre Mooroak Aristocrat
      - Ardoch Mansebrae Melody
- Ch. Heathcote Enchantress
  - Ch. Deko Dragoon
    - Eng. Ch. Zeloy Emperor
      - Eng. Ch. Zeloy Endevour
      - Zeloy Rhapsody
    - Deko Dieudonne
      - Zeloy Select
      - Deko Drambuie
  - Ch. Meritor Zeloy Sunflower
    - Eng. Ch. Zeloy Endevour
      - Eng. Ch. Wyretex Wyns Wun Dar
      - Supremacy's Smart Girl
    - Zeloy Roxville Rainbow
      - Eng. Ch. Zeloy Emperor
      - Zeloy Roxville Rainbow

W-22: Ch. Raylu Recharge, 9/8/76

- Eng. & Am. Ch. Gosmore Kirkmoor Craftsman
  - Eng. Ch. Kirkmoor Speculation
    - Homwire Contender
    - Plata Star Princess
  - Kirkmoor Cygnet
    - Eng. & Am. Ch. Kirkmoor Coachman
    - Exelwyre Luella
- Am., Can. & Bda. Ch. Bev-Wyre's Conbrio Tim
  - Can. Ch. Deko Defiant
    - Vingo's Verge
    - Paltendale Prima Donna
  - Ch. Glory R's Kantankerous
    - Ch. Merrybrook's Dancing Master
    - Derbyshire Donation
- Ch. Bev-Wyre's Can Anima
  - Ch. Raylu's Realization
    - Ch. Raylu Romantic Raider
      - Ch. Glynhir Great Guns
      - Raylu Resemblance
    - Travella Duchess
      - Ch. Forest Fighting Fox
      - Miller Haven's Larryette
  - Ch. Raylu Reality
    - Ch. Raylu Raconteur
      - Ch. Berylean Eclipse
      - Ch. Raylu Rendition
  - Ch. Raylu Repartee
    - Ch. Raylu Remember Me
      - Ch. Glynhir Great Guns
      - Raylu Resemblance